RELIGION

WITHIN THE LIMITS OF REASON ALONE

RELIGION
WITHIN THE LIMITS
OF REASON ALONE

By

IMMANUEL KANT

Translated with an Introduction and Notes

by THEODORE M. GREENE and HOYT H. HUDSON

with a new essay

"The Ethical Significance of Kant's *Religion*"

by JOHN R. SILBER

HARPER TORCHBOOKS
Harper & Row, Publishers
New York, Hagerstown, San Francisco, London

TABLE OF CONTENTS

INTRODUCTION

by

Theodore M. Greene *and* John R. Silber

THE HISTORICAL CONTEXT AND RELIGIOUS SIGNIFICANCE OF KANT'S *RELIGION*

by Theodore M. Greene

The Enlightenment, which began in the seventeenth century and flourished in the eighteenth, constitutes one of the great spiritual movements of modern Europe. In it we see the Renaissance working itself out through the agencies of its scientific and philosophical discoveries. Because of its influence on Kant, who was in so many essential respects a thinker of the Enlightenment, we should recall at the outset the main characteristics of this movement. It was essentially revolutionary, directed against the authority of intellectual and religious tradition. The positive force at its core was a determined assertion of the freedom of the individual—freedom in affairs social and political, intellectual and religious. This spirit expressed itself most emphatically in a new and extravagant belief in the power of reason. Faith in the old presuppositions and authorities, for so long considered valid beyond question, gave way to a spirit of criticism. Faith was now sought exclusively by the path of argument; logical demonstration, like that found in Euclid, was considered the sole adequate basis for conviction; reason claimed to be autonomous and set itself up as the unique court of appeal. And with reason thus ensconced, the mysterious depths of life, the indefinable and incalculable, received scant recognition or appreciation. To strictly religious values the age was for the most part blind. Whatever, from the point of view of reason, had about it an air of mystery fell under suspicion; man's feelings, passions, and sentiments were in ill repute. Thus the movement took on an austere and barren coldness, which was welcomed in the beginning as is the first breath of mountain air after the suffocating heat of the plains; in time, however, it chilled men through and drove them back to a new appreciation of the sunnier and warmer sides of human life.

If ratiocination was the *organon* of the age, humanity, somewhat abstractly viewed, was its chief concern. The Enlightenment fol-

---

[1] The content of this essay has been taken largely from my doctoral dissertation, written under the supervision of Professor Norman Kemp Smith and presented in 1924 at the University of Edinburgh. My thanks are due to Professor Hudson for his invaluable assistance in the selection, condensation, and extensive rewriting of this material. I must assume responsibility for the ideas embodied in this essay; the remainder of the volume, however, is the product of our joint labors together with those of Professor John R. Silber who has made the revisions and additions for the Second Edition.

lowed close upon the heels of religious wars in France and Germany and of the Revolution in England. It was marked, consequently, by a revulsion against the intolerance and persecution which had characterized those conflicts. Lord Herbert of Cherbury, after witnessing the fruitless strife between Catholics and Huguenots in France, wrote *De Veritate* (1624), the earliest classic of modern deism, with a view to establishing a truth which was independent of all religious organizations. Thus men lost interest in the older theological issues; the focus of attention shifted from the next life to this, from the state of man's soul to man's essential humanity. A new spirit of benevolence and philanthropy was abroad; severity was condemned; charity and tolerance became watchwords.

This humanitarianism rested on the newly acquired conviction of the essential goodness and infinite perfectibility of human nature. As God must have created man good, the vitiating causes which had perverted him must be man-made, that is, contingent and removable. What was needed was to purify the race of these evil influences so that human nature might shine forth in its original purity; and reason, it was felt, was qualified to undertake this labor of purification. The long night of spiritual slavery, men believed, neared its end; reason, once freed from all trammels, would prove equal to every demand. Is not the world, men asked, after all a good place to live in? Nay, is it not the best of all possible worlds? Thus arose an optimism and a self-assurance which flourished without serious check until Hume in England and Kant in Germany brought to bear upon it their searching criticism.

The Enlightenment was thoroughly unhistorical in its conception of man's nature, origin, and vocation. This grave limitation of its thinkers is especially noticeable in their usual mode of conceiving the relation of religion to its historical sources. True religion, it was believed, is eternal and unchanging: the propositions essential to religion, its axioms, must have constituted the faith of primitive man. Thus rigidly set in its logical, geometrical mould, and convinced that what is not absolutely true must be absolutely false, the age was, by the very nature of its outlook, unable to understand or wisely to evaluate the religious conceptions of other ages and other races. And because it failed to understand the part played by historical events in shaping the thought of the past, it was equally unsympathetic towards historical influences at work in its own thinking. It failed, in a word, to appreciate the fundamental conception of historical genesis and growth. Even Hume and Kant are by no means free from this characteristic defect of the Enlightenment.

The spirit of emancipation was not restricted to any one phase of human activity. It found expression in the political as well as the religious, in the social as well as the scientific, activities of men. Neither was it limited to any one nation. On its philosophical and religious sides (we are restricting ourselves to these aspects of the movement), it first expressed itself in the Netherlands, where a spirit of toleration early provided a refuge for thinkers who found themselves harassed by the laws and prejudices of their native countries. Signs of the same spirit were soon visible in England; France followed suit; and before long Germany was permeated with the new doctrine. In England, the apostles of the new order were by some called "free-thinkers," while on its religious side the movement came to be connected with the appellation "deism." In France, the spokesman *par excellence* was Voltaire; Rousseau, like Kant, was only partially typical of the age in which he lived. The name *Aufklärung* (enlightenment, illumination)[1] has been given to the parallel movement in Germany. England, it is certain, was one of the sources of the *Aufklärung*, English theology occupying in Germany in those days a position similar to that which German theology held in England in the early twentieth century. Yet, as we shall presently see, the *Aufklärung* was in considerable measure a native growth, the natural outcome of forces at work in German thought itself. Perhaps the more general statement that all the northern countries were in a sense a cultural unit, each to a greater or less extent influencing its neighbors, first through its intellectual pioneers and then through the agency of imported books and pamphlets of a more popular sort, comes nearest to the truth.

[1] The terms *Aufklärung* and "deism" are somewhat hard to define. Without at present going into the various meanings, of greater or lesser scope, which have been assigned to each, I shall use the terms as follows: "deism," as signifying the religious point of view which is opposed both to atheism and to pantheism, and may be thought of as a special form of theism; *Aufklärung*, as applying to the German phase of the general movement of "Emancipation," the equivalent of which in England may be called the movement of Free-thinking. The religious aspect of the *Aufklärung* would then be German deism.

I. Pietism and Rationalism in the German Aufklärung

As an attempt to break down the traditional authority and dogmatism of the church, the *Aufklärung* assumed two mains forms, evangelical pietism and rationalistic deism. Kant, born and nurtured in a deeply pietistic home, and surrounded during his university course and after by strong rationalistic influences, exhibits in many striking ways the deep impression made upon him by both of these aspects of the *Aufklärung*.

By the middle of the seventeenth century the Lutheran church in Germany had become a "creed-bound theological and sacramentarian institution." Müller, one of the forerunners of pietism, trenchantly described the state of affairs by calling the font, the pulpit, the confessional, and the altar "the four dumb idols of the church." Its theology was highly scholastic, the chief interest of its divines attaching to precise and dogmatic formulation of the church's accepted positions; the Bible had fallen from the place of honor to which Luther had raised it; Lutheran pastors had formed themselves into a hierarchy which ruled a subdued flock with almost papal absolutism; and Christian faith, in a word, was no longer a thing of the heart but had deteriorated into a matter of correct ceremonial and orthodox belief.

Against this state of affairs the men who were labelled by their enemies "pietists" arose in protest. The founder of pietism[1] was Philipp Jakob Spener (1635–1705), a man of deep religious zeal. Greatly impressed by the need in which the church stood for moral and religious reform, he began to hold religious meetings in his house, meetings at which the Bible was studied and expounded, a free discussion of religious problems encouraged, and a spirit of prayer and devotion cherished. In 1675 Spener published, partly under the inspiration of Johann Arndt's *True Christianity* (1606–1609), his *Pia Desideria . . .* , or, *An Earnest Desire for a Reform, Pleasing to God, of the True Evangelical Churches*.[2] In this he made six practical proposals which throw into relief the conditions against which he was protesting: (1) that the Bible be earnestly studied; (2) that the laity be given a share in church government; (3) that the practice of Christianity be recognized

---

[1] The movement may be compared to Methodism in England and to the Jansenist movement within the Catholic Church.

[2] *Pia desideria, oder, herzliches Verlangen nach Gottgefälliger Besserung der wahren Evangelischen Kirchen.*

as an essential supplement to a knowledge of Christian doctrine; (4) that sympathetic and kindly treatment of the heterodox be substituted for the usual bitter attacks upon them; (5) that greater emphasis be put, in the universities, upon devotional life; and (6) that, in preaching, rhetorical embellishments give place to a more genuine and devout message. The response to Spener's appeal was considerable, the most notable among his adherents being August Francke, under whose leadership, after Spener's death, the movement grew in influence until Francke's death in 1727. Meanwhile, Frederick III of Brandenburg gave the pietists his active assistance both before and after his accession to the throne of Prussia, and in 1694 founded the pietist University of Halle, all of whose professors, at the beginning, were of that persuasion. This University remained for many years an important center of the movement.

Pietism demanded that justification and rebirth be actually experienced and not merely regarded as orthodox Christian doctrines. It was, in short, an attempt to revive Christianity as a living religion. This end it would achieve by two means—prayer, and a diligent study of the Bible. The Bible was to be regarded, however, not as a source of proof-texts but as a divine revelation capable of providing rich nourishment for the soul. The genuineness of the movement manifested itself in its emphasis upon the practical side of religious life. This took the form of kindliness toward other denominations, an active interest in the needy at home, and a new concern for the heathen abroad. Pietism, finally, proclaimed a new individualism. Religion was no longer to be the concern solely of skilled theologians, but the heritage of the common man, who was now encouraged to find God for himself.

Yet, as often happens, the very strength of pietism soon became its weakness. The laudable importance assigned to the Christian experience developed into an exaggerated, almost fanatical demand (bordering upon superstition) for a certain violent and mystical kind of conversion. Such a new birth, it was thought, must be preceded in all cases by agonies of repentance. The pietists' admirable emphasis upon good works soon grew into an over-emphasis and gave certain color to their opponents' contention that Christianity had become for them a new salvation by works. Their criticism, moreover, of the weaknesses of the Lutheran Church often blinded them to the function and value of the church as such. But their greatest and most fundamental weakness was a tendency to save their own souls and to leave the salvation of the world to the second coming of Christ. Despite their orphanages and their missions, their chief interest lay increasingly not in Christianizing the world by living a Christian life in it and taking an active and conscientious part in its affairs, but rather in withdrawing from the world of men as they withdrew from all carnal pleasures and in achieving for themselves, together with a chosen few, a life of holiness.

The claim that the sources of the *Aufklärung* are to be found exclusively in Germany itself, and primarily in German pietism, is clearly an overstatement. Yet the influence of pietism upon Germany was considerable; in its individualism, its emphasis upon the practical side of religion, and its opposition to the dogmatism of the church, it helped to prepare the way for, and indeed formed part of the vanguard of, the *Aufklärung*. What concerns us more closely, however, is that its influence on Kant's life and teaching was profound. Whereas pietism as a distinct movement ran its course before the middle of the eighteenth century, its indirect influence through men like Kant continued long after it had ceased to be an important element in the religious life of Germany.

The second and far more typical expression of the religious side of the *Aufklärung* was German deism. Though pietism, by weakening the dogmatic armor of the church, helped indirectly to prepare the way for this new theological rationalism, it was, in temper and conception, opposed to the more popular and influential deistic movement, for where the one relied upon religious emotion and the sympathies of men, the other appealed to reason and the intellect. It was only natural, therefore, that the two forces should clash, as indeed they did upon frequent occasions.

The two main roots of German deism were the Leibnizian-Wolffian philosophy and English deism. The influence of the second was felt in Germany toward the end of the seventeenth century and reached its height by the middle of the eighteenth. Lord Herbert of Cherbury was reviewed and criticized[1] as early as 1680. John Toland, Locke's rather disreputable admirer and disciple, lived for a time in Germany after the publication of his *Christianity*

---

[1] By Christian Korthold. Cf. *Religion in Geschichte und Gegenwart* (1908), I, 2012

Not Mysterious,[1] which was respectfully criticized by Leibniz. By 1720 the more erudite had become familiar with the main ideas of Toland and Collins through the writings of Pfaff, Gundling, and Mosheim,[2] and by 1743 English deism had effected a general entrance into Germany through the translation of its main works.[3] Fifteen years later it had attained such popularity that the *Freidenker-lexicon* and the *Freidenker-bibliothek*[4] were not only published with impunity but were well received, and the theologian Baumgarten,[5] one of Wolff's most illustrious disciples, seems to have reviewed almost every English deistic and apologetic work.

The similarity is striking, moreover, between Reimarus, who may be taken as the typical German deist, and Tindal. The general development of deism in the two countries is indeed so nearly the same that a very brief mention of its special German peculiarities will suffice for our present purpose. These are to be found for the most part in the earlier and more indigenous stages of its development, and may be discovered by contrasting Wolff and Locke. The chief difference between them consists in the fact that Locke was an empiricist while Wolff was a dogmatic rationalist. According to the Englishman, our knowledge of God rests on empirical evidence, on a combination of experience and reflection; and the Biblical narratives are just so much documentary evidence from which certain conclusions may legitimately be drawn. Wolff rests his belief in God almost entirely on the *a priori* proofs; God's existence and nature, he argues, may be deduced with certainty and adequacy from the idea of Him which each individual finds implanted in his own mind. Another point of contrast between these two philosopher-theologians appears in their respective attitudes towards the dogmas of the church. Locke ignores current orthodox theology and devotes his attention to the Bible; Wolff pursues the scholastic method of accepting most of the theological propositions of the church and trying to build beneath them a formal and syllogistic foundation.

Christian Wolff (1679–1754) was the most typical and influential thinker in Germany in the first half of the eighteenth century.

---

[1] Published in 1696, a year after Locke's *Reasonableness of Christianity as delivered in the Scriptures.*

[2] Cf. Benno Erdmann, *Martin Knutzen und seine Zeit* (1876), p. 116

[3] *Ibid.*, pp. 45, 119

[4] Published from 1756 to 1765. Cf. *Religion in Geschichte und Gegenwart*, I, 2012

[5] S. J. Baumgarten (1706–1757), brother of Alexander Gottlieb Baumgarten (1714–1762), the philosopher.

Born of humble parents (his father was a tanner), he rose rapidly in the academic world, going in 1706 to the University of Halle, where pietism, after its conflict with Lutheran dogmatism, had itself now assumed the status of a new orthodoxy. Wolff's bold rationalistic claims soon drew down upon him the disfavor and finally the opposition of his theological colleagues, who at last, in 1723, succeeded in persuading the king to expel him from Prussian territory. This struggle with pietism, however, gave Wolff such wide publicity that by 1737 over two hundred books and pamphlets had championed or attacked his philosophy. One of the first acts of Frederick the Great after his accession to the throne in 1740 was to recall him to Halle. His return assumed the nature of a triumphal entry, and within three years he was made chancellor of the University. His influence over German thought was now greater than that of any of his contemporaries, and for years—indeed, until he was displaced by Kant—he held almost undisputed sway. Kant himself was for a time a faithful disciple. It was the Wolffian philosophy which he studied in the University; and it was Wolff's solution of psychological, cosmological and theological problems upon which he later concentrated his attacks in the *Critique of Pure Reason*.

Before Wolff, a knowledge of Leibniz had been restricted to a handful of scholars; now many of Leibniz's ideas became the common property of the nation. Where Leibniz had failed in a marked degree to knit together the various strands of his thought into a simple, unified system, Wolff supplied the lack by giving to as much of his master's philosophy as he could comprehend and assimilate a systematic unity. These portions of Leibnizianism he then offered to his countrymen in German instead of the usual Latin and in a relatively simple and popular form. As was natural, however, "this popularizing was a making shallow, as well; it was the exoteric Leibnizianism which through Wolff was made the dominating mode of thought of the eighteenth-century *Aufklärung*."[1] The reduction of this spirited philosophy to a dogmatic system robbed it, too, of much of its freshness and supplied in its stead "the aridity of a neo-scholastic formalism." The Wolffian framework in which many essentially Leibnizian ideas were set forth is itself symbolic of the spirit of the age of which Wolff was as much the mirror as the fashioner. It was an age for the most part

---

[1] Otto Pfleiderer, *Geschichte der Religionsphilosophie* (1883), p. 94; here translated.

unproductive of new ideas and skillful chiefly in reproducing those of earlier thinkers; it now contented itself with selecting from the Leibnizian philosophy that which suited its own temper, and stating, in a way congenial to itself, what it had thus chosen.

Wolff's theology, predominantly metaphysical in character, looks not to the historical basis or to the empirical manifestations of religion, but to its transcendent metaphysical Object. At the base of his great syllogistic structure of inferences from certain definitions and axioms lie the ontological and cosmological proofs of God's existence and nature. From these Wolff concluded that God is an eternal and unchangeable, intelligent, complete and all-perfect, all-good and omnipotent Spirit, possessing all reality in the highest possible degree. The world in which we live is a perfect machine, created by God out of nothing and running its own course, since that divine event, according to the adequate laws of its own mechanism. Since God is the measure of goodness, wisdom, and power, our world, His handiwork, must necessarily have been selected by Him as, of all possible worlds, the best adapted to His purpose; and this purpose must be to reveal His perfection and glory. To bewail the world's evil is therefore to doubt God's wisdom; for though evil is not directly willed by Him, it appears to be so closely allied to His purposes as to be necessary to their fulfillment. Wolff's teleology is, finally, subjective and anthropocentric in that the purpose and end of things is thought to consist in their usefulness to man.

What place or need is there here for a divine revelation? The possibility of such a revelation Wolff accepts on the grounds, first, that, since God is omnipotent, all things, even the miraculous, are possible to Him; and second, that divine revelation facilitates the task of reason by disclosing to it various propositions which it would, to be sure, eventually have discovered for itself, but only at considerable pains and at a later date. Reason may now accept these revealed truths as given, and may devote its energies to establishing them on a firm philosophical foundation. After admitting the possibility and value of revelation to this extent, however, Wolff robs the admission of all significance by laying down various tests which revelation must satisfy if it is to be considered genuine. There must, in the first place, be a clear need for it. God must have sufficient grounds for interfering with the regular operation of His own world. Again, revelation, to be true, must in no way contradict any aspects of God's nature already known to man; neither can it contradict any of the "necessary truths" of reason or any item of man's "sure experience." The "mysteries" of Christian theology, however, Wolff accepts as being *above* reason and un-discoverable by it. Such mysteries as, for example, the Virgin Birth, are possible because they contradict no "necessary truths" but only certain "contingent truths," the laws of nature being conveniently classed in the second category. A third test of the genuineness of divine revelation may be mentioned as illustrating the pettiness to which Wolff at times descended. Genuine revelation, he holds, must be conveyed to man in unmistakably clear language, as briefly as is consistent with complete clarity, and in sentences whose grammar is unimpeachable—for surely God would not express Himself ungrammatically! Thus supernatural revelation is declared to be possible and yet rendered actually impossible through the imposition of conditions which no one can prove to be fulfilled in the Bible or in any other sacred book. The net result is therefore the invalidation of the concept of external revelation and the establishment of speculative reason as the foundation of theology and the bulwark of religion and the church. It is no wonder that when Kant claimed to have unmasked the pretensions of speculative reason and to have proved its inability to discover truth in the realm of theology, he was accused, far and wide, of undermining religious belief.

What Tindal did for Locke, Reimarus[1] did for Wolff: he accepted, in the main, his master's philosophical position and carried his rationalistic principles to their logical conclusion. He distinguishes himself from Tindal only by the greater thoroughness with which he isolated natural religion from revealed Christianity and the completeness with which he condemned the latter as not only useless but harmful. Wolff had claimed that reason and revelation are reconcilable, at least theoretically, and are mutually advantageous to each other. For Reimarus they stand in flat contradiction. In denying that natural laws are merely contingent he destroyed the ground on which Wolff had accepted the possibility of the miraculous. He declared reasonable proof of a supernatural disturbance in the orderly course of nature to be impossible. Like Tindal, he then concluded, on the one hand, that natural religion, resting exclusively on reason, is universally knowable and is man's

[1] Hermann Samuel Reimarus (1694–1768). Cf. below, p. 76.

sole salvation from the delusions of so-called revealed religions; and, on the other hand, that the Bible, because it claims miraculous authority for itself and reports occurrences of the miraculous, is untrustworthy and at many points harmful to religion. Reimarus goes further than Tindal in frankly charging Christ and his disciples with fraud and ambition. The fall of Christianity he considers both inevitable and desirable. It is interesting to note that while Kant differs from Reimarus in many important respects,[1] particularly in his estimate of Christ's character and of the value of Christianity, he yet speaks of the earlier writer with respect and admiration.[2]

Reimarus had two outstanding weaknesses, both typical of his century and both shared to a degree by Kant, faults which Kant's contemporaries, Semler and Lessing, were able to avoid and partially to remedy. In the first place, Reimarus had no adequate conception of historical criticism and no notion of investigating Biblical sources in a thoroughgoing fashion or of testing their age, peculiar character, and worth. Semler,[3] born thirty-six years after Reimarus, seems to have been the first German to study the Bible from a truly critical standpoint. Where Reimarus had proceeded simply by discarding all references in the Bible to the supernatural and retaining only what was left, Semler acted on the principle that each document and each particular narrative must be judged by itself, with respect to its authority and value. Though little more than a forerunner, Semler thus succeeded in starting, among the Germans, that constructive Biblical criticism which was to develop with such important results in the nineteenth century.

In the second place, Reimarus lacked any conception of the progressive development of man's religious insight. Divine revelation was defined by him, as by the church of his time, as something miraculous, imposed *in toto* upon men from without. The Bible, according to orthodox divines, was in its entirety the explicit Word

[1] When Borowski submitted his biographical essay to Kant for the latter's approval, Kant made the following comment: "The parallels which have been drawn . . . between the Christian ethics and the philosophical ethics which I have sketched might be altered by a few words, so that, instead of the names of those [appearing side by side] of which the one is holy, the other but that of a poor bungler [*ein armer Stümper*] who is trying as best he can to interpret Christ's work, only those expressions which I have indicated be used. . . . " (L. E. Borowski's Preface to his *Darstellung des Lebens und Characters Immanuel Kants* (1804), p. 7; here translated.)

[2] Cf. *Critique of Judgment* (Bernard's tr.), p. 417

[3] Johann Salomo Semler (1725–1791); he published an answer to the *Wolfenbüttel Fragmente* in 1779. Kant seems to have been unacquainted with his writings.

of God, of equal authority and value throughout. Reimarus defended the only alternative he perceived to exist, that the Bible was from end to end nothing but a human document. Between these extreme views there obviously was room for a third position, which Lessing defined by means of the concept, as Pfleiderer describes it, "of a divine revelation which does not descend upon man ready-made from without, but which achieves realization in man through the development of his religious capacity, and which, for that very reason, has at every point a divine and a human aspect, and is never wholly without truth, yet never quite the whole truth."[1]

Kant and Lessing agree chiefly in those respects in which they are typical of their age; they differ most in the particular way in which they transcend the Enlightenment. Both men were born into deeply religious homes; both studied theology in the university;[2] both soon grew impatient with the dogmatic character of contemporary theology and with the narrow intolerance of the clergy, the pressure of whose censorship rested upon each in turn;[3] both preached a gospel of toleration and freedom of conscience; and both, finally, gave their last years to various forms of theological controversy Lessing shared with Kant, moreover, an abiding distrust of history as a vehicle of truth. Can temporal events, he asks, as subsequently recorded and handed down from generation to generation, give us the certainty we crave? Can eternal truth be dependent upon the contingencies of history? His final answer is as definite as Kant's: "Contingent truths of history can never prove necessary truths of reason. That is the horribly wide ditch which I cannot cross, often and earnestly as I have made the spring."[4] Such eternal truths, he feels sure, are discoverable only in the inmost part of the human soul, in the promptings of the heart. Here alone, in one's own inner experience, lies the true basis of faith. And this, as we shall see, is Kant's conclusion when he grounds religious faith upon our inmost moral consciousness.

Lessing, however, is not content to ignore history as unimportant or to use it merely as a source of convenient illustrations

---

[1] *Geschichte der Religionsphilosophie*, p. 106; here translated.

[2] Lessing (1729–1781) entered the University of Leipzig as a theological student in 1746; Kant matriculated at Königsberg in 1740.

[3] Lessing wrote *Nathan der Weise* (1778–1779) after he had been forbidden by the Brunswick government to continue the *"Anti-Göze"* controversy over the *Wolfenbüttel Fragmente*.

[4] Quoted by Pfleiderer, *Geschichte der Religionsphilosophie*, p. 134; here translated.

for moral precepts. He feels, says Oman, that "the Christianity of the Gospels has blood in its veins which never throbs in the pale ghost of Rational Religion."[1] Despite his doubts, to which we have just referred, he sees in history a living reality, and reads in it the great fact of man's slowly developing intellectual and religious faculties, whereby the meaning "of that which God has already furnished us"[2] grows increasingly clear. This is the thesis of his *Education of the Human Race*. Revelation is no longer a gift from some external source but a development from within. "God makes immediate revelations of mere truths of reason, or *has permitted and caused pure truths of reason to be taught, for some time, as truths of immediate revelation*, in order to promulgate them the more rapidly and ground them the more firmly."[3] The genuineness of revelation as the expression of God's guiding and controlling power is not doubted; a new meaning, however, is assigned to the word. "Education is revelation coming to the individual man; and revelation is education which has come, and is yet coming, to the human race."[4] The *preaching* of a truth as a revelation, instead of the *teaching* of it as a product of human reason, is but God's way in dealing with man. At various appointed stages on the road of his progressive development, it is to man's interest to believe that his Primer possesses the absolute and abiding value of an immediate divine revelation; for centuries it was well that the Old Testament should be so accepted, and most Christians still need a similar faith in the New Testament as the *ne plus ultra* of religious knowledge. But philosophers know better—they know that these are but stages on the journey man is travelling, and that in time (that is, when its assurance of future rewards and punishments will no longer be necessary to man) the New Testament too will be transcended even by the masses. Lessing's ideal of human conduct, too, affords interesting comparison with Kant's. "Let us also acknowledge that it is an heroic obedience to obey the laws of God simply because they are God's laws, and not because He has promised to reward the obedience of them here and there; to obey them even though there be an entire despair of future recompense, and uncertainty respecting a temporal one."[5] And to doubt that a time

---

[1] *Problem of Faith and Freedom*, pp. 167–168
[2] *Education of the Human Race* (1780), (Eng. tr., 1858), Preface, p. xii
[3] *Ibid.*, §70; cf. also §71; my italics.
[4] *Ibid.*, §2
[5] *Ibid.*, §32; cf. also §85

will surely come when men will do the right simply because it is
right is to doubt eternal Providence and is nothing short of blas-
phemy. "It will assuredly come—the time of a new eternal Gospel!"[1]

Lessing's view of the development of the religious consciousness
is more truly historical than is Kant's; yet they arrive at the
same goal and conceive the essence of religion to consist in much
the same thing. The piety of their respective homes remained for
each a deep and abiding influence. Both felt for the Jesus of history the most profound respect. Both interpreted the "religion of
Christ," as distinguished from the "Christian religion," in thoroughly moral terms,[2] and neither had the least respect for the
notion of salvation through this or that particular belief. So long
as the adherents of some sect or faith "think that they are favored
children of the Divine Father, whom He regards with a complacency with which He does not view the rest of humanity, so long
is the fulness of God's idea not attained by them."[3] What is left,
then, is essentially a religion of good works, in which virtue is
loved for its own sake—a religion of pure humanity which is the
true religion of Christ.

II. The Aufklärung in Königsberg

The growth of pietism in Germany, and the corresponding rise
of the counter-movement, Wolffian rationalism, the struggle between the two, and the final victory of the second, were in the
main faithfully mirrored in the city and university of Königsberg.
At the beginning of the century the religious life of Königsberg
was completely under the control of Lutheran orthodoxy, while
the philosophical temper of the University was thoroughly Aristo-
telian. By 1724 pietism in religion and Wolffianism in philosophy
had grown strong enough to overthrow the earlier orthodoxies. No
sooner, however, had these simultaneous triumphs occurred than
the two victorious movements joined combat with each other.
Though pietism continued stronger for a few years, it was doomed

[1] *Ibid.*, §86
[2] Cf. a fragment entitled (in translation) *The Religion of Christ and the Christian
Religion*. The former is called by Lessing the religion that Christ, as a man, recognized
and practised. It is the true religion of the Gospels and the religion we must ourselves
desire to practise in proportion as we admire Christ the man. The Christian religion,
in contrast, is that religion which holds Christ to be more than a man, *i.e.*, an object of
worship. This religion is but dimly discernible in the New Testament.
[3] *Education of the Human Race*, Preface, pp. xiv–xv

to a gradual decline, while Wolffianism increased in popularity and influence. Because of the remarkable personality of Franz Albert Schultz, who in 1731 became the champion of pietism in Königsberg, this movement died more slowly here than in other parts of Germany, for his influence lasted, though it waned somewhat, until his death in 1763.

Pietism seems to have owed its entrance into Königsberg to Gehr, a cabinet-maker, who in 1698 secured from Spener a pietist instructor for his children. This private tuition soon developed into a full-fledged school, which, despite the active opposition of older academic institutions, grew in size, in the scope of its curriculum, and in the excellence of its teaching, until it was by acknowledgement the leading school of the city. In 1740 the king made it a royal school, declaring it to be his aim "to extend God's glory and to bring souls to heaven," and gave it the imposing name, Collegium Fridericianum. Its first director, Lysius, was both an excellent scholar and teacher and a man distinguished for his tolerance and kindliness; yet he was above all an ardent pietist whose sole defect, according to his biographer,[1] was that he was "perhaps too strenuous in his zeal for the work of God." Schultz, who succeeded Lysius a year after young Immanuel entered the school as a pupil, was as true a pietist as his predecessor and did all he could to preserve and intensify the school's religious atmosphere.

At the Collegium Fridericianum, which Kant attended as a day-pupil for eight years (1732–1740), the day started at five-thirty with a half-hour of devotions and came to a close with a similar half-hour at nine in the evening. Each class-hour ended with a short but "rousing" prayer; a morning hour was devoted to religious instruction, and for four weeks before every communion service the pupils were assembled frequently to be warned of the evil state of their souls and encouraged to discover and confess their sins. Though the school was the first in the city to teach history, geography, and mathematics, the Bible was as far as possible made the text-book even for secular studies; Greek, for example, was taught solely from the New Testament, and history from Biblical narratives. Sunday was a weary succession of sermons and catechizings.

This religiously saturated atmosphere was not for long confined

---

[1] S. G. Wald; cf. Erdmann, *Martin Knutzen und seine Zeit*, p. 16

to the precincts of the Collegium. It soon pervaded the churches of Königsberg and for a time prevailed in the University itself. For twenty years after his installation (in 1730) as pastor of the *Altstädtische Kirche*, Schultz was the dominant figure in the city. With amazing rapidity he rose from office to office, and undertook with unlimited energy to discharge his numerous duties. Besides serving as pastor, preacher, and school-superintendent, he was one of the chief professors in the University, famous for the clearness and thoroughness of his teaching; yet he attained his highest distinction as a governmental official, effecting various ecclesiastical reforms throughout Prussia and spreading the spirit of a practical pietism with far-reaching results.

The Wolffian philosophy, in the meantime, had secured its first foothold in Königsberg some twenty years later than the advent of pietism. By 1730 several of the professors-extraordinary and lecturers (*Privatdozenten*) of the University were strongly Wolffian, though the weight of pietist influence was sufficient to prevent any man of Wolffian bias from attaining to the position of full-professor, not one of these first disciples of the new philosophy ever achieving that coveted post. They even felt it the part of discretion to keep their philosophical views more or less private. An exception was Fischer, who refused to be tactful and openly avowed his Wolffian sympathies and, as a result, was ordered in 1725 from Königsberg and the state of Prussia and not allowed to return until the turning of the tide some fifteen years later.

During this same period, moreover, the influence of English deism made itself felt. Quandt, Schultz's chief antagonist, was an enthusiastic friend of the English; Rappolt, an important member of the University staff in the early 1730's, had studied for some time in England; and Knutzen, Kant's most cherished teacher, was induced by his interest in theology to read with care the English Free-Thinkers. It is true that in these years English deism was read chiefly that it might be refuted. And when the exiled Fischer published, after his reinstatement at Königsberg, a book in which he treated various Christian doctrines from a deistic standpoint, he was promptly and generally hailed as a dangerous atheist, reprimanded by the government, and enjoined to silence. Yet pietism was on the wane even in this, its former stronghold, and by 1742 it had been forced largely to relinquish its control.

Its decline and fall were in a way expedited by the sympathetic attitude which Schultz and Knutzen, who was also a pietist, adopted toward Wolffian rationalism. For despite their pietism, both were convinced Wolffians who made it their endeavor to effect a reconciliation between the opposing movements. Wolff himself is said to have remarked: "If any one has understood me, it is Schultz in Königsberg." Their friendliness to rationalism was reflected in the city, so that even during the years when it was predominantly pietist in its leanings "its pietism was of such a mild order that it did not oppose the fresh influxes of the new spirit so far as this spirit did not affect destructively the dominant way of thinking."[1]

While Schultz was first a theologian and only secondarily a philosopher, Knutzen's main enthusiasm was always for philosophy, though theology interested him and religion possessed for him, to the end, a vital reality. Like his great pupil, Knutzen was born of poor parents and lived his entire life in Königsberg. He came into contact with pietism at the University where he studied under Schultz, with whom he formed a lasting friendship. Once converted to the movement, Knutzen remained loyal to its principles the rest of his life. Yet, as we have said, he was also an outspoken and zealous Wolffian and became a prominent representative of that philosophy. This double allegiance impeded his academic advancement and prevented his election to the professorial chair to which his brilliance entitled him. Yet he was a real force in the University, so well liked by the students that for years he lectured from four to six hours a day. Though the youthful Kant was undoubtedly impressed more by Knutzen's rational philosophy than by his religious views, he must have been familiar with his teacher's theology and was doubtless influenced by it even in the writing of his later essays on religion.

Knutzen's main work in theology, *A Philosophical Account of the Truth of the Christian Religion*,[2] presents the typical pietist doctrines attired in the Wolffian garb of mathematical formalism. Its constructive purpose was to safeguard from various intellectual doubts those pietist convictions whose basis was faith and whose animating source was a deep-seated religious need, and to find for the Christian religion a sound philosophical basis. Yet it is distinguished from the superstitious excesses of later pietism by its

---

[1] Erdmann, *Martin Knutzen und seine Zeit*, pp. 34–35; here translated.
[2] *Philosophischer Bericht von der Wahrheit der Christlichen Religion* (1740)

forcible protest against all fanaticism and mysticism, all substitution of extreme but unproductive penitence for active well-doing, all self-inflicted punishments which render a man unfit to serve God and his fellows—a protest with which Kant has expressed himself in hearty sympathy. Knutzen gives us a statement of pietism at its best, and as such his book furnishes a standard by which we may decide to what degree Kant's own theological writings are pietistic in character.

Knutzen's doctrine[1] includes three propositions: a divine revelation is necessary; it must satisfy certain conditions; the Christian revelation alone fulfils these conditions. A supernatural revelation Knutzen affirms to be necessary to man's salvation on the ground that unaided human reason cannot discover an adequate means of atoning for man's great guilt. The sin of disobedience is immeasureably great because man's obligation to God is infinite. God's holiness makes it impossible for Him to let this sin go unpunished. The punishments discovered by reason are agonies of repentance, the discipline entailed in leading a better life, sacrifices and ceremonies, and various self-devised and self-inflicted castigations. These, however, fall short of what is required and fail to satisfy divine justice. God must add what man is unable to supply.

A divine revelation, to be adequate and authentic, must in the first place reveal God's holiness and, making plain to man his state of disobedience, provide for his salvation. The genuineness of such a revelation must, furthermore, be attested by some unquestioned miracle.

Christianity is the only religion measuring up to this standard. Christ's sacrificial death reveals God's holiness in the highest possible degree; His supreme sacrifice is a far better means of inspiring man with a wholesome fear of further disobedience than outright punishment would be, for it reveals to man God's inmeasurable love and mercy and awakens in him a blessed and virtuous disposition. God's two-fold purpose in punishing men for their sin is thus satisfied. The Christian revelation is proved to be genuine, moreover, by the fact of Christ's resurrection, which Knutzen believes (on the basis of various historical evidence which he presents) to be an undoubted miracle. Christianity, then, is God's answer to our need. To make clear to us the meaning and

---

[1] The following analysis is based upon Erdmann, *Martin Knutzen und seine Zeit*, p. 116 ff.

significance of Christ's atoning work, God has also revealed to us the mysterious doctrine of the Trinity, which is hardly discoverable by our unaided reason. We become sharers in the divine means of pardon, when, through God's Word and Spirit, and by means of our sincere appeals to Him, we become actively convinced of our guilt and the punishment thereby incurred. This realization brings with it a complete spiritual change—a rebirth into a new and overwhelming allegiance to the God of mercy and a genuine willingness to obey our Saviour's commands. All this expresses itself practically in love for our fellow-men.

These are, in brief, the central doctrines of the pietism in which Kant was nurtured, for which he always preserved a marked respect, and which more deeply influenced his own theology than he perhaps realized.

III. Kant's Religious Training; his Life and Writings up to 1791

"In the year 1724, on Saturday the twenty-second of April at five in the morning my son Immanuel was born into the world and on the twenty-third received holy baptism.... May God preserve him in His covenant of grace unto his blessed end, for Jesus Christ's sake. Amen." With these pious words Anna Regina Reuterin, the mother of Immanuel Kant, recorded his birth in the family Bible. They bespeak the nature of his early training. Both his parents were devout members of the pietist church. The father, a Scotsman by descent and a saddler by trade, reminds one of the father of Thomas Carlyle. He exemplified the virtues of industry and truthfulness; preeminently a moral rather than a religious man, his chief interest was to make his children hard-working and upright. Kant's mother was more ardently and emotionally religious and seems to have had a far more forceful personality than her husband. Kant himself says of her: "My mother was a sweet-tempered, affectionate, pious and upright woman and a tender mother, who led her children to the fear of God by pious teaching and virtuous example. She often took me outside of the city, directed my attention to the works of God, expressed herself with a pious rapture over His omnipotence, wisdom, and goodness, and impressed on my heart a deep reverence for the Creator of all things."[1]

[1] Jachmann, in *Immanuel Kant ... Die Biographien von L. E. Borowski, R. B. Jachmann und A. Ch. Wasianski*, p. 162; here translated.

She was a woman of little education but large natural intelligence and genuine piety, and although she died when Kant was fourteen he never ceased to speak of the profound influence she had upon his life. Yet in spite of his admiration and love for her Kant seems to have attained more nearly to his father's ideal than to hers.

The family life, in spite of considerable poverty and a humble social position, was of a high moral character. This very poverty, indeed, was without doubt the source of Kant's industry and frugality and of his simple tastes and habits in later life. A great influence upon his youth was the friendly patronage of Schultz. As their pastor, he seems to have taken a special interest in the family, finding time to visit them often and assisting them in many ways, even, in the long cold winters, sending them gifts of firewood. He soon became aware that young Immanuel was a boy of marked ability and persuaded his parents to send him, at the age of eight, to the Collegium Fridericianum. He maintained an interest in Kant until his manhood and gave him such good advice and generous assistance that Kant always valued his memory and expressed regret, in old age, that he had never been able to gratify a long-cherished wish to erect a fitting memorial to Schultz as his friend and teacher.

While, in his home, Kant encountered pietism at its best, in the Collegium, he came upon a pietism whose zeal fostered a spirit of hypocrisy. When young and active boys are expected unanimously and daily to give evidence of great religious fervor, they are bound to do so without observing strict proportion to the emotion actually felt. Kant's early-acquired honesty saved him from such short-cuts to favor. "He was quite unable," says Borowski,[1] "to acquire a taste for that form of piety, or rather that affected piety, to which many of his classmates adapted themselves, often from very low motives." This whole experience in the Collegium was for him a painful one, for he was sensitive by nature, and the remark he is said to have made in later life, that "fear and trembling overcame him whenever he recalled those days of youthful slavery,"[2] may well be authentic. Certain it is that he acquired a lasting abhorrence of all religious emotion and would have nothing to do with prayer or the singing of hymns the rest of his life. What

[1] *Op. cit.*, p. 14
[2] Quoted by Vorländer, *Immanuel Kants Leben*, p. 10; here translated.

strikes one with surprise, indeed, is not that he rebelled against certain practices connected with religion[1] but that he did not turn against religion altogether. It was probably the memory of his mother and his acquaintance with men like Schultz and Knutzen that accounted for the relative sanity and justice of his mature estimate of pietism. Instead of condemning it utterly he was able to separate the good from the bad. "Even if the religious consciousness of that time," we find him writing in his old age to his friend Rink,[2] "and the conceptions of what is called virtue and piety were by no means clear and satisfactory, it yet contained the root of the matter. One may say of pietism what one will; it suffices that the people to whom it was a serious matter were distinguished in a manner deserving of all respect. They possessed the highest good which man can enjoy—that repose, that cheerfulness, that inner peace which is disturbed by no passions. No want or persecution rendered them discontented; no controversy was able to stir them to anger or enmity."

In 1740, at the age of sixteen, Kant entered the University of Königsberg and, in conformity with a university ruling that each matriculated student should become a member of one of the faculties, enrolled in the faculty of theology. Thanks to Schultz's liberalizing influence, however, he had the privilege of grounding himself thoroughly in philosophy. We know that Schultz had a warm regard for his old pupil Knutzen, and it may have been at Schultz's instigation that Kant early became Knutzen's disciple. The latter took a special interest in Kant, favored him with personal conferences, gave him the freedom of his excellent library, and in time became his chief inspirer and guide. Kant found Knutzen's lectures of such interest that he presently gave up the plan, formed in the Collegium, of devoting his life to philology and the classics; now it was science and philosophy that called him; he eagerly responded to Knutzen's advances, welcomed his suggestions, and became for the time being a thorough Wolffian.

It was not until late in his university course that he actually attended lectures in theology. Then, partly from a desire to extend

---

[1] After reaching maturity, he never attended church services; he even took special pains to avoid them. When a new rector of the University was inaugurated it was the custom for the professors to march in procession to the cathedral to take part in a religious service. In course of time Kant became rector and duly led the academic procession, but deserted it at the church.

[2] Quoted from Paulsen, *Immanuel Kant, his Life and Doctrine* (Eng. tr. 1902), p. 28.

his general knowledge, and partly from the felt need to master the principles of theology as related to philosophical studies, he attended Schultz's lectures in Dogmatics. He may also have wished to convince his old pastor that he had not grown out of sympathy with the central tenets of the Christian faith. These lectures, we are told, he thoroughly enjoyed; and his work for the course must have been satisfactory, for at the end of it Schultz called in Kant, together with two other students, and offered to secure them good openings and speedy preferment if they cared to enter the ministry. Kant's rationalistic bent and his distaste for the more evangelical aspects of religion were doubtless factors in his decision not to enter the ministry or to pursue his theological studies. These hours with Schultz, indeed, seem to have been the last he spent on Christian theology for many years. Except for certain volumes of church history, which he says he read with pleasure, he felt to the end of his life scant interest in contemporary theological writings, and he is reported to have turned to an old catechism, used in the days of his youth, to refresh his memory before writing, as a man of seventy, his main theological work, the *Religion within the Limits of Reason alone.*

Thus, while he moved from height to height in his strictly philosophical inquiries, his whole conception of Christian theology remained almost unchanged from youth to old age. To the development of Biblical interpretation and criticism in the eighteenth century he seems to have given virtually no attention. The fundamental pietist precepts which had been taught him by his parents and drilled into him at the Collegium were reinforced at the University by Schultz's lectures and, we may imagine, by Knutzen's pietist theology. These essential ideas became and remained identified in his mind with the Christianity of the Bible. It is invariably the pietist version of Christianity that he seems to have in view in his later writings. True, he had early dissociated himself from certain aspects of pietism, but its emphases on the moral or practical side of the religious life and on the doctrines of sin, rebirth, atonement, and the like, became determinants that gave form to his own mature attempt to build, within the limits of reason, the structure of his theology.

We need only mention the main landmarks in Kant's life after he left the University. His poverty obliged him to act as family tutor for several years after completing his university course. Of these years little more is known than that, though he chafed under the restrictions of his post, he performed his duties painstakingly and endeared himself to the families he served. In 1755 he attained a position of greater independence when he began work as *Privatdozent* in the University of Königsberg. For the next fifteen years he lectured to large classes who were attracted by his brilliance and by the inherent interest of the subjects he taught. These included logic and metaphysics, mathematics and natural science, and the new subject of physical geography. Twice during this period he applied in vain for a vacant professorship. In 1765 he sought the help of Schultz toward his desired advancement. Schultz, we are told, apparently alarmed by the complete separation of religion and science which Kant had urged in the introduction to his first publication, the *General History of Nature and Theory of the Heavens* (1755), refused to aid him until he had answered in a satisfactory manner Schultz's solemn question, "Do you fear God with all your heart?" That the question was asked is an indication of the extent to which Kant was drifting away from pietist orthodoxy; but the fact that Kant was apparently able to quiet the fears of his old teacher is proof that he still retained a firm belief in at least this fundamental doctrine of the Christian religion.

In 1770, at the age of forty-six, Kant was at last appointed to the Ordinary Professorship in Logic and Metaphysics at Königsberg. Both before and after this appointment he received tempting calls to other universities. His physical frailty, however, caused him to fear that a change of residence might endanger the labors of composition which he was pursuing with tremendous diligence. During these years his friends complained bitterly of his neglect of them, and every letter he found time to write opens with an apology for his tardiness in replying. In 1781 appeared the *Critique of Pure Reason*, on which he had labored almost continuously for eleven years. The next few years were marked by even greater literary activity; the *Critique of Practical Reason* appeared seven years after the publication of the first *Critique*, and the *Critique of Judgment*, two years after that. Kant had now become the most important figure in the University of Königsberg; and by the last decade of the century his fame had extended throughout Germany and into France and England, and his critical philosophy was being taught in all German universities, whether Catholic or Protestant.

IV. The Publication of "Religion within the Limits of Reason alone"

The publication of the *Religion*,[1] Kant's last major work, precipitated its author into his only serious conflict with official power. The death of Frederick the Great in 1786 brought to the throne the religiously orthodox Frederick William II. Two years later the liberal von Zedlitz, to whom Kant had dedicated *The Critique of Pure Reason*, was replaced, as head of the state department of church and schools, by Wöllner, already known as a bigoted opponent of the *Aufklärung*. On 9 July, 1788, Wöllner issued an edict which threatened civil punishment and dismissal from office to all under his jurisdiction (including teachers) who deviated from adherence to Biblical doctrines. Moreover, all books dealing in any degree with religious subjects were henceforth to be submitted to duly accredited censors and were not to be published until the necessary *imprimatur* had been secured.

In obedience to this decree, Kant in 1791 submitted the first of the four books of the present treatise to Hillmer, one of the official censors in Berlin. This official passed the article as being mainly philosophical in character and as being addressed only to scholars. Accordingly it appeared in the April, 1792, number of the *Berlinische Monatsschrift*. But when Kant submitted Book Two for approval, Hillmer, with the support of his colleague Hermes, refused permission to publish on the ground that the essay controverted the teachings of the Bible.

Kant now found himself in a curious position. As a true son of the Enlightenment, he was a strong advocate of the right and duty of every man to judge for himself in religious as well as in secular matters. In an interesting article entitled *An Answer to the Question, What is Aufklärung?* published eight years earlier (1784) and dedicated to Frederick the Great, he had declared the motto of the Enlightenment to be, "Have courage to make use of your *own* intellect!" Its spirit, he writes, is the spirit of freedom, and only a king who makes it his duty to leave his people free in religious matters is worthy of the appelation *aufgeklärt*.

Yet, as Kant goes on to say in this same article, the business of the state must proceed; and the state must possess a mechanism whose parts are passive in respect to the whole and responsive to

[1] This abbreviation is used in the remainder of the Introduction.

orders from above. "Here, indeed, reasoning is not permitted; one must obey." It is a soldier's duty to obey his commanding officer instantly and implicitly. Now the government, even that of Frederick the Great, held jurisdiction over both the school and the church. In 1766, for example, Frederick had censured severely various professors in the University of Königsberg for neglecting their duties. In his article Kant had approved the official conception of the relation between church and state. "A minister," he says, "is bound, in dealing with his catechumens and his congregation, to conform his discourse to the symbols of the church he serves." As an officer of the church he is not free to teach what he pleases; it is his duty to say, "This is what our church teaches." Thus, to all appearances, Kant had closed his own mouth. The state had decided that what he had written was contrary to the orthodox position; as a professor in an institution under state control his duty was to obey the royal command—royal, though phrased and promulgated by Wöllner.

Kant had left, however, a loophole of escape. A soldier may, as a lecturer on army tactics, express himself freely and openly. So with a cleric: "as a scholar, he has perfect freedom and is indeed under an obligation to make known to the public all his carefully-proved and well-intentioned opinions regarding what is faulty in the ecclesiastical symbols and tenets." Though as a priest he is bound to orthodoxy, as a student he is free.

Such an attitude was far from being agreeable to Wöllner and his associates. Their position was clearly stated in the edict of 1788: "A subject of the Prussian state is declared free to hold what religious views he likes, so long as he quietly performs his duties as a good citizen of the state and so long as he keeps any peculiar opinion to himself and carefully guards himself from spreading it or persuading others, making them uncertain in their faith or leading them astray." Opposed as he was to all the external paraphernalia of churchly Christianity, Kant especially resented this attempt to lay the yoke of orthodoxy so strictly upon a people struggling for intellectual and spiritual freedom. He had, before 1792, openly criticized Wöllner's repressive policy, refraining only from specifically naming that official. The government had at that time shrunk from curbing the literary freedom of so famous a thinker. But when there came before the censors' eyes Book Two of the *Religion*, treating of various biblical doctrines in an unorthodox fashion, this freedom came to an end.

Kant's deep and considered respect for the state's authority made it hard for him to apply himself, as he now did, to evading the prohibition of the Berlin censors. As was well known, the philosophical and theological faculties of several of the German universities were invested with the right to authorize the publication of books dealing with religious subjects. Accordingly, Kant submitted the three unpublished Books of the present work to the philosophical faculty at Jena and, having secured therefrom the necessary *imprimatur*,[1] published the whole at Königsberg in 1793.

But the state was not through with him. In October, 1794, he received the following communication from the king himself: "Our most high person has for a long time observed with great displeasure how you misuse your philosophy to undermine and debase many of the most important and fundamental doctrines of the Holy Scriptures and Christianity; how, namely, you have done this in your book, *Religion innerhalb der Grenzen der blossen Vernunft*, as well as in other smaller works. . . . We demand of you immediately a most conscientious answer and expect that in the future, towards the avoidance of our highest disfavor, you will give no such cause for offense, but rather, in accordance with your duty, employ your talents and authority so that our paternal purpose may be more and more attained. If you continue to resist, you may certainly expect unpleasant consequences to yourself."[2] Thus, as Oman puts it,[3] was "the aged sage and, in his own dry way, the saint of Königsberg treated to a severe spiritual admonition for his dangerous tendencies; the man who spent a laborious life teaching the age the eternal order of personal duty was rebuked by the crude youth whose ill-considered fits of repression were as oil poured upon the furnace of revolt."

Kant answered this communication at length and in a manner for which he has often been censured. The first part of his reply consists in an elaborate defense of himself. He has intended all his writings on religion solely for scholars in the fields of philosophy and theology, whose right to independent thought on these subjects it is to the interest of the government to foster. His only aim

[1] I am following here the note in *Kants Gesammelte Schriften*, Berlin Edition, VI, 499. Previous accounts in English have insisted that he received the *imprimatur* from the University of Königsberg.

[2] Cf. *Vorrede* to *Streit der Facultäten* (Berlin Edition, VII, 316); here translated.

[3] *The Problem of Faith and Freedom*, p. 178

in the *Religion*, he claims, is to discover how religion may be brought clearly and forcefully to the hearts of the people. This is a research which does not interest the public and which does not concern popular teachers. It is the business of these, he admits, to await the orders of the government. As to the actual contents of the book, Kant insists that his sole purpose was to criticize not Christianity but the religion of reason, whose practical sufficiency but speculative inadequacy he claims to have demonstrated. The failure of natural religion to explain such problems as the origin of evil clearly leaves room for a divine revelation. So far from criticizing Christianity adversely, he has shown his high estimation of it by declaring the Bible to be the best vehicle for the instruction of the public in a truly moral religion. His sincerity in expressing these opinions, finally, is vouched for by his age and the consideration that he must look forward to the possibility of soon rendering an account of his life to the Supreme Judge.

Having thus pleaded his innocence, Kant proceeds to pledge himself to future obedience: "I hereby, as Your Majesty's most faithful servant, solemnly declare that henceforth I will entirely refrain from all public statements on religion, both natural and revealed, either in lectures or writings." This promise he kept until the king's death in 1797, when he felt himself relieved of the obligation, on the ground that the phrase, "as your Majesty's most faithful servant," bound him only during the king's lifetime. Nor did he believe that he was bound to suppress the second, slightly enlarged, edition of the present work which appeared in 1794.[1] Wöllner was dismissed from office in 1797 and his edict cancelled shortly after.

The events here recounted will explain the discussion of censorship in Kant's Preface to the First Edition. Much has been said regarding the mental reservation of his promise to the king. The following note was found among his papers after his death: "Recantation and denial of one's inner convictions is base, but silence in a case like the present is a subject's duty. And if all that one says must be true, it does not follow that it is one's duty to tell publicly everything which is true."[2] Some have thought that either

[1] In the meantime, the First Edition had been reprinted at Frankfurt and Leipzig, and at Neuwied. The Second Edition was also reprinted at Frankfurt and Leipzig. A synopsis of the work, intended as a popularization, appeared in 1796 at Riga.
[2] Quoted by Paulsen in *Immanuel Kant, his Life and Doctrine* (Eng. tr.), p. 50. Cf. also below, p. 178, †n. In a letter to Moses Mendelssohn in April, 1766, Kant wrote:

open defiance of the government or else whole-hearted loyalty to the spirit as well as to the letter of his promise would have been more worthy of the real Kant. Yet his course of action is understandable and certainly not wholly indefensible. We know how anxious he was, especially during these last years, that nothing should interfere with the completion of the gigantic intellectual task to which he had devoted his life with unusual single-mindedness. He had always been physically frail, never for a day, he tells us, wholly free from a pain in his chest, and by now (he was seventy-one years old when he wrote his reply to the king) he had fairly worn himself out with his prodigious labors. It is natural that the threat of persecution, with the danger to his continued writing which this entailed, should lead him to avoid political martyrdom and prefer the more prudent solution of his problem. He was also, as we have seen, animated with a genuine sense of civic duty towards governmental decrees and in this instance may well have felt morally bound to obey the king's command. On the other hand, he felt an equally strong sense of duty to give public expression to his ideas and naturally anticipated and, when the time came, welcomed the opportunity provided by the king's death and Wöllner's dismissal to resume the publication of his religious theories.

But whatever judgment we may feel entitled to pass upon Kant's conduct in this controversy, we must recognize that in the *Religion* itself there is no shading or toning with an eye to possible censure by an official. All is forthright and fully expressed. And we may fairly assume that Kant, like any other writer, was content to rest upon the honesty of his work, whatever the circumstances of its publication or whatever its relation to the private scruples or want of scruples of its author. In spite of any disclaimer, furthermore, the essay seems to be directed to the entire learned world and not solely to philosophers and theologians. It is, above the ordinary in Kant's writing, enlivened by apt classical quotations and allusions, by illustrations from human experience, and by material drawn from Kant's continuous reading of explorers

---

"The loss of self-respect, which arises from the consciousness of an insincere mind, would be the greatest evil that could ever befall me, but it is quite certain that it will never happen." He adds: "It is indeed true that I think many things with the clearest conviction and to my great satisfaction which I never have the courage to say; but I never say anything which I do not think." (Here translated.) Cf. his advice to Fichte, following similar lines, in a letter dated February, 1792.

and anthropologists. Plainly, in the author's mind there was no expectation or desire that such light as his labors might cast should be placed under a bushel.

V. *Kant's Philosophy of Religion as Developed in his Writings other than his "Religion within the Limits of Reason alone"*

In the treatise here translated Kant explains fully his conception of the essence and implications of true and false religion and interprets, in the light of this conception, the religion of the New Testament. To restate these ideas here is therefore unnecessary.[1] His formulation and defense of these ideas, however, and his use of technical terms, presupposes a knowledge, on the part of the reader, of the philosophical method and system which he developed in the three *Critiques*. For example, his conception of the nature of the knowing process, his distinction between phenomena and noumena, his treatment of the rationalistic proofs of God's existence, and his own moral argument to God, freedom, and immortality, are all continually relied on as the basis for distinctions and arguments in the *Religion*, although they are nowhere adequately formulated in this work. Many of Kant's minor writings, moreover, provide valuable supplementary material for the study of his ideas on religion. This section of the Introduction is accordingly devoted to a brief critical summary of the pertinent portions of the *Critiques* and of the shorter treatises, preceding and following the *Religion*, which in one way or another deal with religious questions.[2]

The key to Kant's central philosophical thesis is to be found in the first half of the *Critique of Pure Reason*. We have mentioned his early allegiance to Wolff, the systematizer of Leibniz, who, in turn, had developed the doctrines of Continental rationalism in his monadology, as Spinoza, following Malebranche and Geulincx, had developed some of the central Cartesian principles in his

---

[1] Among English summaries and discussions of Kant's religious tenets may be mentioned: C. C. J. Webb, *Kant's Philosophy of Religion* (Clarendon Press, 1926); John Oman, *The Problem of Faith and Freedom* (Hodder and Stoughton, 1906), Lecture IV; F. E. England, *Kant's Conception of God* (Dial Press, 1930) ; A. S. Pringle-Pattison, *The Idea of God in Modern Philosophy* (Oxford, 1920), Chapter II.

[2] For a somewhat fuller summary of the Kantian philosophy as developed in the three *Critiques*, see T. M. Greene's Introduction to his *Selections from Kant* (Scribner's, 1929). Edward Caird's *The Critical Philosophy of Kant* (Two Vols., Maclehose, 1909), which deals with Kant's entire system, and the more recent *Commentary to Kant's Critique of Pure Reason* (Second Edition, Macmillan, 1923) by Norman Kemp Smith, who has also translated this *Critique* (1930), are standard expositions.

pantheistic monism. The hallmark of Cartesian rationalism is a reliance upon reason as man's chief guide to a knowledge of reality and upon the principle of contradiction as the ultimate criterion of truth. The subtle and elaborate philosophies of Descartes and Malebranche, Leibniz and Spinoza, were far richer in content, far more catholic in scope and interest, than this bald statement of the rationalistic *credo* would indicate; Wolff, however, lacking the imaginative depth and metaphysical talent of his predecessors, had fashioned his system narrowly within the lines of this *credo*, and it was Wolff rather than Leibniz who was, for Kant, the spokesman of rationalism. The empiricist, Hume, on the other hand, did most to awaken Kant to the defects of Wolffianism. Kant was familiar with Locke's incomplete but epoch-making attempt to derive all knowledge from sense-experience and with Berkeley's subjective idealism which was based, in part, upon Locke's empirical thesis. But it was Hume who, in his vivid exposition and final *reductio ad absurdum* of the empirical criterion of truth, instilled in Kant what were to remain two lifelong convictions: first, that knowledge of objective reality cannot be spun out of our own heads through the agency of reason alone; second, that "intuition," or first-hand contact with and apprehension of reality, while essential to objective knowledge, does not in itself constitute knowledge but merely furnishes the mind with the raw materials of cognition—a primal datum calling for rational interpretation and systematization before the term "knowledge" may legitimately be applied to it.

Here, then, we have the clue to Kant's epistemological position. Reality can be "known" only so far as we can (a) come into first-hand intuitive contact with it, and (b) rationally apprehend and interpret what such intuition yields. The first half of the *Critique of Pure Reason* is devoted to a brilliant analysis of the nature and implications of our knowledge of the physical world. We establish contact with this world, Kant teaches, through sensuous intuition which, in turn, is possible to us mortals only under the "forms" of space and time. Even in our simplest perceptual experience these sensuous data, in their spatio-temporal patterns, are apprehended and interpreted in terms of certain basic rational concepts, the categories. There results from the organic interplay and cooperation of these diverse mental processes—and one must read the *Critique* to see how complicated and subtle the processes are—our knowledge of the physical world to which we ourselves, as physical beings, belong.

Upon this analysis of the knowing process Kant now bases certain revolutionary conclusions which are of great importance to his philosophy of religion. Deeply impressed with our entire dependence, in cognition, upon *our* finite faculties of sense and reason, which probably are inadequate to give what may be called a cosmic insight into the inner nature of things, he insists upon branding the physical world which *we* can know as merely "phenomenal." This is the world which scientists study with so large a measure of success; and the essential structure and laws of this world philosophy can discover and formulate beyond all peradventure. It is a world of order, untouched by miracles and subject ever to the categories of substance and causality—in short, a world which, philosophy can prove, is necessarily possessed of the essential nature which Newton and his fellow-scientists, in their empirical exploration of its specific character, must and do assume it to have. But—and it is here that Kant, thus far the defender of Newtonian science, limits its scope in the interest of morality, art, and religion—only an unjustifiable materialistic dogmatism will have the temerity to assert that this phenomenal world of ours is the whole of reality. Without denying objective reality to this world, or ascribing to it a Berkeleyan subjectivity, Kant yet insists upon the possibility, suggested to us by our reason, of an ultimate or "noumenal" reality, so constituted that mortal men cannot apprehend it through sensuous intuition or even grasp its essential structure through reason.

The Transcendental Dialectic of the *Critique of Pure Reason* offers, accordingly, a criticism of the complacent theorems of Wolff's rational psychology, rational cosmology, and rational theology.

Kant considers first the claims of rational psychology in his chapter on the paralogisms. Relying solely upon an analysis of the formal judgment "I think," Wolff had claimed that the soul, as the thinking "I," was a simple, numerically identical substance, ultimately distinguishable from things and capable of individual existence. Kant replies that this conclusion is arrived at by means of a fallacious argument, for the unity of self-consciousness, which conditions all perceptual experience, in no way proves the absolute noumenal unity or immortality of the self. The conclusions of rational psychology are therefore wholly unreliable, yielding no knowledge of the final nature, origin, or destiny of the soul. All speculative dogmatism, idealistic and materialistic alike, is unjustifiable, for speculative reason is here confronted by an insurmountable barrier and must for ever remain agnostic.

In the chapter on the antinomies Kant deals with the conclusions of rational cosmology. These he formulates into four theses, in the validity of which, Kant points out, every right-thinking man has a practical interest. "That the world has a beginning, that my thinking self is of simple and therefore indestructible nature, that it is free in its voluntary actions and raised above the compulsion of nature, and finally that all order in the things constituting the world is due to a primordial being, from which everything derives its unity and purposive connection—these are so many foundation stones of morals and religion."[1] To these theses Kant opposes four antitheses which seem to deprive us of a basis for religion, by maintaining, namely, that the world is infinite both spatially and temporally, that there exists in the world no room for human freedom, and that there nowhere exists an absolutely necessary Being. This is the creed of the dogmatic empiricists, the conclusions to which an examination of the empirical world seems to lead. Now both the theses and the antitheses, Kant contends, admit of perfectly valid proofs. Reason thus seems to be at conflict with itself.

The opposition of these two points of view vividly illustrates the dilemma, still present to modern thought, with which Kant and his contemporaries found themselves faced. Science and religion were engaged in mortal combat; it seemed impossible to be at once an honest thinker and observer of nature and a man of faith. Deny the antitheses, doubt the absolute regularity of natural laws or their adequacy to account for all natural phenomena, and science becomes impossible. Admit the validity of the antitheses, on the other hand, and there is nothing left but the mechanistic universe of science.

Kant's solution of these antinomies[2] rests on his distinction be-

---

[1] *Critique of Pure Reason* (Kemp Smith's tr.), p. 424

[2] Kant really solves them in two different ways. His first solution is to declare that they are concerned only with the world of appearance and that both theses and antitheses are meaningless when made to refer to things-in-themselves, for of these speculative reason can know nothing. His second solution, here described, he applies only to the third and fourth antinomies. In view of the fact, however, that this second explanation is the one which points ahead to his later theological views, we shall confine our attention to it.

tween the phenomenal world, or "world of appearance," and a possible noumenal world of ultimate reality—a distinction central to
his later theological thinking. May not *both* theses and antitheses
be true, he asks, the antitheses, if taken to apply solely to phenomena, and the theses as applying to the noumenal world? The
"intelligible" world (as he also calls it, in contrast to the "sensible"
world) and man's "intelligible" nature would, on this hypothesis,
be timeless, unaffected by the world of sense yet conditioning it *as
a whole*. The notion of transcendental freedom, as the law of the
noumenal world, would thus in no way infringe upon, or contradict, the empirical law of causality, which is thus left to reign supreme over the world of nature; and the apparent infinity of the
causal series in nature would no longer make impossible the notion
of an unconditioned Being as the underlying and sustaining ground
of the causal series as a whole. In a word, Kant, like many others
before him and since, proposes completely to separate science and
religion by restricting them to distinct realms, and by this simple
device hopes to reconcile the scientific and the religious interpretations of the world. As Paulsen summarizes it: "By banishing religion from the field of science, and science from the sphere of religion, he afforded freedom and independence to both."[1]

It is important to keep in mind, however, that at this stage Kant
offers his solution as an *hypothesis* only. Speculative reason, he
insists again and again, cannot prove anything regarding man's
immortality, transcendental freedom, an intelligible world, or an
unconditioned Being. It can merely point out that nothing in
the empirical world, as we know it, contradicts these notions, and
that they are therefore plausible possibilities. Thus once again
limits have been set to speculative reason, and the pretensions of
both positive and negative dogmatism have been disclosed. Speculative reason can never afford us knowledge of the nature of ultimate reality; but for identical reasons materialism, too, can never
prove its case. "When empiricism itself, as frequently happens,
becomes dogmatic in its attitude towards ideas, and confidently
denies whatever lies beyond the sphere of its intuitive knowledge,
it betrays the same lack of modesty; and this is all the more reprehensible owing to the irreparable injury which is thereby caused
to the practical interests of reason."[2]

[1] *Immanuel Kant, his Life and Doctrine* (Eng. tr.), p. 7
[2] *Critique of Pure Reason* (Kemp Smith's tr.), p. 427

Kant next proceeds to disprove the conclusions of rational theology by exposing the fallacies of the three traditional proofs of God's existence. The third of these, the physico-theological or teleological proof, is far more adequately treated in the *Critique of Judgment* and may therefore be dealt with conveniently in connection with our summary of the conclusions arrived at in that *Critique*.

Kant states the ontological argument, formulated by Descartes, and, before him, by Anselm and other medieval theologians, after the Wolffian manner. The mind possesses the concept of an *ens realissimum*, a Being which contains all reality in itself. Since non-existence is the negation of reality, not its affirmation, the *ens realissimum* must possess the attribute of existence. Hence the *ens realissimum*, or God, exists. Hume had previously summed up the essence of the argument in the simple sentence, "The idea of infinite perfection implies that of actual existence." The cosmological argument moves in a direction opposite to that of the ontological, and may be analyzed into two distinct stages. The first affirms that if anything contingent exists, there must exist a necessary and unconditioned Being as its cause; the second, that since experience can tell us nothing of the nature of such a Being, we must rely on *a priori* concepts to supply this information. These compel us to identify this necessary Being with the *ens realissimum*, for it alone contains all the conditions of its existence within itself.

Kant now rejects both these proofs as fallacious and denies all objective validity to their conclusions. The ontological argument he condemns on three separate counts,[1] and the first stage of the cosmological on three more.[2] The second stage of the cosmological

[1] First, that the proof rests on a confusion between the logical necessity of thought and the ontological necessity of existence; second, that in an identical judgment, as, for example, that God is omnipotent, *both* subject and predicate may be rejected without contradiction; and third, that existence can never be a predicate—the possible must always include as much as the actual.

[2] (1) The very phrase, "an absolutely necessary yet unconditioned Being," is self-contradictory. Our notion of necessity is bound up completely with our notion of conditions. If, *i.e.*, all conditions are thought away, necessity disappears with them. (2) The underlying assumption, that if the conditioned is given, all the conditions leading up finally to the unconditioned are also given, is disproved by two considerations. (a) The principle, "Everything must have a cause," can be taken to apply, as Kant has previously shown, only to the world of sense, and cannot validly be made to transcend the empirical world and apply to God. The category of causality is valid *only* when limited in its application to the world of sense. (b) The assumption that the causal series cannot be infinite is unjustified—speculative reason can neither assert nor deny such infinity.

argument, moreover, rests on the ontological, and since the latter has been proved invalid, the cosmological argument is still further weakened by its reliance upon it. We may note in passing that one of his objections to the third, or teleological, proof is that it, in turn, is based on the cosmological, which, as he has shown, rests on the ontological proof. The errors of both of the previous arguments are thus inherited by the teleological argument which, in Kant's opinion, is already invalidated by various errors of its own.

Thus does Kant, nurtured in, and, as a young man, sympathetic to, the Leibnizian-Wolffian theology,[1] reject the traditional rationalistic proofs of God's existence and earn for himself the epithet of *"der Allzermalmende,"* the all-destroyer. This accusation, however, left him undisturbed, for throughout the *Critique of Pure Reason* he had had firmly in mind a new *moral* proof of a beneficent and just Deity; in limiting the range of "knowledge" he was but clearing the ground for "faith."

* * * * * * * * * * *

In the *Critique of Judgment* Kant investigates the problems which arise from the fact that the nature of the world in which we live compels us to conceive and interpret it as purposively adapted to certain ends. Natural bodies, in their own objective[2]

---

[1] Cf. his *Principiorum primorum cognitionis metaphysicae nova dilucidatio* ("A New Exposition of the First Principles of Metaphysical Knowledge," translated by England in his *Kant's Conception of God*, 1930), Kant's habilitation essay in 1755, and other early papers, which reveal his strong Leibnizian bent; *Allgemeine Naturgeschichte und Theorie des Himmels* ("General History of Nature and Theory of the Heavens"), 1755, where he argues, along metaphysical lines, for the compatibility of a mechanical explanation of nature with a teleology which regards all nature as depending on God; and especially, *Der einzig mögliche Beweisgrund zu einer Demonstration des Daseins Gottes* ("The only Possible Argument for the Demonstration of the Existence of God," translated by Richardson in *Essays and Treatises*), 1763. Here Kant, while insisting that although it is necessary to be convinced of God's existence it is not so necessary to be able to demonstrate it, yet believes himself to be in a position to offer a genuine *a priori* or speculative proof of His existence. He rejects the Anselmic-Cartesian formulation of the ontological argument; argues, as he did later in the first *Critique*, that existence is not a predicate of anything; and then proceeds to show that it is impossible that nothing should exist, hence that something must necessarily exist, then that such necessary being must be one, as the ultimate ground of all else, and finally that it must be simple, unchangeable and eternal, as well as spiritual, endowed with both understanding and will. Hence there is a God. In an added *Meditation* Kant also advances an *a posteriori*, teleological argument for God's existence.

Note, in contrast, various late essays, such as *Über das Misslingen aller philosophischen Versuche in der Théodicée* ("On the Failure of all the Philosophical Essays in the *Théodicée*," translated by Richardson in *Essays and Treatises*), 1791, where Leibnizian principles are severely criticized.

[2] Apart from this *objective* adaptation to its *own* ends, the natural world as a whole is adapted to the satisfaction of man's *subjective* intellectual and aesthetic needs. To begin with, it is an orderly cosmos whose structure and activity can, to some extent at least,

existence, seem to be inexplicable except in terms of purposiveness or design. Can we imagine that the curious interconnections and subtle adaptations evident everywhere in nature are the result of blind chance or of the play of unintelligent, mechanical forces? But if there is design, must there not be a Designer, and is the Designer not the God we seek?

The distinction must first of all be drawn between external and internal or organic adaptation. Nature supplies innumerable instances of the external adaptation of one natural existence to the needs of another, of plants, for example, to animals, and of both to man. That this must be the outcome of design, that plants must have been created for the benefit of herbivorous animals and the whole world for the sake of man, was the argument upon which metaphysicians had been relying almost entirely for their support of a teleological view of the natural world. Were this a valid argument, we should then be justified in inferring the nature of the Designing Intelligence from the way in which physical nature serves man, the alleged "lord and end of creation." Kant's dismal picture[1] of the treatment man often receives at nature's hands would, indeed, support the inference that this Designing Intelligence is altogether indifferent to man's welfare. Kant, however, makes impossible such an inference by maintaining that the examples in the world of external adaptation may suggest, but can never prove, the existence of a Designing Intelligence as their source.[2]

There are in the world of nature, however, innumerable examples of a different kind of purposiveness. A tree contains within

be comprehended by a rational mind. This compatibility of the physical universe to the mind of man is the fundamental presupposition of all empirical scientific inquiry. Nature, again, is adapted in many of its forms to the satisfying of our aesthetic needs; natural objects are such that man can often derive aesthetic pleasure from their contemplation. Here again is evident a harmony, this time between man's aesthetic sense and the line, form and color of natural objects. How, then, is this two-fold adaptation of man's mind and the world of nature to each other to be explained? Since an adequate explanation of nature's objective or internal purposiveness will serve at the same time to explain nature's adaptation to our subjective needs, we can confine ourselves here to Kant's discussion of the former problem.

[1] Hume had painted as black a one in the *Dialogues on Natural Religion*.

[2] Kant affirms this for two reasons. (a) Since the use of things in such cases is *external* to the things themselves, it determines nothing as to the mode of their origin; the adaptation may always be an accident. (b) None of these adaptations can be regarded as a purpose of nature unless that to which it is immediately advantageous is itself a purpose of nature; and nowhere in the natural world is a final end discoverable which is capable of justifying and accounting for such design. The suffering which nature continually causes man and the calamities with which it is wont to overwhelm him make impossible the designation of man as nature's final end. Cf. *Critique of Judgment* (Bernard's tr.), pp. 268 ff., and 346 ff.

itself both its cause and its effect. It is essentially a self-caused cause. As a genus, it is self-multiplying, itself the source of trees of its own kind. As an individual, it has the faculty of growth, an internal creative process. It and its members are mutually dependent upon each other; a leaf dies when detached from its tree; the tree dies if repeatedly defoliated. Now the origin of such marvelous reciprocal adaptation, in which every part is at once an end and a means, is mechanically inexplicable. Viewed as the chance result of the interplay of blind mechanical forces it is so improbable as to be, to all intents and purposes, impossible.[1] To explain a tree, therefore, we are forced to make use of a special teleological principle according to which a natural "organism" (in which every part is reciprocally end and means) is explained as having been somehow purposed or designed. This principle, then, differs from the mechanical in this, that whereas according to the latter principle an effect follows blindly and automatically in the wake of its cause, in an organized body an *idea* is the basis of its possibility and determines the nature and function of all its parts.[2]

We are now confronted with a dilemma. Both the mechanical and the teleological principles are essential to an explanation of nature, yet the two seem to be in conflict. The mechanical principle, which assumes that nature is wholly explicable in terms of blind mechanical laws, is, for the purposes of exact science, all-important; and since purposiveness implies a reference to the supersensible it constitutes, from the point of view of natural science, an appeal to the unknown and unknowable and so can never be admitted by the man of science as a causal factor. On the other hand, Kant has just shown why natural organisms are, in the last analysis, mechanically inexplicable. "Absolutely no human reason . . . can hope to understand the production of even a blade of grass by mere mechanical causes."[3] "That crude matter should have originally formed itself according to mechanical laws, that life should have sprung from the nature of what is lifeless, that matter should have been able to dispose itself into the form of a self-maintaining pur-

---

[1] Cf. Bergson's similar argument in *Creative Evolution* (Mitchell's tr., 1911).

[2] The mechanical and teleological principles differ in another respect also. A mechanically causal combination is ever progressive—a thing cannot at the same time be the cause and the effect of something else; in a purposively causal combination, on the other hand, the same thing may properly be called both a cause and an effect. A tree's leaves are both the cause and the effect of the tree's continued existence.

[3] *Critique of Judgment* (Bernard's tr.), p. 326

posiveness—this . . . [is] contradictory to reason."[1] The problem of the ultimate origin of natural organisms cannot be solved in purely mechanical terms; the notion of purpose or design, though scientifically incomprehensible and marking, as it were, an unsolved problem, is yet essential to an adequate explanation of the universe. We are faced, therefore, with an antinomy: it is, on the one hand, a necessary law of the human understanding that all natural processes be judged in terms of mechanical laws; all organized products of nature, on the other hand, are mechanically inexplicable and compel us to resort to the teleological principle of design.

While the technical details of Kant's solution of this antinomy does not particularly concern us,[2] the practical relation which the two principles must, in his opinion, be made to bear to each other is of considerable importance. Since each principle is universally extensive, claiming as its domain the entire natural world, they can be reconciled only by the complete subordination of one to the other. Science claims that the teleological principle should be subordinated to the mechanical, the assumption being that as scientific knowledge grows more complete the resort to teleology will gradually become unnecessary, *i.e.*, that an omniscient scientific intelligence in the world would be able to explain all nature mechanically. Kant supports,[3] instead, the "idealistic" position, which wholly subordinates the mechanical to the teleological principle on the ground that the ultimate explanation of nature is more likely to be akin to the teleological than to the mechanical. Of greater interest to us, however, is his suggestion that there may exist a common supersensible source of both mechanism and design. "The principle which should render possible the compatibility of both [principles] in judging of nature must be placed in that which lies outside both . . . but yet contains their ground, *i.e.*, in the supersensible; and each of the two methods of explanation must be referred thereto."[4] Thus, while insisting that we can know nothing

---

[1] *Ibid.*, pp. 345–6

[2] Kant solves the antinomy as follows: These principles are both *subjectively* necessary as "regulative" principles; they are not necessarily valid, however, as "constitutive" principles. The thesis and antithesis of this antinomy may therefore be restated as follows: *Thesis*—investigate nature as if it were wholly explicable in mechanical terms; go as far along these lines as you possibly can: *Antithesis*—you will not be able to explain certain natural products mechanically; you will ultimately have to fall back upon a teleological explanation.

[3] *Critique of Judgment* (Bernard's tr.), pp. 328 ff.

[4] *Ibid.*, p. 329. Cf. pp. 352, 372, etc.

of this hypothetical ultimate principle of explanation which, he says, must remain wholly incomprehensible to both our speculative and our practical reason, Kant honestly recognized our need for a basis of union between the mechanical and teleological principles.

Thus far we have been dealing with the argument *to* design, and we have seen that Kant recognizes in the world of nature the unmistakable marks of some sort of designing hand. He next raises the question, How are these teleological facts to be accounted for? "To explain the purposiveness of nature," he says, "men have tried either *lifeless matter* or a *lifeless God*, or again, *living matter* or a *living God*."[1] The first and second of these attempts he dismisses summarily. The materialistic doctrine[2] that the world reduces ultimately to lifeless matter, a system of mere mechanical causality, is a theory "so plainly absurd that it need not detain us." Organization requires to be explained, not ignored. Opposed to this is the doctrine of fatality, that reality is a lifeless God. Kant takes Spinoza to be the modern exponent of this view. It too fails to give us the explanation we seek; for if the cases of organic adaptation in the world are thought of as having their ultimate source not in the *understanding* of an original Being but in the blind and inexorable necessity of his nature, these purposive combinations are again disregarded and left unexplained. Kant considers the theory of hylozoism (living matter) with greater care. According to this theory, matter either is itself declared to be living and formative, or else it is said to possess an inner and hidden principle of life, a world-soul. As an explanation of our problem, this theory, Kant points out, is inadequate and unsatisfactory. To say that matter is alive amounts to a contradiction in terms, for the fundamental characteristic of matter, as scientifically known, is its inertia, its lifelessness. To resort, on the other hand, to the hypothesis of a world-spirit is nothing but an appeal to the unknown. Hylozoism, therefore, can furnish no *dogmatic* solution to the problem in question. Kant again suggests, however, that organization *may* ultimately not be different in kind from mechanism, and that organisms *may* have arisen from the same hidden source from which the mechanical principle springs, a source which is somehow the supersensible basis of nature. Some form of hylozoism

[1] *Critique of Judgment* (Bernard's tr.), p. 301, n.
[2] Cf. *ibid.*, §§72, 73.

that is, may conceivably be the explanation of which we are in search.

The fourth explanation is theism[1] which "derives [the purposes of nature] from the original ground of the universe, as from an intelligent Being (originally living), who produces them with design."[2] Is this an explanation of whose objective validity we can be dogmatically certain? Kant believes not, for two reasons. There is, in the first place, the fundamental difficulty referred to in our consideration of the *Critique of Pure Reason*, that *no* dogmatic certainty about the noumenal or supersensible is attainable by theoretic reason. Hylozoism cannot be proved right, but neither can it be proved false; it remains, as far as theoretic reason is concerned, an abiding possibility. And theism, he now points out, as he did in the first *Critique*, is equally unprovable. The teleological argument starts from an experience of the phenomena of the present world, their constitution and disposition, and seeks to mount from this empirical base to a supersensible Being, nature's original Cause. But a Being who cannot, like the world of nature, Himself be revealed to us *in experience* is a Being "of no avail for dogmatic determinations."[3] Sense-experience is the sole source of "knowledge"; and since we can have no such experience of the God of theism, we can make no dogmatic assertions as to His existence. "Experience," as Kant summarizes it, " . . . can never . . . raise us above nature to the purpose of its existence, and so to the determinate concept of [a] supreme Intelligence."[4]

A further objection[5] to the theistic explanation of the world is its two-fold inadequacy. It fails, in the first place, to do justice to the *self*-organizing character of natural organisms. It regards them as products of an external design, whereas the creative forces in nature lie within the organism itself. Nature is not merely organized—it is self-organizing. To compare it to a work of art or to a watch is to do less than justice to the distinctive characteristic of

[1] Kant designates the position here discussed as theistic, but it is really typical eighteenth-century deism.
[2] *Critique of Judgment* (Bernard's tr.), p. 301
[3] *Ibid.*, p. 308
[4] *Ibid.*, p. 364
[5] Kant has here stated the teleological proof of God's existence in typical eighteenth-century fashion, where God is thought of as quite distinct from the world and as imposing upon it, from without, a certain preconceived form or arrangement. When the argument is stated in these terms it is not strange that God should be likened to a watchmaker who plans his watch, constructs it, and then casts it off, as it were, to run itself. It is the argument in this form which Kant now rejects.

living organisms. And the notion of a designing Intelligence fails, in the second place, to measure up to our highest ideal of the divine Mind. In *our* thinking we cannot free ourselves from our own mental limitations; we must reason from the parts to the whole, first conceive a plan and then execute it. "We can however think an Understanding which, being, not like ours, discursive, but intuitive, proceeds from the *synthetical-universal* (the intuition of the whole as such) to the particular, *i.e.*, from the whole to the parts";[1] an Understanding for which to have conceived a plan is to have already executed it, one for which the possible and the actual are identical. This concept of an intuitive Understanding for which the whole and the parts mutually and organically involve each other has been described as Kant's conception of God in its profoundest form and an inalienable element in the edifice of modern theism.[2] Kant fails to develop the rich possibilities of this conception or to incorporate it adequately into his moral theology.[3] It serves, nevertheless, to reveal the inadequacy of the notion of a First Cause who first conceives a plan of the universe and then translates that plan into action, and it makes quite impossible a dogmatic acceptance of the deistic hypothesis, in the form stated, as the explanation of natural adaptation.

Kant thus concludes that we cannot explain the purposiveness of nature with any dogmatic certainty. This is why the phrase "*natural* purposiveness" is valuable; it reminds us that we *do* know that nature is somehow purposive but that we *cannot* know the ultimate explanation of this purposiveness. He accepts "theism," however, as "certainly superior to all other grounds of explanation."[4] It is at least non-mechanical, and must be accepted as the best explanation available.

But if we reverse the problem and ask, What basis for a theology is there in natural purposiveness? we see at once that physico-theology must fail to satisfy man's religious needs. For "we may set beneath natural purposes many intelligent original beings or

---

[1] *Critique of Judgment* (Bernard's tr.), p. 322
[2] Mackintosh and Caldecott, *Selections from the Literature of Theism*, p. 182
[3] Cf. however Kant's conception of God as one who views man's endless progress, from the lower to the higher degrees of moral perfection, as a single whole—who in a single intellectual intuition embraces the whole existence of rational beings. Cf. *Critique of Practical Reason* (Abbott's tr.), p. 219; *Religion*, p. 43 below; *Vorlesungen über die philosophische Religionslehre*, p. 168, where God is described as having created the world out of nothing by a single intelligible act.
[4] *Critique of Judgment* (Bernard's tr.), p. 305

only a single one."[1] A demonology, wherein the good in the world is the work of good spirits, the evil, of malignant spirits, is by no means impossible. And even granting the more probable proposition that the world is the result of a single Intelligence, what does this tell us of the nature of such an Intelligence? The utmost that we are justified in inferring is the existence of a very powerful World-Architect,[2] which is wholly different from establishing the existence of an omnipotent Creator of the world. Neither can we, from observation of nature, tell whether this Intelligence is infinite or eternal, or (and this concerns the religious consciousness most of all) whether it possesses a moral nature and is attentive to our moral needs. "Physical teleology impels us, it is true, to seek a theology; but it cannot produce one, however far we may investigate nature by means of experience. . . . "[3] The utmost it can do is to give "sufficient ground of proof to our theoretical *reflective*[4] judgment to *assume* the being of an intelligent World-Cause."[5]

Kant has now completed his work of destruction. He has shown that speculative reason is unable to attain to a sure or adequate conception of God, whether by the *a priori* or the *a posteriori* road. The teleological argument, he admits, "always deserves to be mentioned with respect. It is the oldest, the clearest, and the best suited to ordinary human reason."[6] And moreover, he continues in an eloquent passage, it would be "utterly vain to attempt to diminish in any way the authority of this argument. Reason, constantly upheld by this ever-increasing evidence, which, though empirical, is yet so powerful, cannot be so depressed through doubts suggested by subtle and abstruse speculation, that it is not at once aroused from the indecision of all melancholy reflection, as from a dream, by one glance at the wonders of nature and the majesty of the universe—ascending from height to height up to the all-highest, from the conditioned to its conditions, up to the supreme and unconditioned Author [of all conditioned being]."[6] Yet as argument it is fallacious and unsatisfactory in many ways. Kant ably defends himself, however, against his critics. "All lamentation or impotent anger," he says to the defenders of the

---

[1] *Ibid.*, p. 367
[2] Cf. *Critique of Pure Reason* (Kemp Smith's tr.), p. 522
[3] *Critique of Judgment* (Bernard's tr.), p. 367
[4] *i.e.*, regulative judgment, expressing subjective, not objective, necessity.
[5] *Ibid.*, p. 377; my italics.
[6] *Critique of Pure Reason* (Kemp Smith's tr.), p. 520

traditional proofs, "on account of the alleged mischief of rendering doubtful the coherency of your chain of reasoning, is vain pretentiousness, which would fain have us believe that the doubt here freely expressed as to your argument is a doubting of sacred truth, in order that under this cover the shallowness of your argument may pass unnoticed."[1] But, he continues, for the encouragement of the more sincere seekers after God, "even if the concept of the original Being could be also found determinately by the merely theoretical path . . . it would afterwards be very difficult—perhaps impossible . . . to ascribe to this Being by well-grounded proofs a causality in accordance with moral laws; and yet without this that quasi-theological concept could furnish no foundation for religion."[2] Once prove God's existence out of the mouth of non-moral nature and you have a non-moral God of no use to the religious consciousness. In Kant's opinion, then, it is all to the good that man is forced to depend upon the moral proofs of God's existence and nature for an adequate theology and a sound basis for religious faith.

* * * * * * * * * *

The *Critique of Practical Reason* (1788) and the somewhat earlier *Fundamental Principles of the Metaphysic of Morals*[3] contain Kant's description of the essential characteristics of morality and his account of the inferences to God, freedom, and immortality, which, he believes, may properly be based upon the moral experience. In view of his virtual reduction of religion to morality in the *Religion* and the importance, in his philosophy of religion, of his moral proof of God's existence, it will be necessary to note the salient features of his ethical theory.

The basis of this theory is man's moral experience. Kant describes this experience as an immediate intuition of the value and importance of moral goodness; as a spontaneous feeling of respect for the moral law and an innate sense of "ought" or obligation to obey the law's behests. He believes that this moral faculty is as inexplicable as is man's capacity for sensuous intuition, but he accepts it as an ultimate, incontrovertible fact and regards it with awe and wonder. "*Duty!* Thou sublime and mighty name that dost embrace nothing charming or insinuating, but requirest sub-

---

[1] *Critique of Judgment* (Bernard's tr.), p. 422
[2] *Ibid.*, p. 423
[3] *Grundlegung zur Metaphysik der Sitten*, 1785. Cf. also the *Metaphysik der Sitten* ("Metaphysic of Morals"), 1797, and Kant's minor ethical writings.

mission, and yet seekest not to move the will by threatening aught that would arouse natural aversion or terror, but merely holdest forth a law which of itself finds entrance into the mind . . . a law before which all inclinations are dumb, even though they secretly counter-work it; what origin is there worthy of thee . . . ?"[1]

Kant does not conceive of moral intuition as a direct irrational insight into the rightness or wrongness of any *particular* act; it is "intuitive" only in that man's sense of the reality and vast significance of the *general* distinction between right and wrong is immediate, irreducible, and not itself debatable. Each specific moral decision, however, calls for the active use of reason. Here reason becomes "practical." Whereas "speculative" reason aims solely at knowledge for its own sake, "practical" reason competes with the inclinations in determining man's will and guiding his conduct. It is thus the rational expression of his moral consciousness, the moral law become articulate in him. In this account of moral cognition Kant is obviously remaining true to the central epistemological thesis of the first *Critique*. There a knowledge of the physical world was found to arise solely through the cooperation of *sensuous* spatio-temporal intuition and reason (the understanding), the former providing the raw material or content of perceptual knowledge, the latter organizing this crude sensuous awareness categorically into a rational knowledge of an orderly world of nature. Here *moral* intuition, the immediate and irresistible apprehension of moral value, takes the place of, or at least constitutes an essential supplement to, sensuous intuition, and "practical" reason, whose law (the moral law) is the analogue to the categories of the understanding, organizes blind moral intuition into a rational moral apprehension. Kant does, indeed, refuse to call this apprehension "knowledge" on the ground that we are here in the realm of moral "faith." We can, however, ignore this distinction for the time being[2] and proceed with our account of his ethical theory.

Reason interprets man's innate sense of duty as an obligation to obey the moral law. In describing this law, which is the foundation-stone of his theories of morality and religion alike, Kant gives it two distinct but complementary formulations. The first is designed to bring out the fact that it is, in contrast to the hedonistic principle of the satisfaction of private inclinations, the law of im-

[1] *Critique of Practical Reason*, tr. in Abbott's *Kant's Theory of Ethics*, p. 180
[2] Cf. below, p. lxxv.

partial justice: "Act only on that maxim [or principle of conduct] whereby thou canst at the same time will that it should become a universal law."[1] That is, appraise your contemplated act objectively, as you might the act of another, and not subjectively, with an eye merely to private gain. The second formulation defines the law's social setting. "So act as to treat humanity, whether in thine own person or in that of any other, in every case as an end withal, never as means only."[2] That is, regard all men, including yourself, as human beings of intrinsic worth, and do not use them, like physical objects, merely as a means to non-moral ends; remember your own and their moral nature and destiny. These formulae lead to the important concept of men as citizens in a "kingdom of ends,"[3] that is, a union of rational beings each of whom is a free and responsible moral agent, yet all subject to the moral law. This concept is the ethical basis of Kant's significant interpretation of the "kingdom of God" in Book Three of the *Religion*.

The moral law possesses four characteristics which are implicit in its formulations but deserve special mention. (1) It is distinguished from the laws of nature in defining what *ought* to be, not what is. Man, it says, ought to obey moral reason instead of following sensuous inclination; he ought, as a morally rational being, to look upon the law of reason as the object of his *highest* allegiance. The voice of duty, accordingly, is a "categorical imperative" which men cannot ignore; whereas prudential considerations take the form of "hypothetical imperatives" which may be disregarded with impunity. We do, as sentient beings, desire happiness, and its attainment rests on certain conditions which prudence seeks to satisfy; but happiness and its conditions may both be waived without incurring moral blame. Duty, on the other hand, is morally inescapable and its demands are absolute. (2) It is dictated to each individual by his *own* moral reason. Thus man, as a moral agent, is autonomous and his reason is self-legislative. Man is under no absolute obligation to obey the laws of another, not even the laws of God *because* they are God's laws. Man's own conscience is the highest moral tribunal. (3) Yet since the moral law is the law of reason it is universally and necessarily binding upon all rational beings alike, finite and infinite. It is the same

[1] Cf. *Fundamental Principles of the Metaphysic of Morals*, tr. in Abbott's *Kant's Theory of Ethics*, p. 38
[2] *Ibid.*, p. 47
[3] *Ibid.*, pp. 51 ff.

law for all men because the moral faculty is, in essence (though
not necessarily in strength) the same in all;[1] and it is God's law
because He is a righteous God.[2] (4) The moral law can only be
known *a priori* and cannot be derived from experience. This is a
doctrine which has caused ethicists great perplexity and has
evoked many heated protests. Neither here nor in the first *Critique* is the concept of the *a priori* wholly free from ambiguity. It
is reasonable, however, to interpret the *a priori* to mean that
which is the logical (not necessarily the *temporally* antecendent)
condition of experience, its universal and necessary basis, and *a
priori* knowledge as the awareness of such conditions. Both the
categories and the moral law are *a priori* in this sense, as is our
knowledge of them. It is possible, that is, to review past experience
in recollection and survey it in a superficial manner without pene-
trating, with moral insight, into its inner structure and conditions.
Yet just as the categories are found by philosophical insight to
condition all perception, so moral insight reveals the fact that the
moral law lies at the heart of morality as its *a priori* condition.

Kant now goes on to develop the implications of man's moral
experience, as he has described it, and to base upon it certain
important inferences. The prime condition of moral obligation is
freedom to act in accordance with its requirements. Now man,
regarded merely as a physical being, is subject to the mechanical
laws of nature which Kant has shown to be invariable in their operation. As part of the phenomenal world, therefore, he is not free. In
the *Critique of Pure Reason* it was shown, however, that speculative
reason conceives of a possible noumenal realm underlying the
phenomenal realm as its non-spatial and non-temporal ground, and
suggests that man may be possessed of a dual nature, "sensible"
and "intelligible," thus enabling him to participate in both realms
and to achieve "intelligible" freedom while still subject to "sensible" determinations. What speculative reason could advance
merely as an hypothesis, practical reason now asserts to be morally
certain. Kant's proof of this is very ingenious. The starting point
is the conviction that moral obligation is not illusory but supremely real and significant. But obligation implies freedom. Freedom, in turn, is possible only if man is more than a merely phenomenal being. Hence there must be a noumenal realm and he

---

[1] This is one of Kant's basic assumptions.
[2] This is proved later. Cf. below, p. lx.

must possess a noumenal nature by virtue of which he is free. Thus freedom is the *ratio essendi* of the obligation to obey the moral law; our respect for and duty toward this law, in turn, is the *ratio cognoscendi* of freedom. Though the sense of duty is a direct intuition, and freedom but an inference, their organic inter-relation enables us to be as sure of the latter as we are of the former. Kant thus attaches to freedom an importance and a cognitive certainty which is concealed by his oft-repeated phrase, "God, freedom, and immortality." The idea of freedom, he says explicitly, "is the *only* concept of the supersensible which . . . proves its objective reality in nature . . . "[1] and is, as he puts it elsewhere, "to be reckoned under the *scibilia*." God and immortality, on the other hand, can merely be postulated[2] as the most likely solutions of difficulties which present themselves to the moral consciousness.

Freedom, in its negative aspect, is thus an "independence of everything empirical," *i.e.*, the freedom *from* the mechanical necessitation of natural laws. On its positive side it is the ability to think and act in conformity with moral standards. Despite, or perhaps because of, his dualism, however, Kant fails, in the present writer's judgment, to render his concept of freedom intelligible. Conceiving of determinism as a purely mechanical determinism, he does not see that genuine self-determinism can take place within a larger idealistically interpreted deterministic system, and he cannot appreciate the elements of strength in such a deterministic theory. Therefore, instead of defining freedom along deterministic lines, as the progressive achievement of moral value in the phenomenal world and in strict conformity with its laws, he seeks to preserve man's *absolute* autonomy by cutting him off from all influences, divine, human and physical alike, and requires him to act morally despite, rather than in and through, the larger whole. It is not strange that Kant is, in the end, unable to explain how one and the same man (for all his two-fold nature) can both be free and yet not free in one and the same act, and that, like other libertarians, he has finally to confess that man's freedom, as he conceives of it, is ultimately a mystery not to be fathomed by the human mind.

Kant next bases upon the moral experience two further inferences which are developed in his doctrine of the *Summum Bonum*,

---

[1] *Critique of Judgment* (Bernard's tr.), p. 413, my italics. Cf. p. 406.
[2] Cf. below, pp. lviii ff.

or, as he designates this idea in the *Religion*, the world's highest good—a doctrine which is the connecting link between his ethics and an important aspect of his theology. The *Summum Bonum* is man's morally rational ideal of the complete and perfect goal of human life; and its two ingredients are *virtue*, that is, moral worth attained by obedience to the moral law, and *happiness*, "the condition of a rational being in the world with whom everything goes according to his wish and will."[1] Virtue is definitely the more important of the two. The moral law must be the *sole* determining principle of a will that is to be judged good; it is even dangerous to allow other motives to *cooperate* with the moral law. Man, Kant is never weary of declaring, must do his duty out of pure respect for the law of reason and never from inclination, never from an ulterior motive such as the anticipation of happiness. "Duty for duty's sake" never had a stronger champion. And yet, though virtue, taken by itself, must remain the *supreme* good, it is nevertheless not the *whole and perfect* good. For man's ideal of the highest human good includes happiness as well as virtue. His moral reason demands as the goal of humanity a *Summum Bonum* consisting not only of virtue but of happiness exactly proportioned to virtue, always subordinate to it and conditioned by it, yet making, in conjunction with it, a complete and balanced whole. The introduction of happiness into the *Summum Bonum* is a recognition on Kant's part that even in the purest morality happiness must not be ignored. "Our weal and woe are of *very great* importance in the estimation of our practical reason,"[2] he says; "to need happiness, to deserve it, and yet at the same time not to participate in it, cannot be consistent with the perfect volition of a rational being."[3] Since, however, man must exclude the desire for his own happiness from his motives, if his will is to be pure, this demand for happiness is never merely the subjective desire of the individual that his own inclinations be satisfied. Rather, *"reason*, in prescribing the moral law, prescribes, as the final and complete end of all our actions, the *Summum Bonum, i.e.*, happiness proportioned to moral worth."[4] The inclusion of happiness as an element in the *Summum Bonum* is therefore reason's demand and the *Summum Bonum* is man's *rational* ideal.

[1] *Critique of Practical Reason* (Abbott's tr.), p. 221
[2] *Ibid.*, p. 152
[3] *Ibid.*, p. 206
[4] Kemp Smith, *Commentary to Kant's Critique of Pure Reason*, p. 574; my italics.

Kant now argues that the *Summum Bonum*, so conceived, is absolutely necessary to moral belief. It is, as it were, a pledge that the universe is systematically ordered according to moral purposes. Unless man can be assured by faith in the *Summum Bonum* that he is living under a just moral order and can thus be saved from the inhibiting fear that virtue itself may in the end be of no avail, he has not the heart to exert himself to the performance of duty. It is not enough, Kant told his students in his *Lectures on the Philosophy of Religion*,[1] for me merely to feel under obligation to obey the moral law; I must *want* to obey it. There are moral motives "which, as objective, bind me to do something, yet fail to furnish me with the necessary strength and incentives to action [*Triebfeder*]. For if actions which I recognize to be good and lawful are to materialize, certain subjective motives in me are requisite to drive me to bring them about. It is not enough for me merely to judge the act to be noble and beautiful; my choice must also be determined to this end."[2] Thus a faith in the *Summum Bonum* is the result of man's rational conviction that only if happiness is ultimately proportioned to virtue can his sense of justice be satisfied.

An observation of the state of affairs on earth, however, at once reveals a difficulty. Virtue does not invariably bring with it, in this life, a proportionate quota of happiness; "we cannot expect in the world by the most punctilious observance of the moral laws any necessary connection of happiness with virtue adequate to the *Summum Bonum*."[3] Now this apparent impossibility of the attainment of the *Summum Bonum* threatens the very foundations of morality. For "as the promotion of this *Summum Bonum* . . . is *a priori* a necessary object of our will, and inseparably attached to the moral law, the impossibility of the former must prove the falsity of the latter. If then the supreme good is not possible by practical rules, then the moral law also which commands us to promote it is directed to vain imaginary ends, and must consequently be false."[4] But to have to believe that the moral law is false would obviously, from Kant's point of view, be the greatest calamity that could overtake us.[5]

[1] *Vorlesungen über die philosophische Religionslehre* (edited by Politz and published in 1817, with a second edition in 1830), First Edition, p. 174.
[2] *Ibid.*, p. 174; here translated.
[3] *Critique of Practical Reason* (Abbott's tr.), p. 210
[4] *Ibid.*, p. 210
[5] J. S. Mackenzie, in his *Manual of Ethics* (Fifth Edition), pp. 206–207, summarizes

To avert this misfortune Kant makes his two famous postulates, *viz.*, the existence of a God to equate virtue and happiness, and of a future life in which man may attain to perfect virtue and receive its adequate reward. These postulates, he argues, are the necessary conditions of the *Summum Bonum*, and since it is man's duty to promote the latter he is under a moral obligation to postulate the conditions which will give it reality. The *basis* of the postulates is thus a necessity arising from man's moral nature and the requirements of the moral law. This basis is itself not a postulate but shares the objective validity which man's moral consciousness and freedom, its metaphysical counterpart, possess.[1] The *nature* of the postulates, on the other hand, like the nature of the *Summum Bonum*, is defined subject to the limitations of our minds. We have found that the *Summum Bonum* is a necessary ideal of reason; we now discover that reason finds it impossible to render the *Summum Bonum* conceivable in any way other than in terms of these postulates.[2] Kant thus distinguishes the ideal of the *Summum Bonum* and the postulates of God and immortality from the moral law and freedom, calling the former "objects of faith," regarding whose specific character we must remain in some doubt, while the latter are designated as "facts" to which we are entitled to attach the highest moral certainty.

Why, now, are man's immortality and God's existence necessary postulates of practical reason and objects of faith? Each is required to guarantee one of the two ingredients of the *Summum Bonum*. The first of these is *virtue*, the perfect harmony of man's mind with the moral law. Such harmony is obviously unattainable by a finite being during his lifetime. Yet it is required of him, for the moral law ordains that man ought to be perfectly virtuous, and what is thus required must somehow be possible, else the moral order, by demanding the impossible of man, proves itself fundamentally

the whole situation in a few words. "Kant considers that though the virtuous man does not aim at happiness, yet the complete well-being of a human being includes happiness as well as virtue. And apparently he thought that if we had no ground for believing that the two elements are ultimately conjoined, the ground of morality itself would be removed. For morality rests on a demand of reason; and the possibility of attaining the *summum bonum* is also a demand of reason. If the demands of reason were chimerical in the latter case, they would be equally discredited in the former."

[1] Cf. *Critique of Practical Reason* (Abbott's tr.), p. 242, n.: "It is a duty to realize the *summum bonum* to the utmost of our power, therefore it must be possible, consequently it is unavoidable for every rational being in the world to assume what is necessary for its objective possibility. The assumption is as necessary as the moral law, in connection with which alone it is valid."

[2] *Ibid.*, p. 243

unreasonable and non-moral. *We* can conceive of only one solution to the problem. "For a rational but finite being, the only thing possible is an endless progress from the lower to the higher degrees of moral perfection."[1] But infinite progress is possible only if our existence is infinite, that is, if our souls are immortal. "The *Summum Bonum*, then, practically is only possible on the supposition of the immortality of the soul; consequently this immortality, being inseparably connected with the moral law, is a postulate of pure practical reason."[2]

Kant tells us little about the nature of this future state. His general attitude is expressed in his own statement that "we can know nothing of the future, and we ought not to seek to know more than what is rationally bound up with the incentives of morality and their end."[3] In general he conceives of the next life as a continuation of this. "At least, man has no ground for believing that a sudden change will take place. Rather, experience of his state on earth and the ordering of nature in general gives him clear proofs that his moral deterioration, with its inevitable punishments, as well as his moral improvement and the well-being resulting therefrom, will continue endlessly, *i.e.*, eternally."[4] Kant attaches no importance to the resurrection of the body; "for who is so fond of his body that he would wish to drag it about with him through all eternity if he could get on without it?"[5] Yet his argument for believing in a future life at all would seem to carry with it the implication that the empirical self will survive the death of the body. The notion of a future state in which virtue will still be sought after with varying success, and happiness, virtue's reward, or its opposite, be awarded in recompense, certainly suggests that we shall be as eager for happiness then as now, and as susceptible to pain. Kant's attitude, however, is not that this conception of a future state possesses any peculiar value in itself but merely that we must conceive the future state in this manner if morality and religion are to be practically efficient in our lives.

Kant defines happiness, the second ingredient of the *Summum Bonum*, as the object of man's desire "that can be satisfied by nature in its beneficence."[6] It has to do with man's sentient nature,

[1] *Ibid.*, p. 219
[2] *Ibid.*, p. 219
[3] Cf. below, *Religion*, p. 149, n.
[4] *Vorlesungen über die philosophische Religionslehre*, p. 150; here translated.
[5] *Streit der Facultäten* (Berlin Edition) VII, 40; here translated.
[6] *Critique of Judgment* (Bernard's tr.), p. 353

and is quite impossible of attainment without the cooperation of his environment. A perfect harmony between physical nature and the moral law is needed. The moral law, however, commands quite independently of nature. "Nature," on the other hand, "has not taken [man] for her special darling."[1] On the attainability of a hedonistic goal Kant is a profound pessimist. Because of man's fickleness and natural perversity in the ways in which he seeks his own happiness and destroys the happiness of other men, and because of nature's indifference to our sentient needs, a balance of happiness over unhappiness is not to be counted on. "The value of life for us, if it is estimated by that *which we enjoy* (. . . *i.e.*, happiness), is easy to decide. It sinks below zero; for who would be willing to enter upon life anew under the same conditions?"[2] Thanks to the thoroughgoing separation which Kant has effected between the intelligible and sensible worlds and between man's rational and sensible natures, it is inevitable that he should find no essential harmony between them. In the *Summum Bonum*, however, just such an harmonious connection is declared to be necessary. We must therefore postulate the existence of a Being who acts in harmony with the moral law and who is also the ground and cause of nature.

The nature of this Being is determined solely by an analysis of the task to secure the performance of which His existence has been postulated. He must be moral, for it is His function to make the ethical *Summum Bonum* possible. He must possess intelligence in order to conceive of laws, both natural and moral. He must be endowed with a will capable of acting in accordance with a certain ideal, for the original creation of the world of nature must have been an act of His will, and the actualizing of the *Summum Bonum* must depend upon His volition. Other sides of God's nature are determined in a similar manner. "The moral principle admits as possible only the conception of an Author of the world possessed *of the highest perfection*. He must be *omniscient*, in order to know my conduct up to the inmost root of my mental state in all possible cases and into all future time; *omnipotent*, in order to allot to it its fitting consequences; similarly He must be *omnipresent*, *eternal*, etc. Thus the moral law, by means of the conception of the *summum bonum* as the object of a pure practical reason,

[1] *Ibid.*, p. 353
[2] *Ibid.*, p. 358, n.

determines the concept of the First Being *as the Supreme Being*."[1]

Kant faces squarely the disadvantages of such an anthropomorphic conception of God and deals with them in a manner consistent with his general point of view. "It is in general to be observed that one should in theory take pains to purify the concept of God of all such human ideas and keep it free from them, though one may, from a practical consideration, think to oneself and represent to others such predicates (as God's immortality, *i.e.*, His eternity) in human fashion, if the idea of God thereby attains to a greater power and strength for our morality."[2] In the *Critique of Practical Reason* he states his position more explicitly. We must, first of all, refrain from attributing to God any characteristic which we recognize to be definitely finite. When we think of Him as intelligent, for example, we must not conceive that intelligence as discursive, like our own, but intuitive. But there are three attributes which can be ascribed to God uniquely. "He is the *only holy*, the *only blessed*, the *only wise*, because these conceptions already imply the absence of limitation. In the order of these attributes He is also the *holy lawgiver* (and creator), the *good governor* (and preserver) and the *just judge*, three attributes which include everything by which God is the object of religion."[3] Other attributes we can conceive of only by raising human qualities to their highest degree, as, for example, power to omnipotence, knowledge to omniscience, and the like. Yet whatever be the qualities that we attribute to Him, our conception of the God of the moral argument necessarily remains anthropomorphic. For "if we abstract from it everything anthropomorphic, nothing would remain to us but the mere word, without our being able to connect with it the smallest notion by which we could hope for an extension of theoretical knowledge."[4] Kant's conclusion is not, however, that our moral idea of God is therefore useless. Rather, such a God is admirably suited to the satisfaction of our moral needs. These very anthropomorphisms prove that our conception of God is one that belongs not to speculative reason but to morals. "Natural theology" he considers a "singular name," a contradiction in terms. Theology

---

[1] *Critique of Practical Reason* (Abbott's tr.), p. 238. Cf. *Critique of Pure Reason* (Kemp Smith's tr.), pp. 641 ff.

[2] *Vorlesungen über die philosophische Religionslehre*, p. 156; here translated. Cf. below, *Religion*, pp. 156 ff.

[3] *Critique of Practical Reason* (Abbott's tr.), p. 228, n.

[4] *Ibid.*, p. 236

cannot be based on nature, but on morality alone. The existence
of God can be established only by practical reason and the only
God we can know is a moral God.

God, freedom and immortality are thus the only objects of a
moral faith. In regard to these three alone may man transcend
experience; and even with regard to these, the assurance he arrives
at is not a cognitive or scientific but only a moral certainty. To go
further than this is nothing but *Schwärmerei*, the indulgence in
fanciful dreams. "Here are the limits of our reason clearly deline-
ated. Whoever presumes to overstep them will be punished for his
zeal by reason itself with disgust and error. But, if we remain
within these limits,[1] we shall be rewarded by becoming both wise
and good."[2]

Kant's *Summum Bonum* proof of God's existence is probably
the weakest of his theological doctrines. The root of the difficulty
lies in his dualistic view of man's nature. In order to secure human
freedom he has analyzed man into two irreconcilable natures, the
one abstractly rational and noumenal, the other phenomenal and
purely sentient. The former is completely severed from the empirical world and all empirical motives, desires and impulses, and
is intent only upon the performance of what is often described by
Kant as a joyless duty. The latter is empty of all moral reasonableness and is concerned solely with irrational sensuous satisfaction.
Man thus bifurcated is a thoroughly unreal creature of Kant's own
imagination. Consequently both virtue and happiness tend to
be conceived of in an artificial manner. Virtue is defined in purely
rationalistic terms. The moral law is first declared to be capable
of determining man's will independently of all external aid such as
the empirical inclination to happiness, and the will is said to be
truly virtuous only so long as the categorical imperative remains
its *sole* motive to action; to *want* to do one's duty is to Kant a cause
for suspicion that the will is not as purely virtuous as it might
be. In short, morality is said to be the concern of a purely autonomous rational will. Kant's introduction of happiness into this
moral scheme is therefore inconsistent with his own principles,
and is highly detrimental to them. The *Summum Bonum*, with
happiness equated with virtue, is indeed said to be merely an

---

[1] *Innerhalb dieser Grenzen* [*i.e., der blossen praktischen Vernunft*]. The significance of the title of Kant's treatise is here apparent.
[2] *Vorlesungen über die philosophische Religionslehre*, pp. 159–160; here translated.

ideal of reason which must not be made a motive of action. Yet
without the assurance of its reality reason *cannot* be practical.
Kant states this very plainly in his *Lectures*. There *must* be a
Being who rules the world with reason and according to moral
principles and who has decreed a future state where virtue shall
be rewarded, "for otherwise all the subjectively necessary duties
which I am under obligation as a rational being to perform lose
their objective reality. Why should I make myself worthy of happiness by means of moral conduct if there exists no Being who can
secure me this happiness? Thus without God I should have to be
either a visionary or a scoundrel."[1] "If morality can offer me no
prospect that my need to be happy will be satisfied, neither can it
command me."[2] Professor Pringle-Pattison's remark is well justified: " . . . the preacher of duty for duty's sake, who had so
rigorously purged his ethics of all considerations of happiness or
natural inclination, surprises us with the baldly hedonistic lines on
which he rounds off his theory. Job is not to serve God for naught
after all. . . . An unkind critic might say that although the primacy is accorded to virtue as the supreme condition, yet the definition of virtue as 'worthiness to be happy' seems, on the other hand,
to put virtue in a merely instrumental relation towards happiness,
as the real object of desire and the ultimate end of action."[3]

The attempt has been made to defend Kant by saying that he
intends the individual to seek virtue for himself, happiness only
for others. But even if this were Kant's meaning his position would
be no more defensible. For he never tired of insisting that *any* appeal to empirical motives, such as happiness, is a pollution of
morality and a vitiation of the good will. And if happiness is never
to be the motive of action, why should an exception be made with
regard to the happiness of others? It is a Kantian principle that
what is right for one must also be fair for others and that reason
is equally and indiscriminatingly legislative for *all* rational beings.
If the moral law is really to be kept pure it must have nothing to
do with happiness, whether my happiness or that of others. How
can it be right for me to promote in others what I must strenuously
avoid seeking for myself?

The artificiality of Kant's position shows itself further in his

---

[1] *Vorlesungen über die philosophische Religionslehre*, p. 129; here translated.
[2] *Ibid.*, p. 199
[3] *The Idea of God*, pp. 32-3

view of the nature of happiness. The *Summum Bonum* argument rests on the assumption that the happiness man craves now, and will continue to desire after death, is exclusively sentient in character and unrelated to his higher nature in any internal or organic way. But he has previously shown that man's sentient nature is phenomenal, that is, temporal, and not eternal. He cannot, therefore, consistently maintain now that this phenomenal self will continue after death or that in the next life man will continue to desire the happiness which he craves in this. Kant does, indeed, occasionally[1] speak of a self-satisfaction (*Selbstzufriedenheit*, as opposed to his usual term *Glückseligkeit*, happiness) which arises directly from a consciousness of one's own inner worth. This feeling *is* related to man's moral nature and *is* the natural accompaniment of virtue, and Kant might plausibly have argued that we have a right to expect such a feeling as this to continue after death. Had Kant started with the concrete unity of the whole man he might have realized that reason's demand for a happiness proportioned to virtue is met by certain natural human instincts and feelings and that the fulfilment of moral obligations is inevitably accompanied by a satisfaction superior to, and more lasting than, a purely phenomenal or sentient happiness. His dualistic presuppositions, however, usually led him to make happiness the antithesis of virtue, not its correlate, and he certainly introduces happiness into his account of the *Summun Bonum* in such a way as to make it either superfluous, if the moral will is indeed autonomous, or, if it is not, noxious and destructive to pure morality.

His erroneous account of happiness, in turn, greatly weakens his postulate of God's existence. For, in the first place, God is introduced to guarantee to men a mental satisfaction too closely allied to our lower nature to evoke respect or moral approbation. And, in the second place, however we conceive of the reward which He is postulated to guarantee in the next life, God still remains, in Kant's argument, a *deus ex machina* introduced to resolve our moral perplexities, the great Paymaster who is to reward us for our moral efforts. But surely, if, on Kant's own principles, it is wrong to use men merely as means to our own ends, we are not entitled to bring God into our scheme of things primarily as a means to our ultimate happiness. Once again, had Kant been able

[1] Cf. *Vorlesungen über die philosophische Religionslehre*, pp. 157–8, and below, *Religion*, pp. 18, *n.; 41, n.; and 61.

to conceive of happiness in a profounder and more realistic way
he might have thought of God as the guarantee of the genuineness
and durability of the moral order as a whole. To quote Professor
Pringle-Pattison: "The real postulate or implied presupposition
of ethical action is simply that we are not acting in a world which
nullifies our efforts, but that morality expresses a fundamental aspect of reality, so that in our doings and strivings we may be said,
in a large sense, to have the universe somehow behind us. . . . And
of course that was the general idea which Kant intended to express—the broad idea of a universe as a divine moral order, not as
a power hostile or indifferent to the life of ethical endeavour."[1] This
conception, however, Kant fails to make explicit, and the argument directed against him by Galloway constitutes a fair criticism
of his *Summum Bonum* argument and its postulates: "Moral conduct, I agree, is an essential duty. But the reality and value of
my moral duties in no way depend on their being regarded as commands of God. As for happiness, it is a minor matter which per-
tains to the phenomenal world. An empirical and sensuous product
which, on your own showing, does not belong to the real world at
all, is a slender and uncertain basis on which to ground the mo-
mentous inference that God exists. I therefore decline to make the
inference and maintain that religion is not essential, for it is neither
the ground of moral obligation, nor does it affect the inner worth
of the man who reverently obeys the moral law."[2]

* * * * * * * * * * *

The critical analysis of Kant's *Opus Postumum*, published by
Erich Adickes in 1920, reveals the interesting and significant fact
that Kant himself, in his later thinking, found his ethical proof of
God's existence unsatisfactory, discarded it, and engaged during
his last years in the difficult task of redefining his faith in God and
seeking for it a more adequate foundation. "The whole teaching
of the highest good," says Adickes, "together with the proofs based
thereon of God and immortality has now . . . practically disap-
peared."[3] Kant's chief reason for making this change, Adickes
feels, was the desire to purify his ethical system of the heteronomy
and hedonism which had crept into it through his doctrine of the
Summum Bonum. Purged of this subversive element, Kant's view

[1] *Idea of God*, p. 35
[2] George Galloway, *Religion and Modern Thought*, p. 63
[3] Cf. *Opus Postumum*, pp. 846, 848-9, 832; here translated.

of moral duty regains its original consistency and rigorous purity. By the phrase "recognition of all human duties *as* divine commands," to which Kant still clings, he now means, Adickes believes, nothing but that "the moral individual is to do what is good *only* because it is good; he is thus to act without reference to any external ends whatsoever, in this life or the next, but absolutely autonomously, conformable to, and simply because of, the categorical command of his practical reason. As a religious person, however, he simultaneously recognizes that the ideals and ends which he has himself chosen, and the laws which he has himself imposed, are also God's ideals, ends, and laws, and through this recognition his motives to do good are appreciably strengthened."[1]

But Kant goes even further than this. Having consigned his long-loved *Summum Bonum* proof of God's existence, along with the classical proofs which he has demolished in the first *Critique*, to the limbo of false hopes, he now, for the first time in his life, suggests that the moral experience *itself* may legitimately be regarded as an experience of the Divine. May it not be that the virtuous individual experiences directly, in the categorical imperative, the voice of his God and that he apprehends Him, with the certainty of a personal faith, as a transcendental reality?[2] "The categorical imperative," he is now tempted to believe, "leads directly to God, yes, serves as a pledge of His reality;"[2] "in morally-practical reason and in the categorical imperative God reveals Himself."[2] Thus, instead of arguing from duty to God by way of the *Summum Bonum*, he now tends to find immediately present in man's moral experience a God who reveals Himself to man in and through the moral law.

This suggests that there is to be found in Kant's moral philosophy the germ of a theism very different from the deism of his published writings. For the very notion of a moral law implies an objective standard, a reality revealing itself to man in and through this law. Absolute moral obligation surely implies a relation between him who is obligated and an objective reality capable of evoking this sense of duty. Kant's doctrine of the legislative will would thus seem to lead naturally to some form of divine immanence. During the productive years of his life, however, he had

[1] *Ibid.*, p. 847; here translated.
[2] *Ibid.*, pp. 847, 801, 806; here translated. Cf. Kemp Smith, *Commentary to Kant's Critique of Pure Reason*, Second Edition, Appendix C, for a summary of Kant's various attempts in the *Opus Postumum* to relate God to the moral law along these lines.

always looked upon the idea of divine immanence with profound distrust. While writing the three *Critiques* and the *Religion* his ardent individualism had impelled him to cherish above all else the individual's freedom and autonomy. He was so anxious to maintain that the moral law is man's own law that he could not seriously entertain the idea of its being, in its very essence, the voice of God. He was influenced, too, by his opposition to pantheism, with its corollary of cosmic or divine determinism, which he always interpreted as fatalism. And, finally, the doctrine of an immanent Spirit, dwelling in the hearts and minds of men, had savored too much of the mysticism of which he was a life-long enemy. One needed but go a step further and admit the possibility of being immediately conscious of this indwelling Spirit, he had felt, to be ensnared in the coils of the doctrine of the Inner Light— a doctrine for which he entertained nothing but suspicion and contempt. He admits in the *Religion* that man *may* ultimately need divine assistance, but even here he still insists that we can never directly be conscious of such assistance and that we should resolutely train ourselves to ignore its possibility. Thus Kant failed to appreciate the theistic implication of his own ethical doctrines until age and ill-health had made an adequate examination of such an implication impossible.

Mention may also be made, at this point, of two other aspects of Kant's larger philosophical system which contain fruitful theistic possibilities, although these, again, were not developed by him in any consistent or extended fashion. The first is his conception of the Unconditioned or the Absolute as he formulates it in the later portions (chiefly in the introductory sections of the *Transcendental Dialectic*) of the *Critique of Pure Reason*. All perception, he showed in the *Transcendental Analytic*, involves the cooperation of the understanding and sensuous intuition, and the objective validity of the categories rests on their being the necessary conditions of our experience of the physical world. He now distinguishes reason from the understanding and defines it as the faculty whereby we conceive the idea of Totality, of the Whole. He goes on to say that this idea of the Unconditioned is so fundamental to our thinking that without it all thought, and even our perceptual experience of the phenomenal world, would be impossible. Just as we cannot be conscious of the self without a not-self in contrast with which it acquires its selfhood and individuality, so we cannot think of the self and the not-self without presupposing an underlying Absolute, which somehow embraces both within itself and makes possible their relation to one another. Thus the idea of the Infinite becomes the fundamental condition of all thought of the finite. This idea, it is true, is empty of all content and seems meaningless; but that is only because it is so fundamental that it cannot be described in terms of any other concepts. It is, in a word, unique; and it is the basis of all rational thought and experience.[1]

This is, of course, the source in Kant of the Hegelian Absolute which played so important a role in the idealist movements in Germany and England in the nineteenth century. Edward Caird[2] formulates Kant's idea in a manner prophetic of its later development by the Hegelians. "The consciousness of objects is prior to the consciousness of self, and . . . the consciousness of the unity of subject and object, or, in other words, the consciousness of God, presupposes both." Caird here assumes the identity of the God of religion and the metaphysical Absolute, an assumption which Kant would hardly have sanctioned even in his most idealistic moments. For Kant's thought tended always to conceive of God in terms of the basic concept of personality, which differs significantly from the concept of the Absolute. In his most characteristic utterances, moreover, he maintained that this idea is no more than regulative, subjectively valuable in helping us to form some sort of concept of the whole of which we and the world are parts, but lacking dependable objective validity. The concept of the Unconditioned, then, is merely a brief beginning, soon abandoned, of a metaphysical approach to a Supreme Being; its theistic implications are never developed and it remains unrelated by Kant to his specifically religious doctrines.

The other aspect of his philosophy which contains theistic possibilities is his notion,[3] most fully stated in the *Critique of Judgment*, of a supersensible substratum of the mechanical and teleological aspects of the physical world and of the sensible and intelligible natures in man. This idea is offered as a possible solution of the problem with which man finds himself faced when he realizes that

[1] Cf. Kemp Smith, *Commentary to Kant's Critique of Pure Reason*, p. 559
[2] *Critical Philosophy of Immanuel Kant* (1889), II, 644. See the entire section beginning on p. 589.
[3] Cf. Bernard's Introduction to his translation of the *Critique of Judgment*, pp. xxxviii ff.; and Pfleiderer, *The Philosophy of Religion on the Basis of History*, I, 153 ff., and *The Development of Theology*, pp. 12 ff.

organic nature is only explicable teleologically and must yet be conceived of mechanistically. How are these opposing principles, mechanism and design, matter and mind, blind physical causality and purpose, to be reconciled to each other? May there not, he now asks, be a common principle underlying both? Such a supersensible basis might be thought of as the ground of the *whole* world of nature and responsible both for its mechanical laws and also for the evidences of purpose which it exhibits. Purpose, however, implies an end, and man, the only being on earth with the capacity of envisaging certain ends and applying himself to their attainment, can alone be regarded as nature's own end, her highest product. "Without men the whole creation would be a mere waste, in vain, and without final purpose. But it is not in reference to man's cognitive faculty (theoretical Reason) that the being of everything else in the world gets its worth; he is not there merely that there may be someone to *contemplate* the world."[1] But neither is it as a being capable of happiness that man is nature's final end. Man's moral nature alone can be said to possess intrinsic worth; only man as a free moral agent can be judged the "lord of creation," nature's highest product. To account for nature's purposiveness, however, the supersensible substratum must be conceived of as an intellect, not discursive, like ours, but intuitive; and to be the source of man's moral nature it must itself be moral, the supreme lawgiver in the moral kingdom of ends. In a word, it must be conceived as containing within itself the ultimate explanation of *all* the principles applicable to the world of which man is a part —mechanism, teleology and morality. "It is at least possible," says Kant in his most characteristic, and what may be called his semi-cautious[2] mood, "to consider the material world as mere phenomenon, and to think as its substrate something like a thing in itself (which is not phenomenon), and to attach to this a corresponding intellectual intuition (even though it is not ours). Thus there would be, although incognisable by us, a supersensible real ground for nature, to which we ourselves belong."[3] And again, in less guarded fashion; "There must . . . be a ground of *unity* of

---

[1] *Critique of Judgment* (Bernard's tr.), p. 370

[2] When completely cautious or sceptical, Kant declares that both mechanism and teleology are principles which are only subjectively necessary and are valid only regulatively, for the understanding of the phenomenal world. The possibility of a substratum is, from this point of view, altogether ignored.

[3] *Ibid.*, p. 325

the supersensible, which lies at the basis of nature, with that which the concept of freedom practically contains."[1] "This inductive method of arriving at the idea of God," remarks Pfleiderer,[2] "contrasts favourably with [the *Summum Bonum* method]; whilst by the [latter] God was postulated only for the dubious object of adding happiness to our autonomous morality, by the [former] His existence is inferred from a comprehensive survey of external and internal experience as the necessary condition of a teleological system of things, uniting the natural and moral worlds as means and end. . . . A corollary of this thought is, that man, not only as a natural, but also as a moral being, is dependent upon the Divine Cause of the universe, and that his autonomy must therefore at the same time be an actual (not merely subjectively conceived) theonomy."

This would seem to be a promising attempt to explain the relation of Kant's worlds of nature and freedom to one another. It suggests that these worlds are not utterly disparate, nor wholly alien to one another; the intelligible realm of freedom is the more essential, the locus of the world's value, and somehow expresses itself in the realm of nature without interfering with the regular operation of the latter's mechanical laws. Likewise, man's moral nature is somehow the basis of his physical nature through which it attains to phenomenal expression. This is perhaps hardly an adequate solution of the difficulties arising out of Kant's cosmological and psychological dualism but it does something to bridge the gap left in his philosophical system by the doctrines of the first and second *Critiques*, and it seems to point out a way of escape from deism by suggesting a possible relation between God and the world. Yet Kant handles the conception very gingerly. He seems, says Goethe, to have "woven a certain element of sly irony into his method. For, while at one time he seemed to be bent on limiting our faculties of knowledge in the narrowest way, at another time, he pointed, as it were with a side gesture, beyond the limits which he himself had drawn."[3] Here again his characteristic position is sceptical—since knowledge is strictly limited to the phenomenal world of sense. all assurance of the reality of such a substrate is impossible. And, perhaps because of the curious compartmental

---

[1] *Ibid.*, p. 12
[2] *The Development of Theology* etc. (J. F. Smith's tr.), p. 14
[3] Quoted by Caird, *The Critical Philosophy of Immanuel Kant* (1889), II, 507.

nature of his thinking, the idea of the supersensible ground of nature, like the idea of the Unconditioned, is nowhere related to the God of his ethical faith.

* * * * * * * * * * *

We have referred, in passing, to various of Kant's minor works on or touching religion. After the publication of the *Religion* his thinking seems to have dwelt, to a certain extent, upon religious and theological topics. His brief informal essay entitled *Das Ende aller Dinge* ("The End of all Things," by Richardson in his *Essays and Treatises*), which appeared in the June, 1794, issue of the *Berliner Monatschrift*, deals with the subjects of the last judgment and the future life. Kant raises the difficulties inherent in the concept of an eternal life, beginning with the observation that eternity cannot be merely an infinite continuation of time but must rather be the transcending of time. Hence life, which we can think of as existing only under the form of time, cannot be conceived of as persisting in eternity. Kant partially resolves the difficulty by pointing out that the good disposition may be thought of as already an eternal thing, or as unaffected by a change from time to eternity, and as belonging to the noumenal man "whose life is in heaven." But this is a transcendent idea of not much more claim upon reason than those many other fancies concerning the future life (many of which Kant lists) indulged in by religious thinkers and seers of all ages and peoples. After interpreting rationalistically several expressions from the Book of Revelations, Kant turns to the question, whether the world must grow worse and worse before the last day, or whether we may hope for moral progress. "In spite of everything," he says, "the heroic faith in virtue seems to have, subjectively, no such all-powerful influence for the conversion of the human heart as does the thought of events accompanied with horror leading up to the world's end." The essay ends with a discussion of the special power and hope implicit in Christianity. Here the author follows out some suggestions of the *Religion* but goes further in his commendation of the Christian religion. For this religion, he says, adds to the motives arising from respect for duty those arising from love;[1] and he admits that, because of man's weakness, such an addition is a necessary one. He saves his doctrine of the primacy of respect for the

[1] Cf. below, *Religion*, p. 6, n.

moral law by pointing out that there can be no love without respect. And then he turns to what may embody the real purpose of the essay, the consideration that love cannot be forced; and he says emphatically that if the Christian church attempts to depend upon authority, backed by any sort of forceful coercion, it denies its essential character and throws away its richest treasure. "Then Christianity, which was indeed designed to become the universal religion, would no longer be thus favored by destiny; we should witness, from the moral point of view, a preposterous *end of all things!*"

In 1798 Kant published his *Streit der Facultäten* ("Conflict of the Faculties"). This is essentially a polemic against the current tendency of Biblical theologians in the universities to usurp authority in the fields of religion, philosophy and other secular subjects, and to impede the investigations of scholars in these fields. The essay contains no important new ideas and is merely a reiteration of Kant's views on the nature of true religion, its relation to morality, and the manner in which Biblical narratives and doctrines, and the character and significance of Christ, should be appraised—views already stated clearly, and more fully, in the *Religion.* He mentions a variety of objections, from various sources, to his interpretation of religion, and answers them as we might expect. The work was doubtless read with interest at the time of its publication, but it adds little to our knowledge of Kant's thought.

Of greater interest are his *Vorlesungen über die philosophische Religionslehre,* which have already been quoted from in this Introduction. These lectures were delivered as part of his university instruction over a period of years before 1788. They were edited after Kant's death by Pölitz and published at Leipzig in 1817 (Second Edition, 1830). Pölitz explains in his Preface that he made use of a manuscript belonging to a colleague of Kant in Königsberg, and that he copied it with only a few minor corrections of obvious errors. He adds this comment: "It is very interesting to compare these lectures with Kant's *Religion,* because the former were delivered during the reign of Frederick II while the latter appeared under Wöllner's ministry. Those who understand the sage of Königsberg according to the spirit of his system will not be in doubt as to which views conform better to that system— those expressed in the lectures here published, or those in the later work just mentioned." This suggestion, that Kant expressed himself more boldly in the *Lectures* than in the *Religion*, is hardly borne out by a study of the *Lectures*. They were prepared, we must remember, for the class-room; and Kant, who was always careful not to undermine the moral and religious beliefs of immature students, took pains to express in these *Lectures* the positive and constructive aspects of his philosophy of religion. The *Religion*, on the other hand, was written for scholars, concerning whom he felt no such scruples. There is every reason to believe that in writing this book he did not allow the threat of censorship and royal displeasure to obstruct the free development and expression of his ideas; he frequently indulges here in a bold and trenchant criticism, not to be found in the *Lectures*, of contemporary beliefs and institutions.

These *Lectures*, however, possess for the modern reader a peculiar interest and value. They are written in a clear and flowing style, with many illustrations; the sentences are short and forceful. They offer us the simplest and most direct statement of what may be called Kant's central orthodox theological beliefs, many of which he himself later criticized. As printed, they fall into two parts. Part I, on Transcendental Theology, follows the old tripartite division of *Ontotheologie*, *Kosmotheologie*, and *Physikotheologie*, and summarizes the theological conclusions arrived at in the first and third *Critiques*. Part II, on *Moraltheologie*, contains the central ethico-religious doctrines of the *Critique of Practical Reason* and the *Religion*. After an introductory statement on the moral approach to the knowledge of God, Kant describes God's moral attributes, His holiness, goodness, and justice, and His relation to evil. Then comes a discussion of the certainty of this knowledge of God. This is followed by a consideration of God's relation to the world as its Cause, Creator, and Ruler. The *Lectures* end with a brief examination of revelation and a very sketchy history of natural theology.

VI. Estimate of Kant's Theory of Religion

No exhaustive appraisal of Kant's conception of religion need here be attempted. Its elements of strength are not far to seek. His efforts to separate the form of religion from its substance, the transitory from the abiding, are as significant today as they were at the close of the eighteenth century. Not only was he, in com-

pany with many other religious reformers, fearless in the denounce-
ment of hypocrisy in religious practices; he also gave repeated evidence of a profound insight into the human heart and offered what
may well be accepted as a classic exposition of the place of morality in the religious experience. Furthermore, readers of the *Religion* and his minor works on religion will notice his impressive
familiarity with the Scriptures and his appreciative interpretation
of many important doctrines in Christian theology. His treatment,
for example, of revelation, Providence, the Trinity, the Kingdom
of God, and the church visible and invisible, reveal an understanding for, and a sympathy with, Christian dogmas far deeper than
that commonly found in the deistic literature of the period. For
evidence of this and other marks of Kant's attitude toward the
Christian faith the reader need but study the work here translated.

Brief mention may be made, however, of what, from a genuinely
religious point of view, must be regarded as serious defects in
Kant's account of the religious consciousness. These defects mirror, in part, the limitations of his age; in part they are the products
of certain characteristics of his own temperament and training.

The eighteenth century, we have said,[1] was distinguished for its
uncritical individualism, its lack of historical imagination, and its
exaggerated reliance upon reason as the cure of human ills and the
guide to all truth. These are but aspects of a single attitude toward life, and Kant shows himself to be a true child of the Enlightenment in his willing acceptance of this attitude. He gives
voice to the individualism of the period in his doctrine of man's
moral autonomy and freedom. Believing that man should recognize no authority in heaven or on earth superior to his own conscience, Kant requires him to make his own moral and religious
decisions and work out his own salvation. Historical events and
personages may yield man an occasional clue; certain institutions
may afford him a modicum of social support; and even revelation,
were its authority beyond cavil, might hasten his discovery of the
eternal verities: yet all these aids are no more than adventitious,
and the strong man will avoid undue reliance upon them, trusting,
so far as possible, in himself alone. For, irrespective of racial
heritage, social environment, or personal traits, the inner voice of
reason is always his surest guide; and the fact that his own con-

[1] Above, pp. ix ff.

science commands him to be perfect bespeaks a corresponding ability to obey its behest through his own efforts.

Such ideas as these echo the age in which Kant lived and thought; but in him they developed into convictions also because of their congeniality to his nature. His Protestant upbringing, his early poverty and long battle with ill-health, his unhappy contact with religious fanaticism in the Collegium, the loneliness incident to his solitary and confining labors, and the mental discipline of his philosophical inquiries—all these were factors productive of an ever increasing self-reliance. Endowed, moreover, with a remarkable intellect, and devoting his life, as he did, to the enhancement of this power, he naturally tended to ascribe to reason supreme authority in every phase of experience. This professional search for unalterable philosophical truth produced, in turn, a comparative indifference to the unfolding of historical events and a certain lack of sympathetic understanding toward imaginative portrayals of life in secular and religious literature. Finally, his unflagging interest in science and his desire to provide a philosophical validation for its inquiries, disposed him to look upon the kind of thinking here employed as alone able to yield the highest intellectual assurance.

This respect for scientific method would seem to provide the ultimate explanation for Kant's sharp distinction between knowledge and faith. We have mentioned his willingness to apply the term knowledge solely to the joint product of sense and reason; morality, no doubt, yields supreme pragmatic assurance, yet its judgments lack for him the certainty which characterizes propositions relating to the phenomenal world. This is a doctrine still claiming many adherents, for our own age in numerous ways resembles the Enlightenment. Yet, as nineteenth-century philosophers in Germany and England were to argue, Kant may plausibly be criticized for restricting the realm of knowledge illegitimately, even according to the criteria of some of his own philosophical tenets. He did, indeed, assign an ethical primacy to faith over knowledge; and it may be urged that he employed the term faith, in this connection, merely to indicate the essential difference between man's sensuous and his moral intuitions, without intending to discount the cognitive significance of the latter. The place of honor to which he assigns moral values in his larger philosophical system would seem to justify such an interpretation. Yet the main tenor of his writings indicates a prior philosophical allegiance to the insight based on reason and sensation alone. In any case, it is open to us to suggest that Kant could have remained true to his early belief that knowledge can arise only through first-hand contact with reality, and still have maintained that man achieves such contact preeminently in the moral experience and that, in it, he acquires a vision of objective reality at least as worthy of the appellation knowledge as any apprehension of the phenomenal world.

This criticism of Kant's use of the terms knowledge and faith must, if valid, carry with it implications of great import; yet it is, in a sense, less fundamental to the evaluation of his philosophy of religion as a whole than is the recognition of his indifference, or blindness, to what has been judged, by its chief spokesmen, to be religion's distinctive characteristic. This may be designated in a variety of ways—as a sense of communion with God, as an immediate, intuitive knowledge of Him, or as the worship of Him in private prayer and through the agency of public ceremony. Kant's absolute insistence upon the reduction of true religion to morality, arising from his distrust of mysticism and a stiff-necked refusal to bow down even before God Himself, rendered him incapable of appreciating true religious devotion. In his definition of the religious attitude as obedience to moral duties regarded "as divine commands," the added phrase has the appearance of an afterthought. Such reference of the moral law to a divine legislation adds nothing to the law's authority, and undue regard to God's relation to the law is judged by Kant to be even dangerous. His whole religious theory, then, is anthropocentric, not theocentric, and despite his eulogy of theism as the belief in a "living God," his God is certainly, by all religious standards, related to the world and man in no vital way. He failed to comprehend that mystic communion with God which the devout have signalized as the essence of prayer and ceremonial worship and which they have always sought to distinguish from cringing flattery or a mere request for desired favors; for him it remained but superstitious fanaticism.

The crux of the matter is obviously Kant's inability to recognize a distinctive religious experience, which is akin to that moral experience which he himself describes in such detail, yet is not identical with it. This religious experience implies a knowledge of God as real as Kant's own apprehension of the moral law. Kant himself, we have seen, tended during his last years to interpret the moral experience as a direct revelation of God to man. Yet his characteristic belief is that God is not directly knowable. "Our consciousness of all existence . . . belongs exclusively to the unity of experience" (*i.e.*, sensuous experience); "any [alleged] existence outside this field, while not indeed such as we can declare to be absolutely impossible, is of the nature of an assumption which we can never be in a position to justify."[1] To this a modern theologian pertinently replies: "If knowledge is indissolubly wedded to sense, of course it is vain to speak of our 'knowing' God."[2] But if God is not knowable, faith in Him must indeed be blind, reliance on His assistance hazardous, and communion with Him impossible.

We must conclude, then, that Kant's explicit account of religion is in many ways a typical product of a scientific age and a rationalistic mood. It is an account which harmonizes with an important, perhaps the dominant, aspect of the modern temper; many who read this volume will unquestionably welcome it as giving expression to their own convictions on religion. If this is true, the *Religion*, while lacking the stature of a fourth *Critique*, is yet a treatise of major importance, worthy of being regarded as a deistic classic. Those, on the other hand, who, in their study of the world's religious literature and in their own experience, find in religion far more than Kant was able to record in this and other essays on the subject, will doubtless feel that he comes closest to a recognition of the religious spirit in other portions of his philosophical writings. For despite his opposition to mysticism, he seems always to have been haunted by a sense of cosmic mystery. The starry heavens in their incalculable immensity, the inescapable finitude of all human cognition, the paradox of artistic genius, the sublimity of the moral law, the baffling complexity of life and human consciousness—all this awakens in Kant a spirit of reverence. With every advance in knowledge we must, he feels, preserve an essential modesty of utterance and maintain a basic piety toward the larger whole. It is perhaps significant that his friend and biographer, Jachmann, was able to testify that, during all Kant's destruction and construction of proofs of God's existence, and in the presence of every intellectual doubt, he was ever "con-

---

[1] *Critique of Pure Reason* (Kemp Smith's tr.), p. 506
[2] H. R. Mackintosh in his and A. Caldecott's *Selections from the Literature of Theism*, p. 199, n. 18

vinced in his heart that the world is in the hands of a wise Providence"; that, in private conversation with his friends, "the philosopher and the man spoke out in undeniable testimony to an inner feeling and a genuine conviction [of God's existence]"; and that "in the true sense of the word he was a worshipper of God."[1]

[1] *Immanuel Kant—Die Biographien von L. E. Borowski, R. B. Jachmann und A. Ch. Wasianski*, pp. 169, 172; here translated.

THE ETHICAL SIGNIFICANCE OF
KANT'S *RELIGION*

By John R. Silber

That Kant was a religious man there can be little doubt. Incidents from his life in which he exhibited or confessed a faith in God are reported by Greene in Part I. One passage in the *Religion* suggests that Kant may have retained unwittingly more of the simple Biblical faith of his mother than most scholars have supposed. In a note, on page 154 of the present translation, Kant credits the Bible with importance as an historical document whose credibility extends "into epochs of antiquity (even to the beginning of the world)." Though this passage was written in the 18th Century, which was notoriously unhistorical in orientation, Kant —who also anticipated La Place in the formulation of the nebular hypothesis—does seem here to have accepted as historical the Biblical account of human affairs from their very beginning.

Granting that Kant was genuinely religious, it does not follow that his writings on the subject of religion are presented from a religious viewpoint or that they are important primarily as they relate to religion. There are three important passages in Kant's writings which have a distinctly religious flavor. One of these is his famous statement at the end of the *Critique of Practical Reason* that two things, the starry heavens above him and the moral law within him, fill his mind with ever new and increasing awe. An Old Testament psalmist might have said the same. Equally renowned is Kant's hymn of praise to duty: "Duty, thou sublime and mighty name, that dost embrace nothing charming or insinuating but requirest submission and yet seekest not to move the will by threatening . . . but only holdest forth a law which of itself finds entrance into the mind and gains reluctant reverence . . . : what origin is worthy of thee?"[1] The third passage, in the *Religion*, is less well-known but equally important: "O Sincerity! Thou Astraea, that hast fled from earth to heaven, how mayest thou (the basis of conscience, and hence, all inner religion) be drawn down thence to us again?"[2]

[1] *Critique of Practical Reason* (Beck's tr.), p. 193. Subsequent references to this work will give only the translator's name and the page number. This practice will be followed generally when referring to translations.

[2] P. 178. All references to Kant's *Religion* will be to the present translation. See also *Critique of Teleological Judgement* (Meredith's tr.), p. 130.

These are Kant's "devotionals," his most important public expressions of a religious awareness and concern. Yet, as is evident in all these passages, his is essentially a religion of ethics. Kant does not turn to religion for divine guidance in the determination of duty; he turns instead to the moral law to determine our duty and to provide the only sound argument for the existence of God and the sole valid means of discerning His will. Kant says, moreover, that certain knowledge of God's existence would destroy man's freedom and reduce human experience to a show of puppets frantically currying the favor of the Almighty.[3]

So close, then, in Kant's thinking is the relation of religion to ethics and so dependent is the former upon the latter, that Kant could scarcely have written a book on religion without simultaneously illuminating and expanding his ethical theory. Kant's *Religion* merits, therefore, careful examination and evaluation from the standpoint of its ethical significance. Such an endeavor, briefly undertaken, is the purpose of this essay.

Kant's *Religion*, we may say without exaggeration, compares in importance for the understanding of his ethics with his *Groundwork of the Metaphysic of Morals* and the second *Critique*. Kant's ethical statics, to borrow a term from physics, may be found in varying degrees of systematization in most of his post-critical works. Only in the *Religion*, however, do we find what might be called Kant's ethical dynamics. Kant had discussed the nature of the good, the character of imperatives, and the methodology of moral inquiry in his earlier works; in the *Religion* he addresses himself to the problem of evil—its nature, its origin, and the possibility of its eradication. In the process he raises questions which necessitate an understanding of the will in its full complexity and dynamic unity. We therefore find, in the *Religion*, in his struggle with the problem of evil, Kant's most explicit and systematic account of the will and of human freedom—an account which, in turn, clarifies his entire system of ethics.

I. *The Theoretical Background of the* Religion

Confronting the problem of evil, Kant was concerned, not with natural disasters and faulty natural faculties, but with the power of free beings to misuse their freedom. He sought a rational account of moral obligation while admitting as brute fact that men

[3] Beck, p. 248.

can disregard it. How is categorical obligation possible? Since a *categorical* relation is a necessary one and since *obligation* presupposes freedom, Kant had to show how necessity can be combined with freedom in a single relationship.

Kant thus set himself a task far more difficult than that undertaken by Plato and ethical naturalists on the one hand, or by Christians and religious non-naturalists on the other. Plato argued that the Good is necessary to the soul as a condition of its being because irrationality and injustice, in their disregard of the Good, destroy the soul. His demonstration depends, however, upon his assumption that the Good is homogeneous and the natural object of the soul's desire. Having made this assumption, Plato had to conclude that knowledge leads inevitably to virtue, that one who knows the Good will act accordingly, and that no one can intentionally be ignorant of the Good. This conclusion reduces the experience of moral obligation, which presupposes that one can knowingly reject the Good, to an illusion and fails to explain why the illusion should so commonly occur. The Christian tradition can account for the experience of obligation because it understands the awful power of freedom, that is, man's ability to rebel against the Good and its Creator. But it does not explain why men are necessarily or categorically obligated to obey God or seek the Good. The fact that men can live and flourish in a state of rebellion shows that obedience to the Good is not a necessary condition of self-fulfillment, at least in this life; the obligation to God and His commands remains merely hypothetical. It obligates only those who feel a prudential concern for the hereafter or who, out of purity of heart, prefer obedience to rebellion. Dissatisfied with Plato's cavalier rejection of man's experience of moral obligation and with all Christian attempts to reduce moral obligation to a hypothetical imperative subservient to a Divine decree, Kant tried to explain categorical moral obligation in such a way as to make it consistent with the Christian insight into the dark and irrational depths of human nature and, simultaneously, with Platonic confidence that freedom and obligation are both ultimately grounded in reason.

Kant was aware that his earlier attempt in the *Groundwork* to explain how the categorical imperative is possible was a failure[4] because his comprehension of freedom and the will was still too fragmentary. In the *Groundwork* Kant defined the will as "the

[4] See H. J. Paton's *The Categorical Imperative*, pp. 202–206.

power of a being to act in accordance with his idea of laws"[5] and as the "kind of causality belonging to living beings so far as they are rational."[6] So defined, the will could be nothing other than practical reason, free in the negative sense that it is "able to work independently of *determination* by alien causes" and in the positive sense that it is autonomous, "in all its actions a law to itself."[7] According to these definitions, a free will and a will acting according to laws, that is, maxims capable of universalization, were one and the same. Kant therefore concluded, in a manner reminiscent of Plato, that the free will is the will acting according to moral laws.

But what of the will that rejects the moral law in its actions? This question exposes the incompleteness of Kant's early understanding of freedom. Such a will, said Kant in the *Groundwork,* is heteronomous; that is, the "will does not give itself the law, but the object [of desire] does so in virtue of its relation to the will."[8] If the object gives the will its laws, then the will acts in accordance with the laws of nature and hence is not free but a slave of its inclinations. The heteronomous will, inasmuch as its actions are not free, cannot be held responsible for its unlawful acts, cannot be guilty, and cannot, therefore, be will at all. Kant did not leave place for the introduction of desires into the will nor for the capacity of the will to act in opposition to the law when he defined the will as practical reason. The intrusion of desire and opposition to the law must, however, be reckoned with if man's experience of moral obligation in which the moral law confronts the human will as a categorical imperative is to be explained. Kant himself stated, without squaring his statement with his definition of the will, that the moral law is related to the human will as an imperative only because the will has the *power* and the *temptation* to reject the law.[9] Kant was on solid ground in arguing that freedom involves rationality. But in the *Groundwork* he fails to see that the irrational is a mode of the rational, that heteronomy is a mode of free willing, and that the will must be defined in terms of desire as well as in terms of practical reason. He therefore fails to explain how the categorical imperative is possible.

Kant's advance toward the solution to this problem is clearly

[5] *Groundwork of the Metaphysics of Morals* (Paton's tr.), p. 80.
[6] *Ibid.*, p. 114.
[7] *Idem.*
[8] *Ibid.*, p. 108, cf. p. 111.
[9] *Ibid.*, pp. 80–81.

visible in the second *Critique*. In the first place, Kant now sees that the moral law is given as a *fact* of pure reason and is so firmly established that it can provide the foundation for a transcendental deduction of freedom. In an epigram of uncommon perspicuity he says that "though freedom is certainly the *ratio essendi* of the moral law, the latter is the *ratio cognoscendi* of freedom."[10] Man's freedom is a fact "which, without the moral law, would have remained unknown to him."[11] Kant thus finds that a rational account of the experience of obligation, in which the moral law is legislative for the human will, necessarily presupposes and therefore transcendentally justifies the concept of freedom.[12]

With this starting point firmly established Kant, in the second place, clarifies his conception of freedom. He continues to hold, as he had in the *Groundwork*, that freedom must be understood positively as autonomy, as the capacity of the will (as practical reason) to act in accordance with universal law.[13] Kant now insists, however, that freedom in the negative sense—now called transcendental freedom—involves more than mere independence of the will from causal necessity in time and nature: transcendental freedom also involves absolute spontaneity.[14] And the will, possessed of freedom in this more radical sense, also has the capacity to reject the law. When the will acts in terms of its sensuous desires, it is, as Kant put it, "pathologically affected" but not "pathologically determined—and thus still free."[15] When merely subjective interests are made the basis of action, heteronomy results; heteronomy, however, is now a mode of freedom.[16]

[10] Beck, p. 119.
[11] *Ibid.*, p. 142; cf. *Critique of Teleological Judgement* (Meredith's tr.), p. 142.
[12] Beck, pp. 156, 157; cf. pp. 141–143. Earlier Kant had vacillated on this point by seeking a transcendental deduction of the moral law (Paton, pp. 86 ff.). Kant always insisted, however, that his theory of ethics was to provide a rational account of ordinary moral experience, not to create a new morality (Paton, p. 60; Beck, p. 123.).
[13] *Ibid.*, p. 144.
[14] *Ibid.*, pp. 200–205 ff.; cf. pp. 122, 140, 158 *passim*. The term "transcendental freedom" is apt in view of the deduction of that concept, even though Kant, lapsing into an earlier viewpoint, occasionally refers to it as transcendent (p. 209). It is transcendent if regarded as a theoretical concept. But the concept of freedom is as thoroughly deduced from the standpoint of moral experience as is the concept of causality from the standpoint of scientific experience (pp. 141, 142).
[15] *Ibid.*, p. 144.
[16] *Ibid.*, p. 145; cf. p. 204 *passim*. Kant says that when maxims of merely subjective validity are acted upon "the heteronomy of *Willkür* results" (p. 145). The term *"Willkür"* could mean in this context either "choice" (as Beck translates it) or "the faculty of choice," that is, the will itself. There is no adequate way to determine either from the immediate context or from the second *Critique* as a whole what this particular usage of *"Willkür"* means or how it should be translated. At the

In the third place, Kant's advance in the second *Critique* may be seen in his recognition that the will which is categorically obligated is not the will of a rational being as such but of a rational and sensible being—a human being torn between the demands of his sensible and rational natures. Kant recognized this to a degree in the *Groundwork* when he distinguished between the holy will and the moral will, but he did not sustain this distinction by defining the moral will in terms of the human will. Instead, he persisted in defining the will and its relation to the law in a way that was supposed to be valid for all rational beings as such. Kant did not realize then that if the moral law "when applied to man . . . does not borrow in the slightest from the acquaintance with him (in anthropology), but gives him laws *a priori* as a rational being"[17] it cannot confront man as the categorical imperative. Yet this confrontation is precisely Kant's methodological starting point and the basis of his distinction between the moral will and the holy will. In the second *Critique* Kant faced the fact that if desires are to tempt the will, thereby transforming the moral law into a categorical imperative, they must have access to the will. The will, accordingly, is now defined both as practical reason and as the faculty of desire—a definition that is neither drawn from, nor applicable to, mere rational beings.[18] The will, under this modified definition, is caught between the commands of reason and the attractions of sensible inclinations;

---

time Kant was writing the second and third *Critiques* he had not settled upon a distinct technical meaning for either *"Wille"* or *"Willkür"* but used them almost interchangeably in certain contexts. The discovery and formulation of meanings for these terms was, moreover, one of Kant's foremost achievements in the *Religion* and in the *Metaphysic of Morals*. In light of the meanings given there we can quite easily discern both Kant's use and misuse of these terms as he groped for insight into the nature of the will without foreknowledge of his goal, and we can settle upon the correct interpretation of passages such as the one just quoted. In this passage *"Willkür"* must be translated as "the faculty of choice" or the "choosing will" or some reasonable equivalent. The evolving complexity of Kant's theory of the will is missed by English readers unless they can know when Kant is using *"Wille"* and when he is using *"Willkür."* The practice of translating *"Willkür"* by terms used to translate *"Wille"* or *"Wahl"* is, unfortunately, as prevalent among English translators as it is misleading. A notable exception is T. K. Abbott, who usually followed the practice of translating *"Willkür"* as the "elective will" and *"Wille"* either as "will" or "rational will."

[17] Paton, p. 57; cf. pp. 78–81, 92.

[18] Beck, pp. 123–124, 131–136, 144, 164, 167, 169; cf. *Critique of Teleological Judgement* (Meredith's tr.) p. 109, *passim.* Kant knew from pre-critical days that all objects of the will are in some way related to desire. He disassociated himself from the "moral feeling" school of ethics by insisting that desire cannot determine the will inasmuch as such determination would destroy the will's freedom. To relate the will to desire seemed, therefore, both necessary and impossible.

it is obligated but not compelled to subordinate itself as a faculty of desire to its own legislation as pure practical reason.

Partial answers, however, have a way of raising new problems in the place of those they resolve. Unable to sustain his new insights (excepting the first) with an adequately complex understanding of freedom, the will, and the role of desire in the determination of the will, Kant still occasionally qualifies and contradicts many of the ideas he advanced previously, leaving parts of the second *Critique* in confusion bred of his indecision.

On the basis of his insight that heteronomy is a mode of freedom and that the will is both practical reason and the faculty of desire, Kant could account for the will's being torn between the moral law and its natural desires. War "within the members" (which Plato had ascribed to ignorance) Kant, with St. Paul, ascribes to the human situation. There are incompatible goods competing for man's favor; hard choices must be made in terms of diverse standards of value; and virtue, if attained at all, is a victory over mighty odds.[19] But if the heteronomous will is free even as it rejects the moral law in favor of sensible inclinations, what then is the foundation of the categorical demand that the will obey the law? When Kant argues, as he did in the *Groundwork*, that by rejecting the law the moral agent ceases to be free and loses his personality, he can indeed demonstrate that the law is an essential condition of personal existence. On this view the repudiation of the law involves the repudiation of oneself. But this view, as we have noted, makes the imputation of guilt impossible. Overcoming this difficulty in the second *Critique* by defining heteronomy as a mode of freedom, Kant faced the dismaying consequence that a person is still a person in possession of his freedom even if he rejects the law. Thus the law no longer appears to be related to the will as a condition of its being. The categorical imperative seems to resolve itself into a hypothetical one: if one wishes to be moral he must obey the moral law; if, however, one is not dismayed by the disapprobation of the moral law and superior moral beings, he can still be a person and indulge his subjective fancies. Unable to anticipate his own later discoveries, and unwilling to accept such a conclusion, Kant occasionally reverted in the second *Critique* to his earlier position and defined freedom as action determined solely by the moral law.[20]

[19] *Ibid.*, pp. 122, 146–147, 149, 214–217, 230 *passim.*
[20] *Ibid.*, p. 186, 200, *passim.*

The relation of pleasure and desire to the will was even more‧ troubling to Kant. He never seemed fully clear in the second *Critique* about the status of the faculty of desire: sometimes he refers to it as an aspect of the will; at other times he refers to it as no more than a sensibly determined faculty of appetition.[21] He was similarly unsure regarding the role of pleasure in the moral determination of the will: he flatly contradicts himself by both affirming and denying that moral satisfaction can be a kind of pleasure and a determinant of the will as the faculty of desire.[22]

Despite his own uncertainty, Kant's insights that heteronomy is a mode of freedom, that the faculty of desire is an aspect of the will, and that moral satisfaction and dissatisfaction are legitimate moral incentives were essentially sound. And Kant was able, in large measure, to demonstrate their soundness by means of his extended examination of the dynamic inner workings of the will and the character of its motivations in the *Religion*. To this examination, interpreted in the light of its partial systematization in the *Metaphysic of Morals*, we must now turn.

II. *Freedom*

What does it mean to be a willing being, an individual, a person? This question is central to the understanding of Kant's ethics, for in order to answer it one must understand the nature of freedom, the nature of the will and volition, and the nature of incentives. This question provides not merely a unifying thread on which to string the diverse aspects of Kant's ethical thought; if answered fully, it secures Kant's methodological starting point in moral experience by showing how the categorical imperative is possible.

Before this question can be answered, however, it must be stripped of certain pretensions which may accompany it. The question does not concern the nature of personality in pure, rational beings, nor are we asking what is the nature of the will as such. Kant's ethics, like his theory of cognition and his aesthetics, is grounded in and limited to human experience; it consists in the transcendental deduction of those concepts and relations which

---

[21] *Ibid.*, pp. 171, 182, 218; cf. 123, 124, 133–134, 145, 166, 183, 203 ff.
[22] *Ibid.*, pp. 181, 182, 185, 187; cf. *Critique of Aesthetic Judgement* (Meredith's tr.) p. 48.

must be presupposed in order to give a rational account of moral obligation.[23] If we accept the limitations of Kant's method we must limit our inquiry to the nature of the human will and human personality. We will do well to start with a systematic statement of personality in terms of the concept of freedom which it presupposes, and then discuss the manifold relations of the human will.[24]

The moral law, according to Kant, reveals the fact and the meaning of human personality. By telling us what we *ought* to do regardless of what our inclinations and desires may bid us do, the moral law forces us to be aware of ourselves as agents rather than as mere creatures of desire. We are not, like Buridan's ass, determined to act by our strongest desire or immobilized between two desires of equal strength. We are, rather, willing beings who, while acting according to desire, determine or choose for ourselves that which shall be irresistibly desirable. The moral law thus informs us, through the voice of categorical duty, of our control over and responsibility for our actions. Such responsibility is the mark of personality. "A person," as Kant puts it, "is the subject whose actions are capable of *imputation*."[25]

Freedom is necessarily presupposed by such accountability. In order to be responsible for his actions, a person must be able to institute effects for which he can be legitimately singled out as the cause. But there is no way to restrict the extension of causal influence (and hence to give limit and meaning to personality) apart from the assumption that persons, as causes, are themselves free. If there were no free causes, we would have no rational justification for limiting responsibility to beings whom we designate as persons. The only truly responsible agent or person, if we deny that there are free causes, would be the entire universe extended in space to infinity and in time to the farthest reaches of the past. Responsibility can not be personal unless it can be concentrated in free individuals who can act without being determined to action by external and antecedent causes.

[23] For a fuller discussion of Kant's method in ethics, see my article, "The Context of Kant's Ethical Thought—Part I," *The Philosophical Quarterly*, July 1959.

[24] The following systematic statement of Kant's conception of freedom is drawn from most of his post-critical writings. Of special importance are the chapter on "The Canon of Pure Reason" from the first *Critique*, Chapters II and III of the *Groundwork*, and the section on "The Critical Examination of the Analytic of Pure Practical Reason" from the second *Critique*. Most important are Book One of the *Religion* and the "Introduction" to the *Metaphysic of Morals*.

[25] *Metaphysic of Morals* (Abbott's tr.), p. 279; cf. pp. 280, 283; cf. *Religion*, pp. 20, 21*n*, 26, 40, 45.

That freedom involves the independence of the will from external influences has been generally recognized. It has not been so clearly seen that freedom involves independence from all antecedent determination as well. It has often been supposed, for example, that individuality, personality, and responsibility can be understood as the self-determination of beings in a non-mechanical but nonetheless deterministic universe. On this view, the responsible, free person is said to be determined by his own nature and by nothing alien to his nature. His action, it is argued, flows through and expresses the core of his being.

Kant saw through this subterfuge which he called the "freedom of the turnspit" and which we might call "the freedom of the thermostat."[26] Self-determination on this theory is not merely unfree; it is not even self-determination. Genuine self-determination does not consist in the determination of effects *through* the self; it requires rather the determination of effects *by* a self which is not determined by anything else—not even by its own prior nature. Self-determination is fully compatible with freedom; in fact, it presupposes freedom. When, however, self-determination is conceived to preclude all causes which cannot be accounted for by antecedent conditions, self-determination is a misnomer because it is incompatible with freedom. Such self-determination is actually self-predetermination and is therefore obviously not free. Freedom and determinism, Kant insists, are fully compatible; the actions of moral beings are determined by the wills of those beings and express their characters. But freedom and predeterminism— and predeterministic elements are nearly always to be found in deterministic systems—are fundamentally incompatible. "What we wish to understand and never shall understand," Kant notes, "is how predeterminism, according to which voluntary (*willkürliche*) actions, as events, have their determining grounds *in antecedent time* (which, with what happened in it, is no longer within our power), can be consistent with freedom, according to which the act as well as its opposite must be within the power of the subject at the moment of its taking place."[27] A person capable of responsible action must be free in the transcendental meaning of the term. Freedom must secure him both spatially and temporally from determination by all factors alien or antecedent to himself in

---

[26] Beck, pp. 200–211.

[27] *Religion*, p. 45n. The objection that a subject who is free in this way can never be responsible for his actions will be considered in Section III, *vi*, following.

the moment of action; it must endow him with the power of his
own decision. If a person is not free in this mode of radical independence and spontaneity, then, according to Kant, he is not free
at all, and his self-determination, responsibility, and moral identity are as illusory as his freedom.[28]

Transcendental freedom establishes the basis for moral individuality and endows the individual with many potentialities, the
realization or rejection of which are left to him in the exercise of
his freedom. Heteronomy and autonomy are the two primary
modes of expressing transcendental freedom.

In every decision he makes, the individual must have an end,
that is, he must have some specific intention in the act of willing:
in order to will, he must will something. Just as every volition must
have an object, every object of volition must have content or material; it must be sufficiently concrete and determinate to enable
the individual to know what he is willing.[29] But the desires and
inclinations and contents of experience which provide the material
for the object of volition do not determine the individual either
in framing or in willing that object. As a transcendentally free
being, the individual is determined neither by desires and inclinations nor by his own past character and habits. The individual himself proposes his object of volition and gives it determinate content by his free selection from, and arrangement of, the contents of
experience. The structure or form of the object of volition, that is,
the principle that guides the individual in the determination of
the content of that object, is called by Kant the maxim of choice.
Selection of the maxim and determination of the object of volition
in terms of it are aspects of individual self-determination. If in an
act of volition the individual merely accepts his strongest desire
as the basis for action, he acts on the maxim that he wills to do
that which he most strongly desires to do. He thinks of himself
passively as if he were determined by laws other than those of his
own choosing; he acts as if he were determined by the same laws
of nature that determine the behavior of animals. By acting in

[28] Kant does not deny that there are influences on the will and limitations on the
expression of freedom. Moral instruction, temptation, disease, health, intelligence,
and stupidity influence the will by increasing or decreasing or modifying its power
of self-expression. Kant speaks, consequently, of the direct proportion between
accountability and freedom (Abbott, p. 284). Kant does deny, however, that such
factors can *determine* the will without destroying it. If a person is free and responsible, then his freedom is unqualified and absolute, although the possibilities for
its expression may vary considerably.
[29] Abbott, pp. 290–292, 295 ff.; cf. *Religion,* p. 4 ff.; Beck, pp. 145, 146.

terms of a law other than his own, his action is heteronomous. But the decision to act heteronomously is nonetheless his own decision. The adoption of the heteronomous maxim is an expression of transcendental freedom, the actualization of one of its potentialities.

The actualization of heteronomy is not, however, a fulfilling realization of transcendental freedom; on the contrary, heteronomy involves its abnegation. The individual in adopting a heteronomous maxim freely renounces his power as a free being to act independently of desires. He freely chooses to act just the way he would act if he had no such freedom at all. Heteronomy is thus one but not the only possible mode of free expression. Were it the only potential mode of expression, transcendental freedom would be hollow and meaningless, for the positive realization of spontaneous action in independence of natural determination would not be possible. Transcendental freedom would involve no more than the independence and power willfully to act as if there were no such independence and power. Choice and freedom would be defined so as to preclude their possible fulfillment. The potentiality of freedom would be identical with the potentiality of life for a man who could do nothing but choose between alternative means of suicide.

The transcendentally free individual, potentially heteronomous, is likewise potentially autonomous. He need not abnegate his freedom by heteronomous willing; he is able to affirm in volition his independent and spontaneous nature. While influenced by desires and inclinations, he can positively maintain his unconditional and continuing independence from them by willing in accordance with the demands of universal law. Desires and habits are ineluctably subjective and particular. Consequently, they can never be viewed as the determinants of a universal maxim or of an object of volition based on such a maxim. If, therefore, instead of adopting a maxim expressing determination by desire, the individual adopts a maxim which has been framed out of concern for its universal validity as a law of volition for all willing beings such as he, the very universality of his maxim establishes his transcendence of and independence from determination by desire. The individual continues to be influenced by desires and inclinations and must draw upon them in giving content to his object of volition. But the content of the object is determined by the universal maxim which guides the will in the evaluation and selection of the contents of sensibility. The maxim therefore determines the presence and composition of desires and inclinations in the object of volition; neither the object nor the maxim is determined by desires and inclinations. Any object willed on the basis of a universal maxim demands the approbation of all men who express their freedom positively and not merely the approbation of those beings, animals or men, whose desires may be gratified by the object.[30] When an individual so wills that the maxim of his act is in accord with the universality of law, he is then autonomous, that is, he acts according to the law of his own free nature.

It must seem initially odd to say that an individual who rejects maxims based upon the strength of desires in order to act on universal maxims acts in terms of a law of his own nature. His desires and habits would seem to be also a part of his nature. Indeed, Kant would insist, desires and inclinations may and do influence one's maxims and contribute to the content of the object of one's volitions. But desires and inclinations cannot provide the determining principle of volition for an individual who would assert his individuality rather than abnegate it. His nature as a person, as a responsible individual, is grounded in his freedom. Only his nature as an animal, a turnspit, or a thermostat can be positively expressed by maxims asserting nothing more than his decision to be determined by his strongest desires and inclinations. His free and responsible nature is not positively expressed in his free acts unless the maxims of his acts, by virtue of their conformity to universal law, assert his actualized power to act in independence from determination by desires. By adopting maxims in accordance with universal law he expresses positively the unconditionedness of his will; he takes as his object of volition the concrete realization of unconditioned free willing—that is, he wills the realization of himself as a free being. Thus the law in accordance with which he wills is the law of his nature.

We can now observe the thorough interpenetration of reason and freedom. Rationality is involved in both the heteronomous and the autonomous modes of free expression. It is not merely from im-

[30] An object determined by the will on the basis of a universal maxim and thus claiming universal approbation by men is morally good. The morally good, according to Kant, is an object which, like the object of experience, is determined in part by the subject as a moral agent. The morally good is therefore either the good will itself or the concrete expression of good willing, i.e., the concrete object of volition of a good will. For an extended treatment of these issues, see my article, "The Copernican Revolution in Ethics: the Good Reexamined," *Kant-Studien*, Fall 1959.

pulse that an individual acts from impulse. Even heteronomous action involves the use of reason, independent from inclinations, to determine maxims that negate both freedom and rationality by following inclinations. Autonomous action, in turn, expresses the universality of reason which is the sole means whereby the will can positively assert its creative independence. Both heteronomy and autonomy are modes of rationality just as both are modes of freedom; in essence, Kant holds, they are spontaneity itself. This aspect of Kant's thought can easily be overlooked since he frequently discusses reason as the canon for the exercise of spontaneity. So considered, reason is merely the structure and form of the sound use of our faculties in logic, science, moral conduct, aesthetic creation, and matters of taste; reason, so regarded, appears static. But reason is also dynamic when it functions in understanding as imagination and judgment, in volition as will and judgment, and in artistic creation and appreciation as genius, taste, and judgment. In all of these areas reason functions as *spontaneity*, the inscrutable power of the mind, of the will, and of genius.[31] Reason, in Kant's philosophy, is essentially free; freedom is essentially rational; and both consist ultimately in spontaneity.[32] Inasmuch as spontaneity constitutes the power of both freedom and reason, heteronomy and irrationality no less than autonomy and rationality are possible modes of their expression: heteronomy must not be reduced to complete determination by natural causality, nor should irrationality be confused with the non-rational. (The rational in the generic sense in which Kant often uses it includes both the rational in the honorific sense and the irrational, just as freedom in its transcendental meaning includes both autonomy and heteronomy.) Heteronomous and irrational actions involve the denial and misuse of the power of spontaneity, the failure to actualize its potentialities, and, therefore, the destruction of the person as a spontaneous being. By rejecting through irrationality and heteronomy the realization of that power which enables him to be himself, the indi-

[31] *Critique of Pure Reason* (Kemp Smith's tr.), pp. 130–131, 151–153, 183, 465 *passim;* Paton, pp. 57, 80, 108, 120, 130–131, 158; Beck, pp. 122, 140, 158, 176, 204–206; Abbott, p. 289; *Religion*, pp. 19, 40, 45n, 134; *Critique of Aesthetic Judgement* (Meredith's tr.), pp. 39, 151–152, 168 ff., 180 ff., 192 *passim; Critique of Teleological Judgement* (Meredith's tr.), pp. 62, 142 *passim.* Germane to this point is Kant's division of knowledge into rational and historical modes, the former being creative and active, the latter being slavish and passive (Kemp Smith, p. 656).

[32] Only the desire to avoid needless conflict in an essay too brief to allow for adequate defense prevents my saying that spontaneity is the *ontological* foundation of both rationality and freedom in Kant's philosophy.

vidual denies himself.[33] The moral law, which demands that the individual act according to a maxim that is capable of universalization, is a law that defines the conditions for the fulfillment of personality, just as the law of non-contradiction and the rules of sound understanding define the conditions for the fulfillment of mind. The moral law is a normative law for the will of an individual, just as the law of non-contradiction is normative for his mind.

Kant's theoretical advance beyond Plato in the understanding of freedom is now apparent. Like Kant, Plato identified freedom and rationality. Unlike Kant, however, Plato understood reason only in its honorific meaning. Anything that was not in accord with the fulfillment of reason as a canon, as the static form of the good, was non-rational, determined either by non-rational desires or non-rational spirit or blind necessity, but not by the misuse of reason itself. For a misuse of reason would imply that irrationality, the boundless and the dark forces of necessity, could be found within reason itself—a thought which Plato could not abide. Thus, having identified freedom with rationality and having only an honorific conception of reason, Plato was limited to an honorific conception of freedom as rational freedom. As a consequence, ignorance, whether moral or intellectual, became for Plato a mode of the non-rational and the non-free, and guilt and culpable irrationality were simply not possible. Kant, recognizing what he took to be the actuality of both, defined freedom and reason as spontaneity and pointed to rationality and autonomy as fulfilled and to irrationality and heteronomy as deficient modes of its expression.

Recognizing that any rejection of reason is irrational and, therefore, a mode of the rational (because that which violates or rejects the laws of reason must be subject to them and hence rational), Kant discovered that the moral law is a part of the internal structure of human personality. As such, the moral law is both the descriptive condition for personal self-fulfillment (without any reference to obligation) and the categorical imperative for those individuals tempted to reject it. A person is not *obligated* to be *actually* transcendentally free and *potentially* either

---

[33] The self-rejection of the individual is, from the standpoint of his theoretical faculties, his irrationality, and from the standpoint of his moral nature, his heteronomy. Since reason and freedom have a common essence in spontaneity, however, it is just as correct to speak of the heteronomous uses of the mind and the irrational expressions of the will.

autonomous or heteronomous. Either his given nature as a free being *includes* these factors, or he is not a person, a being whose actions can be imputed to him. To speak in the language of the *Groundwork*, a person is not obligated to be a member and ruler in a kingdom of ends: either he is both member and ruler or he is not a person. Obligation enters as a relation between the subject and the ruler, as the duty of the subject to obey himself as ruler when as subject he is tempted to disobey. A transcendentally free human being, if tempted to abnegate his freedom in the expression of it, is categorically obligated to actualize his free nature. He is obligated to be autonomous, to be the spontaneous individual he is, and to avoid self-rejection in heteronomy. And because his personality wanes as the law of his nature and the condition of its fulfillment is denied, the law has an inescapable jurisdiction over him. He has the freedom to reject the law but he cannot escape its condemnation and its punishment in the destruction of his personality. The imperative issuing from this law is therefore categorical. Without appeal to divine decree or contingent facts of desire, Kant's theory thus provides a theoretical but non-theological foundation in the very nature of free volition and personality for the moral law and its power to obligate categorically.

III. *The Human Will*

Though Kant's conception of freedom thus clarifies the nature of personality and moral obligation, its full interpretive power is not apparent until it is considered in the context of his analysis of the human will in moral struggle. The will according to Kant is a unitary faculty. But, like reason and the understanding, it is subject to division into "parts" for the purpose of analysis. These parts, to which Kant refers by the terms *"Willkür," "Wille,"* and *"Gesinnung,"* are aspects or specific functions of this essentially unified faculty of volition.[34]

[34] Since Kant gives the terms *"Willkür"* and *"Wille"* technical meanings not recognized in ordinary German usage, and since there are no English equivalents for these terms, I shall adapt them to English usage without translating them. The term *"Gesinnung"* is adequately translated by the English term "disposition;" the latter is as imprecise in English as the former in German, but Kant's technical meaning can be derived, as is true of *"Willkür"* and *"Wille"*, from his usage. I shall use the English term "will" to refer to human volition as a unified function including *Willkür, Wille,* and disposition. Kant occasionally uses *"Wille"* in this sense, which is ordinary German usage.

i

Willkür

When Kant refers to the will in its familiar aspect as the power to choose between alternatives, he calls it *Willkür*. As such, it is a faculty of desire, for Kant held that the *Willkür* is determined according to the strength of the pleasures or displeasures it anticipates in connection with the alternatives open to it.[35] But the human *Willkür* is not an animal *Willkür*, an *arbitrium brutum*. The animal *Willkür*, like an iron filing drawn to the strongest magnet, is directly determined by the strongest impulse. The human *Willkür* is influenced but not wholly determined by impulses: its actions are always determined according to the strongest impulse, but only after the *Willkür* itself has made the decision by which the strongest impulse is determined. Thus the human *Willkür* determines itself and is free, an *arbitrium liberum*. "The freedom of the *Willkür*," Kant held, "is of a wholly unique nature in that an incentive can determine the *Willkür* to an action *only so far as the individual has incorporated it into his maxim* (has made it the general rule in accordance with which he will conduct himself)."[36] No impulse or desire can be a determining incentive for the *Willkür* until the *Willkür* chooses to make it so. The irresistible strength of the incentive that determines the action of the *Willkür* (when the latter is viewed psychologically) derives from the decision of the *Willkür* (viewed morally) to give it determining strength. Unless this power to *choose* its determining incentives is attributed to *Willkür*, it cannot be both free and yet under the influence of desires and incentives: "Only thus," Kant argued, "can an incentive, whatever it may be, coexist with the absolute spontaneity of the *Willkür*."[37] We know that sensible incentives and absolute freedom do coexist in the human *Willkür* for they are co-present in the experience of obligation from which our awareness of *Willkür* arises. The moral law, as Kant states

---

[35] Abbott, p. 310; cf. p. 268; cf. *Religion*, p. 26. Because *Willkür* acts in accordance with the strongest desire Kant insisted that whatever is good must be in some way the object of desire and that "the supreme ground of morality must not only permit a conclusion in the direction of delight, but must itself afford delight in the highest degree." (Letter to Marcus Herz, 1773.) See also the *Groundwork* (Paton's tr.), p. 128: "It is admittedly necessary that reason should have the power of *infusing a feeling of pleasure* or satisfaction in the fulfillment of duty, and consequently that it should possess a kind of causality by which it can determine sensibility in accordance with rational principles."

[36] *Religion*, p. 19; cf. Abbott, pp. 267, 268.

[37] *Idem*.

it, "informs us of the independence of our *Willkür* from determination by all other incentives (of our freedom) and at the same time of the accountability of all our actions."[38]

The *Willkür* is thus the core of personality and responsibility. Just as man, the being who experiences moral obligation, must stand in two worlds—the natural and the moral—in order to experience as obligation the conflict between them, the *Willkür* must be found in both realms as well. Man as a natural being, no less than man as a moral being, has *Willkür*. The *Willkür* of man as a natural being is the ground of human action and human virtue as phenomena (*virtus phænomenon*). The *Willkür* of man as a moral being is the ground of the adoption of maxims on which action is based and the source of intelligible virtue (*virtus noumenon*).[39] The distinction that Kant draws between events and acts is this: an event is that which occurs according to determination by causal laws; an act, or deed, has as its author a free cause (*causa libera*). In moral conduct, the individual is responsible for his actions because they are the effects of the individual himself as *causa libera*. His actions in the phenomenal world which are contrary to the demands of the moral law are actions of his *Willkür* and therefore attributable to him as vices. Similarly the actions of his *Willkür* which accord with the demands of the moral law are attributable to him as virtues. But the motives behind his phenomenal acts, that is, the maxims upon which they are based, can never be observed by others and are only sometimes apparent to the individual himself in inner sense.[40] Yet the actions which his *Willkür* performs in the phenomenal world issue from the maxims of the self-same *Willkür* in the intelligible world. Otherwise they could have no moral significance, for the individual could not be held accountable for them.[41] The *Willkür*—which is the expression of man's transcendental freedom, his ultimate spontaneity—is thus, like man himself, inextricably involved in both the phenomenal and the noumenal orders.

[38] *Ibid.*, p. 21; cf. *Ibid.*, p. 45: "The concept of the freedom of the *Willkür* does not precede the consciousness of the moral law in us, but is deduced from the determinability of our *Willkür* by this law as an unconditional command."

[39] *Ibid.*, pp. 13, 26, 27, 43, *passim;* cf. Abbott, pp. 282, 293, *passim.*

[40] *Religion*, p. 16. Later I shall refer to motives, maxims, and moral awareness as moral phenomena.

[41] *Ibid.*, p. 26, *passim;* cf. Abbott, p. 283, *passim.*

ii

The Problem of Two Standpoints

At this point we must interrupt our exposition of Kant's analysis of the will in order to consider a problem which is of interest to anyone concerned with the relation of moral theories to those of science and of overwhelming interest and importance to students of Kant. In order to resolve the Third Antinomy (and for other reasons which we need not here consider) Kant decided, in the first *Critique,* to bifurcate reality into the phenomenal world of appearances and the noumenal world of things in themselves. All events in the phenomenal order, he said, are necessarily related in terms of the category of causality and are in principle fully predictable. In the noumenal order, on the other hand, free causes can express themselves; that is, events may take place in the absence of any antecedent causal determinants. Scientific experience and knowledge pertain to the phenomenal world; moral experience and knowledge pertain to the noumenal. Kant thus asserted that all of the phenomenal actions of men are fully predictable in principle, and, were human knowledge sufficient, would be predicted;[42] yet he insisted no less strenuously that man's moral acts are free and not predetermined, hence unpredictable in principle.[43]

Kant could never adjust himself, however, to the bifurcation of human experience and human nature which this "two standpoints theory" requires. Although he asserted that the two realms exist "independently of one another and without interfering with each other,"[44] he found it impossible to speak of moral problems without presupposing their complete interaction.

The experience of moral obligation is a prime example of thorough interaction. If the same human being (and, therefore, the same *Willkür*) were not both moral and natural, existing fully and simultaneously in both realms, moral experience would be impossible. This experience presupposes the temptation of the moral self in the noumenal world by his natural self in the phenomenal world; it also presupposes the capacity of the moral self in the noumenal world to reorder the natural, phenomenal world according to the demands of the moral law. According to Kant the moral

---

[42] *Critique of Pure Reason* (Kemp Smith's tr.), p. 474; cf. Beck, pp. 204–205.
[43] *Religion,* p. 45, *passim.*
[44] Kemp Smith, p. 279; cf. Beck, p. 209.

individual in the numenal world is obligated (*a*) to seek the reordering of the sensible world in terms of the idea of the highest good (which requires the union of the two worlds), (*b*) specifically, to will as a numenal being to seek the happiness of other human beings in the phenomenal world, (*c*) to so act in the phenomenal world as not to contribute to the moral downfall of others as numenal beings, and (*d*) to rear his children, after their physical procreation in the phenomenal world, so that their moral natures are fulfilled in the numenal world, etc. Further examples could be given almost *ad infinitum*.[45]

The "two standpoints theory" fails to support the facts of everyday life unless one assumes that a pre-established harmony coordinates the phenomenal and numenal worlds. On the presupposition that such a harmony obtains, there is nothing incredible about the fact that whenever a murderer in the numenal order freely wills to kill a victim, a gun in the phenomenal order is predetermined to go off in his hand. But while the interworkings of the two orders seem no longer incredible, nothing can lend credibility to the presupposition itself. Kant, in discussing Leibniz, clearly indicates his lack of sympathy for such *ad hoc* solutions.[46]

Kant attempted to resolve the problems of interaction without resorting to the theory of pre-established harmony by holding that the numenal world is timeless and therefore that decisions made therein (having no causal antecedents) can be regarded regulatively as causes of temporal sequences in the phenomenal world.[47] But the results of this attempt are disastrous. In the first place, if the series of phenomenal events is in no way altered by the intrusion of numenal free causes, the latter are clearly superfluous. As long as the acts of moral volition cannot alter the determination of events in the phenomenal world, all categorical demands that they do so are vain. Second, Kant erred either in designating the moral realm as the numenal realm or in denying that the numenal realm is temporal, for moral volition is ineluctably temporal. The will is tempted in time, decides in time,

---

[45] See Kemp Smith, pp. 633–634, 637 ff.; Paton, pp. 75, 81, 89, 106; Beck, pp. 144, 154, 165 ff., 175–176, 180–182, 185, 190 ff., 210, 215 ff.; *Critique of Aesthetic Judgement* (Meredith's tr.), pp. 9, 10, 13, 14, 37, *passim*; *Critique of Teleological Judgement* (Meredith's tr.), pp. 14, 94–96, 99, 109, 113, 142; *Religion*, pp. 6, 7, 13, 17, 26, 28, 29, 34, 42–45, 65, 69, 71, 81, 88, 98, 130, 148, 158, *passim*; Abbott, pp. 272–279, 282–284, 292, 302–303, 308, 322, *passim*; *Metaphysic of Morals, Philosophy of Law* (Hastie's tr.), Sections 28–29, pp. 114 ff.

[46] Kemp Smith, p. 293; cf. p. 175.

[47] *Ibid.*, pp. 474, 476 ff.; Beck, p. 154 ff.

and, depending on its decision, feels guilty or satisfied in time. The pilgrim's and the rake's progress are, as the word "progress" indicates, thoroughly temporal adventures. In the *Religion,* no less than in the *Groundwork* and second *Critique,* Kant again and again refers in temporal terms to the problems of moral volition, improvement, and decline. When Kant tried to conceive of moral experience apart from time, he was so deeply involved in the highly abstract problems of the Third Antinomy (or in remaining consistent with his solution of them) that he forgot the plain facts of moral experience of which he himself on most occasions was acutely aware.

If we are to understand Kant's ethics and, specifically, his theory of the will as developed in the *Religion,* we must recognize that interaction between the phenomenal and noumenal worlds is required—even though Kant himself has denied that such interaction is possible. We cannot conclude our discussion of this problem by saying, "Kant never properly faces this difficulty."[48] We have to face this difficulty just because Kant did not do so and because no comprehension of his ethics is possible unless we do. Indeed, we have already done so to this extent: we have seen that Kant's ethics necessarily involves the proposition that the human will (particularly as *Willkür*) exists in time and acts in both the phenomenal and noumenal worlds. But the difficulty of incorporating this conclusion into the remainder of Kant's thought without contradiction and without destruction of any of the essential characteristics of his critical philosophy must be faced.[49] Although the problem, considered for itself, calls for a prolonged investigation, a mere suggestion of its possible resolution will suffice to remove it as an obstacle to our further examination of the will.

First, we must revise some of Kant's views in the first and second *Critiques* in light of his views in the third. Kant's early confidence that in principle science can predict all human activity is absent in the third *Critique.* Aware of the implications of man's purposeful activity in art and morality, Kant conceived of the principle of finality on the analogy of such activities and regarded

[48] For an excellent statement of the difficulty, without however any suggestion as to its resolution, see Paton, H. J., *The Categorical Imperative,* p. 277.
[49] Kant explicitly called upon his readers to assist him as co-workers (Kemp Smith, p. 14). He knew that there were contradictions in his writings, but he was confident that they could be resolved by readers who mastered his position in its entirety (*Ibid.,* p. 37; Beck, pp. 124–125). Kant also believed that we can often understand an author better than he has understood himself (Kemp Smith, p. 319); cf. p. 654.).

nature in terms of this principle as a work of art.[50] He argued that scientific investigation is dependent upon this principle for three reasons:

(a) Scientific method rests upon assumptions which regard nature as an artist or work of art—Occam's razor and the saying "nature takes the shortest route" are examples.[51] This assumption is a necessary guiding thread in empirical observation and hypothesis formation.

(b) The special sciences, while achieving islands of determinately ordered experience, have no means for uniting their knowledge into an overall system of nature apart from the use of the principle of finality.[52]

(c) Most important for our investigation, Kant denied that science would ever produce a Newton "to make intelligible to us even the genesis of a blade of grass from natural laws that no design has ordered."[53] Natural laws, having no reference to desire or intention, cannot account for the possibility of organic phenomena in which teleological relations of causes to effects are necessarily involved.[54] Much less can natural causation account for the prediction of organic behavior.

The extension of scientific inquiry to organic nature and to man as an organic and purposive being requires the adoption by scientists of the principle of finality. Through the use of this teleological principle, scientists may extend the use of the principle of natural causality and may *aspire* to predictive knowledge of organic life in terms of these principles. But there is no guarantee of success; furthermore, the principle of finality (unlike that of natural causality) is only a regulative principle for reflective judgement and can not provide determinate knowledge. It is an objective principle, for its use is necessary to the acquisition of knowledge of organic nature and the unification of the sciences. But finality is constitutive and provides determinate knowledge of nature only when employed from the moral standpoint. There it is used constitutively, in connection with the moral argument, to regard nature as ultimately rational and directed toward the fulfillment of the moral aims of men.[55]

[50] *Critique of Teleological Judgement*, pp. 24, 34.
[51] *Ibid.*, p. 21, *passim.* See also the First Introduction to the *Critique of Judgement,* Sections IV, V, X. Unfortunately, this important work, which Kant abandoned only because of its excessive length, has never been translated into English.
[52] See Section IX, First Introduction to the *Critique of Judgement.*
[53] *Critique of Teleological Judgement*, p. 54.
[54] *Ibid.*, pp. 40–47, 66, 67, 81, 82; and Section IV of the First Introduction.
[55] *Critique of Teleological Judgement*, p. 128.

The unjustified metaphysical assumption that science can predict the course of human affairs in principle if not in practice—which Kant took for granted in the first and second *Critiques*—is thus rejected in the third *Critique*. The fact that science requires the use of the principle of finality in order to extend its investigation to organic nature and to man has the consequence of leaving room in the phenomenal world for the effects of free causes. Finality, which interprets nature in terms of intentions and goals, is a regulative, reflective principle when used at the behest of science. And as a reflective principle it does not conflict with either a reflective or even a determinate employment of the idea of freedom: both principles may be used to interpret the same action. Kant does not deny that explanation in terms of natural causality is the continuing aim of science and the only "knowledge of nature in the true sense of the term."[56] But he does deny that this aim can be attained without the employment of reflective, non-determinate principles. This late development must not be overlooked.

Second, Kant's conception of the phenomenal and noumenal realms must be revised to account for the existence of the moral will in time and for its capacity to act in the phenomenal order. In the first *Critique* Kant introduced the distinction between phenomena and noumena for two reasons: (*a*) he wanted to emphasize the fact that the mind is passive in sensation and that knowledge resulting from the articulation of the data of sensibility by the categories of the understanding is merely knowledge of the appearance of reality; (*b*) he wanted to resolve the Third Antinomy by establishing independent orders for freedom and natural causality. The former insistence upon the finitude of human knowledge and its dependence upon the knower is an essential—perhaps *the* essential—tenet of Kant's philosophy. The latter insistence upon separate realms for the employment of free and natural causation is unessential and even inimical to Kant's thought. It is unnecessary because the third *Critique* suggests an alternative solution to the Third Antinomy on the basis of the limitations of natural causality and the regulative employment of finality. It is inimical because moral experience involves, as we have seen, the temporal awareness of duty and the involvement of the moral agent in the phenomenal world.

In the first *Critique* Kant defined noumena as things in themselves, as objects of non-sensible intuition, and he denied that

[56] *Ibid.*, p. 37. See *Religion*, p, 65*n*.

human beings were capable of non-sensible intuition. Moreover, he
defined phenomena as objects of appearance which are known by
applying the categories of the understanding to sensible intuition.[57] In terms of these definitions there is obviously no place for
moral experience in either realm. The noumenal realm is closed to
all human experience through the lack of intellectual intuition,
and the phenomenal realm is limited to experience conceptualized
by the categories of the understanding. We cannot object to Kant's
insistence on sensible intuition, on the perceptual, as a condition
for knowledge: Kant has amply described the dangers of superstition and fanaticism which accompany merely conceptual flights
into the transcendent.[58] We must question, however, his assumption that everything given in sensibility, in the matrices of space
or time, has to be conceptualized by categories of the understanding. Kant did not err in his definition of the noumenal; he erred,
rather, in placing arbitrary and uncritical limits on the phenomenal, for they forced him mistakenly and contradictorily to locate
moral experience in the noumenal realm. The experience of moral
obligation—which Kant called the one fact of pure reason—occurs
in time, in inner sense, and therefore involves sensible intuition.
Any principle or concept which must necessarily be presupposed in
order to give determinate structure to this experience has, by
virtue of that necessity, its own transcendental justification. Thus
the experience of duty provides the basis for the transcendental
deduction of freedom and the transcendental analysis of will. We
have no reason to say that this knowledge stems from an intellectual intuition of noumena. Kant rightly insists in the *Religion,*
as in most of his ethical writings, that we know ourselves morally
only as we appear to ourselves, that we can never know the secret
motives of the heart or the character of our dispositions except by
indirect reasoning from our moral actions.[59] Our knowledge of
freedom, the will, and ourselves as moral beings would seem, consequently, to be a knowledge of moral phenomena and a part of
our knowledge of the phenomenal realm as a whole. By broadening
the conception of the phenomenal world to include all aspects of
human experience—the moral, aesthetic, and organic, no less than
the theoretical[60]—we pose many tasks for Kant's interpreters, but
no insurmountable problems for Kant's system. Here we can

[57] Kemp Smith, pp. 265–267, 271 ff.
[58] *Ibid.,* pp. 257 ff., 264.
[59] *Religion,* pp. 46, *passim.* Cf. pp. 16, 42, 43.
[60] It may be wondered why religious experience is not included. Although Kant

merely take the first step toward realigning his theory of phenomena and noumena to fit his actual practice in their regard.

In resuming our interrupted analysis of the will in the light of this brief sketch—we need not be troubled by Kant's insistence on the presence of *Willkür* in both phenomenal and noumenal orders. We recognize the temporal nature of *Willkür*[61] and its presence in both moral and theoretical aspects of the phenomenal world. *Willkür* can be regarded from a theoretical standpoint as a theoretical phenomenon or from a moral standpoint as a moral phenomenon. Because these orders are not mutually exclusive, the ultimate unity of the will, which is essential to morality, is not impaired. This interpretation is required by Kant's ethical position and reflects the direction taken by Kant in his later writings. It is noteworthy that in the *Religion* Kant put no stock in his earlier technical distinction between phenomena and noumena; he remarks, with some suggestion of impatience, that "these expressions ["phenomena" and "noumena"] are used only because of the schools."[62] In order to follow Kant's usage in the *Religion,* we shall have to continue to speak occasionally of the phenomenal and noumenal actions of the *Willkür,* but we must bear in mind that, strictly speaking, all so-called noumenal acts should be regarded as morally phenomenal acts of inner sense which are not publicly observable, and that the noumenal realm should be regarded as the locus of the will only when it is considered as transcending human knowledge as a thing-in-itself.

iii

Wille

In our discussion of the human will, to which we now return, we have considered the will merely in terms of its radical capacity

---

recognized the autonomy of moral and aesthetic experience and the knowledge of organic nature (hence our extension of the concept of the phenomenal to include this wider range of experience) he refused to admit that religious experience is a genuine, autonomous aspect of human experience. The reasons are these: (*a*) Kant found nothing in religious experience as such to restrain the fanatical and superstitious tendencies of religious imagination. The concepts of religion would seem to be blind, empty, and often perverse without the restraining correction of moral principles. And, as Greene points out, (*b*) Kant was far too rationally inclined to believe that truth might be essentially historical and dependent for its discovery on non-rational revelation. One of many clear instances in the *Religion* of Kant's refusal to recognize the legitimacy of religious data that can be supported by neither theoretical nor moral experience is found on p. 48.

[61] This is not to say that there is a temporal origin, i.e. an antecedent determination, of the acts of *Willkür*. But these acts all take place freely in a temporal continuum. See *Religion*, p. 35.

[62] *Religion*, p. 13.

of free choice—that is, as *Willkür*. The analysis of the will in terms of this single aspect is by no means complete. The moral law awakens the *Willkür* to its transcendental freedom, to its power as a free faculty of desire. But the moral law is not the *Willkür*: it is not the transcendental freedom to act autonomously or heteronomously. The moral law expresses, rather, the rational conditions for the existence and realization of transcendental freedom and confronts *Willkür* with these conditions in the form of the categorical imperative. Kant makes room in the will for the presence of the moral law by introducing the concept of *Wille* which refers to the purely rational aspect of the will. *Wille* is as much a part of the will as *Willkür*, for without it there could be no rational structure for freedom, no experience of obligation, and hence no awareness of the power of volition.

Unlike *Willkür*, however, *Wille* does not make decisions or adopt maxims; it does not act. Rather it is the source of a strong and ever present incentive in *Willkür*, and, if strong enough to be adopted by *Willkür* into the maxim of its choice, *Wille* "can determine the *Willkür*" and then "it is practical reason itself."[63] *Wille* expresses the possibility of autonomy which is presupposed by transcendental freedom. The *Wille* represents the will's own demand for self-fulfillment by commanding *Willkür*, that aspect of the will which can either fulfill or abnegate its freedom, to actualize its free nature by willing in accordance with the law (and condition) of freedom. The most important difference between *Wille* and *Willkür* is apparent here. Whereas *Willkür* is free to actualize either the autonomous or heteronomous potentialities of transcendental freedom, *Wille* is not free at all. *Wille* is rather the law of freedom, the normative aspect of the will, which as a norm is neither free nor unfree. Having no freedom of action, *Wille* is under no constraint or pressure. It exerts, instead, the pressure of its own normative rational nature upon *Willkür*.[64]

In order to influence *Willkür*, which is a faculty of desire, *Wille* must be able to arouse desires or aversions in *Willkür*. The feeling which can be aroused by *Wille* is called moral feeling and consists in the "simple respect for the moral law."[65] The presence of *Wille* in the will, and specifically in relation to *Willkür*, constitutes what

---

[63] Abbott, p. 268. I have substituted the terms *"Wille"* and *"Willkür"* respectively for Abbott's phrases "rational will" and "elective will" in order to avoid needless duplication of terms.

[64] Abbott, p. 282.

[65] *Religion*, p. 23; cf. pp. 26, 31, 42–44, *passim*.

Kant calls the predisposition of the will to personality. This predisposition "is the capacity for respect for the moral law as *in itself a sufficient incentive of the Willkür.*"[66] This predisposition is appropriately named because personality involves freedom and because the capacity to be motivated to action simply by the universality of one's maxim, i.e., by its accordance with the moral law, is a necessary condition for the possession of transcendental freedom and the potentiality of autonomy. The capacity to act merely according to the demands of the moral law regardless of the motivation to such action is a capacity shared by trained animals. But the capacity to act from the *incentive* of universal law, and thereby to transcend determination by particular inclinations and habits, is a capacity enjoyed only by free, responsible beings; it is the capacity to act from the incentive of willing one's own nature as a person. "The moral law," said Kant, "with the respect which is inseparable from it, . . . is personality itself (the idea of humanity considered quite intellectually)."[67]

The determination of *Willkür* by *Wille* can occur in varying degrees, with the general provision that nothing determines *Willkür* unless *Willkür chooses* to be so determined. The natural predisposition to personality (the capacity of the *Willkür* to make the law a sufficient incentive for action) can be fulfilled "only when the *Willkür* incorporates such moral feeling into its maxim."[68] Nonetheless, the *Willkür* can never be totally devoid of moral feeling for then it would cease to be itself. If *Willkür* did not make the moral law (*Wille,* as the rational structure of its own nature) a determinant of action at least to the extent of feeling categorically obligated to do so, whether that obligation were fulfilled in action or not, the *Willkür* would cease to be itself. "No man," Kant argued, "is wholly destitute of moral feeling, for if he were totally unsusceptible to this sensation he would be morally dead; and to speak in the language of physicians, if the moral vital force could no longer produce any effect on this feeling, then his humanity would be dissolved (as it were by chemical laws) into mere animality."[69] To this minimal extent *Wille* necessarily determines *Willkür.* Although the agency of determination is on

[66] *Idem.*
[67] *Idem.*
[68] *Idem.;* cf. pp. 17, 19; Abbott, pp. 267–268.
[69] Abbott, pp. 310–311. Kant writes: "The incentive which consists in respect for the moral law we have never been able to lose, and were such a thing possible, we could never get it again." (Cf. *Religion,* p. 30.)

the side of *Willkür*, when for purposes of analysis these aspects of volition are separated, the necessity of this determination derives from the dependence of *Willkür* on *Wille*. This dependence, as we have seen, is grounded in the inseparability of freedom and rationality. A *Willkür* totally unresponsive to *Wille* would be a freedom totally dirempted from rationality. Of such a freedom we have neither experience nor knowledge. As Kant put it: "To conceive of oneself as a freely acting being and yet as exempt from the law which is appropriate to such a being (the moral law) would be tantamount to conceiving of a cause operating without any laws whatsoever (for determination according to natural laws is excluded by the fact of freedom); this is a self-contradiction."[70]

iv

Moral Feeling

Since moral feeling is not merely an incentive for *Willkür* but expresses, in addition, the *Wille's* relation to *Willkür*, its delineation and careful examination constitute an essential part of Kant's analysis of the will. Moral feeling can be experienced in a variety of pleasant or unpleasant forms: (*a*) it can be painful frustration when respect for the law demands the rejection of the objects of sensible desires; (*b*) it can be the painful feeling of moral dissatisfaction when it forces the *Willkür* to reflect upon its past betrayals or present temptations to betray its own free nature through heteronomous action; (*c*) it can be the pleasant feeling of moral satisfaction in having affirmed one's freedom through autonomous action; or (*d*) it can be the pleasant and painful experience of the sublimity of personality, the experience of the power of the human will to assert its rational independence from the forces of sensibility even at the cost of nappiness or of life itself.[71]

It is far easier to describe the various ways in which moral feeling can be experienced by the will than to specify with precision how it is to be distinguished from all other feelings. It would seem possible, for instance, to distinguish moral feeling from non-moral feelings by noting that the former, unlike the latter, does not *affect* the *Willkür* but is *effected* by it. In a sense, however, this

[70]*Religion*, p. 30.
[71] Beck, pp. 180–195; *Critique of Aesthetic Judgement*, Sections 27, 28, 29; *Religion*, p. 45, *passim*.

can be said for all feelings if the *Willkür* is regarded from both theoretical (psychological) and moral standpoints. If the *Willkür* is regarded from the former standpoint, it is thought to be *affected* by its strongest desire. Regarded from the latter, it is thought to *effect* its strongest desire as its act of free volition. All desires and feelings would seem to be alike, therefore, in their relation to *Willkür:* from one standpoint all of them seem to affect the *Willkür;* from the other, the basic moral standpoint, all are effected by it.

But the foregoing observations, while sound, are superficial. For despite the observed similarities in the relation of moral feeling and non-moral feeling to *Willkür*, there are also radical differences: whereas the non-moral feelings of sensible desire influence the *Willkür* to varying degrees both before and after the decision of the *Willkür* in which the determining incentive is chosen, the moral feeling of respect for the law is not originally an incentive at all. Respect for the moral law is a feeling that is aroused in the *Willkür* only when it recognizes the law as a condition of its own being and the necessary standard of judgment in all its decisions. The *Willkür* first recognizes and accepts the law in this sense and only thereafter *effects* this feeling of respect in the process of expressing its free nature. Viewed phenomenally, this feeling *effected* by *Willkür* may then appear to affect *Willkür* in determining its choice. But this feeling never appears at all except as an effect of the *Willkür*.[72]

The distinction between moral feeling and sensible feelings and desires can be seen more clearly perhaps by means of an example. Suppose X obeys the moral law in situation A in which such action is profitable to him in terms of happiness, gratification of

[72] It is apt to be misleading to say that the feeling of respect is an effect of *Willkür;* it is sounder perhaps to say that this feeling is an effect of the will as a whole. Moral feeling involves the dynamic unity of the parts of the will and is as much the effect of *Wille* as of *Willkür*. When the examination of *Wille* is extended, *Wille* is seen to be merely the internal rational conditions of the existence of *Willkür*. Hence, when Kant says that *Wille* determines *Willkür* through moral feeling, he is saying that *Willkür* determines itself according to its rational nature. And when Kant denies that *Wille* can determine *Willkür* unless the latter freely accepts such determination, he is merely following the line of his analysis of the will, in terms of which the radically self-determining aspect of will, the choosing will, is called *Willkür*. These complications are not theoretical difficulties. No analysis of a dynamic unitary function into static parts can be immune from distortion. But distortion can be held to a safe minimum as long as one does not hypostatize or concretize the isolated abstractions. To pretend that *Wille* and *Willkür* are perfectly discrete and separate parts of the will involves precisely such erroneous hypostatization. Some flexibility of usage is required to convey Kant's analysis with precision.

desires, etc. If we are asked to explain why X obeys the law we can say, from a theoretical perspective, that he is motivated to this action by desires. Although this explanation is by no means complete or exhaustive[73] it has considerable plausibility. Here the *Willkür* is viewed as if it were determined by sensible desires (pathological desires, as Kant curiously calls them) which *affect* and influence its behavior.

But now let us suppose (ruling out, by hypothesis, all prudential concern for the hereafter) that X obeys the moral law in situation B in which his action causes him much suffering, loss of property, happiness, and perhaps the loss of life itself. The interpretation of the action of X in this situation reveals concretely the difference between moral and pathological pleasure. From the theoretical perspective—in which all pleasures are assumed to be of the same sort (pathological, in Kantian terms)— we explain X's action by saying that X obeyed the moral law because he was happy doing so or because he was afraid of a guilty conscience if he did not. Here moral feeling is treated as if it were like other sensible feelings, as if—prior to the decision of *Willkür* to make it so—it were a natural desire or incentive of the will. It is said that X is determined *by desire* to obey the law in situation B just as he was in situation A. This explanation, too, has an initial plausibility. But, as Kant saw quite clearly, it is one of the world's oldest, most popular and enduring varieties of circular reasoning.

In situation A, X has grounds for desiring to obey the law. We can point to the happiness and prosperity that are his by such obedience. In situation B, however, no ground other than X's desire to obey the law itself is brought forward to explain his action. It is explained that X desires to obey the law because X desires to obey the law. This circularity is obscured in the statement that X obeys the law because of his "fear of a guilty conscience." But does not the fear of a guilty conscience derive from the recognition of the authority of the moral law, and is it not the resulting

[73] From a moral perspective Kant would supplement this explanation by saying that as long as X is a responsible person, he has to will that some desire have determining strength. And he would observe that since the demands of the moral law and of self-interest coincided in situation A, it is possible that a moral incentive was also involved. But Kant would regard the judgment as theoretically sound because it was made within the limits of theoretical presuppositions and did not have to borrow surreptitiously from moral ones. Finally, since such an explanation involves no trace of prediction, it poses no difficulties for the moral presupposition of freedom.

desire to obey it? We cannot argue that X recognized the authority of the moral law and made obedience to it the condition of his
happiness because he was afraid of a guilty conscience. He would
have had no conscience—clear or guilty—until after he recognized
the law. An amoral man does not become moral for fear of having
a guilty conscience. Such fear follows from but can never precede
his being moral.[74]

The difference between pathological pleasure and moral pleasure is thus a difference in kind. But the difference cannot be observed from the theoretical standpoint, from which all pleasures
and incentives appear alike as influences which affect and ultimately determine *Willkür*. The individual who feels respect for
the moral law appears to the theoretical observer simply as one
of those rare persons who, as a matter of fact, likes to do his duty.
The difference between moral and pathological feeling cannot be
observed on this level because the free moral power of *Willkür* is
not a theoretical phenomenon. From the moral phenomenal standpoint, however, the difference between, no less than the similarity
of, these kinds of pleasure is observable. From the moral
phenomenal standpoint of inner sense we observe: (*a*) the
recognition by *Willkür* of its own rational nature and the emer-
gence of moral feeling which accompanies it; (*b*) the fact that the
Willkür is passively affected by a vast array of desires and is
sorely tempted to renounce its power of self-determination to the
most alluring to them; and (*c*) the decision of *Willkür* which
potentiates one of these influences, either the moral or the pathological, to determining force (thus accounting for the appearance
of the dynamics of choice from the theoretical perspective). Passing over the similarity of these pleasures, which poses no problem, we find that the basis of their difference lies in their mode
of origination within *Willkür*. Pathological pleasure originates in
the sensible nature of the human will, in *Willkür* as the merely
passive recipient of sensuous influences (which can never be determinants of *Willkür* without its active cooperation but which,
regardless of its action, never cease to be influences). Moral pleasure, in contradistinction, originates in the rational nature of the

[74] The attempt to persuade an amoral being to be moral by threatening him with
a guilty conscience or tempting him with a clear one is as foolish as the attempt to
use reason to persuade a non-rational being to be rational. To be sure, both pro-
cedures are often effective when dealing with immoral or irrational beings respectively, for only a moral being (in the generic sense) can be immoral, just as only
a rational being (in the generic sense) can be irrational.

human will, in *Willkür* as the active, self-originating, spontaneous (hence, rational) aspect of the will.

By establishing the difference between these kinds of pleasure through his prolonged analysis of the human will, Kant realized a theoretical ambition of long standing.[75] On the basis of this distinction, Kant could admit that the moral law issues in a sensible delight and thereby has a practical influence in the sensible world without jeopardizing the rational foundation of obligation and transforming his ethics into an empirical one of the "moral sense" variety. He was concerned never to confuse these kinds of pleasure because the foundation of his ethics, in the experience of obligation, depends upon their clear distinction,[76] and their confusion, he held, leads to "the euthanasia (quiet death) of all morality."[77] Although Kant offered many clear statements of the nature of moral feeling prior to Book One of the *Religion,* and what are perhaps his finest statements concerning it thereafter, he rightly said, "I have in another place [Book One of the *Religion*], reduced, as I believe, to the simplest expressions the distinction between *pathological* and *moral* pleasure."[78] These other statements are verbal conquests apart from his careful analysis of the various structures and functions of the human will upon which the distinction between moral and pathological pleasure depends.[79]

Before leaving the question of moral feeling, we may be tempted to inquire about the incentive that prompts *Willkür* to recognize the authority of the moral law and thus to experience moral feeling. Once moral feeling is present in *Willkür,* then *Willkür* (viewed psychologically) is determined by it. But what incentive, we may ask, can prompt *Willkür* to recognize the authority of the law in the first place? Our question, however, is mistakenly raised. In asking this question, we are looking for the antecedent conditions from which *Willkür*'s free acceptance of the law must follow. But

[75] See our note above referring to Kant's letter of 1773 to Marcus Herz.

[76] Beck, pp. 147, 149, 216, 230, *passim.*

[77] Abbott, p. 289.

[78] *Ibid.,* pp. 288–289. In the Preface to the *Metaphysic of Morals* Kant referred to his article in the *Berlinische Monatsschrift* on the subject of radical evil in human nature. He later published this article as Book One of the *Religion.*

[79] Furthermore, on the basis of his clarifying analysis of the will in the *Religion* one can decide which of Kant's conflicting statements in the second *Critique* on the nature of moral feeling are sound. For what I consider to be Kant's finest statement concerning moral feeling, a statement published after Book One of the *Religion* and in the light of it, see *"Über den Gemeinspruch: Das mag in der Theorie richtig sein, taugt aber nicht für die Praxis,"* (hereafter referred to as "Theory and Practice"), Cassirer edition, Vol. VI, pp. 366–367.

if such conditions could be found, then *Willkür* would not be free, since freedom involves the capacity to act independently of such conditions. When we look for such conditions, Kant argued, we reveal our failure to comprehend the nature of freedom, that is, we fail "to comprehend its incomprehensibility."[80] For the scientifically inclined, the incomprehensibility of freedom is usually enough to warrant its peremptory dismissal.[81] But Kant refused to dismiss one of the necessary presuppositions of man's moral experience merely because that presupposition was incomprehensible. Kant was far too empirical and skeptical to accept the metaphysical position that the universe is necessarily and exhaustively comprehensible. He left to rationalistic philosophers and, surprisingly, to many of the empirical scientists the promethean metaphysic in terms of which one rejects as illusory all that he cannot comprehend. Kant's awareness of the finitude of human knowledge was built into his philosophy in the concept of the thing-in-itself.

v

The Origin of Evil

From the inscrutable depths of freedom, which Kant will neither dismiss nor pretend to understand, issue the moral qualities of the will, both good and evil. "Man *himself*," Kant says, "must make or nave made himself into whatever, in a moral sense, whether good or evil, he is or is to become. Either condition must be an effect of his *Willkür;* for otherwise he could not be held responsible for it and could therefore be *morally* neither good nor evil."[82] The moral quality of the will is completely self-acquired. No matter how bountifully or stepmotherly a human being is treated by nature, he is fundamentally the equal of, and his opportunities are basically the same as those of, all other men in the development

[80] Paton, p. 131; cf. Beck, p. 202; *Religion*, pp. 17, 20, 35, 36, 38, 45, *passim;* Abbott, p. 290.. In his discussion of the incomprehensibility of freedom on page lv above, Greene seems to overlook the fact that it is logically necessary that freedom be incomprehensible; its incomprehensibility does not follow from Kant's disastrous "two standpoints theory." If freedom and *pre*determination are incompatible (and Kant holds that they are), and if explanation consists in specifying the set of conditions from which an act or event necessarily follows (and this is the only kind of explanation which Kant refers to), then since such explanation involves predetermination, such explanation cannot be offered for freedom. This obstacle to the comprehension of freedom can be removed if freedom is defined in such a way that it is compatible with predeterminism. But when freedom is so defined, Kant insisted, it is not explained but is explained away. (See Section II above.)

[81] Abbott, p. 289.

[82] *Religion*, p. 40; cf. pp. 26, 38, 52.

and expression of his moral personality. Until by his own free action he acquires a good or evil will, he is innocent; thereafter, he is still free to be different from what he has been. Hence, every "action [whether good or evil] must be regarded as though the individual had fallen into it directly from a state of innocence. For whatever natural causes may have been influencing him, and whether these causes were to be found within him or outside him, his action is yet free and determined by none of these causes."[83] There is no original sin and no original goodness in man except in the sense that sins and virtues *originate* in his free *Willkür*.

If there is no original evil in man until he originates it, how does he happen to become corrupted? The human *Willkür*, on Kant's analysis, comes to self-awareness in relation to *Wille*, the voice of its rational nature, which instills in *Willkür* respect for the moral law as a part of *Willkür*'s self-recognition. Possessed of moral feeling, and in a state of innocence, why should *Willkür* ever choose to be evil? What is the occasion or condition of its choosing an evil maxim? It cannot be found in a defective or morally corrupt *Wille*. The presence of an inviolate *Wille* is a necessary presupposition of the existence of free choice: the universality of law (as discussed in Section II above) is the necessary condition for the expression of freedom. Were this law itself corrupted, the necessary conditions of freedom, and hence of good or evil, would not be present.[84]

Many moralists and theologians have sought the condition or occasion of evil in man's sensible nature. Kant, however, explicitly rejects this position and argues that man's sensible nature, neither evil in itself nor the occasion of evil, is good and worthy of fulfillment:[85] "Natural inclinations, *considered in them-*

---

[83] *Ibid.*, p. 36; cf. p. 17.

[84] *Religion*, pp. 30–31; *passim*.

[85] Kant has been signally unsuccessful in getting the attention of his readers on this point (though he made it often enough and with sufficient eloquence). Convinced that Kant's ethics is a formalistic ethic of duty and virtue alone, many critics have refused to accept as "Kantian," or have regarded as anomalous and inconsistent, all of Kant's doctrines and texts which insist upon the goodness of happiness and express a concern for its fulfillment. (See page lxii ff. above and the discussion of Erich Adickes' attempt, summarized in the Preface to the Second Edition of this Translation, to find a repudiation by Kant of his own moral argument.)

Kant encountered this critical reaction in his own lifetime. In his essay "Theory and Practice" (Cassirer, ed., Vol. VI, here translated in parts) Kant noted that a respected contemporary, Garve, interpreted him to hold that "even where there is no question of duty, and he will not contradict duty, the virtuous man should still take no regard for happiness" ("Theory and Practice," p. 363). Having clearly stated in the second *Critique* (and elsewhere) that "Pure practical reason does not

selves are good, that is, not a matter of reproach, and it is not only
futile to want to extirpate them but to do so would be harmful
and blameworthy. Rather, let them be tamed, and instead of
clashing with one another they can be brought into harmony in
a wholeness which is called happiness."[86] The goodness of man's
sensible nature is essential, moreover, to the expression of virtue,
for it provides the content for the moral object of volition.
Furthermore, the attribution of evil to man's sensuous nature rests
on the assumption that men can be moved to action by their senses
alone—without their willful cooperation—and thus reduces human nature to an animal level on which evil is impossible.[87] The
Stoics, Kant observed, located the cause of evil in man's careless-

require that we should renounce the claims of happiness" (Beck, p. 199), Kant
added in "Theory and Practice" with some show of emotion, "These objections
are not misunderstandings. . . . Their possibility must remain a mystery, unless
such phenomena are adequately explained by the human tendency to follow one's
own accustomed thought patterns even in the judgment of strange views, and to
carry over the former into the latter" (pp. 363–364). It is easy enough to find isolated passages in Kant's writings where he speaks as if the moral good were the
only good. Such passages are relatively few, however, and passages which insist
upon the goodness of happiness are far more numerous.

Aside from textual proofs alone, which can never be decisive in themselves apart
from their relation to his theory as a whole, Kant's ethical position requires the
existence of two basically different kinds of goodness—moral goodness and natural
(*physische*) goodness: (1) The experience of obligation occurs when the moral individual confronts genuine but conflicting values. Kant took issue with Stoic and
Epicurean ethicists for trying to collapse the difference between virtue and happiness, thereby denying the distinct goodness of one or the other. (2) He recognized
that the material of moral volition must be determined by the formal principle of
the law in relation to the content of man's sensuous nature; hence the direct duty
to seek the happiness of others and the indirect obligation to seek one's own. (3)
He offered a moral theory of punishment which presupposes non-moral values with
which to reward and penalize. (4) In each of the *Critiques* and in most of his
ethical writings, Kant argued that the moral purpose of creation and man's ultimate object of moral volition consists in seeking the highest good—the realization
of virtue and happiness in proper proportion to one another. The close theoretical
bond of happiness and virtue in Kant's ethics (which follows from the close bond
of man's rational and sensible natures) is reflected in Kant's definition of virtue
as the worthiness to be happy, and in his phrasing of the categorical imperative
as the duty to "Do that through which thou becomest worthy to be happy" (Kemp
Smith, p. 638). (See *Ibid.,* pp. 636 ff.; Paton, pp. 61, 83, 109; Beck, pp. 130, 148,
149, 184, 190, 198 ff., 215 ff.; *Critique of Teleological Judgement* (Meredith's tr.),
pp. 114 ff.; *Religion,* pp. 4 ff., 19, 22, 23, 30, 51, *passim;* Abbott, pp. 295 ff.;
"Theory and Practice," pp. 360–372.)

Many of Kant's readers, (like Schopenhauer, who was influential in establishing
this popular misinterpretation), have accepted the *Groundwork* (which offers only
the formalistic foundation for Kant's ethics) as Kant's authoritative and complete
work on ethics. They have ignored or rejected as mistaken those parts of the first
and second *Critiques,* the *Religion* and the *Metaphysic of Morals* which deal with
the material component of Kant's ethics; and some of them have then criticized
Kant for his failure to recognize the legitimate place of happiness in the moral life.
(See Schopenhauer, A., *The Basis of Morality,* (Bullock's tr.), p. 26.)

[86] *Religion,* p. 51.
[87] *Ibid.,* p. 30; cf. pp. 22–27.

ness, in his neglect to combat his sensible inclinations. But, he added, "this neglect is itself contrary to duty (a transgression) and no mere lapse of nature. . . . Genuine evil consists in this, that a man does not *will* to withstand those inclinations when they tempt him to transgress."[88]

Willkür is confronted by the demands of its own rational nature, present in *Wille*, and by the demands of its sensuous nature, present in its natural desires and inclinations. *Willkür* is not torn between good and evil but rather confronts two basically different kinds of good. And while immediately tempted to act upon its natural desires and inclinations, *Willkür* recognizes the categorical obligation to assert its own personality in the determination of its actions, and therefore to act in accordance with the universal demands of the moral law. All men, whether good or evil, have within them the good incentives of happiness and of virtue. The difference between good and evil men depends upon the order of subordination within their wills of the moral and natural incentives. The evil man is one who freely decides to subordinate the demands of the law to the demands of his sensible nature.[89] By expressing no more of his personality than is expressed in its abnegation, he fails as a free person and is evil. The good man, conversely, subordinates the natural incentives to the moral incentive and thus positively expresses in his action his power as a free being. Thus the ground of evil is found in man's tendency or *disposition* to will the rejection of himself as a self-determining personality, as a free being, for the sake of himself as a creature of nature.[90]

vi

Disposition

With the introduction of the concept of the disposition (*Gesinnung*), the analysis of human volition takes on still greater complexity. The development of this concept is, perhaps, the most important single contribution of the *Religion* to Kant's ethical

[88] *Ibid.*, p. 51.
[89] *Ibid.*, p. 31 ff.
[90] *Ibid.*, pp. 51, 78, *passim*. Man's proper aim is the fulfillment of himself in both aspects, though the fulfillment for the moral is a necessary condition of the personal fulfillment of the natural. The moral fulfillment is fundamental to the individual while the natural, though to be desired, is not. Thus Kant writes in "Theory and Practice" (p. 366), "Happiness contains all (but not more than) that which nature provides us; virtue, however, contains that which no one other than the person himself can give or take from himself."

theory, for by means of it he accounts for continuity and responsibility in the free exercise of *Willkür* and for the possibility of ambivalent volition, as well as the basis for its complex assessment. In defining the disposition, Kant says, "The disposition, i.e., the ultimate subjective ground of the adoption of maxims, can be only one and applies universally to the whole use of freedom."[91] And since each individual is morally responsible for his disposition, the disposition itself must be freely adopted by his *Willkür*. As the ultimate subjective ground of decision, the disposition is a maxim influencing or directing the adoption of the particular maxims on which individual decisions are based. In discussing evil in man, for example, Kant refers to the disposition as "a maxim of all particular morally-evil maxims" and points out that it is not observable but can be only inferred from the maxims of particular actions which in turn are inferred from particular actions which are observable: "In order to call a man evil, it would have to be possible *a priori* to infer from several acts done with a consciousness of their evil, or from one such act, an underlying evil maxim; and further, from this maxim to infer the presence in the agent of an underlying common ground, itself a maxim, of all particular morally-evil maxims."[92] The disposition is this underlying common ground. In discussing the return of the *Willkür* from evil to good, Kant speaks of the revolution that takes place in the disposition which consists in "going over to the *maxim* of the holiness of the disposition."[93] But, he notes, the "man who adopts this purity into his maxim is indeed not yet holy by reason of this act (for there is a great gap between the maxim and the deed)."[94] That is to say, there is a difference between the dispositional act of *Willkür* and its particular acts that may, if the dispositional act is firm, follow from it.

The nature of the disposition is further clarified by Kant's discussion of the two kinds of action that *Willkür* performs. "The term 'act,' " he writes, "can apply in general to that exercise of freedom whereby the supreme maxim (in harmony with the law or contrary to it) is adopted by the *Willkür* [the dispositional act], but also to the exercise of freedom whereby the actions themselves

---

[91] *Religion,* p. 20; cf. 64. Unfortunately, Kant was never systematic in his discussion of disposition; hence, we must fit together a picture from widely separated passages.

[92] *Ibid.,* p. 16; cf. pp. 32, 34, 65.

[93] *Ibid.,* p. 43. (The italics are mine.) A change of disposition, according to Kant, involves a "change of heart," not a "change of practices."

[94] *Ibid.,* p. 42; cf. p. 43.

(considered materially, i.e., with reference to the objects of *Willkür* [the specific acts]) are performed in accordance with that maxim."[95] The dispositional act involves the decision of the *Willkür* to subordinate either its sensible nature to its moral nature or its moral nature to its sensible nature; that is, the dispositional act determines the basic motivation of *Willkür*. It determines whether the specific actions of *Willkür* are to stem from a virtuous respect for the law (and hence are to be done for the sake of the law) *or* whether they are to stem from subjective interests (and hence conform to the law only when there is a coincidence of moral and subjective interests). The dispositional act concerns the willing or the rejecting of the spirit of the moral law and establishes the *morality* of the acts of the *Willkür*, the underlying intentional ground of all its specific acts and therefore its character.[96] The specific acts of *Willkür*, on the other hand, do not establish the motive of action but are largely the products of the motivational force of the dispositional act. As concrete expressions of the dispositional motive, they may express that motive accurately or with a distortion resulting from the influence of intervening forces within the *Willkür* (as we shall consider later). But they can never fail entirely to reflect their dispositional ground inasmuch as their occurrence depends primarily upon the potentiating dispositional act. In its specific acts, the *Willkür* wills or refuses to will in accordance with the demands of the moral law; these acts reveal the decision of the *Willkür* regarding the letter, rather than the spirit, of the law, and establish the *legality* of the acts of *Willkür*. Although the dispositional act can be intuited only by an omniscient being and merely inferred (and with considerable inaccuracy) by human beings, the specific acts of *Willkür* are observable either in inner or outer sense. To the extent that the dispositional act can be grasped by inference, it is a part of moral experience. Beyond that, it is a noumenal thing-in-itself. The specific acts of *Willkür*, however, are all aspects of the morally phenomenal order, and when the intentions of these acts are carried out, some of them can be experienced as theoretical phenomena. The dispositional act establishes the intelligible or noumenal character of the *Willkür*, whereas the specific acts establish its phenomenal character.[97]

[95] *Ibid.*, p. 26.
[96] *Ibid.*, pp. 27, 42, 43; cf. p. 16, *passim;* cf. Abbott, pp. 282 ff.
[97] *Idem.*

The disposition is thus the enduring aspect of *Willkür;* it is *Willkür* considered in terms of the continuity and fullness of its free expression. It is the enduring pattern of intention that can be inferred from the many discrete acts of *Willkür* and reveals their ultimate motive.[98] To use a military analogy, the disposition is the strategic *Willkür,* as opposed to the tactical *Willkür* of specific actions. Since *Willkür* is free, its dispositional aspect is alterable from one moment to the next. In each moment, *Willkür* is not predetermined by what it was. On the other hand, and this point is frequently overlooked, *Willkür* is not undetermined nor indetermined. Freedom is itself a mode of causality with its own law.[99] The acts of the moral individual are *determined* by what the individual himself *is.* Admittedly, Kant refused to deny the spontaneous agency of the individual; he refused to fossilize him in a predeterministic scheme which makes him the expression of what he was, or more accurately, the expression of what *he* never was but only of what *nature* was and continues to be. The moral agent is responsible for his actions because he is the author of them and because they express what he is. But we must not suppose, Kant insists, that what a person *is* (and therefore what is within his power and for which he is responsible) is expressed exhaustively in each discrete act of volition. Kant knew that we discover what we are not merely by observing our many discrete actions[100] but by inferring from them the quality of our disposition or moral character.[101] Our disposition reveals much more about what we are than our individual actions taken in isolation or aggregate. The disposition is not the compulsive carry-over of our past nature into our present nature but the indication of our true and full nature freely, though not always consciously, willed in every present moment. It is the endurance or perseverance of our intentional, volitional commitment. Though a free and hence precarious continuity, the disposition is a *de facto* continuity in volition, a continuity whose existence does not cease merely because it is unsupported by predeterministic forces.

Continuity in disposition is essential to moral self-identity. Our

[98] *Ibid.,* p. 65. Although the disposition cannot be divided into temporal parts and is not in the scientifically determinate temporal order (since it cannot be intuited in time and since it is the maxim of the complete free expression of *Willkür*), it has nonetheless the temporal properties of endurance and change. (*Idem.;* cf. pp. 34, 43, 46, 60, 68, 69, *passim.*)

[99] *Ibid.,* pp. 30, 45; cf. Beck, p. 175 ff.; Paton, pp. 80 ff., 114 ff. See also Section II above.

[100] Several of these can occur simultaneously as subsequent discussion will indicate.

[101] See *Anthropologie,* (Cassirer, ed., Vol. VIII), pp. 187 ff.

moral self-consciousness would be fractured and dissipated into isolated intentions and actions if we did not relate them to one another by reference to their common ground of intention in disposition. Specific acts of *Willkür* have in themselves no direct interrelation. Each is a free decision of *Willkür* and none is the cause of another. The establishment of a *moral* (intentional, motivational, and not merely legal) relation between our actions depends upon viewing them as expressing, more or less accurately, the dispositional act of which we are not directly aware.

This extended-present nature of the *Willkür* (what it is in its full being as disposition, and not merely what it is in specific actions) is thus, on Kant's view, the ground of moral responsibility. The *Willkür* acts on the basis of what it freely chooses to be, and because it freely asserts its fuller being in disposition, in addition to the part of its being which is asserted in specific moral choices, it is an enduring moral self. As such it is responsible for its actions despite the non-predictable spontaneity of its freedom.[102]

This complex analysis of *Willkür* into an aspect of dispositional volition and an aspect of individual volition also enabled Kant to resolve another problem which confronted his theory. Having admitted that both moral and sensuous incentives are good and that moral evil consists merely in the decision to subordinate the former incentive to the latter, while moral goodness consists in the subordination of the latter to the former, he was left with a rigoristic (he used the term with pride) conception of the will. Although there is always a mixture of incentives in the *Willkür*, the *Willkür* must reflect one to which all others are subordinated: only one of these basic incentives can be made the determining foundation of action. Kant therefore concluded that there can be no middle ground of moral mediocrity: either the will is good or it is evil. But Kant had to admit that in everyday life we find men of gray morality (and in all shades from light to dark) without ever finding the whites and blacks demanded by his rigoristic theory.[103] Kant resolved this problem by arguing that these judgments are made from two different moral standpoints. Our

[102] The criticism that Kant's theory of freedom precludes the responsibility of the moral agent has usually been directed against an oversimplified conception of Kant's theory that omits all reference to the dispositional aspect of the free will. (See C. D. Broad, "Determinism, Indeterminism, and Libertarianism" in *Ethics and the History of Philosophy*.)

[103] *Ibid.*, pp. 17–20, 31; cf. Abbott, pp. 294, 300.

everyday judgments are made on the basis of empirical observation and concern the phenomenal virtue of the will and the legality of its actions. We can only conjecture about the motives behind the actions of others, and we can never be sure of the motives behind our own, although we can be aware of some of them introspectively. On the level of mere observation, then, we judge the will on the basis of its specific actions, and we conclude that most if not all wills are both good and evil. Had we the omniscience of a divine judge, however, to observe the dispositional act, the basic intention which is the ultimate motive behind all specific acts, this judgment would be supplemented. The disposition would be found to be either good or evil and its moral quality only more or less distorted by the specific acts which follow from it when the *Willkür* applies its dispositional intention in concrete moral situations. From the standpoint of such an omniscient judge, we would judge the noumenal nature of the will and the morality of its actions; we would observe that the dispositional act—which is the adoption of the maxim of the entire exercise of freedom—was one in which the intention to subordinate the law to the senses, or the reverse, was present. From this viewpoint, the will would thus be judged either good or evil.[104]

In addition to providing the continuity essential to moral self-identity and the basis for two distinct judgments of the quality of the will, Kant's analysis of *Willkür* into its enduring dispositional act and its immediate specific acts provides the foundation for the interpretation of the complexity and ambivalence of volition. That his analysis of the will enables him to interpret the full range of human volition is best demonstrated by his examination of the stages in the decline of moral goodness in volition.[105] This discussion divides itself naturally into two main parts: the discussion of the declining quality of the will while the *Willkür* remains good in its dispositional aspect, followed by the discussion of the will's further decline after *Willkür* has become evil in disposition. The discussion thus derives its basic structure from Kant's rigoristic account of the moral quality of disposition as either good or evil, while within this structure the relative pro-

---

[104] *Ibid.*, pp. 20, 34, 42, 46, 65–71, *passim;* cf. Abbott, p. 282.

[105] See *ibid.*, pp. 24, 31–33. In order to give systematic completeness to Kant's analysis of the decline of the moral quality of the will, we shall begin our discussion with the examination of the fully autonomous will. Kant did not consider this stage in connection with the subsequent stages because his discussion occurs in the context of an inquiry into the propensity to evil; hence he began with the first stage of evil, the stage just inferior to complete autonomy.

portion of good to evil in specific acts and in the relation of specific acts to the disposition itself is amenable to a sliding scale.

The optimum stage of volition is one in which there is the closest approximation in the concrete acts of *Willkür* to the purity and goodness of its dispositional act. This is the stage of volition in which *Willkür* acts both in accordance with and for the sake of the moral law. In its dispositional act, *Willkür* here wills to subordinate all inclinations and sensuous desires to the demands of the moral law; that is, *Willkür* wills to meet the conditions for the fulfillment of itself as a free being. Furthermore, this dispositional intention, which establishes the morality of *Willkür*, provides the motivational force for its specific concrete actions. They, in turn, express transparently the intention of the disposition through their legality, through their conformity to the demands of the moral law. In this stage, reason is fully practical, as *Wille* instills moral feeling in *Willkür*.

Even at this stage of the most complete realization of autonomy, however, there may be some difference between the intention of the disposition and its expression in concrete volition. This difference, which may involve a deviation from the demands of the law, does not necessarily imply any moral inferiority on the part of the will. Kant recognized two legitimate causes for deviation from the demands of the law. First, in any specific volition *Willkür* must adapt the essentially timeless intention of its disposition to the conditions of temporal (and sometimes spatial) realization. Distortion inevitably results, and its inevitability precludes its being imputed to *Willkür*.[106] Second, in any act of volition, judgment is required in order to determine the specific demands of the universal law. Such judgment may err through inexperience, and unless *Willkür* ought to have gained the requisite experience prior to the action in question, the errors in judgment due to inexperience cannot be imputed to *Willkür*.[107] No deviation of *motives* from the strict demand of the law is permitted, however, for motives are fully within the power of *Willkür*. If the will is fully autonomous the basic dispositional motive will be faithfully revealed in each specific act.

The first stage in the decline of autonomous volition is occasioned by that capacity for evil which Kant called the "weakness" or "frailty" of human nature. At this level, the dispositional act

[106] *Ibid.*, p. 61.
[107] *Ibid.*, p. 176, and Paton, p. 57.

is steadfastly good, although *Willkür* does not succeed in expressing its dispositional motive without distortion and ambivalence. Here the plaint of St. Paul, "What I would do, that I do not" becomes relevant. Although the will has adopted the good as a dispositional maxim, this maxim is not followed in the specific acts of *Willkür*. Out of weakness *Willkür* abandons the difficult course of willing the law of its rational nature and freely gives its strongest momentary desires mastery over its actions.

At first glance this may seem to be a clear case of abject heteronomy. The specific act following inclinations is neither in accordance with the moral law nor done for the sake of it. Here, however, as Kant subtly and correctly observes, more than one act is involved.[108] *What Willkür would do* in terms of its dispositional intention—which it positively expresses in the lawful act of self-condemnation—*it does not do* in the specific act in which the domination of particular pathological incentives is willed. The same *Willkür* that wills immorally to betray the demands of the law in a specific act wills morally, in the very same act,[109] to condemn itself for so willing. St. Paul, and any individual on this level, is so virtuous that he cannot even enjoy his vice. The voice of *Wille*, still expressing the dispositional intention, is willed so strongly by *Willkür* that *Wille* cautions the *Willkür* prior to the act, palls its enjoyment in the midst of the act, and condemns it subsequent to the act. All these expressions of *Wille* are also specific acts of the *Willkür*, and in them the dispositional act is faithfully and autonomously expressed. The goodness of the weak will is revealed by the continuing prominence and even dominance (when one thinks of the great moral suffering in comparison with the slight satisfaction of the illegal desires) of *Wille*. When, for example, Major Barbara quickens the conscience of Bill Walker, she rightly concludes that his redemption has begun. As Kant put it: "Only the virtuous person, or one on his way to becoming so, is capable of this pure moral dissatisfaction (which [stems] from the action's very opposition to the law)."[110] Because the strength of the disposition is judged in temptation, *Willkür* on this level acquires a very clear picture of the strength and weak-

[108] *Ibid.*, p. 25.

[109] One can regard the decision of *Willkür* at any moment of action either as a complex single act or as a group of simultaneous but individual acts. I think the former description is both simpler and closer to the facts. I do not think our simultaneous acts of volition are normally sufficiently examined and analyzed to be regarded as an aggregate of individually considered decisions.

[110] "Theory and Practice," p. 366.

ness of its disposition and its own power to express it faithfully.[111] There is no confusion of motives in this *Willkür*. The clarity of its moral awareness is another mark of its essential autonomy.

The next lower stage in moral volition, that of the impurity of the will, is occasioned by the capacity for evil stemming from the failure of *Willkür* to distinguish between moral and non-moral motives in its action. At this level the *Willkür* may adopt a good maxim and intend to observe the demands of the law; it may act "with good intent and under the maxims of the good."[111] But in neglecting to make its dispositional maxim, to act for the sake of the law, the *"all-sufficient"* motive of action, *Willkür* fails to live up to the full demands of the law. At this level *Willkür* usually acts according to the demands of the moral law but the motive power of its volition does not stem from its respect for the law of its own freedom. Its lawful actions are motivated, rather, by the happy coincidence, never rare in civilized society, of moral and non-moral incentives. Viewed externally, the impure will may seem morally superior to the weak will; the impure will acts legally and *what it would do, it does*. The hell-fearing cate-chumen and the self-satisfied tradesman usually appear more righteous than the sinners in whose ranks are found the saints. The legality of its specific actions and the goodness of its dispositional intent belie the moral weakness of the impure will. Whereas the weak-willed individual is strengthened by the knowledge of his weakness and purified by the *Wille* that condemns his vice, the impure individual is dying the quiet death (euthanasia) of morality through his confusion of moral and non-moral incentives. The impure *Willkür* does not even know that it follows the law without ever obeying it. The correcting voice of *Wille* is virtually silent, though uncorrupted, for the law is not violated. The disposition, whose strength grows and is measured in moral struggle against conflicting motives, wastes away. It is not rejected through evil intent; it atrophies from disuse.

Autonomy and moral goodness decline to a vanishing point in impure volition. Subsequent decline in moral quality involves the radical shift of the disposition itself from good to evil. No longer indiscriminate about motive, *Willkür* now deliberately subordinates its moral incentive to its non-moral ones. Its specific actions

---

[111] *Religion*, p. 23; cf. p. 24. See pp. 32–33 for a further discussion of this stage of volition. Page 32 of this later material must be used with caution, however, because Kant confuses there the impurity of the will with its wickedness. The various strands of the discussion must be carefully separated.

may be either legal or illegal, depending upon what *Willkür* must do in order to express its evil dispositional intent. Wickedness can be pursued single-mindedly or haphazardly. The former type may require the scrupulous observance of proprieties and the external signs of moral goodness. As Thrasymachus and Callicles knew, the successful scoundrel must have a reputation for moral goodness; the exploiter of the public must be renowned for his philanthropy.[112] Despite the apparent variety in the specific acts of the wicked *Willkür*, however, all of them issue from the evil disposition. The change in disposition from good to evil may not be fully recognized (and perhaps can never be fully recognized) by the wicked individual himself. The clarity of such recognition may vary from time to time within the individual and between different individuals. A person who, in reflecting on an immoral act in his past, says "I am glad I had that experience before I recognized how wrong it was" is conscious of his ambivalent wickedness. He tacitly admits that he preferred moral ignorance when knowledge would have forced him openly to reject the law or to forego the object of desire. He thus prefers the evil order in the subordination of incentives, although his practical reason is still too strong for him openly to reveal his evil disposition. For such an individual, says Kant, "who despite a corrupted heart [disposition] yet possesses a good *Wille*, there remains hope of a return to the good."[113]

The presence and expression of the uncorrupted *Wille* in the acts of the wicked *Willkür* is clearly evident in the life of St. Augustine. Unlike St. Paul, who merely suffered the weakness of an otherwise good will, St. Augustine plunged to the depths of wickedness crying, "Lord, save me! But not now!" The ambivalence of his wicked *Willkür* is apparent: the *Wille*, incorruptible so long as the *Willkür* retains its self-awareness as a free being, is expressed in the *Willkür's* specific plea "Lord, save me!"; simultaneously, the evil dispositional act is expressed in the *Willkür's* more forceful objection "But not now!" Thus *Wille* preserves the moral feeling in specific acts after it has been banished from the disposition. The dispositional act is wicked, and specific acts express faithfully its evil intent; co-present with them, nonetheless, are specific morally good acts which express a subdued but audible

---

[112] The ambivalent expression of evil thus renders uncertain the moral judgment of men and, as Kant said, "constitutes the foul taint in our race." *Ibid.*, p. 34.

[113] *Ibid.*, p. 39. Kant's use here of *"Wille"* rather than *"Willkür"* is noteworthy.

conscience. Although the wicked man can enjoy his vices because his disposition favors them, he cannot forget completely that the law that he is rejecting is the condition of his own personal self-realization. In the midst of increasing animality, *Wille* keeps alive in the *Willkür* the last vestige of personal realization.

There is no stage in the decline of the moral volition beyond that of wickedness. Kant denied that the deliberate rejection of the law itself is possible for men. Not even a wicked man wills evil for the sake of evil. His evil consists in his willing to ignore the moral law and to oppose its demands when it interferes with his non-moral incentives. His evil consists in his abandonment of the conditions of free personal fulfillment in favor of the adoption of the conditions of his fulfillment as a natural creature of desire.[114] This represents the ultimate point in the abnegation of personality. In wickedness, the only *personal* assertion consists in *Willkür's* free resignation of its power of self-determination in the adoption of natural, non-moral incentives, and in its awareness through *Wille* of what it is doing. Once *Wille* is completely silent, the free *Willkür* loses its freedom altogether and becomes mere animal *"Willkür";* the weakness of personality is finally replaced by mere animal strength.[115]

In this review of the decline of volition, we have observed the concomitant diminution of virtue and personal power. In this parallel movement we have an intuitively clear answer to the question, How is the categorical imperative possible?[116] The necessity

[114] *Ibid.*, pp. 30–32. Kant, unlike Plato, recognized that men can will evil intentionally. But Kant agrees with Plato by denying that men will evil for its own sake. Both assertions can be made with consistency by Kant because he recognizes the heterogeneity of the good and hence can designate the natural good as the object of volition of the wicked will which is fully conscious that willing that object is morally wrong.

[115] Abbott, pp. 282–283.

[116] When Kant asked, 'How is the categorical imperative possible' (Paton, pp. 84, 121 ff.), he might have been asking any or all of three different questions: He could have been asking (1) How can reason be practical by issuing such an imperative? or (2) Why is the moral law a categorical imperative for the human will? or (3) Why is the moral law bound to the will with necessity? The first question (though Kant asked it) is mistakenly asked because the starting point of his ethics (see Section I above) is found in the experience of obligation in which reason is practical, since any further explanation of how it is practical involves an explanation of freedom. The second question is properly asked but readily answered; the moral law is an imperative for man merely because the human will is both rational and sensible and is tempted to subordinate the moral law to non-moral incentives. The third question is the important and difficult one whose answer requires that one explain why the judgment which expresses the necessary obligation of the will to an act is synthetic *a priori* (Ibid., pp. 87 ff., 94). The answer is found in the analysis of the concept of freedom which is, in this instance, the third thing "X" in terms of which the proposition expressing the synthetic relation of the concept of the will to the concept of the moral law is found to be transcendentally analytic—hence, a successfully deduced synthetic *a priori* judgment.

of the conformity to law as a condition for the expression of freedom is graphically expressed. The will, always transcendentally free to reject the moral law, can never escape its jurisdiction and punishment. The will escapes the law only in the sense that a prisoner who is shot to death as he goes over the wall of a prison can be said to have escaped. The categorical imperative is inescapable because its violation, according to Kant, destroys the personality of the violator. Since freedom is a power whose fulfillment depends upon the structure of rationality, its irrational misuse results in impotence. Thus the categorical imperative, grounded in freedom, is necessary. The question, How is the categorical imperative possible? is thus answered.

To assert, then, as is often done in literature and in the popular imagination, that there can be devilish beings who defiantly and powerfully reject the moral law itself, presupposes a conception of freedom which, according to Kant, is hopelessly transcendent and without foundation in human experience. In human experience, he insists, our knowledge of freedom is revealed exclusively by the moral law and its realization depends upon the incorporation of that law in volition. Hence, speculation about devilish beings is either transcendent superstition, or, since the most evil mode of free expression is wickedness, devils must be responsibly portrayed in the weakness of wickedness. The Satan of "Paradise Lost" is an example of the transcendent sort. He is asserted to be powerfully free without any indication as to the source of a freedom that is unrelated to the conditions of lawfulness. Such an image beckons to men with its romantic illusions about the grandeur and heroism of wickedness. Milton's Satan, towering in his solitary, defiant rage, consumed by a hatred of everything God-like save God-like power, differs in kind from the obsequious, knavish seducer of men and young girls whom Goethe calls Mephistopheles. Faithful (whether or not intentionally) to Kant's analysis of extreme wickedness as a weakness in personality, Goethe, in Part I of *Faust*, portrays the devil as one who serves the moral purposes of God by trying the dispositions of men, quickening them to their moral destiny or allowing them to damn themselves. Sometimes, out of human compassion, Mephistopheles even feels sorry for men and their sorry lot. And, shameless, he appreciates the fact that God, whom he affectionately calls *"Der Alte,"* condescends to speak with him. Goethe's Mephistopheles, though less imaginatively drawn than Satan and far less attractive, has the weakness of personality required by Kant's analysis.

This extended, though still sketchy, review of the stages in volition can best be summarized and brought into focus by means of the following diagram. Reading from left to right, we observe the struggle of the human will toward the realization of its full power as a responsible person. Reading from right to left we observe the gradual decline and final loss by the will of its personality.[117]

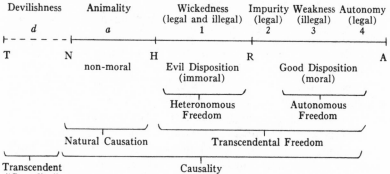

The diagram is largely self-explanatory. Line HRA represents the *constant* presence of transcendental freedom with its basic modes of potential expression—autonomy and heteronomy. It is constant because it is the *sine qua non* of responsibility and personality.

Specific positions on this line represent the degree to which the positive expression of transcendental freedom (autonomy) has been attained. The points on this line are read in an ascending scale from left to right, or a descending scale from right to left.

Point H represents the minimal limit in the realization of freedom beyond which freedom ceases and natural causality begins. Point A represents the maximal limit. Point R represents the point of revolution in the disposition where its quality changes from being morally evil to being morally good.

Line HR represents the heteronomous expression of freedom by the *Willkür* with an evil disposition. This line represents the minimal realization of autonomy even though *Willkür* is heteronomous: autonomy is minimally present here in the form of *Wille* which confronts *Willkür* with the actual possibility of autonomous volition. The specific acts of the heteronomous *Willkür* are read at point 1 and are evil. The designation in parentheses, which indicates the predominant relation of the specific acts to the demands of the law, shows that acts done in wickedness may be either legal or illegal; they vary widely depending upon the non-moral interests of the evil disposition.

Line RA represents the autonomous expression of the *Willkür* with a good disposition, from its minimal realization of autonomy at point R to its maximal realization at point A. The presence of the good disposition sustains the judgment of any expression of *Willkür* on this line as moral rather than immoral and as autonomous. Point 2 represents a partial realization of personality in specific acts which are predominantly legal: there is no testing here of the disposition because of the impurity of the motives and the negligible activity of *Wille* due to the predominant legality of actions. Point 3 represents the confirmation in moral conflict of the autonomous nature of the disposition. *Wille* becomes strong and purifies

[117] I wish to thank Dr. Klaus Hartmann of the University of Bonn for suggestions on the design of this diagram.

the motives of *Willkür* so that moral self-awareness and critical self-judgment together with consequent fulfillment of personality follow. The typical specific act of the weak will is illegal, though a mixture of legal and illegal acts can occur. Point 4 represents *Willkür's* achievement of mastery over its momentary inclinations so that the good dispositional intent is transparently reflected in specific actions. Specific actions are predominantly legal.

Point *a* on line NH represents action of *Willkür* after *Wille* has ceased to function and *Willkür* has become a mere animal *Willkür* causally determined by its incentives.

Point *d* on line TN represents the expression of a transcendent, merely conceptual, idea of a devilish freedom with power apart from any conception of law.

The rigorism of Kant's analysis is represented in the division of the exercise of freedom into autonomous (good) and heteronomous (evil) sections, line HR and line RA. And the common sense judgment of the mixture of good and evil in men and the opinion that men are better or worse than one another to different degrees is represented in the numbered positions showing the greater or lesser realization of autonomy.

IV. *Estimate of the Contribution of the* Religion *to Ethics*

The contribution of the *Religion* to Kant's own theory of ethics should now be apparent. My assertion that the *Religion* compares in importance for Kant's ethics with the *Groundwork* and the second *Critique*—which, coming at the beginning of this study, may have seemed exaggerated—is, I believe, accurate. The rationale of Kant's ethics turns upon the interrelation of freedom, rationality and sensibility. Yet prior to the *Religion* Kant offered virtually no analysis of the human will which provides the foundation for the interrelation of these factors. He merely defined the will as practical reason and as the faculty of desire, without showing how these diverse conceptions can be united in a single faculty of volition. Without the establishment of the unity of these conceptions, however, no account can be given of the experience of obligation on which Kant's ethics is grounded. In the second *Critique* Kant argued that the will is either heteronomous or autonomous. In the common moral experience of guilt, however, the will is obviously both—heteronomous in the acquisition of guilt and autonomous in the recognition and acceptance of it. The conception of the will prior to its development in the *Religion* was insufficiently complex to account for this experience. In all the *Critiques* Kant argued that man is obligated to seek the realization of both happiness and virtue; nevertheless, the *Religion* presents his earliest sustained account of a faculty of volition capable of willing these heterogeneous elements.

The capital importance of the *Religion* to Kant's ethics consists in the fact that the *Religion* offers us his only sustained analysis of the human will—an analysis which resolves several of these problems and removes many of the superficialities involved in his earlier statements. *Willkür* is analyzed in the *Religion* as a unitary faculty in which the forces of sensibility and rationality have a common meeting place. It thus provides the basis for an understanding of the experience of obligation as the constraint of the law upon a will tempted to reject it. Through the development of the important dispositional aspect of *Willkür*, moreover, Kant provides a theoretical account of the duplicity and ambivalence of human volition, a foundation for enduring moral character, and a basis for the rigoristic judgment of the will in terms of its entire exercise of freedom. Kant also now provides a dramatic confirmation of his conception of the categorical imperative by showing, in his analysis of the stages of evil volition, the concomitant decline of virtue and power. All this should amply assure the *Religion* a place of major importance in Kant's ethics.

The *Religion* is no less important for its contribution to ethics in general. One aspect of this latter contribution consists, paradoxically, in the fact that the *Religion,* while purportedly strengthening Kant's conception of freedom, exposes its ultimate flaw in two quite independent ways.[118] The first turns on Kant's rejection of devilish volition as an illusion, the second, on his handling of the problem of forgiveness.

Kant's theoretical advance over Plato in the understanding of freedom was discussed in Section II. We noted Kant's acceptance of the fact that men knowingly do evil, his argument that freedom is essentially rational, his crucially important expansion of the concept of the rational to include irrational as well as rationally sound modes, and his conclusion that freedom, as rational, has the irrational mode of heteronomy no less than the sound rational mode of autonomy. We observed that, in terms of his conception of freedom, the will is free to reject the rational moral law but must pay the price in self-abnegation, in the loss of freedom. And we saw, in Section III, that Kant offered experiential support for his concept of freedom by showing, in the *Religion*, the concomitant decline of virtue and personality. This demonstration reached its critical point in the discussion of wickedness and devilishness. Wickedness was shown to be a weakness, because freedom is a power and the rejection of its rational nature is

---

[118] Due to limitations of space, this estimate, which is neither exhaustive nor balanced, is directed to only one aspect (and that a weakness) of Kant's position.

therefore an impotence. Devilishness was shown to be an illusion, because no one can deliberately reject the law since the power (the freedom) to reject anything is derived from the law. Kant thus seemed to offer in the *Religion* a final clarification and experiential support for his conception of freedom.

But in dismissing the devilish rejection of the law as an illusion, Kant called attention to the limitations of his conception of freedom rather than to the limits of human freedom itself. In denying the power of men to reject the law deliberately, Kant repeated the methodological mistake that Plato made when he denied that men can knowingly do evil. Kant, like Plato before him, explicitly considered the data which seemed contrary to his theory and, like Plato, used his theory to dismiss the contravening evidence as illusory.[119] He gave his theory momentary support, but he exposed its ultimate weakness.

Kant's insistence to the contrary, man's free power to reject the law in defiance is an ineradicable fact of human experience. St. Paul consolidated the opposition to Plato's moral optimism in asserting the power of men knowingly to do evil; Kierkegaard consolidated the opposition to Kant's moral optimism in asserting the power of men to fulfill their personalities in the despair of defiance.[120] Nietzsche joined Kierkegaard in affirming that man's freedom can be diabolically, no less than heteronomously, expressed. Novelists and historians have supplemented their arguments with many observations and facts. Melville created Ahab who, having thrown prudence as well as morality to the winds, stalks the deck of the *Pequod* in deliberate search of destruction— his own, the ship's, and Moby Dick's. Far from languishing in the impotency of personality demanded by Kant's conception of freedom, Ahab infuses the excess of his personal strength into the spirits of his men, into the rigging of his ship, and even into the artificial limb on which he stamps out his defiance of the law. History in turn records the deeds of Hitler and Napoleon. No weak personality loses an entire army in Egypt only to lose yet another in Russia; no weak personality leads a civilized nation to moral disaster and a continent to ruin.

[119] The use of one's theory to establish the factual value of data is nonetheless unavoidable. The frequent occurrence of this practice in science is considered by Michael Polanyi in *Personal Knowledge*. See also Chapter One of *Reality*, by Paul Weiss, for a general statement of the interdependence of fact and theory.

[120] See *Sickness unto Death*.

Kant was right, perhaps, to insist with Plato that the realization of freedom depends on rationality. He was certainly right in going beyond Plato to distinguish the volitional and theoretical uses of reason and to argue that the former provides the foundation and direction of the latter (the primacy of practical reason). But Kant erred in failing to note that the power of volitional rationality can be fully asserted either in irrationality or in sound rationality. Because the power of theoretical reason depends upon its observance of the laws of thought and is reduced to incoherence when these laws are violated, Kant thoughtlessly assumed that volitional rationality [121] loses its power in the violation of the moral law. But although theoretical irrationality is an impotence, since it is separated from its source of power in the law, volitional irrationality can derive its power elsewhere. One source of its free power is doubtlessly the theoretical employment of reason itself. The industrial and financial tyrants of the 19th Century may have been ruthless, but they were never stupid and rarely imprudent in the rational determination of their plans. Ahab abandoned the prudential use of reason, but he took prodigious care in charting the habits of Moby Dick and in judging the temper of his crew. Volitional irrationality, whether the subordination of the law to non-moral interests, or the willful rejection of the law itself—finds power of realization in a parasitic use of theoretical reason. I should argue, furthermore, that there are other non-rational sources for the power of freedom and personality. But even if we agree with Kant that reason supplies the power of freedom, we must still conclude that his conception of freedom is inadequate. On Kant's own premises we must admit that personal fulfillment is possible for the irrational will as long as it uses the theoretical and prudential capacities of rationality to its perverse ends.

The implications of this conclusion for Kant's answer to the question, How is the categorical imperative possible? are plain: the concept of freedom does not relate the will to an action required by the moral law with necessary obligation. The will is free to fulfill itself without the law, for it has a source of free power apart from its observance of the law.[122]

---

[121] I am using rationality in a generic sense which includes both the rationally sound and the irrational.

[122] Some interpreters hold that Kant never conceived of the force of the categorical imperative in anything other than logical terms. This interpretation is over-intellectual. Of course it is illogical to reject the moral law when the law is a condition of one's being. But Kant did not intend to say that a wicked man is guilty

Suppose we grant for the sake of argument, however, that Kant's analysis of wickedness and devilishness is sound. We still encounter a difficulty with his view of freedom: it shatters on the problem of forgiveness. Kant holds in the *Religion*, as elsewhere, that man's freedom involves absolute spontaneity. The moral individual makes himself into whatever he is from a moral standpoint. He acquires his own virtues and vices through his own free actions. Others may force him to act contrary to the moral law, but no one can make him violate it. Violation of the moral law can result only from a free decision and never from force. An individual himself must fall into sin from a state of innocence. If his acts can be imputed to him, they must follow from the exercise of his own freedom.

It follows from this conception of freedom that no man can be good for another. Kant rejected the doctrine of vicarious atonement because it runs counter to the nature of freedom. No matter how good another person is, his excess of goodness (were such an excess possible) would in no way remove another person's lack of goodness nor redeem his evil. Any notion of forgiveness or absolution, moreover, would seem impossible in terms of this conception of freedom. A good man has the right to be proud of his virtue. But even God cannot help the guilty individual without violating the moral law. If a man is guilty, it is his own fault, and he must bear the full and non-transferable burden. Kant sought a means of sustaining man's hope of forgiveness and absolution from guilt

merely of an intellectual *faux pas*. Such a man has lost the worthiness to be happy, though he may continue to be happy; he has lost all that makes life worthwhile, though he may continue to live; he has bankrupted himself as a person and is worthless as a human being, though because of his power other persons may defer to him. In all these ways, Kant speaks of the here-and-now enforcement of the demand of the moral law. If one rejects the moral law, he forfeits personal fulfillment, fulfillment as a free being, in favor of fulfillment as an animal. In his discussion of the impotence of immorality in the *Metaphysic of Morals* Kant speaks of immorality as the destroying disease of the will much in the way that Plato speaks of injustice as the disease of the soul. (Abbott, pp. 282–283.) The force of Kant's answer to the question, How is the categorical imperative possible? consisted in his showing that freedom is of such a nature that to disobey the moral law involves the loss of one's freedom. And since freedom is the basis of individuality, the individual who loses his freedom loses his own self. Kant's demonstration of the categorical imperative fails, I think, but not because it never aimed to succeed. Even its success, on the logical interpretation, would be a gross failure, for in the heights of personal fulfillment a wicked person could ask, "Why be logical?" And such a person could not be told that anything essential to his personal fulfillment was lacking. Kant had more to say than this. He was convinced that the universe was sufficiently rational to assure the payment of a penalty for irrational behavior even without appeal to a God to restore the balance of happiness and virtue.

without compromising the absolute purity of the moral law.[123] By means of an imaginative interpretation of the mystery of atonement, Kant offered a plausible solution to the problem of forgiveness as it relates to guilt deriving from an evil disposition. He considered the change of disposition from ill to good to be so radical that it could accurately be called a new birth. And he thought that the difference between an evil and a good disposition is so great that the new *Willkür*, structured by a good disposition, is justified in denying identity with its preceding evil disposition. Since the disposition is itself the only basis for moral self-identity, this conclusion has an initial credibility.

Kant could see clearly the incompatibility of forgiveness and absolute freedom. And this incompatibility troubled him because he realized that an inescapable guilt could lead the moral individual to despair and far greater guilt. But how is man to gain absolution from the guilt that follows from the impurity and weakness of his will? His disposition is already good when, through weakness or impurity, he violates the demands of the law. Kant was sorely troubled on this point. The problem is insoluble in terms of absolute freedom. Yet he argues that man may, through effort, acquire *grace;* that is, he may become worthy of receiving aid or absolution should the one who judges him be disposed to offer it.[124] But why should God or any righteous judge decide to qualify the requirements of the moral law or fail to hold the absolutely free being responsible for his exercise of freedom? Kant himself knew, I think, that he was in trouble. On the same page in which he speaks of the possibility and necessity of grace in order to give hope to guilty moral beings so that they will not slacken their efforts, he also says, "The accuser within us would be more likely to propose a judgment of condemnation." [125]

When Kant confronted the Antinomies, he presented thesis and antithesis and then offered a resolution. On this issue he merely vacillates. There is neither antinomy nor resolution. His absolute conception of freedom precludes the need for grace, since every guilty man freely wills to become guilty; the purity of the moral law precludes the granting of grace, for grace violates the uncompromising nature of the law. But despite these theoretical implications of Kant's conceptions of absolute freedom and the law, which

[123] *Religion*, p. 70.
[124] *Ibid.*, pp. 62, 64, 66, 70.
[125] *Idem.*, cf. pp. 60–69, 70–77, 133–137, 106–108, 159, 168.

are clear, consistent, and precise on the issue, Kant insisted on the possibility of grace. He insisted that the individual of good disposition who strives hard to live up to the moral law has the right to hope that his shortcomings will be excused or that the demands of the law will be reduced to his measure. Kant tries to reassure himself by saying that this of course implies that the individual has done all that he can. But if the individual has done all that he can, he does not need grace. And if he has not, even Kant agrees he should not get it.

If Kant had recognized this problem as a genuine antinomy he would have been on sounder ground. In order to make sense of the idea of personal responsibility, Kant argued that freedom is absolute. Yet by holding that man's responsibility is absolute, he condemned man to an insufferable burden of guilt. The guilt may not be predetermined or logically necessary. Nevertheless, all men seem to find themselves guilty. The realization of oneself depends upon the recognition of absolute freedom; yet the recognition of absolute freedom precludes the realization of oneself by destroying the individual through an overburdening guilt. Here is a moral antinomy worthy of Kant.

It is a tribute to Kant's reasonableness and humanity that he contradicted his theory by admitting the possibility of grace. But the contradiction involved is a serious one whose resolution demands either the drastic redefinition of freedom or obligation or the introduction of the miracle of forgiveness.

If Kant had consistently held to his theory of unqualified freedom, he would have followed the line of argument taken by Ivan Karamazov.[126] In discussing the evil in this world, Ivan insisted that he would accept no Euclidian (i.e. scientific) nonsense about there being no freedom. And he saw quite clearly that if there is freedom (the absolute freedom of which Kant speaks), there can be no forgiveness. Consider the man who orders ravenous hunting dogs to tear a naked little boy to shreds because he accidentally hit a dog in the foot. Shall this man be forgiven, Ivan asked? Suppose the mother forgives? Suppose the boy forgives? How dare they forgive! Forgiveness, as Ivan observed following Kantian principles, is a moral outrage; it is itself a violation of the moral law.[127]

---

[126] See the "Pro and Contra" from *The Brothers Karamazov*, by F. Dostoevsky.
[127] Kierkegaard's discussion of the offense of Christianity is illuminating on this point. Cf. *op. cit.*, Appendix II, 2.

What then is the penalty of guilt? Ivan proposes three alternatives: sensuality, suicide, or insanity. Alyosha, his brother, proposed a fourth: the acceptance of a divine and miraculous forgiveness. Ivan rejected this fourth alternative. His rejection did not follow from the fact that a miracle is involved (although this in itself would have posed a serious obstacle for Kant). He refused to accept forgiveness on moral principle. In so doing he remained faithful to the implications of Kant's view of the purity of the law and the absolute nature of freedom.

We cannot ignore the problem of forgiveness nor can we accept Kant's futile resolution of it. It calls for a serious reconsideration of Kant's assumptions that freedom is absolute and that freedom is essentially rational—even if rationality be expanded to admit of the full potentiality of irrationality as one mode of expression. When freedom is considered in terms of rationality, it is inevitably narrowed to the limits of conscious intention and made far too intellectual.[128]

This discussion of the problem of forgiveness leads us once again to the conclusion of the preceding discussion of wickedness and devilishness: two independent lines of inquiry suggest the inadequacy of Kant's conception of freedom.

Our estimate of the contribution of the *Religion* to ethics has been little more than a sketch. Yet in order to discuss this question we have had to touch upon issues of the greatest importance in the understanding of man. We have been forced to these issues by the *Religion* itself. In the *Religion* Kant enriches our conception of freedom and volition, of good and evil, and of the nature of responsibility to a surprising degree. Despite the fact that his conclusions are not final, he points to areas for fruitful continuing research. We are bound to profit from further exploration of the relation of freedom and rationality, from a further examination of the nature and power of the irrational, and from continuing inquiry into the possibility of non-rational sources of free personal expression. We do not question but rather confirm Kant's greatness by pursuing these lines of inquiry from the point at which his efforts terminated.

---

[128] At this point I concur in part with Greene's criticism of Kant's view of freedom. See p. lv above.

TRANSLATORS' PREFACE

An inaccurate English translation of some parts of this treatise was made by John Richardson, a Scot, and printed in 1798 under the title, *Religion within the Sphere of Naked Reason.*[1] The only attempt at a complete translation was made by William Semple, a Scottish barrister, who published his work at Edinburgh in 1838, with the title, *Religion within the Boundary of Pure Reason.* It seems to have attracted little attention and to have had a limited circulation. Semple's version is always spirited and occasionally eloquent, but is in many passages free to the point of license. The translator considered himself at liberty to omit phrases or even whole sentences and paragraphs (these last usually in foot-notes); while at times he made explanatory additions of his own, without notice to the reader. The present translators should acknowledge, however, some debt to Semple, since in the main he appears to have got the sense of the original, and his diction, which reflects his nationality and his legal vocation, is a continual source of interest. As a specimen of his style, we would quote the following, which represents a passage here translated on p. 9: "Thus no one would ever think of saying, that Teachers of International Law, when citing classical passages or formulae out of the Code or Digest, for the behoof of a philosophical theory of their subject, are guilty of invading or violating the majesty of the CORPUS JURIS, although those passages be accommodated or understood in a sense slightly varying from that in which Justinian or Ulpian may have employed them; nor could they, with any colour of reason, be accused of tampering with, or trespassing on, the Civil Law, provided they did not insist that the Bench and Bar should receive their gloss as the strict and proper meaning of the words."

A passage translated by an anonymous writer from Book Three, Part One, Section VI, appears in the *British Quarterly* for 1845 (pp. 310–312). T. K. Abbott included an English rendering of Book One in his volume, *Kant's Theory of Ethics* (1889). Abbott made a competent and readable version, though occasionally by his concision he over-simplifies the text, and he sometimes fails to resolve ambiguities or uncertainties of reference which appear

---

[1] In the second volume of Richardson's collected translations of Kant, entitled *Essays and Treatises.*

in the original. In our work upon Book One we could not avoid, without falling into mere singularity, reproducing words and phrases from Abbott's translation.

In addition to these English renderings, we have made some slight use of A. Tremesaygues' *La religion dans les limites de la raison* (Paris, 1913), a skilful and fairly accurate French version, with an excellent introduction by the translator.[1]

Throughout our attempt "to make Kant speak English" we have emphasized fidelity to the original, sometimes at the expense of smoothness and immediate clarity. The German of Kant's essay is not distinguished, save in occasional passages, for straightforwardness, grace, or concision; it tends rather to be pleonastic and awkwardly involuted. Marks of haste appear, so that more than once the reader gets the impression that Kant worked with a sense that his time was short, but also with a sense of the great importance of his ideas. He crowds his sentences, often repeating a few fundamental ideas as if afraid that in their first statement they had not been made emphatic enough. Studiously to have disguised these faults would have been a form of freedom which might have led to actual misrepresentation of our author's meaning.

There is also some awkwardness in our version due to the inherent difficulty of finding English equivalents for certain words and expressions much affected by Kant. *Triebfeder*, for example, we have sometimes translated by "motivating force," or "motive," but more often by "incentive," since no single English term seemed adequate in every passage. The very title of the book raised a difficulty: *der blossen Vernunft* cannot well be rendered in English as "of *mere* reason" or as "of *bare* reason." We rejected Richardson's "naked reason" and Semple's suggestion of "unassisted reason" (frequently appearing in his text) in favor of "reason alone"; though elsewhere in our version "mere," "bare," and "unassisted" do appear as translations of *bloss*. The difficulty here touched upon, however, we share with all translators of Kant and, to be sure, with all other translators; and it is hardly necessary to repeat the *apologia* that no rendering from a foreign tongue can be at once wholly exact and yet satisfactory as a composition in English.

[1] The French translation by J. Trullard (Paris, 1841) is poor in comparison with that of Tremesaygues. There is also a French rendering by Lortet (Paris and Lyons, 1842) of the popularized summary of the *Religion*, mentioned in an earlier foot-note (above, p. xxxv).

For our text we have followed the Berlin Edition (1907), and we have translated some of the excellent interpretative notes written for that edition by Georg Wobbermin. All notes or insertions not in Kant's own text are indicated by square brackets. Kant's foot-notes are always indicated by an asterisk (*) or, if added in the Second Edition, by a dagger (†). Other additions which he made in the Second Edition are plainly indicated.

We have capitalized references to the Supreme Being (except in exact quotations from the Bible), and to Christ when he is spoken of definitely as the Son of God. In many passages, however, where Kant discusses Christ as a personification of man's predisposition to good, or as the archetype of perfected humanity, we have deemed it more accurate not to capitalize pronouns or other references. Parentheses and italicizations of the Berlin Edition have been followed faithfully though not blindly.

We wish to acknowledge the aid, in translating several difficult passages, of our colleagues, Professor George M. Priest, a recent translator of Goethe's *Faust*, and of Professor Hans Jaeger. We also wish to thank our colleague, Professor Warner Fite, and Professor Charles W. Hendel Jr. of McGill University, both of whom offered valuable suggestions some years ago when the task of translation was first undertaken. Our greatest indebtedness, however, is to Professor Norman Kemp Smith of Edinburgh, at whose suggestion this translation was first undertaken, and whose general advice and numerous detailed criticisms we have found most helpful. He should, of course, not be held responsible for any of the work's imperfections.

Princeton, 1934.

PREFACE TO THE SECOND EDITION
OF THIS TRANSLATION

The continuing and growing interest of scholars in Kant's *Religion* dictates a second edition of this translation. My colleague, Hoyt H. Hudson, died in 1944. I wish to record my continuing gratitude to him for his invaluable collaboration in the original translation. I have been fortunate in securing the help of my friend, John R. Silber, now at The University of Texas, for the revision of the translation and for his essay, Part II of the Introduction, on "The Ethical Significance of Kant's *Religion*." This essay, which examines the *Religion* primarily from the standpoint of its ethical rather than its religious significance, provides a valuable supplement to my earlier Introduction, now Part I. My own more recent reflections on Kant's *Religion* are to be found in *Moral, Aesthetic, and Religious Insight*, Rutgers University Press, 1957, Chapter V. What follows in this preface is Professor Silber's contribution.

Scripps College, 1960

Theodore M. Greene

In the first edition of this translation the word *"Willkür"* is variously translated as "choice," "power of choice," "will," and "volition." Professor Greene agrees with me that this translation of *"Willkür"* as "will" is very misleading because *"Wille"* is also translated as "will." Since the correct interpretation of Kant's theory of the will depends upon a careful distinction between *"Wille"* and *"Willkür"* the reader should know when the words *"Wille"* and *"Willkür"* occur in the German text. A small "w" has therefore been inserted after every English word or phrase which translates *"Willkür."* When the English word "will" occurs without the following "w" the reader can assume that it is a translation of the German word *"Wille."*

Apart from the alterations relating to *"Wille"* and *"Willkür,"*

I have made very few revisions in the translation since few seemed to be required.

The reader's attention is also called to recent developments in Kantian scholarship which necessitate some re-evaluation of Professor Greene's Introduction. Professor Greene, along with N. Kemp Smith, A. H. Dakin, C. C. J. Webb, and other Kant scholars, accepted Erich Adickes' contention that Kant repudiated his "moral argument" for the existence of God and immortality and extensively revised his doctrine of the highest good in the *Opus Postumum*. It was not until 1938—four years after the publication of Greene's Introduction—that the complete text of the *Opus Postumum* became available for independent study. After a careful examination of that text, Professor G. A. Schrader demonstrated the inadequacy of Adickes' interpretation. A brief summary of Schrader's critique of Adickes is indicated.

Schrader notes[1] the difficulty of proving on the basis of the *Opus Postumum*, which was composed for the most part after 1800, that such a radical shift in Kant's thought occurred. In order to understand and interpret the *Opus Postumum* one must distinguish Kant's own views from the mass of theses and countertheses which he presents in this series of dialectically developed reflections. A guiding principle of interpretation is required. Adickes, who first edited and commented on the *Opus Postumum*, wisely decided to interpret individual passages, in the *Opus Postumum* and elsewhere, in the light of Kant's entire conceptual framework.

Although it is difficult on the basis of this sound principle to show that Kant repudiated a central and oft repeated part of his ethical and metaphysical system, Adickes concluded nonetheless that the moral argument did not fit into the larger context of Kant's thought. He found the moral argument unacceptable for two reasons: (1) it failed to recognize the personal, subjective character of religious faith, and (2) it introduced an unfortunate hedonistic element into Kant's ethics. Pursuant to the first objection, Adickes interpreted those statements in the *Opus Postumum* which stress the subjective character of faith as evidence that Kant saw the error in his earlier position. Schrader points out that from the first *Critique* onward Kant presented the moral argument both as subjective, in the sense that it was not and never could be a

[1] "Kant's Presumed Repudiation of the 'Moral Argument' in the *Opus Postumum*: an Examination of Adickes' Interpretation," *Philosophy*, July 1951. This important article should be read in conjunction with Greene's statements on pp. lxv ff. of the Introduction.

theoretical proof, and also as objective, as a necessary condition of rational, moral volition.[2] He rejects Adickes' second objection because (a) Adickes failed to prove that the moral argument actually constituted an unfortunate hedonistic intrusion in Kant's ethics, and because (b) such a proof, even if forthcoming, would have been inconclusive for the purpose of the argument unless it could also be shown that Kant agreed. The avoidance of this "hedonistic intrusion" could not have served Kant as a motive for the repudiation of the moral argument unless he had realized that the moral argument involved this consequence. Kant, however, gave no indication of such "insight." In the *Opus Postumum*, as in earlier works, Kant argued that the moral law is not obligatory either because God commands it or because He rewards and punishes men in accordance with their observance of it. On the the contrary, he argued that God must exist because the moral law issues categorical commands for whose fulfillment His existence is required.[3]

(Although Schrader did not pursue this issue further, he might also have questioned Adickes' assumption, which is shared by the majority of Kant's interpreters, that hedonism has no place in Kant's ethics. This interpretation oversimplifies and distorts Kant's actual position. Although Kant did insist repeatedly that one cannot fulfil his duty when duty is made a mere means to happiness, he was equally insistent that a good man, fulfilling his duty by seeking the happiness of others and his own perfection,[4] *deserves* to be happy and is rationally compelled to believe that he *will* be happy. Thus Kant argued—without making happiness the motive of moral conduct—that the good man who deserves happiness has the rational ground to "will that there be a God" and that his own "duration be endless."[5])

Schrader also rejects the evidence purporting to show that Kant actually repudiated the moral argument in the *Opus Postumum*. Adickes' positive proof rests on three considerations: (1) that

[2] For a fuller discussion of the objectivity, from a non-theoretical standpoint, of Kant's moral argument, see "The Metaphysical Importance of the Highest Good as the Canon of Pure Reason in Kant's Philosophy," by J. R. Silber, in *Texas Studies in Literature and Language*, Summer 1959.

[3] An extended discussion of the relative ultimacy in Kant's thought of the moral law and God and of the necessity of God's existence as a condition for the realization of the *summum bonum*, which the moral law commands, may be found in "Kant's Conception of the Highest Good as Immanent and Transcendent," by J. R. Silber, in *The Philosophical Review*, October 1959.

[4] *Metaphysic of Morals*, (Abbott's tr.), pp. 295–300.

[5] *Critique of Practical Reason*, (Beck's tr.), p. 245.

Kant fails to restate the argument in the *Opus Postumum*, (2) that Kant declares that no proof of the existence of God can be offered, and (3) that in the *Opus Postumum* Kant argues that God is directly revealed in the categorical imperative. Schrader dismisses the first consideration on the grounds that, if true, it would be inconsequential but that, as a matter of fact, recognizable restatements of the moral argument are present in the *Opus Postumum*. The second consideration lacks substance because Kant never presented the moral argument as a theoretical proof and never believed that a theoretical proof of God's existence is possible. Hence, there is nothing new or revolutionary about Kant's denial of the possibility of such a proof in the *Opus Postumum*. Adickes' third objection fails because Kant continued to insist in the *Opus Postumum* that the existence of God, like the concept of freedom, can never be known or presented directly but only through the mediation of a necessary principle. The moral law, even as it reveals man's freedom, leads the mind to the necessary hypothesis of God's existence, and thus provides the necessary mediation.

In the light of Schrader's argument and analysis, it is necessary to reject Adickes' interpretation and once again to take seriously the moral argument as an enduring and unrepudiated part of Kant's philosophy.

In Part I of the Introduction Professor Greene examines and evaluates Kant's *Religion* as a work on religion *per se*. He does not discuss the significance of this work as an extension of Kant's ethical writings. The *Religion* is, however, very important for the understanding of Kant's ethics for at least two reasons. First, the *Religion* presents Kant's most careful and systematic analysis of the will and its degrees of potency in moral and immoral volition; and second, "Book One" contains what Kant considered his clearest and simplest statement of the nature of moral incentives and of the way in which moral pleasure is to be distinguished from pathological pleasure. Part II of the Introduction, entitled "The Ethical Significance of Kant's *Religion*", has therefore been added to the Second Edition.

The University of Texas, 1960

John R. Silber

1724 Born in Königsberg
1732 Entered the *Collegium Friedericianum*
1740 Matriculated at the University of Königsberg
1754 Appointed *Privatdozent* in the University of Königsberg
1755 Anonymous publication of *Allgemeine Naturgeschichte und Theorie des Himmels* (General History of Nature and Theory of the Heavens)
1755 *Principiorum primorum cognitionis metaphysicae nova dilucidatio* (A New Exposition of the First Principles of Metaphysical Knowledge, tr. by England in Kant's Conception of God, 1930)
1759 *Versuch einiger Betrachtungen über den Optimismus* (An Attempt at some Considerations on Optimism)
1763 *Der einzig mögliche Beweisgrund zu einer Demonstration des Daseins Gottes* (The only Possible Argument for the Existence of God, tr. by Richardson, 1798)
1763 *Untersuchung über die Deutlichkeit der Grundsätze der natürlichen Theologie und Moral,* etc. (An Inquiry into the Distinctness of the Principles of Natural Theology and Morals, tr. by Beck, 1949; also by Richardson, 1798)
1764 *Beobachtungen über das Gefühl des Schönen und Erhabenen* (Observations on the Sense of the Beautiful and the Sublime, tr. by Friedrich, 1949)
1766 *Träume eines Geistersehers* (Dreams of a Spirit-seer, tr. by Friedrich, 1949; also by Goerwitz, 1900)
1770 Appointed Ordinary Professor of Logic and Metaphysics in the University of Königsberg
1775 *Von den verschiedenen Racen der Menschen* (Concerning the different Races of Mankind)—announcement of lectures in 1775
1781 *Kritik der reinen Vernunft,* Second Edition 1787 (Critique of Pure Reason, tr. by Kemp Smith, 1929; also by Müller, 1896, and by Meiklejohn, 1871)
1783 *Prolegomena zu einer jeden künftigen Metaphysik* etc. (Prolegomena to any Future Metaphysic, tr. by Mahaffy and Bernard, 1915, also by Carus, 1902)

may be true in Theory but does not hold good in Practice, tr. by Richardson, 1798) in *Berlinische Monatsschrift*, Sept. 1793

1793 RELIGION INNERHALB DER GRENZEN DER BLOS-SEN VERNUNFT (Religion within the Limits of Reason Alone—for translations, see above, pp. cxxxv) Second Edition, 1794

1795 *Zum ewigen Frieden* (Eternal Peace, tr. by Beck and Friedrich, 1949; also by Hastie, 1914)

1796 Discontinued his university lectures

1797 *Metaphysik der Sitten* (Metaphysic of Morals, General Introduction and Introduction to Part II, tr. in part by Abbott, 1889, Part I, tr. by Hastie, 1887, and Part II, tr. by Semple, 1836)

1797 Death of Frederick William II; Wöllner dismissed

1797 *Ueber ein vermeintes Recht, aus Menschenliebe zu lügen* (On a Supposed Right to Lie from Altruistic Motives, tr. by Beck, 1949, also by Abbott, 1889) in *Berlinische Blätter*, Sept. 1797

1798 *Der Streit der Facultäten* (The Conflict of the Faculties)

1798 *Anthropologie in pragmatischer Hinsicht abgefasst*, Second Edition, 1800 (Anthropology, Considered from a Pragmatic Viewpoint)

1800 *Vorrede zu Jachmanns Prüfung der Kantischen Religionsphilosophie in Hinsicht auf die ihr beigelegte Aenlichkeit mit dem reinen Mysticismus* (Preface to Jachmann's Examination of the Kantian Philosophy of Religion with regard to its alleged Similarity to pure Mysticism)

1803 *Ueber Pädagogik* (The Educational Theory of Immanuel Kant, tr. by E. F. Buchner, 1904) edited by Rink

1804 Died in Königsberg

1817 *Vorlesungen über die philosophische Religionslehre* (Lectures on the Philosophy of Religion) edited by Pölitz. Second Edition, 1830

1920 *Kants Opus Postumum dargestellt und beurteilt* by Erich Adickes

1924 *Eine Vorlesung Kants über Ethik* (Lectures on Ethics, tr. by Infield, 1930) edited by Menzer

1936 *Opus Postumum, Erste Hälfte*, edited by Buchenau

1938 *Opus Postumum, Zweite Hälfte*, edited by Lehmann

RELIGION
WITHIN THE LIMITS OF REASON ALONE

PREFACE TO THE FIRST EDITION

So far as morality is based upon the conception of man as a free agent who, just because he is free, binds himself through his reason to unconditioned laws, it stands in need neither of the idea of another Being over him, for him to apprehend his duty, nor of an incentive other than the law itself, for him to do his duty. At least it is man's own fault if he is subject to such a need; and if he is, this need can be relieved through nothing outside himself: for whatever does not originate in himself and his own freedom in no way compensates for the deficiency of his morality. Hence for its own sake morality does not need religion at all (whether objectively, as regards willing, or subjectively, as regards ability [to act]); by virtue of pure practical reason it is self-sufficient. For since its laws are binding, as the highest condition (itself unconditioned) of all ends, through the bare form of universal legality of the maxims, which must be chosen accordingly, morality requires absolutely no material determining ground of free choice^w,* that is, no end, in order either to know what duty is or to impel the performance of duty. On the contrary, when it is a question of duty, morality is perfectly able to ignore all ends, and

* Those who, in the conception of duty, are not satisfied with the merely formal determining ground as such (conformity to law) as the basis of determination, do indeed admit that such a basis cannot be discovered in *self-love* directed to one's own *comfort*. Hence there remain but two determining grounds: one, which is rational, namely, one's own *perfection*, and another, which is empirical, the *happiness* of others.[1] Now if they do not conceive of the first of these as the moral determining ground (a will, namely, unconditionally obedient to the law) which is necessarily unique—and if they so interpreted it they would be expounding in a circle—they would have to have in mind man's natural perfection, so far as it is capable of enhancement, and this can be of many kinds, such as skill in the arts and sciences, taste, bodily adroitness, etc. But these are always good only on the condition that their use does not conflict with the moral law (which alone commands unconditionally); set up as an end, therefore, perfection cannot be the principle of concepts of duty. The same holds for the end which aims at the happiness of other men. For an act must, first of all, itself be weighed according to the moral law before it is directed to the happiness of others. The requirement laid down by this end, therefore, is a duty only conditionally and cannot serve as the supreme principle of moral maxims.

[1] [*fremde Glückseligkeit*. We have almost always translated *Glückseligkeit* as *happiness*.]

^w For an explanation of the "w" see the "Preface to the Second Edition of this Translation," page cxxxix.

it ought to do so. Thus, for example, in order to know whether I should (or indeed can) be truthful in my testimony before a court, or whether I should be faithful in accounting for another man's property entrusted to me, it is not at all necessary for me to search for an end which I might perhaps propose to achieve with my declaration, since it matters not at all what sort of end this is; indeed, the man who finds it needful, when his avowal is lawfully demanded, to look about him for some kind of [ulterior] end, is, by this very fact, already contemptible.

But although for its own sake morality needs no representation of an end which must precede the determining of the will, it is quite possible that it is necessarily related to such an end, taken not as the ground but as the [sum of] inevitable consequences of maxims adopted as conformable to that end. For in the absence of all reference to an end no determination of the will can take place in man, since such determination cannot be followed by no effect whatever; and the representation of the effect must be capable of being accepted, not, indeed, as the basis for the determination of the will^w and as an end antecedently aimed at, but yet as an end conceived of as the result ensuing from the will's^w determination through the law (*finis in consequentiam veniens*). Without an end of this sort a will^w, envisaging to itself no definite goal[1] for a contemplated act, either objective or subjective (which it has, or ought to have, in view), is indeed informed as to *how* it ought to act, but not *whither*, and so can achieve no satisfaction. It is true, therefore, that morality requires no end for right conduct; the law, which contains the formal condition of the use of freedom in general, suffices. Yet an end does arise out of morality; for how the question, *What is to result from this right conduct of ours?* is to be answered, and towards what, as an end—even granted it may not be wholly subject to our control—we might direct our actions and abstentions so as at least to be in harmony with that end: these cannot possibly be matters of indifference to reason. Hence the end is no more than an idea of an object which takes the formal condition of all such ends as we *ought* to have (duty) and combines it with whatever is conditioned, and in harmony with duty, in all the ends which we *do* have (happiness proportioned to obedience to duty)—that is to say, the idea of a highest good in the world for whose possibility we must postulate a higher, moral,

[1] [*Gegenstand*]

most holy, and omnipotent Being which alone can unite the two elements of this highest good. Yet (viewed practically) this idea is not an empty one, for it does meet our natural need to conceive of some sort of final end for all our actions and abstentions, taken as a whole, an end which can be justified by reason and the absence of which would be a hindrance to moral decision. Most important of all, however, this idea arises out of morality and is not its basis; it is an end the adoption of which as one's own presupposes basic ethical principles. Therefore it cannot be a matter of unconcern to morality as to whether or not it forms for itself the concept of a final end of all things (harmony with which, while not multiplying men's duties, yet provides them with a special point of focus for the unification of all ends); for only thereby can objective, practical reality be given to the union of the purposiveness arising from freedom with the purposiveness of nature, a union with which we cannot possibly dispense. Take a man who, honoring the moral law, allows the thought to occur to him (he can scarcely avoid doing so) of what sort of world he would create, under the guidance of practical reason, were such a thing in his power, a world into which, moreover, he would place himself as a member. He would not merely make the very choice which is determined by that moral idea of the highest good, were he vouchsafed solely the right to choose; he would also will that [such] a world should by all means come into existence (because the moral law demands that the highest good possible through our agency should be realized) and he would so will even though, in accordance with this idea, he saw himself in danger of paying in his own person a heavy price in happiness—it being possible that he might not be adequate to the [moral] demands of the idea, demands which reason lays down as conditioning happiness. Accordingly he would feel compelled by reason to avow this judgment with complete impartiality, as though it were rendered by another and yet, at the same time, as his own; whereby man gives evidence of the need, morally effected in him, of also conceiving a final end for his duties, as their consequence.

Morality thus leads ineluctably to religion, through which it extends itself* to the idea of a powerful moral Lawgiver, outside

---

* If the proposition, There is a God, hence there is a highest good in the world, is to arise (as a dogma) from morality alone, it is a synthetic *a priori* proposition: for even though accepted only for practical reference, it does yet

of mankind, for Whose will that is the final end (of creation) which at the same time can and ought to be man's final end.

* * * * * * * * * * *

pass beyond the concept of duty which morality contains (and which presupposes merely the formal laws, and not the matter, of choice[w]), and hence cannot analytically be evolved out of morality. *But how is such a proposition a priori possible?* Agreement with the bare idea of a moral Lawgiver for all men is, indeed, identical with the general moral concept of duty, and so far the proposition commanding this agreement would be analytic. But the acknowledgment of His existence asserts more than the bare possibility of such a thing. The key to the solution of this problem, so far as I believe myself to understand it, I can only indicate here and not develop.

An *end* is always the object of an *inclination*, that is, of an immediate craving for possession of a thing through one's action, just as the *law* (which commands practically) is an object of *respect*. An objective end (*i.e.,* the end which we ought to have) is that which is proposed to us as such by reason alone. The end which embraces the unavoidable and at the same time sufficient condition of all other ends is the *final end*. The subjective final end of rational worldly beings is their own happiness (each of them *has* this end by virtue of having a nature dependent upon sensuous objects, and hence it would be absurd to say that anyone *ought* to have it) and all practical propositions which are based on this final end are synthetic, and at the same time empirical. But that everyone ought to make the highest *good* possible in the world a *final end* is a synthetic practical proposition *a priori* (and indeed objectively practical) given by pure reason; for it is a proposition which goes beyond the concept of duties in this world and adds a consequence (an effect) thereof which is not contained in the moral laws and therefore cannot be evolved out of them analytically. For these laws command absolutely, be the consequence what it will; indeed, they even require that the consideration of such consequence be completely waived when a particular act is concerned; and thereby they make duty an object of highest respect without offering or proposing to us an end (or a final end) such as would have to constitute duty's recommendation and the incentive to the fulfilment of our duty. All men could have sufficient incentive if (as they should) they adhered solely to the dictation of pure reason in the law. What need have they to know the outcome of their moral actions and abstentions, an outcome which the world's course will bring about? It suffices for them that they do their duty; even though all things end with earthly life and though, in this life, happiness and desert may never meet. And yet it is one of the inescapable limitations of man and of his faculty of practical reason (a limitation, perhaps, of all other worldly beings as well) to have regard, in every action, to the consequence thereof, in order to discover therein what could serve him as an end and also prove the purity of his intention—which consequence, though last in practice (*nexu effectivo*) is yet first in representation and intention (*nexu finali*). In this end, if directly presented to him by reason alone, man seeks something that he can *love;* therefore the law, which merely arouses his *respect,* even

If morality finds in the holiness of its law an object of the great-est respect, then at the level of religion it presents the ultimate cause, which consummates those laws, as an object of *adoration* and thus appears in its majesty. But anything, even the most sub-lime, dwindles under the hands of men when they turn the idea of it to their own use. What can truly be venerated only so far as re-spect for it is free must adapt itself to those forms which can be rendered authoritative only by means of coercive laws; and what of its own accord exposes itself to the public criticism of everyone must submit itself to a criticism which has power, *i.e.*, a censor-ship.

Meanwhile, since the command, Obey the authorities! is also moral, and since obedience to it, as to all injunctions of duty, can be drawn into religion, it is fitting that a treatise which is dedicated to the definite concept of religion should itself present an example of this obedience, which, however, can be evinced not through at-tention merely to law in the form of a single state regulation and blindness with respect to every other, but only through combined respect for all [regulations] taken together.

Now the theologian who passes on books can be appointed either as one who is to care for the soul's welfare alone or as one who is also to care for the welfare of the sciences; the first judge is ap-

---

though it does not acknowledge this object of love as a necessity does yet ex-tend itself on its behalf by including the moral goal of reason among its de-termining grounds. That is, the proposition: Make the highest good possible in the world your own final end! is a synthetic proposition *a priori*, which is introduced by the moral law itself; although practical reason does, indeed, extend itself therein beyond the law. This extension is possible because of the moral law's being taken in relation to the natural characteristic of man, that for all his actions he must conceive of an end over and above the law (a char-acteristic which makes man an object of experience). And further, this ex-tension (as with theoretical propositions *a priori* which are synthetic) is pos-sible only because this 'end embraces the *a priori* principle of the knowledge of the determining grounds in experience of a free will[w], so far as this experi-ence, by exhibiting the effects of morality in its ends, gives objective though merely practical reality to the concept of morality as causal in the world. But if, now, the strictest obedience to moral laws is to be considered the cause of the ushering in of the highest good (as end), then, since human capacity does not suffice for bringing about happiness in the world proportionate to worthiness to be happy, an omnipotent moral Being must be postulated as ruler of the world, under whose care this [balance] occurs. That is, morality leads inevitably to religion.

pointed merely as a divine; the second, as a scholar also. It rests with the second, as a member of a public institution to which (under the name of a university) all the sciences are entrusted for cultivation and defense against interference, to limit the usurpations of the first by the stipulation that his censorship shall create no disturbance in the field of the sciences. And when both judges are Biblical theologians, the superior censorship will pertain to the second as a member of the university and as belonging to the faculty which has been charged with the treatment of this theology: for, as regards the first concern (the welfare of souls), both have a mandate alike; but, as regards the second (the welfare of the sciences), the theologian in his capacity as university scholar has, in addition, a special function to perform. If we depart from this rule things must finally come to the pass to which they came of yore (for example, at the time of Galileo), where the Biblical theologian, in order to humble the pride of the sciences and to spare himself labor in connection with them, might actually venture an invasion into astronomy, or some other science, as for example the ancient history of the earth, and—like those tribes who, finding that they do not have either the means or the resolution sufficient to defend themselves against threatened attacks, transform all about them into a wilderness—might arrest all the endeavors of human reason.

Among the sciences, however, there is, over and against Biblical theology, a philosophical theology, which is an estate entrusted to another faculty. So long as this philosophical theology remains within the limits of reason alone, and for the confirmation and exposition of its propositions makes use of history, sayings, books of all peoples, even the Bible, but only for itself, without wishing to carry these propositions into Biblical theology or to change the latter's public doctrines—a privilege of divines—it must have complete freedom to expand as far as its science reaches. And although the right of censorship of the theologian (regarded merely *as a divine*)[1] cannot be impugned when it has been shown that the philosopher has really overstepped his limits and committed trespass upon theology, yet, the instant this is in doubt and a question arises whether, in writing or in some other public utterance of the philosopher, this trespass has indeed occurred, the superior censorship can belong only to the Biblical theologian, and to him *as a member of his faculty;* for he has been assigned to care

[1] [Italics not in the text.]

for the second interest of the commonwealth, namely, the prosperity of the sciences, and has been appointed just as legally as has the other [the theologian regarded as a divine].

And under such circumstances it is indeed to this faculty and not to the philosophical that the ultimate censorship belongs; for the former alone is privileged in respect of certain doctrines, while the latter investigates its doctrines freely and openly; hence only the former can enter a complaint that its exclusive rights have been violated. But despite the approximation of the two bodies of doctrine to one another and the anxiety lest the philosophical faculty overstep its limits, doubt relating to such trespass is easily prevented if it is borne in mind that the mischief occurs not through the philosopher's *borrowing* something from Biblical theology, in order to use it for his purpose—even granting that the philosopher uses what he borrows from it in a meaning suited to naked reason but perhaps not pleasing to this theology—but only so far as he *imports* something into it and thereby seeks to direct it to ends other than those which its own economy sanctions. For Biblical theology will itself not want to deny that it contains a great deal in common with the teachings of unassisted reason and, in addition, much that belongs to historical and philological lore, and that it is subject to the censorship of these [disciplines].

Thus, for example, we cannot say that the teacher of natural rights, who borrows many a classical expression and formula for his philosophical doctrine of rights from the codex of the Romans, thereby trespasses—even if, as often happens, he does not employ them in exactly the same sense in which, according to the expositors of Roman Law, they were to be taken—so long as he does not wish jurists proper, and even the courts of law, also to use them thus. For were that not within his competence, we could, conversely, accuse the Biblical theologian or the statutory jurist of trespassing countless times on the province of philosophy, because both must borrow from philosophy very often, though only to mutual advantage, since neither can dispense with reason, nor, where science is concerned, with philosophy. Were Biblical theology to determine, wherever possible, to have nothing to do with reason in things religious, we can easily foresee on which side would be the loss; for a religion which rashly declares war on reason will not be able to hold out in the long run against it.

I will even venture to ask whether it would not be beneficial, upon completion of the academic instruction in Biblical theology, always to add, by way of conclusion, as necessary to the complete equipment of the candidate, a special course of lectures on the purely *philosophical* theory of religion (which avails itself of everything, including the Bible), with such a book as this, perhaps, as the text (or any other, if a better one of the same kind can be found). For the sciences derive pure benefit from separation, so far as each first constitutes a whole by itself; and not until they are so constituted should the attempt be made to survey them in combination. Let the Biblical theologian, then, be at one with the philosopher, or let him believe himself obliged to refute him, if only he hears him. Only thus can he be forearmed against all the difficulties which the philosopher might make for him. To conceal these, or indeed to decry them as ungodly, is a paltry device which does not stand the test; while to mix the two—the Biblical theologian, for his part, casting but an occasional fleeting glance at philosophy—is to lack thoroughness, with the result that in the end no one really knows how he stands towards the theory of religion as a whole.

In order to make apparent the relation of religion to human nature (endowed in part with good, in part with evil predispositions), I represent, in the four following essays, the relationship of the good and evil principles as that of two self-subsistent active causes influencing men. The first essay has already been printed in the *Berlinische Monatsschrift* of April, 1792, but could not be omitted here, because of the close coherence of the subject-matter in this work, which contains, in the three essays now added, the complete development of the first.

The reader is asked to forgive the orthography of the first sheets (which differs from mine) in view of the variety of hands which have worked on the copy and the shortness of time left me for revision.

PREFACE TO THE SECOND EDITION

For this Edition nothing has been altered except misprints and a few expressions which have been improved. New supplementary material, indicated by a dagger (†), is placed at the foot of the text.

Regarding the title of this work (for doubts have been expressed about the intention concealed thereunder) I note: that since, after all, *revelation* can certainly embrace the pure religion of reason, while, conversely, the second cannot include what is historical in the first, I shall be able [experimentally] to regard the first as the *wider* sphere of faith, which includes within itself the second, as a *narrower* one (not like two circles external to one another, but like concentric circles). The philosopher, as a teacher of pure reason (from unassisted principles *a priori*), must confine himself within the narrower circle, and, in so doing, must waive consideration of all experience. From this standpoint I can also make a second experiment, namely, to start from some alleged revelation or other and, leaving out of consideration the pure religion of reason (so far as it constitutes a self-sufficient system), to examine in a fragmentary manner this revelation, as an *historical system*, in the light of moral concepts; and then to see whether it does not lead back to the very same pure *rational system* of religion. The latter, though not from the theoretical point of view (and the technico-practical point of view of pedagogical method, as a *technology*, must also be reckoned under this head) may yet, from the morally practical standpoint, be self-sufficient and adequate for genuine religion, which, indeed, as a rational concept *a priori* (remaining over after everything empirical has been taken away), obtains only in this [morally practical] relation. If this experiment is successful we shall be able to say that reason can be found to be not only compatible with Scripture but also at one with it, so that he who follows one (under guidance of moral concepts) will not fail to conform to the other. Were this not so, we should have either two religions in one individual, which is absurd, or else one *religion* and one *cult*,[1] in which case, since the second is not (like religion) an end in itself but only possesses value as a means, they would often have to be shaken up together

[1] [*Cultus*, ceremonial worship]

that they might, for a short while, be united; though directly, like oil and water, they must needs separate from one another, and the purely moral (the religion of reason) be allowed to float on top.

I noted in the first Preface that this unification, or the attempt at it, is a task to which the philosophical investigator of religion has every right, and is not a trespass upon the exclusive rights of the Biblical theologian. Since then I have found this assertion made in the *Moral* (Part I, pp. 5–11) of the late Michaelis,[1] a man well versed in both departments, and applied throughout his entire work; and the higher faculty did not find therein anything prejudicial to their rights.

In this Second Edition I have not been able, as I should have liked, to take cognizance of the judgments passed upon this book by worthy men, named and unnamed, since (as with all foreign literary intelligence) these arrive in our parts very late. This is particularly true of the *Annotationes quaedam theologicae*, etc. of the renowned Hr. D. Storr[2] in Tübingen, who has examined my book with his accustomed sagacity and with an industry and fairness deserving the greatest thanks. I have it in mind to answer him, but cannot venture to promise to do so because of the peculiar difficulties which age sets in the way of working with abstract ideas. But there is a review in Number 29 of the *Neueste Kritische Nachrichten*, of Greifswald,[3] which I can despatch as briefly as the reviewer did the book itself. For the book, in his judgment, is nothing but an answer to the question which I myself posed: "How is the ecclesiastical system of dogmatics, in its concepts and doctrines, possible according to pure (theoretical and practical) reason?" This essay [he claims] does not concern those[4] who have no knowledge and understanding of his (Kant's) system and have no desire to be able to understand it—by them it may be looked upon as non-existent. I answer thus: To understand this book in its essential content, only common morality is needed, without meddling with the *Critique of Practical Reason*, still less with the theoretical Critique. When, for example, virtue as skill in *actions*

---

[1] [Johann David Michaelis, 1717–1791; celebrated Orientalist and Biblical scholar; the book referred to was published posthumously in 1792.]

[2] [Gottlob Christian Storr, 1746–1805, Professor of Theology in Tübingen, and later court-preacher in Stuttgart. His *Annotationes*, directed against Kant, appeared in 1793, with a German translation in 1794.]

[3] [For 1793; pp. 225–229]

[4] [Reading *diejenigen* for *diejenige*, as in Kehrbach's Leipzig Edition.]

conforming to duty (according to their legality) is called *virtus phænomenon*, and the same virtue as an enduring *disposition* towards such actions from *duty* (because of their morality) is called *virtus noumenon*, these expressions are used only because of the schools; while the matter itself is contained, though in other words, in the most popular children's instruction and sermons, and is easily understood. Would that as much could be said for the mysteries concerning the divine nature which are numbered among religious teachings, mysteries introduced into the catechism as though they were wholly popular, but which, ultimately, must first be transformed into moral concepts if they are to become comprehensible to everyone!

Königsberg, 26 January, 1794.

BOOK ONE

CONCERNING THE INDWELLING OF THE EVIL PRINCIPLE WITH THE GOOD, OR, ON THE RADICAL EVIL IN HUMAN NATURE

That "the world lieth in evil"[1] is a plaint as old as history, old even as the older art, poetry; indeed, as old as that oldest of all fictions, the religion of priest-craft. All agree that the world began in a good estate, whether in a Golden Age, a life in Eden, or a yet more happy community with celestial beings. But they represent that this happiness vanished like a dream and that a Fall into evil (moral evil, with which physical evil ever went hand in hand) presently hurried mankind from bad to worse with accelerated descent;* so that now (this "now" is also as old as history) we live in the final age, with the Last Day and the destruction of the world at hand. In some parts of India the Judge and Destroyer of the world, Rudra (sometimes called Siwa or Siva), already is worshipped as the reigning God—Vishnu, the Sustainer of the world, having some centuries ago grown weary and renounced the supreme authority which he inherited from Brahma, the Creator.

More modern, though far less prevalent, is the contrasted optimistic belief, which indeed has gained a following solely among philosophers and, of late, especially among those interested in education—the belief that the world steadily (though almost imperceptibly) forges in the other direction, to wit, from bad to better; at least that the predisposition to such a movement is discoverable in human nature. If this belief, however, is meant to apply to *moral* goodness and badness (not simply to the process of civilization), it has certainly not been deduced from experience; the history of all times cries too loudly against it. The belief, we

---

[1] [Cf. I John V, 19]

* *Aetas parentum peior avis tulit*
Nos nequiores, mox daturos
Progeniem vitiosiorem.

Horace [*Odes*, III, 6.

. . . Our father's race
More deeply versed in ill
Than were their sires, hath borne us yet
More wicked, duly to beget
A race more vicious still.

(Martin)]

may presume, is a well-intentioned assumption of the moralists, from Seneca to Rousseau, designed to encourage the sedulous cultivation of that seed of goodness which perhaps lies in us—if, indeed, we can count on any such natural basis of goodness in man. We may note that since we take for granted that man is by nature sound of body (as at birth he usually is), no reason appears why, by nature, his soul should not be deemed similarly healthy and free from evil. Is not nature herself, then, inclined to lend her aid to developing in us this moral predisposition to goodness? In the words of Seneca: *Sanabilibus ægrotamus malis, nosque in rectum genitos natura, si sanari velimus, adiuvat.*[1]

But since it well may be that both sides have erred in their reading of experience, the question arises whether a middle ground may not at least be possible, namely, that man as a species is neither good nor bad, or at all events that he is as much the one as the other, partly good, partly bad. We call a man evil, however, not because he performs actions that are evil (contrary to law) but because these actions are of such a nature that we may infer from them the presence in him of evil maxims. In and through experience we can observe actions contrary to law, and we can observe (at least in ourselves) that they are performed in the consciousness that they are unlawful; but a man's maxims, sometimes[2] even his own, are not thus observable; consequently the judgment that the agent is an evil man cannot be made with certainty if grounded on experience. In order, then, to call a man evil, it would have to be possible *a priori* to infer from several evil acts done with consciousness of their evil, or from one such act, an underlying evil maxim; and further, from this maxim to infer the presence in the agent of an underlying common ground, itself a maxim, of all particular morally-evil maxims.

Lest difficulty at once be encountered in the expression *nature*, which, if it meant (as it usually does) the opposite of *freedom* as a basis of action, would flatly contradict the predicates *morally* good or evil, let it be noted that by "nature of man" we here intend only the subjective ground of the exercise (under objective moral laws) of man's freedom in general; this ground—whatever is its character—is the necessary antecedent of every act apparent to the senses. But this subjective ground, again, must itself always be

---

[1] [*De ira*, II, 13, 1: "We are sick with curable diseases, and if we wish to be cured, nature comes to our aid, *for we were born to health.*"]

[2] [*nicht allemal*]

an expression[1] of freedom (for otherwise the use or abuse of man's power of choice[w] in respect of the moral law could not be imputed to him nor could the good or bad in him be called moral). Hence the source of evil cannot lie in an object *determining* the will[w] through inclination, nor yet in a natural impulse; it can lie only in a rule made by the will[w] for the use of its freedom, that is, in a maxim. But now it must not be considered permissible to inquire into the subjective ground in man of the adoption of this maxim rather than of its opposite. If this ground itself were not ultimately a maxim, but a mere natural impulse, it would be possible to trace the use of our freedom wholly to determination by natural causes; this, however, is contradictory to the very notion of freedom. When we say, then, Man is by nature good, or, Man is by nature evil, this means only that there is in him an ultimate ground (inscrutable to us)* of the adoption of good maxims or of evil maxims (*i.e.*, those contrary to law), and this he has, being a man; and hence he thereby expresses the character of his species.

We shall say, therefore, of the character (good or evil) distinguishing man from other possible rational beings, that it is *innate* in him. Yet in doing so we shall ever take the position that nature is not to bear the blame (if it is evil) or take the credit (if it is good), but that man himself is its author. But since the ultimate ground of the adoption of our maxims, which must itself lie in free choice[w], cannot be a fact revealed in experience, it follows that the good or evil in man (as the ultimate subjective ground of the adoption of this or that maxim with reference to the moral law) is termed innate only in *this* sense, that it is posited as the ground antecedent to every use of freedom in experience (in earliest youth as far back as birth) and is thus conceived of as present in man at birth—though birth need not be the cause of it.

Observation

The conflict between the two hypotheses presented above is based on a disjunctive proposition: *Man is* (by nature) *either morally good or morally evil*. It might easily occur to any one, how-

---

* That the ultimate subjective ground of the adoption of moral maxims is inscrutable is indeed already evident from this, that since this adoption is free, its ground (why, for example, I have chosen an evil and not a good maxim) must not be sought in any natural impulse, but always again in a

[1] [*Aktus*]

ever, to ask whether this disjunction is valid, and whether some might not assert that man is by nature neither of the two, others, that man is at once both, in some respects good, in other respects evil. Experience actually seems to substantiate the middle ground between the two extremes.

It is, however, of great consequence to ethics in general to avoid admitting, so long as it is possible, of anything morally intermediate, whether in actions (*adiophora*) or in human characters; for with such ambiguity all maxims are in danger of forfeiting their precision and stability. Those who are partial to this strict mode of thinking are usually called *rigorists* (a name which is intended to carry reproach, but which actually praises); their opposites may be called *latitudinarians*. These latter, again, are either latitudinarians of neutrality, whom we may call *indifferentists*, or else latitudinarians of coalition, whom we may call *syncretists*.*

According to the rigoristic diagnosis,** the answer to the question

maxim. Now since this maxim also must have its ground, and since apart from maxims no *determining ground* of free choice^w can or ought to be adduced, we are referred back endlessly in the series of subjective determining grounds, without ever being able to reach the ultimate ground.

* If the good = a, then its diametric opposite is the not-good. This latter is the result either of a mere absence of a basis of goodness, = 0, or of a positive ground of the opposite of good, = − a. In the second case the not-good may also be called positive evil. (As regards pleasure and pain there is a similar middle term, whereby pleasure = a, pain = − a, and the state in which neither is to be found, indifference, = 0.) Now if the moral law in us were not a motivating force of the will^w, the morally good (the agreement of the will^w with the law) would = a, and the not-good would = 0; the latter, as merely the result of the absence of a moral motivating force, would = a × 0. In us, however, the law is a motivating force, = a; hence the absence of agreement of the will^w with this law (= 0) is possible only as a consequence of a real and contrary determination of the will^w, *i.e.*, of an *opposition* to the law, = − a, *i.e.*, of an evil will^w. Between a good and an evil disposition (inner principle of maxims), according to which the morality of an action must be judged, there is therefore no middle ground.

A^1 morally indifferent action (*adiaphoron morale*) would be one resulting merely from natural laws, and hence standing in no relation whatsoever to the moral law, which is the law of freedom; for such action is not a morally significant fact at all and regarding it neither *command*, nor *prohibition*, nor *permission* (legal *privilege*) occurs or is necessary.

** Professor Schiller, in his masterly treatise (*Thalia*, 1793, Part III) on *grace* and *dignity* in morality, objects to this way of representing obligation,

¹ [Added in the Second Edition.]

at issue rests upon the observation, of great importance to morality, that freedom of the will[w] is of a wholly unique nature in that an incentive can determine the will[w] to an action *only so far as the individual has incorporated it into his maxim* (has made it the general rule in accordance with which he will conduct himself); only thus can an incentive, whatever it may be, co-exist with the absolute spontaneity of the will[w] (*i.e.*, freedom). But the moral law, in the judgment of reason, is in itself an incentive, and who-

---

as carrying with it a monastic cast of mind. Since, however, we are at one upon the most important principles, I cannot admit that there is disagreement here, if only we can make ourselves clear to one another. I freely grant that by very reason of the dignity of the *idea of duty* I am unable to associate *grace* with it. For the idea of duty involves absolute necessity, to which grace stands in direct contradiction. The majesty of the moral law (as of the law on Sinai) instils awe (not dread, which repels, nor yet charm, which invites familiarity); and in this instance, since the ruler resides within us, this *respect*, as of a subject toward his ruler, awakens a *sense of the sublimity* of our own destiny which enraptures us more than any beauty. *Virtue*, also, *i.e.*, the firmly grounded disposition strictly to fulfil our duty, is also *beneficent* in its results, beyond all that nature and art can accomplish in the world; and the august picture of humanity, as portrayed in this character, does indeed allow the attendance of the *graces*. But when duty alone is the theme, they keep a respectful distance. If we consider, further, the happy results which virtue, should she gain admittance everywhere, would spread throughout the world, [we see] morally-directed reason (by means of the imagination) calling the sensibilities[1] into play. Only after vanquishing monsters did Hercules become Musagetes, leader of the Muses,—after labors from which those worthy sisters, trembling, draw back. The attendants of Venus Urania become wantons in the train of Venus Dione as soon as they meddle in the business of determining duty and try to provide springs of action therefor.

Now if one asks, What is the *aesthetic character*,[2] the *temperament*, so to speak, *of virtue*, whether courageous and hence *joyous* or fear-ridden and dejected, an answer is hardly necessary. This latter slavish frame of mind can never occur without a hidden *hatred* of the law. And a heart which is happy in the *performance* of its duty (not merely complacent in the *recognition* thereof) is a mark of genuineness in the virtuous disposition—of genuineness even in *piety*, which does not consist in the self-inflicted torment of a repentant sinner (a very ambiguous state of mind, which ordinarily is nothing but inward regret at having infringed upon the rules of prudence), but rather in the firm resolve to do better in the future. This resolve, then, encouraged by good progress, must needs beget a joyous frame of mind, without which man is never certain of having really *attained a love* for the good, *i.e.*, of having incorporated it into his maxim.

[1] [*Sinnlichkeit*]
[2] [*Beschaffenheit*]

ever makes it his maxim is *morally* good. If, now, this law does not determine a person's will^w in the case of an action which has reference to the law, an incentive contrary to it must influence his choice^w; and since, by hypothesis, this can only happen when a. man adopts this incentive (and thereby the deviation from the moral law) into his maxim (in which case he is an evil man) it follows that his disposition in respect to the moral law is never indifferent, never neither good nor evil.

Neither can a man be morally good in some ways and at the same time morally evil in others. His being good in one way means that he has incorporated the moral law into his maxim; were he, therefore, at the same time evil in another way, while his maxim would be universal as based on the moral law of obedience to duty, which is essentially single and universal, it would at the same time be only particular; but this is a contradiction.*

To have a good or an evil disposition as an inborn natural constitution does not here mean that it has not been acquired by the man who harbors it, that he is not author of it, but rather, that it has not been acquired in time (that he has *always* been good, or evil, *from his youth up*). The disposition, *i.e.*, the ultimate subjective ground of the adoption of maxims, can be one only and applies universally to the whole use of freedom. Yet this disposition itself must have been adopted by free choice^w, for otherwise it could not be imputed. But the subjective ground or cause of this adoption cannot further be known (though it is inevitable that we should inquire into it),[1] since otherwise still another maxim would have to be adduced in which this disposition must have been

---

* The ancient moral philosophers, who pretty well exhausted all that can be said upon virtue, have not left untouched the two questions mentioned above. The first they expressed thus: Must virtue be learned? (Is man by nature indifferent as regards virtue and vice?) The second they put thus: Is there more than one virtue (so that man might be virtuous in some respects, in others vicious)? Both questions were answered by them, with rigoristic precision, in the negative, and rightly so; for they were considering virtue *as such*, as it is in the idea of reason (that which man ought to be). If, however, we wish to pass moral judgment on this moral being, man *as he appears*, *i.e.*, as experience reveals him to us, we can answer both questions in the affirmative; for in this case we judge him not according to the standard of pure reason (at a divine tribunal) but by an empirical standard (before a human judge). This subject will be treated further in what follows.

[1] [Kant closes this parenthesis at the end of the sentence; our alteration seems necessitated by the meaning.]

incorporated, a maxim which itself in turn must have its ground. Since, therefore, we are unable to derive this disposition, or rather its ultimate ground, from any original act of the will[w] in time, we call it a property of the will[w] which belongs to it by nature (although actually the disposition is grounded in freedom). Further, the man of whom we say, "He is by nature good or evil," is to be understood not as the single individual (for then one man could be considered as good, by nature, another as evil), but as the entire race; that we are entitled so to do can only be proved when anthropological research shows that the evidence, which justifies us in attributing to a man one of these characters as innate, is such as to give no ground for excepting anyone, and that the attribution therefore holds for the race.

I. Concerning the Original Predisposition to Good in Human Nature

We may conveniently divide this predisposition, with respect to function, into three divisions, to be considered as elements in the fixed character and destiny[1] of man:

(1) The predisposition to *animality* in man, taken as a *living* being;

(2) The predisposition to *humanity* in man, taken as a living and at the same time a *rational* being;

(3) The predisposition to *personality* in man, taken as a rational and at the same time an *accountable* being.*

* We cannot regard this as included in the concept of the preceding, but necessarily must treat it as a special predisposition. For from the fact that a being has reason it by no means follows that this reason, by the mere representing of the fitness of its maxims to be laid down as universal laws, is thereby rendered capable of determining the will[w] unconditionally, so as to be "practical" of itself; at least, not so far as we can see. The most rational mortal being in the world might still stand in need of certain incentives, originating in objects of desire, to determine his choice[w]. He might, indeed, bestow the most rational reflection on all that concerns not only the greatest sum of these incentives in him but also the means of attaining the end thereby determined, without ever suspecting the possibility of such a thing as the absolutely imperative moral law which proclaims that it is itself an incentive, and, indeed, the highest. Were it not given us from within, we should never by any ratiocination subtilize it into existence or win over our will[w] to it; yet this law is the only law which informs us of the independence of our will[w] from determination by all other incentives (of our freedom) and at the same time of the accountability of all our actions.

[1] [Our phrase "fixed character and destiny" translates *Bestimmung*.]

1. The predisposition to *animality* in mankind may be brought under the general title of physical and purely *mechanical* self-love, wherein no reason is demanded. It is threefold: first, for self-preservation; second, for the propagation of the species, through the sexual impulse, and for the care of offspring so begotten; and third, for community with other men, *i.e.*, the social impulse. On these three stems can be grafted all kinds of vices (which, however, do not spring from this predisposition itself as a root). They may be termed vices of the coarseness[1] of nature, and in their greatest deviation from natural purposes are called the *beastly* vices of *gluttony* and *drunkenness*,[2] *lasciviousness*, and *wild lawlessness* (in relation to other men).

2. The predisposition[3] to humanity can be brought under the general title of a self-love which is physical and yet *compares* (for which reason is required); that is to say, we judge ourselves happy or unhappy only by making comparison with others. Out of this self-love springs the inclination *to acquire worth in the opinion of others*. This is originally a desire merely for *equality*, to allow no one superiority above oneself, bound up with a constant care lest others strive to attain such superiority; but from this arises gradually the unjustifiable craving to win it for oneself over others. Upon this twin stem of *jealousy* and *rivalry* may be grafted the very great vices of secret and open animosity against all whom we look upon as not belonging to us—vices, however, which really do not sprout of themselves from nature as their root; rather are they inclinations, aroused in us by the anxious endeavors of others to attain a hated superiority over us, to attain for ourselves as a measure of precaution and for the sake of safety such a position over others. For nature, indeed, wanted to use the idea of such rivalry (which in itself does not exclude mutual love) only as a spur to culture.[4] Hence the vices which are grafted upon this inclination might be their termed vices of *culture*;[4] in highest degree of malignancy, as, for example, in *envy, ingratitude, spitefulness*, etc. (where they are simply the idea of a maximum of evil going beyond what is human), they can be called the *diabolical vices*.

3. The predisposition to *personality* is the capacity for respect

---

[1] [*Rohigkeit*]

[2] [The two English words translate *Völlerei*.]

[3] [Reading *Anlage* for *Anlagen*.]

[4] [*Kultur*. Cf. below, p. 29, where these vices are referred to as vices of culture and civilization (*Kultur und Zivilisierung*).]

for the moral law as *in itself a sufficient incentive of the will*^{w}. This capacity for simple respect for the moral law within us would thus be moral feeling, which in and through itself does not constitute an end of the natural predisposition except so far as it is the motivating force of the will.^{w} Since this is possible only when the free will^w incorporates such moral feeling into its maxim, the property of such a will^w is good character. The latter, like every character of the free will^w, is something which can only be acquired; its possibility, however, demands the presence in our nature of a predisposition on which it is absolutely impossible to graft anything evil. We cannot rightly call the idea of the moral law, with the respect which is inseparable from it, *a predisposition* to *personality;* it is personality itself (the idea of humanity considered quite intellectually). But the subjective ground for the adoption into our maxims of this respect as a motivating force seems to be an adjunct to our personality, and thus to deserve the name of a predisposition to its furtherance.

If we consider the three predispositions named, in terms of the conditions of their possibility, we find that the first requires no reason, the second is based on practical reason, but a reason thereby subservient to other incentives, while the third alone is rooted in reason which is practical of itself, that is, reason which dictates laws unconditionally. All of these predispositions are not only *good* in negative fashion (in that they do not contradict the moral law); they are also predispositions *toward good* (they enjoin the observance of the law). They are *original*, for they are bound up with the possibility of human nature. Man can indeed use the first two contrary to their ends, but he can extirpate none of them. By the predispositions of a being we understand not only its constituent elements which are necessary to it, but also the forms of their combination, by which the being is what it is. They are *original* if they are involved necessarily in the possibility of such a being, but *contingent* if it is possible for the being to exist of itself without them. Finally, let it be noted that here we treat only those predispositions which have immediate reference to the faculty of desire and the exercise of the will^w.

II. *Concerning the Propensity to Evil in Human Nature*

By *propensity* (*propensio*) I understand the subjective ground of the possibility of an inclination (habitual craving, *concupis-*

centia)[1] so far as mankind in general is liable to it.† A propensity is distinguished from a predisposition by the fact that although it can indeed be innate, it *ought* not to be represented merely thus; for it can also be regarded as having been *acquired* (if it is good), or *brought* by man *upon himself* (if it is evil). Here, however, we are speaking only of the propensity to genuine, that is, moral evil; for since such evil is possible only as a determination of the free will,^{w} and since the will^{w}can be appraised as good or evil only by means of its maxims, this propensity to evil must consist in the subjective ground of the possibility of the deviation of the maxims from the moral law. If, then, this propensity can be considered as belonging universally to mankind (and hence as part of the character of the race), it may be called a *natural* propensity in man to evil. We may add further that the will's^{w}capacity or incapacity, arising from this natural propensity, to adopt or not to adopt the moral law into its maxim, may be called *a good or an evil heart.*

In this capacity for evil there can be distinguished three distinct degrees. First, there is the weakness of the human heart in the general observance of adopted maxims, or in other words, the *frailty* of human nature; second, the propensity for mixing unmoral with moral motivating causes (even when it is done with good intent and under maxims of the good), that is, *impurity;*[3] third, the propensity to adopt evil maxims, that is, the *wickedness* of human nature or of the human heart.

First: the frailty (*fragilitas*) of human nature is expressed even

---

† A *propensity* (*Hang*) is really only the *predisposition*[2] to crave a delight which, when once experienced, arouses in the subject an *inclination* to it. Thus all savage peoples have a propensity for intoxicants; for though many of them are wholly ignorant of intoxication and in consequence have absolutely no craving for an intoxicant, let them but once sample it and there is aroused in them an almost inextinguishable craving for it.

Between inclination, which presupposes acquaintance with the object of desire, and propensity there still is *instinct*, which is a felt want to do or to enjoy something of which one has as yet no conception (such as the constructive impulse in animals, or the sexual impulse). Beyond inclination there is finally a further stage in the faculty of desire, *passion* (not *emotion*, for this has to do with the feeling of pleasure and pain), which is an inclination that excludes the mastery over oneself.

[1] [*Concupiscentia* added in the Second Edition.]
[2] [*Predisposition;* not the usual German word *Anlage*, which heretofore we have translated as *predisposition*.]
[3] [*Unlauterkeit, i.e.*, lack of single-mindedness, integrity.]

in the complaint of an Apostle, "What I would, that I do not!"[1] In other words, I adopt the good (the law) into the maxim of my will[w], but this good, which objectively, in its ideal conception[2] (*in thesi*), is an irresistible incentive, is subjectively (*in hypothesi*), when the maxim is to be followed, the weaker (in comparison with inclination).

Second: the impurity (*impuritas, improbitas*) of the human heart consists in this, that although the maxim is indeed good in respect of its object (the intended observance of the law) and perhaps even strong enough for practice, it is yet not purely moral; that is, it has not, as it should have, adopted the law *alone* as its *all-sufficient* incentive: instead, it usually (perhaps, every time) stands in need of other incentives beyond this, in determining the will[w] to do what duty demands; in other words, actions called for by duty are done not purely for duty's sake.

Third: the wickedness (*vitiositas, pravitas*) or, if you like, the *corruption* (*corruptio*) of the human heart is the propensity of the will[w] to maxims which neglect the incentives springing from the moral law in favor of others which are not moral. It may also be called the *perversity* (*perversitas*) of the human heart, for it reverses the ethical order [of priority] among the incentives of a *free* will[w]; and although conduct which is lawfully good (*i.e.*, legal) may be found with it, yet the cast of mind is thereby corrupted at its root (so far as the moral disposition is concerned), and the man is hence designated as evil.

It will be remarked that this propensity to evil is here ascribed (as regards conduct) to men in general, even to the best of them; this must be the case if it is to be proved that the propensity to evil in mankind is universal, or, what here comes to the same thing, that it is woven into human nature.

There is no difference, however, as regards conformity of conduct to the moral law, between a man of good morals (*bene moratus*) and a morally good man (*moraliter bonus*)—at least there ought to be no difference, save that the conduct of the one has not always, perhaps has never, the law as its sole and supreme incentive while the conduct of the other has it *always*. Of the former it can be said: He obeys the law according to the *letter* (that is, his conduct conforms to what the law commands); but of the second: He

[1] [Cf.Romans, VII, 15]
[2] [*in der Idee*]

obeys the law according to the *spirit* (the spirit of the moral law consisting in this, that the law is sufficient in itself as an incentive). *Whatever is not of this faith is sin*[1] (as regards cast of mind). For when incentives other than the law itself (such as ambition, self-love in general, yes, even a kindly instinct such as sympathy) are necessary to determine the will^w to conduct *conformable to the law*, it is merely accidental that these causes coincide with the law, for they could equally well incite its violation. The maxim, then, in terms of whose goodness all moral worth of the individual must be appraised, is thus contrary to the law, and the man, despite all his good deeds, is nevertheless evil.

The following explanation is also necessary in order to define the concept of this propensity. Every propensity is either physical, *i.e.*, pertaining to the will^w of man as a natural being, or moral, *i.e.*, pertaining to his will^w as a moral being. In the first sense there is no propensity to moral evil, for such a propensity must spring from freedom; and a physical propensity (grounded in sensuous[2] impulses) towards any use of freedom whatsoever—whether for good or bad—is a contradiction. Hence a propensity to evil can inhere only in the moral capacity of the will^w. But nothing is morally evil (*i.e.*, capable of being imputed) but that which is our own *act*. On the other hand, by the concept of a propensity we understand a subjective determining ground of the will^w which *precedes all acts* and which, therefore, is itself not an act. Hence in the concept of a simple propensity to evil there would be a contradiction were it not possible to take the word "act" in two meanings, both of which are reconcilable with the concept of freedom. The term "act" can apply in general to that exercise of freedom whereby the supreme maxim (in harmony with the law or contrary to it) it is adopted by the will^w, but also to the exercise of freedom whereby the actions themselves (considered materially, *i.e.*, with reference to the objects of volition^w) are performed in accordance with that maxim. The propensity to evil, then, is an act in the first sense (*peccatum originarium*), and at the same time the formal ground of all unlawful conduct in the second sense, which latter, considered materially, violates the law and is termed vice (*peccatum derivatum*); and the first offense remains, even though the second (from incentives which do not subsist in the law itself) may be repeatedly avoided. The former is intelligible[1]

[1] [Cf. *Romans* XIV, 23]
[2] [*sinnliche, i.e.*, pertaining to sense]

action, cognizable by means of pure reason alone, apart from every temporal condition; the latter is sensible[1] action, empirical, given in time (*factum phænomenon*). The former, particularly when compared with the latter, is entitled a simple propensity and innate, [first] because it cannot be eradicated (since for such eradication the highest maxim would have to be that of the good— whereas in this propensity it already has been postulated as evil), but chiefly because we can no more assign a further cause for the corruption in us by evil of just this highest maxim, although this is our own action, than we can assign a cause for any fundamental attribute belonging to our nature. Now it can be understood, from what has just been said, why it was that in this section we sought, at the very first, the three sources of the morally evil solely in what, according to laws of freedom, touches the ultimate ground of the adoption or the observance of our maxims, and not in what touches sensibility[2] (regarded as receptivity).

III. Man is Evil by Nature

Vitiis nemo sine nascitur.—Horace[3]

In view of what has been said above, the proposition, Man is *evil*, can mean only, He is conscious of the moral law but has nevertheless adopted into his maxim the (occasional) deviation therefrom. He is evil *by nature*, means but this, that evil can be predicated of man as a species; not that such a quality can be inferred from the concept of his species (that is, of man in general) —for then it would be necessary; but rather that from what we know of man through experience we cannot judge otherwise of him, or, that we may presuppose evil to be subjectively necessary to every man, even to the best. Now this propensity must itself be considered as morally evil, yet not as a natural predisposition but rather as something that can be imputed to man, and consequently it must consist in maxims of the will[w] which are contrary to the law. Further, for the sake of freedom, these maxims must in themselves be considered contingent, a circumstance which, on the other hand, will not tally with the universality of this evil *unless* the ultimate subjective ground of all maxims somehow or

---

[1] [*intelligible* and *sensible*]
[2] [*Sinnlichkeit*]
[3] [*Satires*, I, iii, 68: "No one is born free from vices."]

other is entwined with and, as it were, rooted in humanity itself. Hence we can call this a natural propensity to evil, and as we must, after all, ever hold man himself responsible for it, we can further call it a *radical* innate *evil* in human nature (yet none the less brought upon us by ourselves).

That such a corrupt[1] propensity must indeed be rooted in man need not be formally proved in view of the multitude of crying examples which experience *of the actions* of men puts before our eyes. If we wish to draw our examples from that state in which various philosophers hoped preeminently to discover the natural goodliness of human nature, namely, from the so-called *state of nature*, we need but compare with this hypothesis the scenes of unprovoked cruelty in the murder-dramas enacted in Tofoa, New Zealand, and in the Navigator Islands, and the unending cruelty (of which Captain Hearne[2] tells) in the wide wastes of northwestern America, cruelty from which, indeed, not a soul reaps the smallest benefit;* and we have vices of barbarity[3] more than sufficient to draw us from such an opinion. If, however, we incline to the opinion that human nature can better be known in the civilized state (in which its predispositions can more completely develop), we must listen to a long melancholy litany of indictments against humanity: of secret falsity even in the closest friendship, so that a limit upon trust in the mutual confidences of even the best friends is reckoned a universal maxim of prudence in intercourse; of a propensity to hate him to whom one is indebted, for which

---

* Thus the war ceaselessly waged between the Arathapescaw Indians and the Dog Rib Indians has no other object than mere slaughter. Bravery in war is, in the opinion of savages, the highest virtue. Even in a civilized state it is an object of admiration and a basis for the special regard commanded by that profession in which bravery is the sole merit; and this is not without rational cause. For that man should be able to possess a thing (*i.e.*, honor) and make it an end to be valued more than life itself, and because of it renounce all self-interest, surely bespeaks a certain nobility in his natural disposition. Yet we recognize in the complacency with which victors boast their mighty deeds (massacres, butchery without quarter, and the like) that it is merely their own superiority and the destruction they can wreak, without any other objective, in which they really take satisfaction.

[1] [*verderbter;* misprinted *verdorbener* in the First Edition.]
[2] [Samuel Hearne (1745–1792), an English traveller, in the service of the Hudson Bay Company. His *Account of a Journey from Prince of Wales's Fort in Hudson's Bay to the Northwest* was published in 1795. Kant evidently had read the brief account of Hearne's travels in Douglas's Introduction to *Cook's Third Voyage*, London, 1784.]
[3] [*Rohigkeit*]

a benefactor must always be prepared; of a hearty well-wishing which yet allows of the remark that "in the misfortunes of our best friends there is something which is not altogether displeasing to us";[1] and of many other vices still concealed under the appearance of virtue, to say nothing of the vices of those who do not conceal them, for we are content to call him good who is *a man bad in a way common to all;* and we shall have enough of the vices of *culture* and civilization (which are the most offensive of all) to make us rather turn away our eyes from the conduct of men lest we ourselves contract another vice, misanthropy. But if we are not yet content, we need but contemplate a state which is compounded in strange fashion of both the others, that is, the international situation,[2] where civilized nations stand towards each other in the relation obtaining in the barbarous state of nature (a state of continuous readiness for war), a state, moreover, from which they have taken fixedly into their heads never to depart. We then become aware of the fundamental principles of the great societies called *states*†—principles which flatly contradict their public pronouncements but can never be laid aside, and which no philosopher has yet been able to bring into agreement with morality. Nor (sad to say) has any philosopher been able to propose

† When we survey the history of these, merely as the phenomenon of the inner predispositions of mankind which are for the most part concealed from us, we become aware of a certain machine-like movement of nature toward ends which are nature's own rather than those of the nations. Each separate state, so long as it has a neighboring state which it dares hope to conquer, strives to aggrandize itself through such a conquest, and thus to attain a world-monarchy, a polity wherein all freedom, and with it (as a consequence) virtue, taste, and learning, would necessarily expire. Yet this monster (in which laws gradually lose their force), after it has swallowed all its neighbors, finally dissolves of itself, and through rebellion and disunion breaks up into many smaller states. These, instead of striving toward a league of nations (a republic of federated free nations), begin the same game over again, each for itself, so that war (that scourge of humankind) may not be allowed to cease. Although indeed war is not so incurably evil as that tomb, a universal autocracy (or even as a confederacy which exists to hasten the weakening of a despotism in any single state), yet, as one of the ancients put it, war creates more evil men than it destroys.[3]

[1] [La Rochefoucauld, *Maximes*, No. 583: "Dans l'adversité de nos meilleurs amis, nous trouvons toujours quelque chose qui ne nous déplaît pas."]

[2] [*den aüszern Völkerzustand*]

[3] ["This is also cited by Kant in the first Appendix to Section II of *Zum ewigen Frieden*. There the quotation is termed 'a saying of that Greek'; unfortunately, its source has not been found." (Note in Berlin Edition.)]

better principles which at the same time can be brought into harmony with human nature. The result is that the *philosophical millenium*, which hopes for a state of perpetual peace based on a league of peoples, a world-republic, even as the *theological millenium*, which tarries for the completed moral improvement of the entire human race, is universally ridiculed as a wild fantasy.

Now the ground of this evil (1) cannot be placed, as is so commonly done, in man's *sensuous nature*[1] and the natural inclinations arising therefrom. For not only are these not directly related to evil (rather do they afford the occasion for what the moral disposition in its power can manifest, namely, virtue); we must not even be considered responsible for their existence (we cannot be, for since they are implanted in us we are not their authors). We are accountable, however, for the propensity to evil, which, as it affects the morality of the subject, is to be found in him as a free-acting being and for which it must be possible to hold him accountable as the offender—this, too, despite the fact that this propensity is so deeply rooted in the will[w] that we are forced to say that it is to be found in man by nature. Neither can the ground of this evil (2) be placed in a *corruption* of the morally legislative reason—as if reason could destroy the authority of the very law which is its own, or deny the obligation arising therefrom; this is absolutely impossible. To conceive of oneself as a freely acting being and yet as exempt from the law which is appropriate to such a being (the moral law) would be tantamount to conceiving a cause operating without any laws whatsoever (for determination according to natural laws is excluded by the fact of freedom); this is a self-contradiction. In seeking, therefore, a ground of the morally-evil in man, [we find that] *sensuous nature* comprises too little, for when the incentives which can spring from freedom are taken away, man is reduced to a merely *animal* being. On the other hand, a reason exempt from the moral law, a *malignant reason* as it were (a thoroughly evil will[2]), comprises too much, for thereby opposition to the law would itself be set up as an incentive (since in the absence of all incentives the will[w] cannot be determined), and thus the subject would be made a *devilish* being. Neither of these designations is applicable to man.

But even if the existence of this propensity to evil in human nature can be demonstrated by experiential proofs of the real

[1] [*Sinnlichkeit*]

[2] [*Wille*]

opposition, in time, of man's will^w to the law, such proofs do not teach us the essential character of that propensity or the ground of this opposition. Rather, because this character concerns a relation of the will^w, which is free (and the concept of which is therefore not empirical), to the moral law as an incentive (the concept of which, likewise, is purely intellectual), it must be apprehended *a priori* through the concept of evil, so far as evil is possible under the laws of freedom (of obligation and accountability). This concept may be developed in the following manner.

Man (even the most wicked) does not, under any maxim whatsoever, repudiate the moral law in the manner of a rebel (renouncing obedience to it). The law, rather, forces itself upon him irresistibly by virtue of his moral predisposition; and were no other incentive working in opposition, he would adopt the law into his supreme maxim as the sufficient determining ground of his will^w; that is, he would be morally good. But by virtue of an equally innocent natural predisposition he depends upon the incentives of his sensuous nature and adopts them also (in accordance with the subjective principle of self-love) into his maxim. If he took the latter into his maxim *as in themseves wholly adequate* to the determination of the will^w, without troubling himself about the moral law (which, after all, he does have in him), he would be morally evil. Now, since he naturally adopts *both* into his maxim, and since, further, he would find either, if it were alone, adequate in itself for the determining of the will,[1] it follows that if the difference between the maxims amounted merely to the difference between the two incentives (the content of the maxims), that is, if it were merely a question as to whether the law or the sensuous impulse were to furnish the incentive, man would be at once good and evil: this, however, (as we saw in the Introduction) is a contradiction. Hence the distinction between a good man and one who is evil cannot lie in the difference between the incentives which they adopt into their maxim (not in the content of the maxim), but rather must depend upon *subordination* (the form of the maxim), *i.e., which of the two incentives he makes the condition of the other.* Consequently man (even the best) is evil only in that he reverses the moral order of the incentives when he adopts them into his maxim. He adopts, indeed, the moral law along with the law of self-love; yet when he becomes aware that they cannot remain on a par with each other but that one must be subordinated

---

[1] [Our phrase "determining of the will" translates *Willensbestimmung*.]

to the other as its supreme condition, he makes the incentive of self-love and its inclinations the condition of obedience to the moral law; whereas, on the contrary, the latter, as the *supreme condition* of the satisfaction of the former, ought to have been adopted into the universal maxim of the will^w as the sole incentive.

Yet, even with this reversal of the ethical order of the incentives in and through his maxim, a man's actions still may prove to be as much in conformity to the law as if they sprang from true basic principles. This happens when reason employs the unity of the maxims in general, a unity which is inherent in the moral law, merely to bestow upon the incentives of inclination, under the name of *happiness*, a unity of maxims which otherwise they cannot have. (For example, truthfulness, if adopted as a basic principle, delivers us from the anxiety of making our lies agree with one another and of not being entangled by their serpent coils.) The empirical character is then good, but the intelligible character is still evil.

Now if a propensity to this[1] does lie in human nature, there is in man a natural propensity to evil; and since this very propensity must in the end be sought in a will^w which is free, and can therefore be imputed, it is morally evil. This evil is *radical*, because it corrupts the ground of all maxims; it is, moreover, as a natural propensity, *inextirpable* by human powers, since extirpation could occur only through good maxims, and cannot take place when the ultimate subjective ground of all maxims is postulated as corrupt; yet at the same time it must be possible to *overcome* it, since it is found in man, a being whose actions are free.

We are not, then, to call the depravity of human nature *wickedness*[2] taking the word in its strict sense as a disposition (the subjective *principle* of the maxims) to adopt evil[3] *as evil* into our maxim as our incentives (for that is diabolical); we should rather term it the *perversity* of the heart, which, then, because of what follows from it, is also called an *evil heart*. Such a heart may coexist with a will which in general[4] is good: it arises from the frailty of human nature, the lack of sufficient strength to follow out the principles it has chosen for itself, joined with its impurity, the failure to distinguish the incentives (even of well-intentioned ac-

---

[1] [*i.e.*, to the inversion of the ethical order of the incentives.]
[2] [*Bosheit*]
[3] [*Böse*]
[4] [*im Allegemeinen*]

tions) from each other by the gauge of morality; and so at last, if the extreme is reached, [it results] from looking only to the squaring of these actions with the law and not to the derivation of them from the law as the sole motivating spring. Now even though there does not always follow therefrom an unlawful act and a propensity thereto, nämely, *vice*, yet the mode of thought which sets down the absence of such vice as being conformity of the *disposition* to the law of duty (as being virtue)—since in this case no attention whatever is paid to the motivating forces in the maxim but only to the observance of the letter of the law—itself deserves to be called a radical perversity in the human heart.

This *innate* guilt (*reatus*), which is so denominated because it may be discerned in man as early as the first manifestations of the exercise of freedom, but which, none the less, must have originated in freedom and hence can be imputed,—this guilt may be judged in its first two stages (those of frailty and impurity) to be unintentional guilt (*culpa*), but in the third to be deliberate guilt (*dolus*) and to display in its character a certain *insidiousness*[1] of the human heart (*dolus malus*), which deceives itself in regard to its own good and evil dispositions, and, if only its conduct has not evil consequences—which it might well have, with such maxims—does not trouble itself about its disposition but rather considers itself justified before the law. Thence arises the peace of conscience of so many men (conscientious in their own esteem) when, in the course of conduct concerning which they did not take the law into their counsel, or at least in which the law was not the supreme consideration, they merely elude evil consequences by good fortune. They may even picture themselves as meritorious, feeling themselves guilty of no such offenses as they see others burdened with; nor do they ever inquire whether good luck should not have the credit, or whether by reason of the cast of mind which they could discover, if they only would, in their own inmost nature, they would not have practised similar vices, had not inability, temperament, training, and circumstances of time and place which serve to tempt one (matters which are not imputable), kept them out of the way of those vices. This dishonesty, by which we humbug ourselves and which thwarts the establishing of a true moral disposition in us, extends itself outwardly also to falsehood and deception of others. If this is not to be termed wickedness, it at least deserves the name of worthlessness, and is an element in the radi-

[1] [*Tücke*]

cal evil of human nature, which (inasmuch as it puts out of tune the moral capacity to judge what a man is to be taken for, and renders wholly uncertain both internal and external attribution of responsibility) constitutes the foul taint in our race. So long as we do not eradicate it, it prevents the seed of goodness from developing as it otherwise would.

A member of the British Parliament[1] once exclaimed, in the heat of debate, "Every man has his price, for which he sells himself." If this is true (a question to which each must make his own answer), if there is no virtue for which some temptation cannot be found capable of overthrowing it, and if whether the good or evil spirit wins us over to his party depends merely on which bids the most and pays us most promptly, then certainly it holds true of men universally,[2] as the apostle said:[3] "They are all under sin,— there is none righteous (in the spirit of the law), no, not one."*

IV. Concerning the Origin of Evil in Human Nature

An origin (a first origin) is the derivation of an effect from its first cause, that is, from that cause which is not in turn the effect of another cause of the same kind. It can be considered either as an *origin in reason* or as an *origin in time*. In the former sense, regard is had only to the *existence* of the effect; in the latter, to its

---

* The special proof of this sentence of condemnation by morally judging reason is to be found in the preceding section rather than in this one, which contains only the confirmation of it by experience. Experience, however, never can reveal the root of evil in the supreme maxim of the free will[w] relating to the law, a maxim which, as *intelligible act,* precedes all experience. Hence from the singleness of the supreme maxim, together with the singleness of the law to which it relates itself, we can also understand why, for the pure intellectual judgment of mankind, the rule of excluding a mean between good and evil must remain fundamental; yet for the empirical judgment based on *sensible conduct*[4] (actual performance and neglect) the rule may be laid down that there *is* a mean between these extremes—on the one hand a negative mean of indifference prior to all education, on the other hand a positive, a mixture, partly good and partly evil. However, this latter is merely a judgment upon the morality of mankind as appearance, and must give place to the former in a final judgment.

[1] [Sir Robert Walpole. What he said, however, was not so universal: "All those men" (referring to certain "patriots") "have their price."]
[2] [*allgemein*]
[3] [Cf. Romans III, 9–10]
[4] [*sinnlicher That*]

occurrence, and hence it is related as an event to its *first cause in time*. If an effect is referred to a cause to which it is bound under the laws of freedom, as is true in the case of moral evil, then the determination of the will^w to the production of this effect is conceived of as bound up with its determining ground not in time but merely in rational representation; such an effect cannot be derived from any *preceding* state whatsoever. Yet derivation of this sort is always necessary when an evil action, as an *event* in the world, is referred to its natural cause. To seek the temporal origin of free acts as such (as though they were natural effects) is thus a contradiction. Hence it is also a contradiction to seek the temporal origin of man's moral character,[1] so far as it is considered as contingent, since this character signifies the ground of the *exercise* of freedom; this ground (like the determining ground of the free will^w generally) must be sought in purely rational representations.

However the origin of moral evil in man is constituted, surely of all the explanations of the spread and propagation of this evil through all members and generations of our race, the most inept is that which describes it as descending to us as an *inheritance* from our first parents; for one can say of moral evil precisely what the poet said of good:[2] *genus et proavos, et* quae non fecimus ipsi, *vix ea nostra puto.** Yet we should note that, in our search for the origin of this evil, we do not deal first of all with the propensity thereto (as *peccatum in potentia*); rather do we direct our attention to the actual evil of given actions with respect to its inner possibility—to what must take place within the will^w if evil is to be performed.

---

* The three so-called "higher faculties" (in the universities) would explain this transmission of evil each in terms of its own specialty, as *inherited disease, inherited debt,* or *inherited sin.* (1) The *faculty of medicine* would represent this hereditary evil somewhat as it represents the tapeworm, concerning which several naturalists actually believe that, since no specimens have been met with anywhere but in us, not even (of this particular type) in other animals, it must have existed in our first parents. (2) The *faculty of law* would regard this evil as the legitimate consequence of succeeding to the *patrimony* bequeathed us by our first parents, [an inheritance] encumbered, however, with heavy forfeitures (for to be born is no other than to inherit the use of

[1] [*Beschaffenheit*]
[2] [Ovid, *Metamorphoses*, XIII, 140–141: "Race and ancestors, and those things *which we ourselves have not made,* I scarcely account our own."]

In the search for the rational origin of evil actions, every such action must be regarded as though the individual had fallen into it directly from a state of innocence. For whatever his previous deportment may have been, whatever natural causes may have been influencing him, and whether these causes were to be found within him or outside him, his action is yet free and determined by none of these causes; hence it can and must always be judged as an *original* use of his will[w]. He should have refrained from that action, whatever his temporal circumstances and entanglements; for through no cause in the world can he cease to be a freely acting being. Rightly is it said that to a man's account are set down the *consequences* arising from his former free acts which were contrary to the law; but this merely amounts to saying that man need not involve himself in the evasion of seeking to establish whether or not these consequences are free, since there exists in the admittedly free action, which was their cause, ground sufficient for holding him accountable. However evil a man has been up to the very moment of an impending free act (so that evil has actually become custom or second nature) it was not only his duty to have been better [in the past], it is *now* still his duty to better himself. To do so must be within his power, and if he does not do so, he is susceptible of, and subjected to, imputability in the very moment of that action, just as much as though, endowed with a predisposition to good (which is inseparable from freedom), he had stepped out of a state of innocence into evil. Hence we cannot inquire into the temporal origin of this deed, but solely into its rational origin, if we are thereby to determine and, wherever possible, to elucidate the propensity, if it exists, *i.e.*, the general subjective ground of the adoption of transgression into our maxim.

The foregoing agrees well with that manner of presentation which the Scriptures use, whereby the origin of evil in the human

---

earthly goods so far as they are necessary to our continued existence). Thus we must fulfil payment (atone) and at the end still be dispossessed (by death) of the property. How just is legal justice! (3) The *theological faculty* would regard this evil as the personal participation by our first parents in the *fall* of a condemned rebel, maintaining either that we ourselves then participated (although now unconscious of having done so), or that even now, born under the rule of the rebel (as prince of this world), we prefer his favors to the supreme command of the heavenly Ruler, and do not possess enough faith to free ourselves; wherefore we must also eventually share his doom.

race is depicted as having a [temporal] *beginning*, this beginning being presented in a narrative, wherein what in its essence must be considered as primary (without regard to the element of time) appears as coming first in time. According to this account, evil does not start from a propensity thereto as its underlying basis, for otherwise the beginning of evil would not have its source in freedom; rather does it start from *sin* (by which is meant the transgressing of the moral law as a *divine command*). The state of man prior to all propensity to evil is called the state of *innocence*. The moral law became known to mankind, as it must to any being not pure but tempted by desires, in the form of a *prohibition* (Genesis II, 16–17). Now instead of straightway following this law as an adequate incentive (the only incentive which is unconditionally good and regarding which there is no further doubt), man looked about for other incentives (Genesis III, 6) such as can be good only conditionally (namely, so far as they involve no infringement of the law). He then made it his maxim—if one thinks of his action as consciously springing from freedom—to follow the law of duty, not as duty, but, if need be, with regard to other aims. Thereupon he began to call in question the severity of the commandment which excludes the influence of all other incentives; then by sophistry he reduced* obedience to the law to the merely conditional character of a means (subject to the principle of self-love); and finally he adopted into his maxim of conduct the ascendancy of the sensuous impulse over the incentive which springs from the law—and thus occurred sin (Genesis III, 6). *Mutato nomine de te fabula narratur*.[1] From all this it is clear that we daily act in the same way, and that therefore "in Adam all have sinned"[2] and still sin; except that in us there is presupposed an innate propensity to transgression, whereas in the first man, from the point

* All homage paid to the moral law is an act of hypocrisy, if, in one's maxim, ascendancy is not at the same time granted to the law as an incentive sufficient in itself and higher than all other determining grounds of the will[w]. The propensity to do this is inward deceit, *i.e.*, a tendency to deceive oneself in the interpretation of the moral law, to its detriment (Genesis III, 5). Accordingly, the Bible (the Christian portion of it) denominates the author of evil (who is within us) as the liar from the beginning, and thus characterizes man with respect to what seems to be the chief ground of evil in him.

[1] [Horace, *Satires*, I, 1. "Change but the name, of you the tale is told." (Conington)]
[2] [Cf. Romans V, 12. "The ἐφ' ᾧ πάντες ἥμαρτον of the Greek text ($= ἐπὶ\ τούτῳ\ ὅτι\ κ.\ τ.\ λ. =$ 'on this ground, that . . ') is rendered in the Latin translation (the Vulgate) by *in quo omnes peccaverunt*; and this *in quo* was in early times taken, as a

of view of time, there is presupposed no such propensity but rather innocence; hence transgression on his part is called a *fall into sin;* but with us sin is represented as resulting from an already innate wickedness in our nature. This propensity, however, signifies no more than this, that if we wish to address ourselves to the explanation of evil in terms of its *beginning in time,* we must search for the causes of each deliberate transgression in a previous period of our lives, far back to that period wherein the use of reason had not yet developed, and thus back to a propensity to evil (as a natural ground) which is therefore called innate—the source of evil. But to trace the causes of evil in the instance of the first man, who is depicted as already in full command of the use of his reason, is neither necessary nor feasible, since otherwise this basis (the evil propensity) would have had to be created in him; therefore his sin is set forth as engendered directly from innocence. We must not, however, look for an origin in time of a moral character[1] for which we are to be held responsible; though to do so is inevitable if we wish to *explain* the contingent existence of this character (and perhaps it is for this reason that Scripture, in conformity with this weakness of ours, has thus pictured the temporal origin of evil).

But the rational origin of this perversion of our will[w] whereby it makes lower incentives supreme among its maxims, that is, of the propensity to evil, remains inscrutable to us, because this propensity itself must be set down to our account and because, as a result, that ultimate ground of all maxims would in turn involve the adoption of an evil maxim [as its basis]. Evil could have sprung only from the morally-evil (not from mere limitations in our nature); and yet the original predisposition (which no one other than man himself could have corrupted, if he is to be held responsible for this corruption) is a predisposition to good; there is then for us no conceivable ground from which the moral evil in us could originally have come. This inconceivability, together with a more accurate specification[2] of the wickedness of our race, the Bible

---

masculine, to mean 'in Adam' (particularly by Augustine, in the interest of his doctrine of inherited sin: in Adam omnes tunc peccaverunt, quando in eius natura illa insita vi, qua eos gignere poterat, adhuc omnes ille unus fuerunt. *De pecc. mer. et rem.,* III, 7, 14). This interpretation continued to be dominant in the older Protestant exegesis. Indeed, even today critical interpreters defend the notion that 'in Adam' may be supplied as really in the thought of Paul." (Note in Berlin Edition.)]

[1] [*Beschaffenheit*]
[2] [*Bestimmung*]

expresses in the historical narrative as follows.* It finds a place for evil at the creation of the world, yet not in man, but in a *spirit* of an originally loftier destiny.[1] Thus is the *first* beginning of all evil represented as inconceivable by us (for whence came evil to that spirit?); but man is represented as having fallen into evil only *through seduction*, and hence as being *not basically* corrupt (even as regards his original predisposition to good) but rather as still capable of an improvement, in contrast to a seducing *spirit*, that is, a being for whom temptation of the flesh cannot be accounted as an alleviation of guilt. For man, therefore, who despite a corrupted heart yet possesses a good will,[2] there remains hope of a return to the good from which he has strayed.

* What is written here must not be read as though intended for Scriptural exegesis, which lies beyond the limits of the domain of bare reason. It is possible to explain how an historical account is to be put to a moral use without deciding whether this is the intention of the author or merely our interpretation, provided this meaning is true in itself, apart from all historical proof, and is moreover the only one whereby we can derive something conducive to our betterment from a passage which otherwise would be only an unfruitful addition to our historical knowledge. We must not quarrel unnecessarily over a question or over its historical aspect, when, however it is understood, it in no way helps us to be better men, and when that which can afford such help is discovered without historical proof, and indeed must be apprehended without it. That historical knowledge which has no inner bearing valid for all men belongs to the class of *adiaphora*, which each man is free to hold as he finds edifying.

[1] [*Bestimmung*]

[2] [*Wille*]

GENERAL OBSERVATION[1]

Concerning the Restoration to its Power of the Original Predisposition to Good

Man *himself* must make or have made himself into whatever, in a moral sense, whether good or evil, he is or is to become. Either condition must be an effect of his free choice[w]; for otherwise he could not be held responsible for it and could therefore be *morally* neither good nor evil. When it is said, Man is created good, this can mean nothing more than: He is created *for good* and the original *predisposition* in man is good; not that, thereby, he is already actually good, but rather that he brings it about that he becomes good or evil, according to whether he adopts or does not adopt into his maxim the incentives which this predisposition carries with it ([an act] which must be left wholly to his own free choice). Granted that some supernatural cooperation may be necessary to his becoming good, or to his becoming better, yet, whether this cooperation consists merely in the abatement of hindrances or indeed in positive assistance, man must first make himself worthy to receive it, and must *lay hold* of this aid (which is no small matter)—that is, he must adopt this positive increase of power into his maxim, for only thus can good be imputed to him and he be known as a good man.

How it is possible for a naturally evil man to make himself a good man wholly surpasses our comprehension; for how can a bad tree bring forth good fruit? But since, by our previous acknowledgment, an originally good tree (good in predisposition) did bring forth evil fruit,* and since the lapse from good into evil (when one remembers that this originates in freedom) is no more comprehensible than the re-ascent from evil to good, the possibility of this last cannot be impugned. For despite the fall, the injunction that we *ought* to become better men resounds unabatedly in our souls; hence this must be within our power, even though what *we* are able to do is in itself inadequate and though we thereby only

---

* The tree, good in predisposition, is not yet good in actuality, for were it so, it could certainly not bring forth bad fruit. Only when a man has adopted into his maxim the incentive implanted in him of allegiance to the moral law is he to be called a good man (or the tree a thoroughly good tree).

[1] [In the First Edition this "General Observation" was designated as section V.]

40

render ourselves susceptible of higher, and for us inscrutable, assistance. It must indeed be presupposed throughout that a seed of goodness still remains in its entire purity, incapable of being extirpated or corrupted; and this seed certainly cannot be self-love* which, when taken as the principle of all our maxims, is the very source of evil.

* Words which can be taken in two entirely different meanings frequently delay for a long time the reaching of a conviction even on the clearest of grounds. Like *love* in general, so also can *self-love* be divided into love of *good will* and love of *good pleasure* (*benevolentiae et complacentiae*), and both (as is self-evident) must be rational. To adopt the former into one's maxim is natural (for who will not wish to have it always go well with him?); it is also rational so far as, on the one hand, that end is chosen which can accord with the greatest and most abiding welfare, and, on the other, the fittest means are chosen [to secure] each of the components of happiness. Here reason holds but the place of a handmaid to natural inclination; the maxim adopted on such grounds has absolutely no reference to morality. Let this maxim, however, be made the unconditional principle of the will^w, and it is the source of an incalculably great antagonism to morality.

A rational love of *good pleasure in oneself* can be understood in either of two ways: first, that we are well pleased with ourselves with respect to those maxims already mentioned which aim at the gratification of natural inclination (so far as that end is attained through following those maxims); and then it is identical with love as good will toward oneself: one takes pleasure in oneself, just as a merchant whose business speculations turn out well rejoices in his good discernment regarding the maxims he used in these transactions. In the second sense, the maxim of self-love as *unqualified good pleasure* in oneself (not dependent upon success or failure as consequences of conduct) would be the inner principle of such a contentment as is possible to us only on condition that our maxims are subordinated to the moral law. No man who is not indifferent to morality can take pleasure in himself, can indeed escape a bitter dissatisfaction with himself, when he is conscious of maxims which do not agree with the moral law in him. One might call that a *rational self-love* which prevents any adulteration of the incentives of the will^w by other causes of happiness such as come from the consequences of one's actions (under the name of a thereby attainable happiness). Since, however, this denotes an unconditional respect for the law, why needlessly render difficult the clear understanding of the principle by using the term *rational self-love,* when the use of the term *moral self-love* is restricted to this very condition, thus going around in a circle? (For only he can love himself in a moral fashion who knows that it is his maxim to make reverence for the law the highest incentive of his will^w.) By our *nature* as beings dependent upon circumstances of sensibility, we crave happiness first and unconditionally. Yet by this same nature of ours (if we wish in general so to term that which is innate). as beings endowed with reason and freedom, this happiness is far from being first. nor indeed is it unconditionally an object of our maxims; rather this object is

The restoration of the original predisposition to good in us is therefore not the acquiring of a *lost* incentive for good, for the incentive which consists in respect for the moral law we have never been able to lose, and were such a thing possible, we could never get it again. Hence the restoration is but the establishment of the *purity* of this law as the supreme ground of all our maxims, whereby it is not merely associated with other incentives, and certainly is not subordinated to any such (to inclinations) as its conditions, but instead must be adopted, in its entire purity, as an incentive *adequate* in itself for the determination of the will^w. Original goodness is the *holiness of maxims* in doing one's duty, merely for duty's sake. The man who adopts this purity into his maxim is indeed not yet holy by reason of this act (for there is a great gap between the maxim and the deed). Still he is upon the road of endless progress towards holiness. When the firm resolve to do one's duty has become habitual, it is also called the *virtue* of conformity to law; such conformity is virtue's *empirical character* (*virtus phænomenon*). Virtue here has as its steadfast maxim conduct *conforming to law;* and it matters not whence come the incentives required by the will^w for such conduct. Virtue in this sense is won *little by little* and, for some men, requires long practice (in observance of the law) during which the individual passes from a tendency to vice, through gradual reformation of his conduct and strengthening of his maxims, to an opposite tendency. For this to come to pass a *change of heart* is not necessary, but only a *change of practices*.[1] A man accounts himself virtuous if he feels that he is confirmed in maxims of obedience to his duty, though these do not spring from the highest ground of all maxims, namely, from duty itself. The immoderate person, for instance, turns to temperance for the sake of health, the liar to honesty for the sake of reputation, the unjust man to civic righteousness for the sake of peace or profit, and so on—all in conformity with the precious principle of happiness. But if a man is to become not merely *legally*, but *morally*, a good man (pleasing to God), that is, a man endowed with

---

worthiness to be happy, *i.e.*, the agreement of all our maxims with the moral law. That this is objectively the condition whereby alone the wish for happiness can square with legislative reason—therein consists the whole precept of morality; and the moral cast of mind consists in the disposition to harbor no wish except on these terms.

[1] [*Sitten*]

virtue in its intelligible character (*virtus noumenon*) and one who, knowing something to be his duty, requires no incentive other than this representation of duty itself, *this* cannot be brought about through gradual *reformation* so long as the basis of the maxims remains impure, but must be effected through a *revolution* in the man's disposition (a going over to the maxim of holiness of the disposition). He can become a new man only by a kind of rebirth, as it were a new creation (John III, 5; compare also Genesis I, 2), and a change of heart.

But if a man is corrupt in the very ground of his maxims, how can he possibly bring about this revolution by his own powers and of himself become a good man? Yet duty bids us do this, and duty demands nothing of us which we cannot do. There is no reconciliation possible here except by saying that man is under the necessity of, and is therefore capable of, a revolution in his cast of mind, but only of a gradual reform in his sensuous nature[1] (which places obstacles in the way of the former). That is, if a man reverses, by a single unchangeable decision, that highest ground of his maxims whereby he was an evil man (and thus puts on the new man), he is, so far as his principle and cast of mind are concerned, a subject susceptible of goodness, but only in continuous labor and growth is he a good man. That is, he can hope in the light of that purity of the principle which he has adopted as the supreme maxim of his will[w], and of its stability, to find himself upon the good (though strait) path of continual *progress* from bad to better. For Him who penetrates to the intelligible ground of the heart (the ground of all maxims of the will[w]) and for whom this unending progress is a unity, *i.e.*, for God, this amounts to his being actually a good man (pleasing to Him); and, thus viewed, this change can be regarded as a revolution. But in the judgment of men, who can appraise themselves and the strength of their maxims only by the ascendancy which they win over their sensuous nature[2] in time, this change must be regarded as nothing but an ever-during struggle toward the better, hence as a gradual reformation of the propensity to evil, the perverted cast of mind.

From this it follows that man's moral growth of necessity begins not in the improvement of his practices but rather in the transforming of his cast of mind and in the grounding of a character; though customarily man goes about the matter otherwise

[1] [*Sinnesart*]   [2] [*Sinnlichkeit*]

and fights against vices one by one, leaving undisturbed their common root. And yet even the man of greatest limitations is capable of being impressed by respect for an action conforming to duty—a respect which is the greater the more he isolates it, in thought, from other incentives which, through self-love, might influence the maxim of conduct. Even children are capable of detecting the smallest trace of admixture of improper incentives; for an action thus motivated at once loses, in their eyes, all moral worth. This predisposition to goodness is cultivated in no better way than by adducing the actual *example* of good men (of that which concerns their conformity to law) and by allowing young students of morals to judge the impurity of various maxims on the basis of the actual incentives motivating the conduct of these good men. The predisposition is thus gradually transformed into a cast of mind, and *duty*, for its own sake, begins to have a noticeable importance in their hearts. But to teach a pupil to *admire* virtuous actions, however great the sacrifice these may have entailed, is not in harmony with[1] preserving his feeling for moral goodness. For be a man never so virtuous, all the goodness he can ever perform is still his simple duty; and to do his duty is nothing more than to do what is in the common moral order and hence in no way deserving of wonder. Such wonder is rather a lowering of our feeling for duty, as if to act in obedience to it were something extraordinary and meritorious.

Yet there is one thing in our soul which we cannot cease from regarding with the highest wonder, when we view it properly, and for which admiration is not only legitimate but even exalting, and that is the original moral predisposition itself[2] in us. What is it in us (we can ask ourselves) whereby we, beings ever dependent upon nature through so many needs, are at the same time raised so far above these needs by the idea of an original predisposition (in us) that we count them all as nothing, and ourselves as unworthy of existence, if we cater to their satisfaction (though this alone can make life worth desiring) in opposition to the law—a law by virtue of which our reason commands us potently, yet without making either promises or threats? The force of this question every man, even one of the meanest capacity, must feel most deeply—every man, that is, who previously has been taught the holiness which inheres in the idea of duty but who has not yet advanced to an

---

[1] [*die rechte Stimmung*]   [2] [*überhaupt*]

inquiry into the concept of freedom, which first and foremost emerges from this law:* and the very incomprehensibility of this predisposition, which announces a divine origin, acts perforce upon the spirit even to the point of exaltation, and strengthens it for whatever sacrifice a man's respect for his duty may demand of him. More frequently to excite in man this feeling of the sublimity of his moral destiny is especially commendable as a method of awakening moral sentiments. For to do so works directly against the innate propensity to invert the incentives in the maxims of our will^w and toward the re-establishment in the human heart, in the form of an unconditioned respect for the law as the ultimate condition upon which maxims are to be adopted, of the original

* The concept of the freedom of the will^w does not precede the consciousness of the moral law in us but is deduced from the determinability of our will^w by this law as an unconditional command. Of this we can soon be convinced by asking ourselves whether we are certainly and immediately conscious of power to overcome, by a firm resolve, every incentive, however great, to transgression (*Phalaris licet imperet, ut sis falsus, et admoto dictet periuria tauro*).[1] Everyone will have to admit that he *does not know* whether, were such a situation to arise, he would not be shaken in his resolution. Still, duty commands him unconditionally: he *ought* to remain true to his resolve; and thence he rightly *concludes* that he must *be able* to do so, and that his will^w is therefore free. Those who fallaciously represent this inscrutable property as quite comprehensible create an illusion by means of the word *determinism* (the thesis that the will^w is determined by inner self-sufficient grounds) as though the difficulty consisted in reconciling this with freedom—which after all never occurs to one; whereas what we wish to understand, and never shall understand, is how *predeterminism*, according to which voluntary[2] actions, as events, have their determining grounds *in antecedent time* (which, with what happened in it, is no longer within our power), can be consistent with freedom, according to which the act as well as its opposite must be within the power of the subject at the moment of its taking place.

To[3] reconcile the concept of freedom with the idea of God as a *necessary* Being raises no difficulty at all: for freedom consists not in the contingency of the act (that it is determined by no grounds whatever), *i.e.*, not in indeterminism (that God must be equally capable of doing good or evil, if His actions are to be called free), but rather in absolute spontaneity. Such spontaneity is endangered only by predeterminism, where the determining ground of the act is *in antecedent time*, with the result that, the act being now no longer in *my* power but in the hands of nature, I am irresistibly determined; but since in God no temporal sequence is thinkable, this difficulty vanishes.

[1] [Juvenal, *Satires* VIII, 81–82: "though Phalaris himself should command you to be false and should bring up his bull and dictate perjuries."]
[2] [*willkürliche*]
[3] [This paragraph added in the Second Edition.]

moral order among the incentives, and so of the predisposition to good in all its purity.

But does not this restoration through one's own exertions directly contradict the postulate[1] of the innate corruption of man which unfits him for all good? Yes, to be sure, as far as the conceivability, *i.e.*, our *insight* into the possibility, of such a restoration is concerned. This is true of everything which is to be regarded as an event in time (as change), and to that extent as necessary under the laws of nature, while at the same time its opposite is to be represented as possible through freedom under moral laws. Yet the postulate in question is not opposed to the possibility of this restoration itself. For when the moral law commands that we *ought* now to be better men, it follows inevitably that we must *be able* to be better men. The postulate of innate evil is of no use whatever in moral *dogmatics*,[2] for the precepts of the latter carry with them the same duties and continue in identical force whether or not there is in us an innate tendency toward transgression. But in moral *discipline*[3] this postulate has more to say, though no more than this: that in the moral development of the predisposition to good implanted in us, we cannot start from an innocence natural to us but must begin with the assumption of a wickedness of the will[w] in adopting its maxims contrary to the original moral predisposition; and, since this propensity [to evil] is inextirpable, we must begin with the incessant counteraction against it. Since this leads only to a progress, endlessly continuing, from bad to better, it follows that the conversion of the disposition of a bad man into that of a good one is to be found in the change of the highest inward ground of the adoption of all his maxims, conformable to the moral law, so far as this new ground (the new heart) is now itself unchangeable. Man cannot attain naturally to assurance concerning such a revolution, however, either by immediate consciousness or through the evidence furnished by the life which he has hitherto led; for the deeps of the heart (the subjective first ground of his maxims) are inscrutable to him. Yet he must be able to *hope* through his *own* efforts to reach the road which leads thither, and which is pointed out to him by a fundamentally improved disposition, because he ought to become a good man and is to be adjudged *morally* good only by virtue of that which can be imputed to him as performed by himself.

[1] [*Satz*]   [2] [*Dogmatik*]   [3] [*Ascetik*]

Against this expectation of self-improvement, reason, which is by nature averse to the labor of moral reconstruction, now summons, under the pretext of natural incapacity, all sorts of ignoble religious ideas (among which belongs the false ascription to God Himself of the principle of happiness as the chief condition of His commandments). All religions, however, can be divided into those which are *endeavors to win favor* (mere worship) and *moral* religions, *i.e.*, religions of *good life-conduct*. In the first, man flatters himself by believing either that God can make him eternally happy (through remission of his sins) without his having *to become a better man*, or else, if this seems to him impossible, that *God* can certainly *make him a better man* without his having to do anything more than to *ask* for it. Yet since, in the eyes of a Being who sees all, to ask is no more than to *wish*, this would really involve doing nothing at all; for were improvement to be achieved simply by a wish, every man would be good. But in the moral religion (and of all the public religions which have ever existed, the Christian alone is moral) it is a basic principle that each must do as much as lies in his power to become a better man, and that only when he has not buried his inborn talent (Luke XIX, 12–16) but has made use of his original predisposition to good in order to become a better man, can he hope that what is not within his power will be supplied through cooperation from above. Nor is it absolutely necessary for a man to know wherein this cooperation consists; indeed, it is perhaps inevitable that, were the way it occurs revealed at a given time, different people would at some other time form different conceptions of it, and that with entire sincerity. Even here the principle is valid: "It is not essential, and hence not necessary, for every one to know what God does or has done for his salvation;" but it is essential to know *what man himself must do* in order to become worthy of this assistance.

This[1] General Observation is the first of four which are appended, one to each Book of this work, and which might bear the titles, (1) Works of Grace, (2) Miracles, (3) Mysteries, and (4) Means of Grace. These matters are, as it were, *parerga* to religion within the limits of pure reason; they do not belong within it but border upon it. Reason, conscious of her inability to satisfy her moral need, extends herself to high-flown[2] ideas capable of supply-

---

[1] [From here to the end of Book One added in the Second Edition.]
[2] [*überschwenglich*]

ing this lack, without, however, appropriating these ideas as an extension of her domain. Reason does not dispute the possibility or the reality of the objects of these ideas; she simply cannot adopt them into her maxims of thought and action. She even holds that, if in the inscrutable realm of the supernatural there is something more than she can explain to herself, which may yet be necessary as a complement to her moral insufficiency, this will be, even though unknown, available to her good will. Reason believes this with a faith which (with respect to the possibility of this supernatural complement) might be called *reflective*; for *dogmatic* faith, which proclaims itself as a form of *knowledge*, appears to her dishonest or presumptuous. To remove the difficulties, then, in the way of that which (for moral practice) stands firm in and for itself, is merely a by-work (*parergon*), when these difficulties have reference to transcendent questions. As regards the damage resulting from these *morally*-transcendent ideas, when we seek to introduce them into religion, the consequences, listed in the order of the four classes named above, are: (1) [corresponding] to imagined inward experience (works of grace), [the consequence is] *fanaticism;* (2) to alleged external experience (miracles), *superstition;* (3) to a supposed enlightening of the understanding with regard to the supernatural (mysteries), *illumination*, the illusion of the "adepts"; (4) to hazardous attempts to operate upon the supernatural (means of grace), *thaumaturgy*—sheer aberrations of a reason going beyond its proper limits and that too for a purpose fancied to be moral (pleasing to God).

But touching that which especially concerns this General Observation to Book One of the present treatise, the calling to our assistance of *works of grace* is one of these aberrations and cannot be adopted into the *maxims* of reason, if she is to remain within her limits; as indeed can nothing of the supernatural, simply because in this realm all use of reason ceases. For it is impossible to find a way to define these things *theoretically* ([showing] that they are works of grace and not inner natural effects) because our use of the concept of cause and effect cannot be extended beyond matters of experience, and hence beyond nature. Moreover, even the hypothesis of a *practical* application of this idea is wholly self-contradictory. For the employment of this idea would presuppose a rule concerning the good which (for a particular end) we ourselves must *do* in order to accomplish something, whereas to await a work of grace means exactly the opposite, namely, that the good (the morally good) is not our deed but the deed of another being, and that we therefore can *achieve* it only by *doing nothing*, which contradicts itself. Hence we can admit a work of grace as something incomprehensible, but we cannot adopt it into our maxims either for theoretical or for practical use.

BOOK TWO

CONCERNING THE CONFLICT OF THE GOOD WITH THE EVIL PRINCIPLE FOR SOVEREIGNTY OVER MAN

To become morally good it is not enough merely to allow the seed of goodness implanted in our species to develop without hindrance; there is also present in us an active and opposing cause of evil to be combatted. Among the ancient moralists it was pre-eminently the Stoics who called attention to this fact by their watchword *virtue*, which (in Greek as well as in Latin) signifies courage and valor and thus presupposes the presence of an enemy. In this regard the name *virtue* is a noble one, and that it has often been ostentatiously misused and derided (as has of late the word "Enlightenment") can do it no harm. For simply to make the demand for courage is to go half-way towards infusing it; on the other hand, the lazy and pusillanimous cast of mind (in morality and religion) which entirely mistrusts itself and hangs back waiting for help from without, is relaxing to all a man's powers and makes him unworthy even of this assistance.

Yet those valiant men [the Stoics] mistook their enemy: for he is not to be sought in the merely undisciplined natural inclinations which present themselves so openly to everyone's consciousness; rather is he, as it were, an invisible foe who screens himself behind reason and is therefore all the more dangerous. They called out *wisdom* against *folly*, which allows itself to be deceived by the inclinations through mere carelessness, instead of summoning her against *wickedness* (the wickedness of the human heart), which secretly undermines the disposition with soul-destroying principles.*

* These philosophers derived their universal ethical principle from the dignity of human nature, that is, from its freedom (regarded as an independence from the power of the inclinations), and they could not have used as their foundation a better or nobler principle. They then derived the moral laws directly from reason, which alone legislates morally and whose command, through these laws, is absolute. Thus everything was quite correctly defined—objectively, with regard to the rule, and subjectively, with reference to the incentive—provided one ascribes to man an uncorrupted will to incorporate these laws unhesitatingly into his maxims. Now it was just in the latter presupposition that their error lay. For no matter how early we direct our attention to our moral state, we find that this state is no longer a *res*

Natural inclinations, *considered in themselves*, are *good*, that is, not a matter of reproach, and it is not only futile to want to extirpate them but to do so would also be harmful and blameworthy. Rather, let them be tamed and instead of clashing with one another they can be brought into harmony in a wholeness which is called happiness. Now the reason which accomplishes this is termed *prudence*. But only what is opposed to the moral law is evil in itself, absolutely reprehensible, and must be completely eradicated; and that reason which teaches this truth, and more especially that which puts it into actual practice, alone deserves the name of *wisdom*. The vice corresponding to this may indeed be termed *folly*, but again only when reason feels itself strong enough not merely to *hate* vice as something to be feared, and to arm itself against it, but to *scorn* vice (with all its temptations).

So when the Stoic regarded man's moral struggle simply as a conflict with his inclinations, so far as these (innocent in themselves) had to be overcome as hindrances to the fulfilment of his duty, he could locate the cause of transgression only in man's *neglect* to combat these inclinations, for he admitted no special, positive principle (evil in itself). Yet since this neglect is itself contrary to duty (a transgression) and no mere lapse of nature,

integra, but that we must start by dislodging from its stronghold the evil which has already entered in (and it could never have done so, had we not ourselves adopted it into our maxims); that is, the first really good act that a man can perform is to forsake the evil, which is to be sought not in his inclinations, but in his perverted maxim, and so in freedom itself. Those inclinations merely make difficult the *execution* of the good maxim which opposes them; whereas genuine evil consists in this, that a man does not *will* to withstand those inclinations when they tempt him to transgress—so it is really this disposition that is the true enemy. The inclinations are but the opponents of basic principles in general (be they good or evil); and so far that high-minded principle of morality [of the Stoics] is of value as an initiatory lesson (a general discipline of the inclinations) in allowing oneself to be guided by basic principles. But so far as specific principles of moral *goodness* ought to be present but are not present, as maxims, we must assume the presence in the agent of some other opponent with whom virtue must join combat. In the absence of such an opponent all virtues would not, indeed, be *splendid vices*, as the Church Father[1] has it; yet they would certainly be *splendid frailties*. For though it is true that thus the rebellion is often stilled, the rebel himself is not being conquered and exterminated.

[1] ["Augustine, to whom tradition ascribes the saying, not traceable, indeed, in any of the works extant to us but corresponding to a tendency of his thought, *virtutes gentium splendida vitia*." (Note in Berlin Edition.)]

and since the cause thereof cannot be sought once again in the inclinations (unless we are to argue in a circle) but only in that which determines the will^w as a free will^w (that is, in the first and inmost ground of the maxims which accord with the inclinations), we can well understand how philosophers for whom the basis of an explanation remained ever hidden in darkness*—a basis which, though inescapable, is yet unwelcome—could mistake the real opponent of goodness with whom they believed they had to carry on a conflict.

So it is not surprising that an Apostle represents this *invisible* enemy, who is known only through his operations upon us and who destroys basic principles, as being outside us and, indeed, as an evil *spirit:* "We wrestle not against flesh and blood (the natural inclinations) but against principalities and powers—against evil spirits."[1] This is an expression which seems to have been used not to extend our knowledge beyond the world of sense but only to make clear *for practical use* the conception of what is for us unfathomable. As far as its practical value to us is concerned, moreover, it is all one whether we place the seducer merely within ourselves or without, for guilt touches us not a whit less in the latter case than in the former, inasmuch as we would not be led

---

* It is a very common assumption of moral philosophy that the existence of moral evil in man may easily be explained by the power of the motivating springs of his sensuous nature on the one hand, and the impotence of his rational impulses (his respect for the law) on the other, that is, by *weakness*. But then the moral goodness in him (his moral predisposition) would have to allow of a still easier explanation, for to comprehend the one apart from comprehending the other is quite unthinkable. Now reason's ability to master all opposing motivating forces through the bare idea of a law is utterly inexplicable; it is also inconceivable, therefore, how the motivating forces of the sensuous nature should be able to gain the ascendancy over a reason which commands with such authority. For if all the world were to proceed in conformity with the precepts of the law, we should say that everything came to pass according to natural order, and no one would think of so much as inquiring after the cause.

[1] [Several of Kant's quotations from the Bible, and this among them, are not accurate reproductions of Luther's translation. Where such discrepancies occur we have given, in the text, a direct translation of Kant's words, using, so far as possible, the language of the King James version, and adding, in a footnote, the King James version of the entire passage which Kant seems to have had in mind. Cf. Ephesians VI, 12: "For we wrestle not against flesh and blood, but against principalities, against powers, against the rulers of the darkness of this world, against spiritual wickedness in high places."]

astray by him at all were we not already in secret league with him.* We will treat of this whole subject in two sections.

* It is a peculiarity of Christian ethics to represent moral goodness as differing from moral evil not as heaven from *earth* but as heaven from *hell*. Though this representation is figurative, and, as such, disturbing, it is none the less philosophically correct in meaning. That is, it serves to prevent us from regarding good and evil, the realm of light and the realm of darkness, as bordering on each other and as losing themselves in one another by gradual steps (of greater and lesser brightness); but rather to represent those realms as being separated from one another by an immeasurable gulf. The complete dissimilarity of the basic principles, by which one can become a subject of this realm or that, and the danger, too, which attends the notion of a close relationship between the characteristics which fit an individual for one or for the other, justify this manner of representation—which, though containing an element of horror, is none the less very exalting.

CONCERNING THE LEGAL CLAIM OF THE GOOD PRINCIPLE TO SOVEREIGNTY OVER MAN

A. The Personified Idea of the Good Principle

Mankind (rational earthly existence in general) *in its complete moral perfection* is that which alone can render a world the object of a divine decree and the end of creation. With such perfection as the prime condition, happiness is the direct consequence, according to the will of the Supreme Being. Man so conceived, alone pleasing to God, "is in Him through eternity";[1] the idea of him proceeds from God's very being; hence he is no created thing but His only-begotten Son, "the *Word* (the *Fiat!*) through which all other things are, and without which nothing is in existence that is made"[2] (since for him, that is, for rational existence in the world, so far as he may be regarded in the light of his moral destiny, all things were made). "He is the brightness of His glory."[3] "In him God loved the world,"[4] and only in him and through the adoption of his disposition can we hope "to become the sons of God";[5] etc.

Now it is our universal duty as men to *elevate* ourselves to this ideal of moral perfection, that is, to this archetype of the moral disposition in all its purity—and for this the idea itself, which reason presents to us for our zealous emulation, can give us power. But just because we are not the authors of this idea, and because it has established itself in man without our comprehending how human nature could have been capable of receiving it, it is more appropriate to say that this archetype has *come down* to us from heaven and has assumed our humanity (for it is less possible to conceive how man, by nature *evil*, should of himself lay aside evil and *raise* himself to the ideal of holiness, than that the latter

[1] [Cf. John I, 1–2: "In the beginning was the Word, and the Word was with God, and the Word was God. The same was in the beginning with God."]

[2] [Cf. John I, 3: "All things were made by him; and without him was not anything made that was made."]

[3] [Cf. Hebrews I, 3]

[4] [Cf. John III, 16: "For God so loved the world, that he gave his only begotten Son, that whosoever believeth in him should not perish, but have everlasting life." Cf. also I John IV, 9–10.]

[5] [Cf. John I, 12: "But as many as received him, to them gave he power to become the sons of God, even to them that believe on his name."]

should *descend* to man and assume a *humanity* which is, in itself, not evil). Such union with us may therefore be regarded as a state of *humiliation* of the Son of God[1] if we represent to ourselves this godly-minded person, regarded as our archetype, as assuming sorrows in fullest measure in order to further the world's good, though he himself is holy and therefore is bound to endure no sufferings whatsoever. Man, on the contrary, who is never free from guilt even though he has taken on the very same disposition, can regard as truly merited the sufferings that may overtake him, by whatever road they come; consequently he must consider himself unworthy of the union of his disposition with such an idea, even though this idea serves him as an archetype.

This ideal of a humanity pleasing to God (hence of such moral perfection as is possible to an earthly being who is subject to wants and inclinations) we can represent to ourselves only as the idea of a person who would be willing not merely to discharge all human duties himself and to spread about him goodness as widely as possible by precept and example, but even, though tempted by by the greatest allurements, to take upon himself every affliction, up to the most ignominious death, for the good of the world and even for his enemies. For man can frame to himself no concept of the degree and strength of a force like that of a moral disposition except by picturing it as encompassed by obstacles, and yet, in the face of the fiercest onslaughts, victorious.

Man may then hope to become acceptable to God (and so be saved) through *a practical faith in this Son of God* (so far as He is represented as having taken upon Himself man's nature). In other words, he, and he alone, is entitled to look upon himself as an object not unworthy of divine approval who is conscious of such a moral disposition as enables him to have a well-grounded confidence in himself and to *believe* that, under like temptations and afflictions (so far as these are made the touchstone of that idea), he would be loyal unswervingly to the archetype of humanity and, by faithful imitation, remain true to his exemplar.

B. *The Objective Reality of this Idea*

From the practical point of view this idea is completely real in its own right, for it resides in our morally-legislative reason. We *ought* to conform to it; consequently we must *be able* to do so. Did

---

[1] [Cf. Philippians II, 6 ff.]

we have to prove in advance the possibility of man's conforming to this archetype, as is absolutely essential in the case of concepts of nature (if we are to avoid the danger of being deluded by empty notions), we should have to hesitate before allowing even to the moral law the authority of an unconditioned and yet sufficient determining ground of our will^w. For how it is possible that the bare idea of conformity to law, as such,[1] should be a stronger incentive for the will than all the incentives conceivable whose source is personal gain, can neither be understood by reason nor yet proved by examples from experience. As regards the former, the law commands unqualifiedly; and as regards the latter, even though there had never existed an individual who yielded unqualified obedience to this law, the objective necessity of being such an one would yet be undiminished and self-evident. We need, therefore, no empirical example to make the idea of a person morally well-pleasing to God our archetype; this idea as an archetype is already present in our reason. Moreover, if anyone, in order to acknowledge, for his imitation, a particular individual as such an example of conformity to that idea, demands more than what he sees, more, that is, than a course of life entirely blameless and as meritorious as one could wish; and if he goes on to require, as credentials requisite to belief, that this individual should have performed miracles or had them performed for him—he who demands this thereby confesses to his own moral *unbelief*, that is, to his lack of faith in virtue. This is a lack which no belief that rests upon miracles (and is merely historical) can repair. For only a faith in the practical validity of that idea which lies in our reason has moral worth. (Only this idea, to be sure, can establish the truth of miracles as possible effects of the good principle; but it can never itself derive from them its own verification.)

Just for this reason must an experience be possible in which the example of such a [morally perfect] human being is presented (so far, at least, as we can expect or demand from any merely external experience the evidences of an inner moral disposition). According to the law, each man ought really to furnish an example of this idea in his own person; to this end does the archetype reside always in the reason: and this, just because no example in outer experience is adequate to it; for outer experience does not disclose the inner nature of the disposition but merely allows of an infer-

[1] [*überhaupt*]

ence about it though not one of strict certainty. (For the matter of that, not even does a man's inner experience with regard to himself enable him so to fathom the depths of his own heart as to obtain, through self-observation, quite certain knowledge of the basis of the maxims which he professes, or of their purity and stability.)

Now if it were indeed a fact that such a truly godly-minded man at some particular time had descended, as it were, from heaven to earth and had given men in his own person, through his teachings, his conduct, and his sufferings, as perfect an *example* of a man well-pleasing to God as one can expect to find in external experience (for be it remembered that the *archetype* of such a person is to be sought nowhere but in our own reason), and if he had, through all this, produced immeasurably great moral good upon earth by effecting a revolution in the human race—even then we should have no cause for supposing him other than a man naturally be-gotten. (Indeed, the naturally begotten man feels himself under obligation to furnish just such an example in himself.) This is not, to be sure, absolutely to deny that he might be a man supernat-urally begotten. But to suppose the latter can in no way benefit us practically, inasmuch as the archetype which we find embodied in this manifestation must, after all, be sought in ourselves (even though we are but natural men). And the presence of this arche-type in the human soul is in itself sufficiently incomprehensible without our adding to its supernatural origin the assumption that it is hypostasized in a particular individual. The elevation of such a holy person above all the frailties of human nature would rather, so far as we can see, hinder the adoption of the idea of such a person for our imitation. For let the nature of this individual pleasing to God be regarded as human in the sense of being encumbered with the very same needs as ourselves, hence the same sorrows, with the very same inclinations, hence with the same temptations to transgress; let it, however, be regarded as superhuman to the degree that his unchanging purity of will, not achieved with effort but innate, makes all transgression on his part utterly impossible: his distance from the natural man would then be so infinitely great that such a divine person could no longer be held up as an *example* to him. Man would say: If I too had a perfectly holy will, all temptations to evil would of themselves be thwarted in me; if I too had the most complete inner assurance that, after a short life on earth, I should (by virtue of this holiness) become at once a partaker in all the eternal glory of the kingdom of heaven, I too should take upon myself not only willingly but joyfully all sorrows, however bitter they might be, even to the most ignominious death, since I would see before my eyes the glorious and imminent sequel. To be sure, the thought that this divine person was in actual possession of this eminence and this bliss from all eternity (and needed not first of all to earn them through such afflictions), and that he willingly renounced them for the sake of those absolutely unworthy, even for the sake of his enemies, to save them from everlasting perdition—this thought must attune our hearts to admiration, love, and gratitude. Similarly the idea of a demeanor in accordance with so perfect a standard of morality would no doubt be valid for us, as a model for us to copy. Yet he himself could *not* be represented to us as an *example* for our imitation, nor, consequently, as a proof of the feasibility and attainability *for us* of so pure and exalted a moral goodness.*

* It is indeed a limitation of human reason, and one which is ever inseparable from it, that we can conceive of no considerable moral worth in the actions of a personal being without representing that person, or his manifestation, in human guise. This is not to assert that such worth is in itself (κατ᾽ ἀλήθειαν) so conditioned, but merely that we must always resort to some analogy to natural existences to render supersensible qualities intelligible to ourselves. Thus a philosophical poet assigns a higher place in the moral gradation of beings to man, so far as he has to fight a propensity to evil within himself, nay, just in consequence of this fact, if only he is able to master the propensity, than to the inhabitants of heaven themselves who, by reason of the holiness of their nature, are placed above the possibility of going astray:

> "The world with all its faults
> Is better than a realm of will-less angels." (Haller)[1]

The Scriptures too accommodate themselves to this mode of representation when, in order to make us comprehend the degree of God's love for the human race, they ascribe to Him the very highest sacrifice which a loving being can make, a sacrifice performed in order that even those who are unworthy may be made happy ("For God so loved the world . . .");[2] though we cannot indeed rationally conceive how an all-sufficient Being could sacrifice a part of what belongs to His state of bliss or rob Himself of a possession. Such is the *schematism of analogy*, with which (as a means of explanation) we cannot dispense. But to transform it into a *schematism of objective determination* (for the extension of our knowledge) is *anthropomorphism*, which has, from the moral point of view (in religion), most injurious consequences.

. [1] [Albrecht Haller, in his poem *Über den Ursprung des Übels* (1734), ii, 33–34.]
[2] [John III, 16 ff.]

Now such a godly-minded teacher, even though he was completely human, might nevertheless truthfully speak of himself as though the ideal of goodness were displayed incarnate in him (in his teachings and conduct). In speaking thus he would be alluding only to the disposition which he makes the rule of his actions; since he cannot make this disposition visible, as an example for others, by and through itself, he places it before their eyes only through his teachings and actions: "Which of you convinceth me of sin?"[1] For in the absence of proofs to the contrary it is no more than right to ascribe the faultless example which a teacher furnishes of his teaching—when, moreover, this is a matter of duty for all—to the supremely pure moral disposition of the man himself. When a disposition such as this, together with all the afflictions assumed for the sake of the world's highest good, is taken as the ideal of mankind, it is, by standards of supreme righteousness, a perfectly valid ideal for all men, at all times and in all worlds, whenever man makes his own disposition like unto it, as he ought to do. To be sure, such an attainment will ever remain a righteousness not our own, inasmuch as it would have to consist of a course of life completely and faultlessly harmonious with that perfect disposition.

At this point let me remark incidentally that while, in the ascent from the sensible to the supersensible, it is indeed allowable to *schematize* (that is, to render a concept intelligible by the help of an analogy to something sensible), it is on no account permitted us to *infer* (and thus to *extend* our concept), by this analogy, that what holds of the former must also be attributed to the latter. Such an inference is impossible, for the simple reason that it would run *directly counter* to all analogy to conclude that, because we absolutely need a schema to render a concept intelligible to ourselves (to support it with an example), it therefore follows that this schema must necessarily belong to the object itself as its predicate. Thus, I cannot say: I can *make comprehensible* to myself the cause of a plant (or of any organic creature, or indeed of the whole purposive world) only by attributing intelligence to it, on the analogy of an artificer in his relation to his work (say a watch); therefore the cause (of the plant and of the world in general) must itself *possess* intelligence. That is, I cannot say that this postulated intelligence of the cause conditions not merely my comprehending it but also conditions the possibility of its being a cause. On the contrary, between the relation of a schema to its concept and the relation of this same schema of a concept to the objective fact itself there is no analogy, but rather a mighty chasm, the overleaping of which (μετάβασις εἰς ἄλλο γένος) leads at once to anthropomorphism. The proof of this I have given elsewhere.

[1] [John VIII, 46]

Yet an appropriation of this righteousness for the sake of our own must be possible when our own disposition is made at one with that of the archetype, although the greatest difficulties will stand in the way of our rendering this act of appropriation comprehensible. To these difficulties we now turn.

C. Difficulties which Oppose the Reality of this Idea, and their Solution

The *first* difficulty which makes doubtful the realization in us of that idea of a humanity well-pleasing to God, when we consider the *holiness* of the Lawgiver and the lack of a righteousness of our own, is the following. The law says: "Be ye holy (in the conduct of your lives) even as your Father in Heaven is holy."[1] This is the ideal of the Son of God which is set up before us as our model. But the distance separating the good which we ought to effect in ourselves from the evil whence we advance is infinite, and the act itself, of conforming our course of life to the holiness of the law, is impossible of execution in any given time. Nevertheless, man's moral constitution ought to accord with this holiness. This constitution must therefore be found in his disposition, in the all-embracing and sincere maxim of conformity of conduct to the law, as the seed from which all goodness is to be developed. Such a disposition arises, then, from a holy principle which the individual has made his own highest maxim. A change of heart such as this must be possible because duty requires it.

Now the difficulty lies here: How can a disposition count for the act itself, when the act is *always* (not eternally,[2] but at each instant of time) defective? The solution rests on these considerations. In our conceptions of the relation of cause and effect we are unavoidably confined to time-conditions. According to our mode of estimation, therefore, conduct[3] itself, as a continual and endless advance from a deficient to a better good, ever remains defective. We must consequently regard the good as it appears in us, that is, in the guise of *an act*,[3] as being *always* inadequate to a holy law. But we may also think of this endless progress of our goodness towards conformity to the law, even if this progress is conceived in terms of actual deeds,[3] or life-conduct, as being judged by Him who knows the heart, through a purely intellectual intuition, as a

---

[1] [Matthew V, 48; Leviticus XI, 44; and I Peter I, 16]
[2] [*überhaupt*]   [3] [*That*]

completed whole, because of the *disposition*, supersensible in its nature, from which this progress itself is derived.* Thus may man, notwithstanding his permanent deficiency, yet expect to be *essentially*[1] well-pleasing to God, at whatever instant his existence be terminated.

The *second* difficulty emerges when we consider man, as he strives towards the good, with respect to the relation of his moral goodness to the divine *goodness*. This difficulty concerns *moral happiness*. By this I do not mean that assurance of the everlasting possession of contentment with one's *physical state* (freedom from evils and enjoyment of ever-increasing pleasures) which is *physical happiness;* I mean rather the reality and *constancy* of a disposition which ever progresses in goodness (and never falls away from it). For *if only one were absolutely assured of the unchangeableness of a disposition of this sort*, the constant "seeking for the kingdom of God"[2] would be equivalent to knowing oneself to be already in possession of this kingdom, inasmuch as an individual thus minded would quite of his own accord have confidence that "all things else (*i.e.*, what relates to physical happiness) would be added unto him."[3]

Now a person solicitous on this score might perhaps be rebuked for his concern, with: "His (God's) Spirit beareth witness to our spirit," etc.;[4] that is to say, he who possesses as pure a disposition as is required will feel of himself that he could never fall so low as again to love evil. And yet to trust to such feelings, supposedly of

* Yet the following must not be overlooked. I do not mean by the above statement that the disposition shall serve to *compensate* for failure in allegiance to duty, or, consequently, for the actual evil in this endless course [of progress] (rather is it presupposed that a moral character in man, which is pleasing to God, is actually to be met with in this temporal series). What I do mean is that the disposition, which stands in the place of the totality of this series of approximations carried on without end, makes up for only that failure which is inseparable from the existence of a temporal being as such, the failure, namely, ever wholly to be what we have in mind to become. The question of compensation for actual transgressions occurring in this course of progress will be considered in connection with the solution of the *third* difficulty.

[1] [*überhaupt*]
[2] [Cf. Matthew VI, 33; Luke XII, 31]
[3] [Cf. Matthew VI, 33: "But seek ye first the kingdom of God, and his righteousness; and all these things shall be added unto you."]
[4] [Cf. Romans VIII, 16, ff. "The Spirit itself beareth witness with our spirit, that we are the children of God."]

supersensible origin, is a rather perilous undertaking; man is never more easily deceived than in what promotes his good opinion of himself. Moreover it does not even seem advisable to encourage such a state of confidence; rather is it advantageous (to morality) to "work out our own salvation *with fear and trembling*"[1] (a hard saying, which, if misunderstood, is capable of driving a man to the blackest fanaticism). On the other hand, if a man lacked *all* confidence in his moral disposition, once it was acquired, he would scarcely be able to persevere steadfastly in it. He can gain such confidence, however, without yielding himself up either to pleasing or to anxious fantasies, by comparing the course of his life hitherto with the resolution which he has adopted. It is true, indeed, that the man who, through a sufficiently long course of life, has observed the efficacy of these principles of goodness, from the time of their adoption, in his conduct, that is, in the steady improvement of his way of life, can still only *conjecture*[2] from this that there has been a fundamental improvement in his inner disposition. Yet he has reasonable grounds for *hope*[2] as well. Since such improvements, if only their underlying principle is good, ever increase his *strength* for future advances, he can hope that he will never forsake this course during his life on earth but will press on with ever-increasing courage. Nay, more: if after this life another life awaits him, he may hope to continue to follow this course still —though to all appearances under other conditions—in accordance with the very same principle, and to approach ever nearer to, though he can never reach, the goal of perfection. All this may he reasonably hope because, on the strength of what he has observed in himself up to the present, he can look upon his disposition as radically improved. Just the reverse is true of him who, despite good resolutions often repeated, finds that he has never stood his ground, who is ever falling back into evil, or who is constrained to acknowledge that as his life has advanced he has slipped, as though he were on a declivity, evermore from bad to worse. Such an individual can entertain no reasonable hope that he would conduct himself better were he to go on living here on earth, or even were a future life awaiting him, since, on the strength of his past record, he would have to regard the corruption as rooted in his very disposition.

[1] [Cf. Philippians II, 12]
[2] [Translators' italics.]

Now in the first experience we have a glimpse of an *immeasurable* future, yet one which is happy and to be desired; in the second, of as *incalculable a misery*—either of them being for men, so far as they can judge, a blessed or cursed *eternity*. These are representations powerful enough to bring peace to the one group and strengthen them in goodness, and to awaken in the other the voice of conscience commanding them still to break with evil so far as it is possible; hence powerful enough to serve as incentives without our having to presume to lay down *dogmatically* the objective doctrine that man's destiny is an eternity of good or evil.* In making

* Among those questions which might well be entitled *childish*, since even if an answer were forthcoming the questioner would be none the wiser, is this: Will the punishments of hell be terminable or everlasting? Were the former alternative to be taught, there would be cause for fear that many (and indeed all who believe in purgatory) would say with the sailor in Moore's *Travels*,[1] "Then I hope that I can stand it out!" If, however, the other alternative were to be affirmed and counted as an article of faith,[2] there might arise the hope of complete immunity from punishment after a most abandoned life, though the purpose of the doctrine would be directly opposed to such a hope. For a clergyman, sought for advice and consolation by a man in moments of tardy repentance at the end of such a wicked life, must find it gruesome and inhuman to have to announce to the sinner his eternal condemnation. And since between this and complete absolution he recognizes no middle ground (but rather that men are punished either through all eternity or not at all), he will have to hold out to the sinner hope of the latter alternative. That is to say, he will have to promise to transform him on the spur of the moment into a man well-pleasing to God. Moreover, since there is now no more time to enter upon a good course of life, avowals of penitence, confessions of faith, nay, even solemn vows to lead a new life in the event of a further postponement of death, must serve as the means to this transformation. Such is the inevitable result when the *eternity* of man's future destiny, conformable to the way of life here led, is set forth as a *dogma*. When, on the contrary, a man is taught to frame *for himself* a concept of his future state from his moral condition up to the present, as the natural and foreseeable result of it, the *immeasurableness* of this series of consequences under the sway of evil will have upon him the same beneficial moral effect (*i.e.*, of impelling him before his life ends to undo so far as possible what he has done, by reparation or compensation proportionate to his actions) as can be expected from proclaiming the eternity of his doom, but without entailing the disadvantages of that dogma (which, moreover, neither rational insight nor Scriptural exegesis warrants). For the consequences of this dogma are that the wicked man either counts in advance, even during the course of *life*, upon this pardon so easily

[Francis Moore, *A New Collection of Voyages and Travels*, 1745; translated into the German in 1748 by G. J. Schwabe in *Allgemeine Historie der Reisen*, III.]
[2] [*zum Glaubensymbol*]

such assertions and pretensions to knowledge, reason simply passes beyond the limits of its own insight.

---

obtainable, or else, at life's close, believes that it is merely a question of the claims of divine justice upon him, and that these claims may be satisfied with mere words. The rights of humanity meanwhile are disregarded and no one gets back what belongs to him. (This is a sequel so common to this form of expiation that an instance to the contrary is almost unheard of.) Furthermore, if anyone is apprehensive that his reason, through his conscience, will judge him too leniently, he errs, I believe, very seriously. For just because reason is free, and must pass judgment even upon the man himself, it is not to be bribed; and if we tell a man under such circumstances that it is at least possible that he will soon have to stand before a judge, we need but leave him to his own reflections, which will in all probability pass sentence upon him with the greatest severity.

I will add here one or two further observations. The common proverb, "All's well that ends well," may indeed be applied to *moral* situations, but only if by ending well is meant the individual's becoming a genuinely good person. Yet wherein is he to recognize himself as such, since he can make this inference only from subsequent persistently good conduct for which, at the end of life, no time remains? The application of this saying to *happiness* may be more easily admitted, but, even here, only relatively to the position from which a man looks upon his life—that is, not if he looks ahead from its beginning but only if he reviews it from its close. Griefs that have been endured leave behind them no tormenting recollections, once we recognize that we are now delivered from them, but rather a feeling of gladness which but enhances the enjoyment of the good fortune which is now becoming ours: for both pleasure and pain are included in the temporal series (as belonging to the world of sense[1]) and so disappear with it; they do not enter into the totality of the present enjoyment of life, but are displaced by it as their successor. If, finally, this proverb is applied in estimating the moral worth of the life we have led up to the present, we may go very far wrong if we accept its truth, even though our conduct at the end of life be perfectly good. For the subjective moral principle of the *disposition*, according to which alone our life must be judged, is of such a nature (being something supersensible) that its existence is not susceptible to division into periods of time, but can only be thought of as an absolute unity. And since we can arrive at a conclusion regarding the disposition only on the basis of actions (which are its appearances), our life must come to be viewed, for the purpose of such a judgment, as a *temporal unity*, a *whole;* in which case the reproaches [of conscience] arising from the earlier portion of life (before the improvement began) might well speak as loudly as the approbation from the *latter* portion, and might considerably repress the triumphant note of "All's well that ends well!"

In conclusion, there is another tenet, closely related to this doctrine regarding the duration of punishments in another world, though not identical with it; namely, that "All sins must be forgiven here," that at the end of life our account must be completely closed, and that none may hope somehow to

[1] [*Sinnlichkeit*]

And so that good and pure disposition of which we are conscious (and of which we may speak as a good spirit presiding over us) creates in us, though only indirectly, a confidence in its own permanence and stability, and is our Comforter (Paraclete) whenever our lapses make us apprehensive of its constancy. Certainty with regard to it is neither possible to man, nor, so far as we can see, [would it be] morally beneficial. For, be it well noted, we cannot base such confidence upon an immediate consciousness of the unchangeableness of our disposition, for this we cannot scrutinize: we must always draw our conclusions regarding it solely from its consequences in our way of life. Since such a conclusion, however, is drawn merely from objects of perception, as the appearances of the good or evil disposition, it can least of all reveal the *strength* of the disposition with any certainty. This is particularly true when we think that we have effected an improvement in our disposition only a short while before we expect to die; because now, in the absence of further conduct upon which to base a judgment regarding our moral worth, even such empirical proofs of the genuineness of the new disposition are entirely lacking. In this case a feeling of wretchedness is the inevitable result of a rational estimate of our moral state (though, indeed, human nature itself, by virtue of the obscurity of all its views beyond the limits of this life, prevents this comfortlessness from turning into wild despair).

The *third* and apparently the greatest difficulty, which represents every man, even after he has entered upon the path of good-

---

retrieve there what has been neglected here. This teaching can no more proclaim itself to us as a dogma than could the previous one. It is only a principle by means of which practical reason regulates its use of its own concepts of the supernatural, while granting that it knows nothing of the objective character of this supersensible realm. That is, practical reason says: We can draw an inference as to whether or not we are persons well-pleasing to God only from the way in which we have conducted our lives; but since such life-conduct ends with life, the reckoning, whose sum total alone can tell us whether we may regard ourselves as justified or not, also closes for us at death.

In general, if we limited our judgment to *regulative* principles, which content themselves with their own possible application to the moral life, instead of aiming at *constitutive* principles of a knowledge of supersensible objects, insight into which, after all, is forever impossible to us, human wisdom would be better off in a great many ways, and there would be no breeding of a presumptive knowledge of that about which, in the last analysis, we know nothing at all—a groundless sophistry that glitters indeed for a time but only, as in the end becomes apparent, to the detriment of morality.

ness, as reprobate when his life-conduct as a whole is judged before a divine *righteousness*, may be stated thus: Whatever a man may have done in the way of adopting a good disposition, and, indeed, however steadfastly he may have persevered in conduct conformable to such a disposition, *he nevertheless started from evil*, and this debt[1] he can by no possibility wipe out. For he cannot regard the fact that he incurs no new debts subsequent to his change of heart as equivalent to having discharged his old ones. Neither can he, through future good conduct, produce a surplus over and above what he is under obligation to perform at every instant, for it is always his duty to do all the good that lies in his power. This debt which is original, or prior to all the good a man may do—this, and no more, is what we referred to in Book One as the *radical* evil in man—this debt can never be discharged by another person, so far as we can judge according to the justice of our human reason. For this is no *transmissible* liability which can be made over to another like a financial indebtedness (where it is all one to the creditor whether the debtor himself pays the debt or whether some one else pays it for him); rather is it *the most personal of all debts*, namely a debt of sins, which only the culprit can bear and which no innocent person can assume even though he be magnanimous enough to wish to take it upon himself for the sake of another. Now this moral evil (transgression of the moral law, called SIN when the law is regarded *as a divine command*) brings with it endless violations of the law and so *infinite* guilt. The extent of this guilt is due not so much to the *infinitude* of the Supreme Lawgiver whose authority is thereby violated[2] (for we understand nothing of such transcendent relationships of man to the Supreme Being) as to the fact that this moral evil lies in the *disposition* and the maxims in general, in *universal basic principles* rather than in particular transgressions. (The case is different before a human court of justice, for such a court attends merely to single offenses and therefore to the deed itself and what is relative thereto, and not to the general disposition.) It would seem to follow, then, that because of this infinite guilt all mankind must look forward to *endless punishment* and exclusion from the kingdom of God.

---

[1] [*Verschuldung*, which, as well as the term *Schuld*, might have been translated throughout this passage as "offense" or "guilt." "Debt" seems suitable to the legalistic nature of Kant's thought.]

[2] ["This is the scholastic-dogmatic view, which had already received classic interpretation in Anselm's discourse, *Cur deus homo?*" (Note in Berlin Edition.)]

The solution of this difficulty rests on the following considerations. The judicial verdict of one who knows the heart must be regarded as based upon the general disposition of the accused and not upon the appearances of this disposition, that is, not upon actions at variance or in harmony with the law. We are assuming, however, that there now exists in man a good disposition having the upper hand over the evil principle which was formerly dominant in him. So the question which we are now raising is: Can the moral consequence of his former disposition, the punishment (or in other words the effect upon the subject of God's displeasure), be visited upon his present state, with its bettered disposition, in which he is already an object of divine pleasure? Since the question is not being raised as to whether, *before* his change of heart, the punishment ordained for him would have harmonized with the divine justice (on this score no one has any doubts), this punishment *must not* be thought of (in the present inquiry) as consummated prior to his reformation. *After* his change of heart, however, the penalty cannot be considered appropriate to his new quality (of a man well-pleasing to God), for he is now leading a new life and is morally another person; and yet satisfaction must be rendered to Supreme Justice,[1] in whose sight no one who is blameworthy can ever be guiltless. Since, therefore, the infliction of punishment can, consistently with the divine wisdom, take place *neither before nor after* the change of heart, and is yet necessary, we must think of it as carried out *during* the change of heart itself, and adapted thereto. Let us see then whether, by means of the concept of a changed moral attitude, we cannot discover in this very act of reformation such ills as the new man, whose disposition is now good, may regard as incurred by himself (in another state) and, therefore, as constituting *punishments*** whereby satisfaction is rendered to divine justice.

* The hypothesis that all the ills in the world are uniformly to be regarded as punishments for past transgressions cannot be thought of as devised for the sake of a theodicy or as a contrivance useful to the religion of priest-craft (or formal worship[2]) for it is a conception too commonly held to have been excogitated in so artificial a manner); rather, it lies in all probability very near to human reason, which is inclined to knit up the course of nature with

[1] ["This is also the basic principle of the orthodox ecclesiastical 'satisfaction-theory' from which Anselm, mistaking the essence of the Christian belief in God, had already deduced the following alternative: *aut poena aut satisfactio.*" (Note in Berlin Edition.)]
[2] [*Cultus*]

Now a change of heart is a departure from evil and an entrance into goodness, the laying off of the old man and the putting on of the new,[1] since the man becomes dead unto sin (and therefore to all inclinations so far as they lead thereto) in order to become alive unto righteousness. But in this change, regarded as an intellectual[2] determination, there are not two moral acts separated by an interval of time but only a single act, for the departure from evil is possible only through the agency of the good disposition which effects the individual's entrance into goodness, and *vice versa*. So the good principle is present quite as much in the desertion of the evil as in the adoption of the good disposition, and the pain, which by rights accompanies the former disposition, ensues wholly from the latter. The coming forth from the corrupted into the good disposition is, in itself (as "the death of the old man," "the crucifying of the flesh"),[3] a sacrifice and an entrance upon a long train of life's ills. These the new man undertakes in the disposition of the Son of God, that is, merely for the sake of the good, though really they are due as *punishments* to another, namely to the old man (for the old man is indeed morally another).

Although the man (regarded from the point of view of his empirical nature as a sentient being) is *physically* the self-same guilty person as before and must be judged as such before a moral tribunal and hence by himself; yet, because of his new disposition, he is (regarded as an intelligible being) *morally* another in the eyes of a divine judge for whom this disposition takes the place of action.

---

the laws of morality and therefore very naturally conceives the idea that we are to seek to become better men before we can expect to be freed from the ills of life or to be compensated for these by preponderating goods. Hence the first man is represented (in Holy Scripture) as condemned to work if he would eat, his wife to bear children in pain, and both to die, *all on account of their transgressions*, although we cannot see how animal creatures supplied with such bodily members could have expected any other destiny even had these transgressions never been committed. To the Hindus men are nothing but spirits (called *devas*) who are imprisoned in animal bodies in punishment for old offenses. Even a philosopher, Malebranche,[4] chose to deny to non-rational animals a soul, and therefore feelings, rather than to admit that horses had to endure so much misery "without ever having eaten of forbidden hay."

[1] [Cf. Colossians III, 9–10: "Lie not one to another, seeing that ye have put off the old man with his deeds; and have put on the new man, which is renewed in knowledge after the image of him that created him." Also Ephesians IV, 22, 24]

[2] [*intellectueller, i.e.,* supersensible, intelligible]

[3] [Cf. Romans VI, 2, 6, and Galatians V, 24]

[4] [*De la recherche de la vérité*, IV, 11]

And this moral disposition which in all its purity (like unto the purity of the Son of God) the man has made his own—or, (if we personify this idea) this Son of God, Himself—bears as *vicarious substitute* the guilt of sin for him, and indeed for all who believe (practically) in Him; as *savior* He renders satisfaction to supreme justice by His sufferings and death; and as *advocate* He makes it possible for men to hope to appear before their judge as justified. Only it must be remembered that (in this mode of representation) the suffering which the new man, in becoming dead to the *old*, must accept throughout life* is pictured as a death endured once for all by the representative of mankind.

* In terms of the actions which are met with in the world of sense, even the purest moral disposition brings about in man, regarded as an earthly creature, nothing more than a continual becoming of a subject pleasing to God. In quality, indeed, this disposition (since it must be conceived as *grounded* supersensibly) ought to be and can be holy and conformable to that of its archetype; but in degree [of manifestation], as revealed in conduct, it ever remains deficient and infinitely removed therefrom. Nevertheless, because this disposition contains the basis for continual progress in the reparation of this deficiency, it does, as an intellectual unity of the whole, take *the place of action* carried to its perfect consummation. But now the question arises: Can he "in whom there is no condemnation,"[1] and in whom there must be none, believe himself justified and at the same time count *as punishment* the miseries which befall him on his way to an ever greater goodness, thus acknowledging blameworthiness and a disposition that is displeasing to God? Yes, but only in his quality of the man whom he is continually putting off. Everything (and this comprises all the miseries and ills of life in general) that would be due him as punishment in that quality (of the old man) he gladly takes upon himself in his quality of new man simply for the sake of the good. So far as he is a new man, consequently, these sufferings are not ascribed to him as punishments at all. The use of the term "punishment" signifies merely that, in his quality of new man, he now willingly takes upon himself, as so many opportunities for the testing and exercising of his disposition to goodness, all the ills and miseries that assail him, which the old man would have had to regard as punishments and which he too, so far as he is still in the process of becoming dead to the old man, accepts as such. This punishment, indeed, is simultaneously the effect and also the cause of such moral activity and consequently of that contentment and *moral happiness* which consists of a consciousness of progress in goodness (and this is one and the same act as the forsaking of evil). While possessed of the old disposition, on the other hand, he would not only have had to count the very same ills as punishments but he would also have had to *feel* them as such, since, even though they are regarded as mere ills, they are the direct opposite of what, in the form of *physical happiness*, an individual in this state of mind makes his sole objective.

[1] [Cf. Romans VIII, 1]

Here, then, is that surplus—the need of which was noted previously[1]—over the profit from good works, and it is itself a profit which is reckoned to us *by grace*. That what in our earthly life (and possibly at all future times and in all worlds) is ever only a *becoming* (namely, becoming a man well-pleasing to God) should be credited to us exactly as if we were already in full possession of it—to this we really have no legal claim,* that is, so far as we know ourselves (through that empirical self-knowledge which yields no immediate insight into the disposition but merely permits of an estimate based upon our actions); and so the accuser within us would be more likely to propose a judgment of condemnation. Thus the decree is always one of grace alone, although fully in accord with eternal justice, when we come to be cleared of all liability by dint of our faith in such goodness; for the decree is based upon a giving of satisfaction (a satisfaction which consists for us only in the idea of an improved disposition, known only to God).

Now the question may still be raised: Does this deduction of the idea of a *justification* of an individual who is indeed guilty but who has changed his disposition into one well-pleasing to God possess any practical use whatever, and what may this use be? One does not perceive what *positive* use could be made of it for religion or for the conduct of life, because the condition underlying the enquiry just conducted is that the individual in question is already in actual possession of the required good disposition toward the development and encouragement of which all practical employment of ethical concepts properly aims; and as regards comfort, a good disposition already carries with it, for him who is conscious of possessing it, both comfort and hope (though not certainty). Thus the deduction of the idea has done no more than answer a speculative question, which, however, should not be passed over in silence just because it is speculative. Otherwise reason could be accused of being wholly unable to reconcile with divine justice man's hope of absolution from his guilt—a reproach which might be damaging to reason in many ways, but most of all morally. Indeed the *negative* benefit to religion and morality which may be derived, to every

* But only a *capability of receiving*, which is all that we, for our part, can credit to ourselves; and a superior's decree conferring a good for which the subordinate possesses nothing but the (moral) receptivity is called *grace*.

[1] [See above, p. 66]

man's advantage, from the deduction of this idea of justification is very far-reaching. For we learn from this deduction that only the supposition of a complete change of heart allows us to think of the absolution, at the bar of heavenly justice, of the man burdened with guilt; that therefore no expiations, be they penances or ceremonies, no invocations or expressions of praise (not even those appealing to the ideal of the vicarious Son of God), can supply the lack of this change of heart, if it is absent, or, if it is present, can increase in the least its validity before the divine tribunal, since that ideal must be adopted into our disposition if it is to stand in place of conduct.

Another point is suggested by the question: What *at life's close* may a man promise himself, or what has he to fear, on the basis of his way of life? To answer this question a man must know his own character, at least to a certain extent. That is, even though he may believe that his disposition has improved, he must also take into consideration the old (corrupt) disposition with which he started; he must be able to infer what, and how much, of this disposition he has cast off, what *quality* (whether pure or still impure) the assumed new disposition possesses, as well as its *degree of strength* to overcome the old disposition and to guard against a relapse. Thus he will have to examine his disposition throughout his whole life. Now he can form no certain and definite concept of his real disposition through an immediate consciousness thereof and can only abstract it from the way of life he has actually followed. When, therefore, he considers the verdict of his future judge (that is, of his own awakening conscience, together with the empirical knowledge of himself which is summoned to its aid), he will not be able to conceive any other basis for passing judgment than to have placed before his eyes at that time *his whole life* and not a mere segment of it, such as the last part of it or the part most advantageous to him. He would of his own accord add to this his prospects in a life continued further (without setting any limits thereto) were he to live longer. Here he will not be able to let a previously recognized disposition take the place of action; on the contrary, it is from the action before him that he must infer his disposition. What, I ask the reader, will be a man's verdict when someone tells him no more than that he has reason to believe that he will one day stand before a judge—and this thought will bring back to his recollection (even though he is not of the worst) much that he has long since light-heartedly forgotten—what verdict, based on the way of life he has hitherto led, will this thought lead him to pronounce upon his future destiny?

If this question is addressed to the judge *within* a man he will pronounce a severe verdict upon himself; for a man cannot bribe his own reason. Place him, however, before another judge—since there are those who claim to know of such a judge through other channels of information—and he will have a store of excuses drawn from human frailty with which to oppose the severity of that judge, and in general his purpose will be to circumvent him. He may plan to anticipate his penalties by offering rueful self-inflicted penances, which do not arise from any genuine disposition toward improvement; or else to mollify him with prayers and entreaties, or with formulas and confessions in which he claims to believe. And if he receives encouragement in all this (in keeping with the proverb, "All's well that ends well"), he will lay his plans betimes so as not to forfeit needlessly too much of the enjoyment of life and yet, shortly before the end, to settle his account in all haste and to his own advantage.*

---

* The purpose of those who at the end of life have a clergyman summoned is usually that they want him as a *comforter*—not for the *physical* suffering brought on by the last illness or even for the fear which naturally precedes death (death itself, which ends these ills, can here be the comforter), but for their *moral* anguish, the reproaches of conscience. At such a time, however, conscience should rather be *stirred up* and *sharpened*, in order that the dying man may not neglect to do what good he still may, or (through reparation) to wipe out, so far as he can, the remaining consequences of his evil actions. This is in accordance with the warning: "Agree with thine adversary" (with him who has a claim against thee) "quickly, whiles thou art in the way with him" (that is, so long as thou art still alive), "lest he deliver thee to the judge" (after death) etc.[1] But, instead of this, to administer a sort of opium to the conscience is an offense both against the man himself and against those who survive him, and is wholly contrary to the purpose for which such an aid to conscience at life's close can be considered necessary.

[1] [Cf. Matthew V, 25]

CONCERNING THE LEGAL CLAIM OF THE EVIL PRINCIPLE TO
SOVEREIGNTY OVER MAN, AND THE CONFLICT OF THE
TWO PRINCIPLES WITH ONE ANOTHER

Holy Scripture (the Christian portion) sets forth this intelligible
moral relationship in the form of a narrative, in which two principles in man, as opposed to one another as is heaven to hell, are
represented as persons outside him; who not only pit their strength
against each other but also seek (the one as man's accuser, the
other as his advocate) to establish their claims *legally* as though
before a supreme judge.

Man was originally constituted the proprietor of all the goods
of the earth (Genesis I, 28), though he was to possess them only
in fee (*dominium utile*) under his Creator and Master as overlord
(*dominus directus*). At once an evil being appears (how he became
so evil as to prove untrue to his Master is not known, for he was
originally good) who, through his fall, has been deprived of whatever estate he might have had in heaven and who now wishes to
win another on earth. But since, as a being of a higher order—a
spirit—he can derive no satisfaction from earthly and material objects, he seeks to acquire a dominion *over spiritual natures*[1] by
causing man's first parents to be disloyal to their Overlord and
dependent upon himself. Thus he succeeds in setting himself up
as the lord paramount of all the goods of the earth, that is, as the
prince of this world. Now one might indeed find it strange that
God did not avail Himself of His might* against this traitor, and
prefer to destroy at its inception the kingdom which he had intended to found. In its dominion over the government of rational
beings, however, Supreme Wisdom deals with them according to

---

* Father Charlevoix[2] reports that when he recounted to the Iroquois, to
whom he was teaching the catechism, all the evil which the wicked spirit had
brought into a world created good, and how he still persistently sought to
frustrate the best divine arrangements, his pupil asked indignantly, "But why
doesn't God strike the devil dead?"—a question for which the priest candidly
admits he could, at the moment, find no answer.

[1] [*Gemüther*, translated here and elsewhere as *spiritual natures;* but on p. 76, below, as *hearts and minds.*]
[2] [Pierre-François Xavier de Charlevoix, 1682–1761, Jesuit missionary in Canada,
who wrote *Histoire et description générale de la Nouvelle-France*, Paris, 1744.]

the principle of their freedom, and the good or evil that befalls them is to be imputable to themselves. A kingdom of evil was thus set up in defiance of the good principle, a kingdom to which all men, descended (in natural wise) from Adam, became subject, and this, too, with their own consent, since the false show of this world's goods lured their gaze away from the abyss of destruction for which they were reserved. Because of its legal claim to sovereignty over man the good principle did, indeed, secure itself through the establishment (in the Jewish theocracy) of a form of government instituted solely for the public and exclusive veneration of its name. Yet since the spiritual natures of the subjects of this government remained responsive to no incentives other than the goods of this world; since consequently they chose to be ruled only by rewards and punishments in this life; and since, therefore, they were suited only for such laws as were partly prescriptive of burdensome ceremonies and observances, and partly ethical, but all purely civil, in that external compulsion characterized them all and the inner essence of the moral disposition was not considered in the least: this institution did no substantial injury to the realm of darkness and served merely to keep ever in remembrance the imprescriptible right of the First Possessor.

Now there appeared at a certain time among these very people, when they were feeling in full measure all the ills of an hierarchical constitution, and when because of this and perhaps also because of the ethical doctrines of freedom of the Greek sages (doctrines staggering to the slavish mind) which had gradually acquired an influence over them, they had for the most part been brought to their senses and were therefore ripe for a revolution,—there suddenly appeared a person whose wisdom was purer even than that of previous philosophers, as pure as though it had descended from heaven. This person proclaimed himself as indeed truly human with respect to his teachings and example, yet also an as envoy from heaven who, through an original innocence, was not involved in the bargain with the evil principle into which, through their representatives, their first parents, the rest of the human race had entered,* and "in whom, therefore, the prince of this world had

---

* To conceive the possibility of a person free from innate propensity to evil by having him born of a virgin mother is an idea of reason accommodating itself to an instinct which is hard to explain, yet which cannot be disowned, and is moral, too. For we regard natural generation, since it cannot occur

no part."[1] Hereby the sovereignty of this prince was endangered. For were this man, well-pleasing to God, to withstand his temptations to enter also into that bargain, and were other men then devoutly to adopt the same disposition, the prince would lose just as many subjects and his kingdom would be in danger of being completely overthrown. The prince accordingly offered to make this person deputy-governor of his entire kingdom if only he would pay homage to him as owner thereof. When this attempt failed he not only took away from this stranger in his house all that could make his eartly life agreeable (to the point of direst poverty), but he also incited against him all the persecutions by means of which evil men can embitter life, [causing him] such sorrows as only the well-disposed can feel deeply, by slandering the pure intent of his teachings in order to deprive him of all following—and finally pursuing him to the most ignominious death. Yet he achieved nothing by this onslaught through the agency of a worthless mob upon his steadfastness and forthrightness in teaching and example for the

without sensual pleasure on both sides and since it also seems to relate us to the common animal species far too closely for the dignity of humanity, as something of which we should be *ashamed* (it is certainly this idea which gave rise to the notion that the monastic state is holy) and which therefore signifies for us something unmoral, irreconcilable with perfection in man, and yet ingrafted in man's nature and so inherited also by his descendants as an evil predisposition. Well suited to this confused view (on one side merely sensuous, yet on the other moral, and therefore intellectual) is this idea of a birth, dependent upon no sexual intercourse (a virgin birth), of a child encumbered with no moral blemish. The idea, however, is not without difficulty in theory (though a decision on this score is not at all necessary from the practical point of view). For according to the hypothesis of epigenesis the mother, who was descended from her parents through *natural* generation, would be infected with this moral blemish and would bequeath it to her child at least to the extent of a half [of his nature], even though he had been supernaturally begotten. To avoid this conclusion, we should have to adopt the theory that the seed [of evil] *pre-existed* in the parents but that it did not develop on the part of the *female* (for otherwise that conclusion is not avoided) but only on the part of the *male* (not in the *ova* but in the *spermatazoa*), for the male has no share in supernatural pregnancy. This mode of representation could thus be defended as reconcilable theoretically with that idea.

Yet of what use is all this theory pro or con when it suffices for practical purposes to place before us as a pattern this idea taken as a symbol of mankind raising itself above temptation to evil (and withstanding it victoriously)?

[1] [Cf. John XIV, 30: ". . . for the prince of this world cometh, and hath nothing in me."]

sake of the good. And now as to the issue of this combat: the event can be viewed either in its *legal*[1] or in its *physical*[2] aspect. When we regard it as a physical event (which strikes the senses) the good principle is the worsted party; having endured many sorrows in this combat, he must give up his life* because he stirred up a rebellion against a (powerful) foreign suzerainty. Since, however, the realm in which *principles* (be they good or evil) have might is a realm not of nature but of freedom, *i.e.*, a realm in which one can control events only so far as one can rule hearts and minds[6] and where, consequently, no one is a slave (or bondsman) but the man

* Not that (as D. Bahrdt[3] fancifully imagined) he *sought* death to further a worthy design through a brilliant and sensational example; that would have been suicide. For one may indeed attempt something at the risk of losing one's life, or even suffer death at the hands of another, when one cannot avoid it, without becoming faithless to an irremissible duty; but one may not dispose of oneself and of one's life as a means, to any end whatever, and so be the *author* of one's own death.

Nor yet (as the writer of the *Wolfenbüttel Fragmente*[4] suspects) did he *stake* his life without moral but merely with political (and unlawful) intent, to the end, perhaps, of overthrowing the priests' rule and establishing himself in worldly supremacy in their stead. This conflicts with his exhortation delivered, after he had already given up hope of such an achievement, to his disciples at the supper, "to do this in remembrance"[5] of him. Intended as a reminder of a worldly design that had miscarried, this would have been a mortifying admonition, provocative of ill-will toward its author and therefore self-contradictory. But it might well refer to the failure of a very good and purely moral design of the Master, namely, the achievement during his lifetime of a *public* revolution (in religion) through the overthrow of a ceremonial faith, which wholly crowded out the moral disposition, and of the authority of its priests. (The preparations for the gathering together at Easter of his disciples, scattered over the land, may have had this purpose.) We may indeed even now regret that this revolution did not succeed; yet it really was not frustrated, for it developed, after his death, into a religious transformation which quietly, despite many misfortunes, continued to spread.

¹ [*rechtlicher*]
² [*physischer*]
³ [Karl Friedrich Bahrdt, 1741–1792, a rationalist. Cf. Chapters IX and X, "Upon the Authority of Jesus, Philosophically Judged," in his *System der moralischen Religion zur endlichen Beruhigung für Zweifler und Denker*, Berlin, 1787.]
⁴ [The main deistic work of Hermann Samuel Reimarus, 1694–1768, written about 1743, and published by Lessing in 1774–8 under the above title. These "fragments" were selections from a book which Reimarus left in manuscript, entitled, *Apologie oder Schutzschrift für die vernünftigen Verehrer Gottes* ("Apology or Defense for the Rational Worshippers of God"). Lessing first issued these anonymously, announcing that he had discovered them in the Wolfenbüttel library where he was at the time engaged.]
⁵ [Cf. Luke XXII, 19]
⁶ [*Gemüther*]

who wills to be one, and only so long as he wills: this death (the last extremity of human suffering) was therefore a manifestation of the good principle, that is, of humanity in its moral perfection, and an example for everyone to follow. The account of this death ought to have had, and could have had, the greatest influence upon human hearts and minds at that time and, indeed, at all times; for it exhibited the freedom of the children of heaven in most striking contrast to the bondage of a mere son of earth. Yet the good principle has descended in mysterious fashion from heaven into humanity not at one particular time alone but from the first beginnings of the human race (as anyone must grant who considers the holiness of this principle, and the incomprehensibility of a union between it and man's sensible nature in the moral predisposition) and it rightfully has in mankind its first dwelling place. And since it made its appearance in an actual human being, as an example to all others, [it may be said that] "he came unto his own, and his own received him not, but as many as received him, to them gave he power to be called the sons of God, even to them that believe on his name."[1] That is, by example (in and through the moral idea) he opens the portals of freedom to all who, like him, choose to become dead to everything that holds them fettered to life on earth to the detriment of morality; and he gathers together, among them, "a people for his possession, zealous of good works"[2] and under his sovereignty, while he abandons to their fate all those who prefer moral servitude.

So the moral outcome of the combat, as regards the hero of this story (up to the time of his death), is really not the *conquering* of the evil principle—for its kingdom still endures, and certainly a new epoch must arrive before it is overthrown—but merely the breaking of its power to hold, against their will, those who have so long been its subjects, because another dominion (for man must be subject to some rule or other), a moral dominion, is now offered them as an asylum where they can find protection for their morality if they wish to forsake the former sovereignty. Furthermore, the evil principle is still designated the prince of this world, where those who adhere to the good principle should always be prepared for physical sufferings, sacrifices, and mortifications of self-love

---

[1] [Cf. John I, 11–12. Kant has changed slightly the order of words and the tenses, and has put *heiszen* = called (the sons of God) instead of *werden* = become.]

[2] [Cf. Titus II, 14: "that he might redeem us from all iniquity and purify unto himself a people for his own possession, zealous of good works."]

—[tribulations] to be viewed, in this connection, as persecutions by the evil principle, since the latter has rewards in his kingdom only for those who have made eartly well-being their final goal.

Once this vivid mode of representation, which was in its time probably the only *popular* one, is divested of its mystical veil, it is easy to see that, for practical purposes, its spirit and rational meaning have been valid and binding for the whole world and for all time, since to each man it lies so near at hand that he knows his duty towards it. Its meaning is this: that there exists absolutely no salvation for man apart from the sincerest adoption of genuinely moral principles into his disposition; that what works against this adoption is not so much the sensuous nature, which so often receives the blame, as it is a certain self-incurred perversity, or however else one may care to designate this wickedness which the human race has brought upon itself—falsity (*fausseté*), Satanic guile, through which evil came into the world—a corruption which lies in all men and which can be overcome only through the idea of moral goodness in its entire purity, together with the consciousness that this idea really belongs to our original predisposition and that we need but be assiduous in preserving it free from all impure admixture and in registering it deeply in our dispositions to be convinced, by its gradual effect upon the spiritual nature, that the dreaded powers of evil can in no wise make headway against it ("the gates of hell shall not prevail against it").[1] Finally, lest perchance for want of this assurance we compensate *superstitiously*, through expiations which presuppose no change of heart,[2] or *fanatically*, through pretended (and merely passive) inner illumination, and so forever be kept distant from the good that is grounded in activity of the self, we should acknowledge as a mark of the presence of goodness in us naught but a well-ordered conduct of life. An attempt such as the present, moreover, to discover in Scripture that sense* which harmonizes with the *most holy* teachings of reason is not only allowable but must be deemed a duty. And we can remind ourselves of what the *wise* Teacher said to His disciples regarding someone who went his own way, by which, however, he was bound eventually to arrive at the same goal: "Forbid him not; for he that is not against us is for us."[3]

---

* And it may be admitted that it is not the only one.

[1] [Cf. Matthew XVI, 18]   [2] [*Sinnesänderung*]

[3] [Cf. Mark IX, 39–40]

GENERAL OBSERVATION

If a moral religion (which must consist not in dogmas and rites but in the heart's disposition to fulfil all human duties as divine commands) is to be established, all *miracles* which history connects with its inauguration must themselves in the end render superfluous the belief in miracles in general; for it bespeaks a culpable degree of moral unbelief not to acknowledge as completely authoritative the commands of duty—commands primordially engraved upon the heart of man through reason—unless they are in addition accredited through miracles: "Except ye see signs and wonders, ye will not believe."[1] Yet, when a religion of mere rites and observances has run its course, and when one based on the spirit and the truth (on the moral disposition) is to be established in its stead, it is wholly conformable to man's ordinary ways of thought, though not strictly necessary, for the historical introduction of the latter to be accompanied and, as it were, adorned by miracles, in order to announce the termination of the earlier religion, which without miracles would never have had any authority. Indeed, in order to win over the adherents of the older religion to the new, the new order is interpreted as the fulfilment, at last, of what was only prefigured in the older religion and has all along been the design of Providence. If this be so it is quite useless to debate those narratives or interpretations; the true religion, which in its time needed to be introduced through such expedients, is now here, and from now on is able to maintain itself on rational grounds. Otherwise one would have to assume that mere faith in, and repetition of, things incomprehensible (which any one can do without thereby being or ever becoming a better man) is a way, and indeed the only way, of pleasing God—an assertion to be combatted with might and main. The person of the teacher of the one and only religion, valid for all worlds, may indeed be a mystery; his appearance on earth, his translation thence, and his eventful life and his suffering may all be nothing but miracles; nay, the historical record, which is to authenticate the account of all these miracles, may itself be a miracle (a supersensible revelation). We need not call in question any of these miracles and indeed may honor the trap-

[1] [Cf. John IV, 48]

79

pings[1] which have served to bring into public currency a doctrine whose authenticity rests upon a record indelibly registered in every soul and which stands in need of no miracle. But it is essential that, in the use of these historical accounts, we do not make it a tenet of religion that the knowing, believing, and professing of them are themselves means whereby we can render ourselves well-pleasing to God.

As for miracles in general, it appears that sensible men, while not disposed to renounce belief in them, never want to allow such belief to appear in practice; that is to say, they believe *in theory* that there are such things as miracles but they do not warrant them *in the affairs of life*.[2] For this reason wise governments have always granted the proposition, and indeed legally recorded it among the public doctrines of religion, that miracles occurred of *old*, but they have not tolerated *new* miracles.* The ancient mira-

---

* Even the teachers of religion who link their articles of faith to the authority of the government (*i.e.*, the orthodox) follow, like it, this same maxim. Hence Hr. Pfenninger,[3] in defending his friend Hr. Lavater, for declaring that belief in miracles was still possible, rightly charged these orthodox theologians with inconsistency (since he specifically excepted those who think *naturalistically* on this topic) in that, while they insisted that there had really been workers of miracles in the Christian community some seventeen hundred years ago, they were unwilling to authenticate any such at the present time; yet without being able to prove from Scripture either that miracles were wholly to cease or at what date they were to cease (for the over-subtle argument that they are no longer necessary involves a presumption of greater insight than man should attribute to himself). Such proof they never gave. The refusal to admit or to tolerate contemporary miracles was therefore merely a maxim of reason and not [an expression of] objective knowledge that there are none. But is not this same maxim, which in this instance is applied to a threatened disorder in the civic life, equally valid for the fear of a similar disorder in the philosophical, and the whole rational contemplative commonwealth? Those who do not admit *great* (sensational) miracles but who freely allow *little* ones under the name of *special Providence*[4] (since this last, as mere guidance, requires only a little application of force on the part of the supernatural cause) do not bear in mind that what matters herein is not the effect, or its magnitude, but rather the form of the course of earthly events,[5] that is, *the way in which the effect occurs*, whether naturally or super-

[1] [*Hülle*]
[2] [*Geschäfte*]
[3] [Johann Konrad Pfenninger, 1747–1792, a pastor at Zürich, author of *Apellation an den Menschenverstand, gewisse Vorfälle, Schriften und Personen betreffend*, Hamburg 1776.]
[4] [*ausserordentliche Direktion*]
[5] [*Weltlauf*]

cles were little by little so defined and so delimited by the authorities that they could cause no disturbance in the commonwealth; the authorities had to be concerned, however, over the effects which the new workers of miracles might have upon the public peace and the established order.

If one asks: What is to be understood by the word *miracle?* it may be explained (since it is really proper for us to know only what miracles are *for us, i.e.,* for our practical use of reason) by saying that they are events in the world the *operating laws* of whose causes are, and must remain, absolutely unknown to us. Accordingly, one can conceive of either *theistic* or *demonic* miracles; the second are divided into *angelic* miracles (of good spirits) and *devilish* miracles (of bad spirits). Of these only the last really come into question because the *good angels* (I know not why) give us little or nothing to say about them.

As regards *theistic* miracles: we can of course frame for ourselves a concept of the laws of operation of their cause (as an omnipotent, etc., and therewith a moral Being), but only a *general* concept, so far as we think of Him as creator of the world and its ruler according to the order of nature, as well as the moral order. For we can obtain direct and independent[1] knowledge of the laws of the natural order, a knowledge which reason can then employ for its own use. If we assume, however, that God at times and under special circumstances allows nature to deviate from its own laws, we have not, and can never hope to have, the slightest conception of the law according to which God then brings about such an event (aside from the *general moral concept* that whatever He does will be in all things good—whereby, however, nothing is determined regarding this particular occurrence). But here reason is, as it were, crippled, for it is impeded in its dealings with respect to known laws, it is not instructed with anything new, and it can never in the world hope thus to be instructed. Among miracles, the demonic are the most completely irreconcilable with the use of our reason. For as regards *theistic* miracles, reason would at least have a negative criterion for its use, namely that even though something is represented as commanded by God, through a direct manifesta-

---

naturally; and that for God no distinction of easy and difficult is to be thought of. But as regards the *mystery* of supernatural influences, thus deliberately to conceal the importance of such an occurrence is still less proper.

[1] [*für sich*]

tion of Him, yet, if it flatly contradicts morality, it cannot, despite all appearances, be of God (for example, were a father ordered to kill his son who is, so far as he knows, perfectly innocent). But in the presence of what is taken to be a demonic miracle even this criterion fails; and were we, instead, to avail ourselves in these instances of the opposite, positive criterion for reason's use— namely, that, when through such an agency there comes a bidding to a good act which in itself we already recognize as duty, this bidding has not issued from an evil spirit—we might still make a false inference, for the evil spirit often disguises himself, they say, as an angel of light.

In the affairs of life, therefore, it is impossible for us to count on miracles or to take them into consideration at all in our use of reason (and reason must be used in every incident of life). The judge (however credulous of miracles he may be in church) listens to the delinquent's claims to have been tempted of the devil exactly as though nothing has been said; although, were the judge to regard this diabolical influence as possible, it would be worthy of some consideration that an ordinary simple-minded man had been ensnared in the toils of an arch-rogue. Yet the judge cannot summon the tempter and confront each with the other; in a word, he can make absolutely nothing rational out of the matter. The wise clergyman will therefore guard himself well against cramming the heads and debasing the imaginations of those committed to his pastoral care with anecdotes from *The Hellish Proteus*.[1] As regards miracles of the good variety, they are employed by men in the affairs of life as mere phrases. Thus the doctor says that there is no help for the patient unless a miracle occurs—in other words, he will certainly die. Among these affairs belongs also the work of the scientist,[2] searching for the causes of events in their own natural laws; in the natural laws of these events, I say, which he can verify through experience, even though he must renounce knowledge of what it is in itself that works according to these laws, or what it might be for us if we had, possibly, another sense. In like manner, a man's own moral improvement is one of the tasks incumbent upon him; and heavenly influences may cooperate with him in this, or may be deemed needful for the explanation of the

---

[1] [*Der höllische Proteus oder tausend-künstige Versteller (nebenst vorberichtlichen Grundbeweis der Gewissheit, dass es wirklich Gespenster gebe) abgebildet durch Erasmum Francisci*, Nürnberg, 1708.]

[2] [*Naturforscher*]

possibility of such improvement—yet man cannot comprehend them; he can neither distinguish them with certainty from natural influences, nor draw them, and thereby, as it were, heaven, down to him. Since, then, he can make no possible use of them he *sanctions** no miracles in this case but instead, should he attend to the commands of reason, he conducts himself as though all change of heart and all improvement depended solely upon his own exertions directed thereto. But to think that, through the gift of a really *firm* theoretical faith in miracles, man could himself perform them and so storm heaven—this is to venture so far beyond the limits of reason that we are not justified in tarrying long over such a senseless conceit.**

* That is to say, he does not incorporate belief in miracles into his maxims (either of theoretical or practical reason), though, indeed, he does not impugn their possibility or reality.

** It is a common subterfuge of those who deceive the gullible with *magic* arts, or at least who want to render such people credulous in general, to appeal to the scientists' confession of their *ignorance*. After all, they say, we do not know the *cause* of gravity, of magnetic force, and the like! Yet we *are* acquainted with the laws of these [phenomena] with sufficient thoroughness [to know] within definite limits the conditions under which alone certain effects occur; and this suffices both for an assured rational use of these forces and for the explanation of their manifestations, *secundum quid, downwards* to the use of these laws in the ordering of experiences thereunder, though not indeed *simpliciter* and *upwards*, to the comprehension of the very causes of the forces which operate according to these laws.

From this an inner phenomenon of the human mind becomes comprehensible—why so-called natural wonders, *i.e.*, sufficiently attested, though irrational appearances, or unexpected qualities of things emerging and not conforming to laws of nature previously known, are eagerly seized upon and *exhilarate* the spirit so long as they are still held to be natural; whereas the spirit is *dejected* by the announcement of a real miracle. For the first opens up the prospect of a new acquisition for the nourishment of reason; that is, it awakens the *hope* of discovering new laws of nature: the second, in contrast, arouses the *fear* that confidence shall be lost in what has been hitherto accepted as known. For when reason is severed from the laws of experience it is of no use whatsoever in such a bewitched world, not even, in such a world, for moral application toward fulfilment of duty; for we no longer know whether, without our being aware, changes may not be occurring, through miracles, among our moral incentives, changes regarding which no one can decide whether they should be ascribed to ourselves or to another, inscrutable cause.

Those whose judgment in these matters is so inclined that they suppose themselves to be helpless without miracles, believe that they soften the blow which reason suffers from them by holding that they happen but *seldom*. If thereby they want to say that this is already implicit in the concept of a miracle (for, were such an event to occur commonly, it would not be accounted a miracle), one can indeed make them a present of this sophistry (of transforming an objective question of what the thing is into the subjective question of what the word, by which we signify the thing, means) and still ask: *How seldom?* Once in a hundred years? Or in ancient times but never now? Here we can determine nothing on the basis of knowledge of the object (which, by our own admission, transcends our understanding) but only on the basis of the maxims which are necessary to the use of our reason. Thus, miracles must be admitted as [occurring] *daily* (though indeed hidden under the guise of natural events) or else *never*, and in the latter case they underlie neither our explanations by reason nor the guiding rules of our conduct; and since the former alternative [that they occur daily] is not at all compatible with reason, nothing remains but to adopt the latter maxim—for this principle remains ever a mere maxim for making judgments, not a theoretical assertion. No one can have such a good conceit of his insight as to wish to assert definitely that, for example, the most admirable conservation of the species in the plant and animal kingdoms, whereby each new generation re-presents, every spring, its original, anew and undiminished, with all the inner perfection of mechanism and (as in the plant kingdom) even with their delicate beauty of color, without the forces of inorganic nature, otherwise so destructive, in the bad weather of autumn and winter being able to harm their seed at all in this respect—no one, I say, will assert that this is a mere result of natural laws; no one, indeed, can claim to *comprehend* whether or not the direct influence of the Creator is required on each occasion.

We do, however, experience all these things; they are *for us*, therefore, nothing but natural effects and *ought* never to be adjudged otherwise; for such [a distinction] the modesty of reason demands in its pronouncements. To venture beyond these limits is rashness and immodesty, although those who support miracles frequently pretend to exhibit a humble and self-renouncing way of thought.

BOOK THREE

THE VICTORY OF THE GOOD OVER THE EVIL PRINCI-
PLE, AND THE FOUNDING OF A KINGDOM OF
GOD ON EARTH

The combat which every morally well-disposed man must sustain in this life, under the leadership of the good principle, against the attacks of the evil principle, can procure him, however much he exerts himself, no greater advantage than freedom from the *sovereignty* of evil. To become *free*, "to be freed from bondage under the law of sin, to live for righteousness"[1]—this is the highest prize he can win. He continues to be exposed, none the less, to the assaults of the evil principle; and in order to assert his freedom, which is perpetually being attacked, he must ever remain armed for the fray.

Now man is in this perilous state through his own fault; hence he is *bound* at the very least to strive with all his might to extricate himself from it. But how? That is the question. When he looks around for the causes and circumstances which expose him to this danger and keep him in it, he can easily convince himself that he is subject to these not because of his own gross nature, so far as he is here a separate individual, but because of mankind to whom he is related and bound. It is not at the instigation of the former that what should properly be called the *passions*, which cause such havoc in his original good predisposition, are aroused. His needs are but few and his frame of mind in providing for them is temperate and tranquil. He is poor (or considers himself so) only in his anxiety lest other men consider him poor and despise him on that account. Envy, the lust for power, greed, and the malignant inclinations bound up with these, besiege his nature, contented within itself, *as soon as he is among men.* And it is not even necessary to assume that these are men sunk in evil and examples to lead him astray; it suffices that they are at hand, that they surround him, and that they are men, for them mutually to corrupt each other's predispositions and make one another evil. If no means could be discovered for the forming of an alliance uniquely designed as a

[1] [Cf. Romans VI, 18: "Being then made free from sin, ye became the servants of righteousness."]

protection against this evil and for the furtherance of goodness in man—of a society, enduring, ever extending itself, aiming solely at the maintenance of morality, and counteracting evil with united forces—this association with others would keep man, however much, as a single individual, he may have done to throw off the sovereignty of evil, incessantly in danger of falling back under its dominion. As far as we can see, therefore, the sovereignty of the good principle is attainable, so far as men can work toward it, only through the establishment and spread of a society in accordance with, and for the sake of, the laws of virtue, a society whose task and duty it is rationally to impress these laws in all their scope upon the entire human race. For only thus can we hope for a victory of the good over the evil principle. In addition to prescribing laws to each individual, morally legislative reason also unfurls a banner of virtue as a rallying point for all who love the good, that they may gather beneath it and thus at the very start gain the upper hand over the evil which is attacking them without rest.

A union of men under merely moral laws, patterned on the above idea, may be called an *ethical*, and so far as these laws are public, an *ethico-civil* (in contrast to a *juridico-civil*) society or an *ethical commonwealth*. It can exist in the midst of a political commonwealth and may even be made up of all its members; (indeed, unless it is based upon such a commonwealth it can never be brought into existence by man). It has, however, a special and unique principle of union (virtue), and hence a form and constitution, which fundamentally distinguish it from the political commonwealth. At the same time there is a certain analogy between them, regarded as two commonwealths, in view of which the former may also be called an *ethical state*, *i.e.*, a *kingdom* of virtue (of the good principle). The idea of such a state possesses a thoroughly well-grounded objective reality in human reason (in man's duty to join such a state), even though, subjectively, we can never hope that man's good will will lead mankind to decide to work with unanimity towards this goal.

PHILOSOPHICAL ACCOUNT OF THE VICTORY OF THE GOOD PRINCIPLE IN THE FOUNDING OF A KINGDOM OF GOD ON EARTH

I. Concerning the Ethical State of Nature

A *juridico-civil* (political) *state*[1] is the relation of men to each other in which they all alike stand socially under *public juridical laws* (which are, as a class, laws of coercion). An *ethico-civil* state[1] is that in which they are united under non-coercive laws, *i.e.*, *laws of virtue* alone.

Now just as the rightful (but not therefore always righteous), *i.e.*, *the juridicial, state of Nature* is opposed to the first, *the ethical state of Nature* is distinguished from the second. In both, each individual prescribes the law for himself, and there is no external law to which he, along with all others, recognizes himself to be subject. In both, each individual is his own judge, and there exists no powerful *public* authority to determine with legal power, according to laws, what is each man's duty in every situation that arises, and to bring about the universal performance of duty.

In an already existing political commonwealth all the political citizens, as such, are in an *ethical state of nature* and are entitled to remain therein; for it would be a contradiction (*in adjecto*) for the political commonwealth to compel its citizens to enter into an ethical commonwealth, since the very concept of the latter involves freedom from coercion. Every political commonwealth may indeed wish to be possessed of a sovereignty, according to laws of virtue, over the spirits [of its citizens]; for then, when its methods of compulsion do not avail (for the human judge cannot penetrate into the depths of other men) their dispositions to virtue would bring about what was required. But woe to the legislator who wishes to establish through force a polity directed to ethical ends! For in so doing he would not merely achieve the very opposite of an ethical polity but also undermine his political state and make it insecure. The citizen of the political commonwealth remains therefore, so far as its legislative function is concerned, completely free

[1] [*Zustand*, condition]

to enter with his fellow-citizens into an ethical union in addition
[to the political] or to remain in this kind of state of nature, as he
may wish. Only so far as an ethical commonwealth must rest on
public laws and possess a constitution based on these laws are
those who freely pledge themselves to enter into this ethical state
bound, not [indeed] to accept orders from the political power as to
how they shall or shall not fashion this ethical constitution internally, but to agree to limitations, namely, to the condition that
this constitution shall contain nothing which contradicts the duty
of its members as *citizens of the state*—although when the ethical
pledge is of the genuine sort the political limitation need cause no
anxiety.

Further, because the duties of virtue apply to the entire human
race, the concept of an ethical commonwealth is extended ideally
to the whole of mankind, and thereby distinguishes itself from the
concept of a political commonwealth. Hence even a large number
of men united in that purpose can be called not the ethical commonwealth itself but only a particular society which strives towards harmony with all men (yes, finally with all rational beings)
in order to form an absolute ethical whole of which every partial
society is only a representation or schema; for each of these societies in turn, in its relation to others of the same kind, can be
represented as in the ethical state of nature and subject to all the
defects thereof. (This is precisely the situation with separate political states which are not united through a public international law.)

*II. Man ought to leave his Ethical State of Nature in order to
become a Member of an Ethical COMMONWEALTH*

Just as the juridical state of nature is one of war of every man
against every other, so too is the ethical state of nature one in
which the good principle, which resides in each man, is continually
attacked by the evil which is found in him and also in everyone
else. Men (as was noted above) mutually corrupt one another's
moral predispositions; despite the good will of each individual, yet,
because they lack a principle which unites them, they recede,
through their dissensions, from the common goal of goodness and,
just as though they were *instruments of evil*, expose one another
to the risk of falling once again under the sovereignty of the evil
principle. Again, just as the state of a lawless external (brutish)
freedom and independence from coercive laws is a state of in-

justice and of war, each against each, which a man ought to leave in order to enter into a politico-civil state*: so is the ethical state of nature one of *open* conflict between principles of virtue and a state of inner immorality which the natural man ought to bestir himself to leave as soon as possible.

Now here we have a duty which is *sui generis*, not of men toward men, but of the human race toward itself. For the species of rational beings is objectively, in the idea of reason, destined for a social goal, namely, the promotion of the highest as a social good. But because the highest moral good cannot be achieved merely by the exertions of the single individual toward his own moral perfection, but requires rather a union of such individuals into a whole toward the same goal—into a system of well-disposed men, in which and through whose unity alone the highest moral good can come to pass—the idea of such a whole, as a universal republic based on laws of virtue, is an idea completely distinguished from all moral laws (which concern what we know to lie in our own power); since it involves working toward a whole regarding which we do not know whether, as such, it lies in our power or not. Hence this duty is distinguished from all others both in kind and in principle. We can already foresee that this duty will require the presupposition of another idea, namely, that of a higher moral Being through whose universal dispensation the forces of separate individuals, insufficient in themselves, are united for a common end.[1] First of all, however, we must follow up the clue of that moral need [for social union] and see whither this will lead us.

---

* Hobbes' statement, *status hominum naturalis est* bellum *omnium in omnes*, is correct except that it should read, *est* status *belli*, etc. For even if one does not concede that actual *hostilities* are continually in progress between men who do not stand under external and public laws, yet the *state* (*status iuridicus*) is the same; *i.e.*, the relationship in and through which men are fitted for the acquisition and maintenance of rights—a state in which each wants to be the judge of what shall be his rights against others, but for which rights he has no security against others, and gives others no security: each has only his private strength. This is a state of war in which everyone must be perpetually armed against everyone else. Hobbes' second statement, *exeundum esse e statu naturali*, follows from the first; for this state is a continual infringement upon the rights of all others through man's arrogant insistence on being the judge in his own affairs and giving other men no security in their affairs save his own arbitrary will[w].

[1] [*Wirkung*]

III. The Concept of an Ethical Commonwealth is the Concept of a PEOPLE OF GOD under Ethical Laws

If an ethical commonwealth is to come into being, all single individuals must be subject to a public legislation, and all the laws which bind them must be capable of being regarded as commands of a common law-giver. Now if the commonwealth to be established is to be *juridical*, the mass of people uniting itself into a whole would itself have to be the law-giver (of constitutional laws), because legislation proceeds from the principle of *limiting the freedom of each to those conditions under which it can be consistent with the freedom of everyone else according to a common law,** and because, as a result, the general will sets up an external legal control. But if the commonwealth is to be *ethical*, the people, as a people, cannot itself be regarded as the law-giver. For in such a commonwealth all the laws are expressly designed to promote the *morality* of actions (which is something *inner*, and hence cannot be subject to public human laws) whereas, in contrast, these public laws— and this would go to constitute a juridical commonwealth—are directed only toward the *legality* of actions, which meets the eye, and not toward (inner) morality, which alone is in question here. There must therefore be someone other than the populace capable of being specified as the public law-giver for an ethical commonwealth. And yet, ethical laws cannot be thought of as emanating *originally* merely from the will of this superior being (as statutes, which, had he not first commanded them, would perhaps not be binding), for then they would not be ethical laws and the duty proper to them would not be the free duty of virtue but the coercive duty of law. Hence only he can be thought of as highest lawgiver of an ethical commonwealth with respect to whom all *true duties*, hence also the ethical,** must be represented as *at the same*

---

* This is the principle of all external rights.

** As soon as anything is recognized as a duty, even if it should be a duty imposed through the arbitrary will[w] of a human law-giver, obedience to it is also a divine command. Of course one cannot call statutory civil laws divine commands; yet, when they are just,[1] *obedience* to them is still a divine command. The saying: "We ought to obey God rather than men,"[2] signifies merely that when men command anything which in itself is evil (directly opposed to the law of morality) we dare not, and ought not, obey them. But conversely, when a politico-civil law, itself not immoral, is opposed to what is held to be a divine statutory law, there are grounds for re-

[1] [*rechtmässig*]
[2] [Cf. Acts V, 29]

time his commands; he must therefore also be "one who knows the heart,"[1] in order to see into the innermost parts of the disposition of each individual and, as is necessary in every commonwealth, to bring it about that each receives whatever his actions are worth. But this is the concept of God as moral ruler of the world. Hence an ethical commonwealth can be thought of only as a people under divine commands, *i.e.*, as a *people of God*,[2] and indeed *under laws of virtue*.

We might indeed conceive of a people of God *under statutory laws*, under such laws that obedience to them would concern not the morality but merely the legality of acts. This would be a juridical commonwealth, of which, indeed, God would be the lawgiver (hence the *constitution* of this state would be theocratic); but men, as priests receiving His behests from Him directly, would build up an aristocratic *government*. Such a constitution, however, whose existence and form rest wholly on an historical basis, cannot settle the problem of the morally-legislative reason, the solution of which alone we are to effect; as an institution under politico-civil laws, whose lawgiver, though God, is yet external, it will come under review in the historical section. Here we have to do only with an institution whose laws are purely inward—a republic under laws of virtue, *i.e.*, a people of God "zealous of good works."[3]

To such a *people* of God we can oppose the idea of a *rabble* of the evil principle, the union of those who side with it for the propagation of evil, and whose interest it is to prevent the realization of that other union—although here again the principle which combats virtuous dispositions lies in our very selves and is represented only figuratively as an external power.

IV. The Idea of a People of God can be Realized (through Human Organization) only in the Form of a Church

The sublime, yet never wholly attainable,· idea of an ethical commonwealth dwindles markedly under men's hands. It becomes an institution which, at best capable of representing only the pure

---

garding the latter as spurious, since it contradicts a plain duty and since [the notion] that it is actually a divine command can never, by any empirical token, be accredited adequately enough to allow an otherwise established duty to be neglected on its account.

[1] [Cf. Acts I, 24; XV, 8; Luke XVI, 15]
[2] [Cf. I Peter II, 10]
[3] [Cf. Titus II, 14]

form of such a commonwealth, is, by the conditions of sensuous human nature, greatly circumscribed in its means for establishing such a whole. How indeed can one expect something perfectly straight to be framed out of such crooked wood?

To found a moral people of God is therefore a task whose consummation can be looked for not from men but only from God Himself. Yet man is not entitled on this account to be idle in this business and to let Providence rule, as though each could apply himself exclusively to his own private moral affairs and relinquish to a higher wisdom all the affairs of the human race (as regards its moral destiny). Rather must man proceed as though everything depended upon him; only on this condition dare he hope that higher wisdom will grant the completion of his well-intentioned endeavors.

The wish of all well-disposed people is, therefore, "that the kingdom of God come, that His will be done on earth."[1] But what preparations must they now make that it shall come to pass?

An ethical commonwealth under divine moral legislation is a *church* which, so far as it is not an object of possible experience, is called the *church invisible* (a mere idea of the union of all the righteous under direct and moral divine world-government, an idea serving all as the archetype of what is to be established by men). The *visible church* is the actual union of men into a whole which harmonizes with that ideal. So far as each separate society maintains, under public laws, an order among its members (in the relation of those who obey its laws to those who direct their obedience), the group, united into a whole (the church), is a *congregation* under authorities, who (called teachers or shepherds of souls) merely administer the affairs of the invisible supreme head thereof. In this function they are all called *servants* of the church, just as, in the political commonwealth, the visible overlord occasionally calls himself the highest servant of the state even though he recognizes no single individual over him (and ordinarily not even the people as a whole). The true (visible) church is that which exhibits the (moral) kingdom of God on earth so far as it can be brought to pass by men. The requirements upon, and hence the tokens of, the true church are the following:

---

[1] [Cf. Matthew VI, 10; Luke XI, 2]

1. *Universality*, and hence its numerical oneness; for which it must possess this characteristic,[1] that, although divided and at variance in unessential opinions, it is none the less, with respect to its fundamental intention, founded upon such basic principles as must necessarily lead to a general unification in a single church (thus, no sectarian divisions).

2. Its *nature* (quality); *i.e.*, *purity*, union under no motivating forces other than *moral* ones (purified of the stupidity of superstition and the madness of fanaticism).

3. Its *relation* under the principle of *freedom;* both the internal relation of its members to one another, and the external relation of the church to political power—both relations as in a *republic* (hence neither a *hierarchy*, nor an *illuminatism*, which is a kind of *democracy* through special inspiration, where the inspiration of one man can differ from that of another, according to the whim of each).

4. Its *modality*, the *unchangeableness* of its *constitution*, yet with the reservation that incidental regulations, concerning merely its *administration*, may be changed according to time and circumstance; to this end, however, it must already contain within itself *a priori* (in the idea of its purpose) settled principles. (Thus [it operates] under primordial laws, once [for all] laid down, as it were out of a book of laws, for guidance; not under arbitrary symbols which, since they lack authenticity, are fortuitous, exposed to contradiction, and changeable.)

An ethical commonwealth, then, in the form of a church, *i.e.*, as a mere *representative* of a city of God, really has, as regards its basic principles, nothing resembling a political constitution. For its constitution is neither *monarchical* (under a pope or patriarch), nor *aristocratic* (under bishops and prelates), nor *democratic* (as of sectarian *illuminati*). It could best of all be likened to that of a household (family) under a common, though invisible, moral Father, whose holy Son, knowing His will and yet standing in blood relation with all members of the household, takes His place in making His will better known to them; these accordingly honor the Father in him and so enter with one another into a voluntary, universal, and enduring union of hearts.

[1] *[Anlage]*

V. The Constitution of every Church Originates always in some Historical (Revealed) Faith which we can Call Ecclesiastical Faith; and this is best Founded on a Holy Scripture

Pure religious faith alone can found a universal church; for only [such] rational faith can be believed in and shared by everyone, whereas an historical faith, grounded solely on facts, can extend its influence no further than tidings of it can reach, subject to circumstances of time and place and dependent upon the capacity [of men] to judge the credibility of such tidings. Yet, by reason of a peculiar weakness of human nature, pure faith can never be relied on as much as it deserves, that is, a church cannot be established on it alone.

Men are conscious of their inability to know supersensible things; and although they allow all honor to be paid to faith in such things (as the faith which must be universally convincing to them), they are yet not easily convinced that steadfast diligence in morally good life-conduct is all that God requires of men, to be subjects in His kingdom and well-pleasing to Him. They cannot well think of their obligation except as an obligation to some *service* or other which they must offer to God—wherein what matters is not so much the inner moral worth of the actions as the fact that they are offered to God—to the end that, however morally indifferent men may be in themselves, they may at least please God through passive obedience. It does not enter their heads that when they fulfil their duties to men (themselves and others) they are, by these very acts, performing God's commands and are therefore in all their actions and abstentions, so far as these concern morality, *perpetually in the service of God*, and that it is absolutely impossible to serve God more directly in any other way (since they can affect and have an influence upon earthly beings alone, and not upon God). Because each great worldly lord stands in special need of being *honored* by his subjects and *glorified* through protestations of submissiveness, without which he cannot expect from them as much compliance with his behests as he requires to be able to rule them, and since, in addition, however gifted with reason a man may be, he always finds an immediate satisfaction in attestations of honor, we treat duty, so far as it is also a divine command, as the prosecution of a *transaction* with God, not with man. Thus arises the concept of a religion of *divine worship* instead of the concept of a religion purely moral.

Since all religion consists in this, that in all our duties we look upon God as the lawgiver universally to be honored, the determining of religion, so far as the conformity of our attitude with it is concerned, hinges upon knowing *how God wishes* to be honored (and obeyed). Now a divine legislative will commands either through laws in themselves *merely statutory* or through *purely moral* laws. As to the latter, each individual can know of himself, through his own reason, the will of God which lies at the basis of his religion; for the concept of the Deity really arises solely from consciousness of these laws and from the need of reason to postulate a might which can procure for these laws, as their final end, all the results conformable to them and possible in a world. The concept of a divine will, determined according to pure moral laws alone, allows us to think of only *one* religion which is purely moral, as it did of only *one* God. But if we admit statutory laws of such a will and make religion consist of our obedience to them, knowledge of such laws is possible not through our own reason alone but only through revelation, which, be it given publicly or to each individual in secret, would have to be an *historical* and not a *pure rational* faith in order to be propagated among men by tradition or writ. And even admitting divine statutory laws (laws which do not in themselves appear to us as obligatory but can be known as such only when taken as the revelation of God's will), pure *moral* legislation, through which the will of God is primordially engraved in our hearts, is not only the ineluctable condition of all true religion whatsoever but is also that which really constitutes such religion; statutory religion can merely comprise the means to its furtherance and spread.

If, then, the question: How does God wish to be honored? is to be answered in a way universally valid for each man, *regarded merely as man*, there can be no doubt that the legislation of His will ought to be solely *moral;* for statutory legislation (which presupposes a revelation) can be regarded merely as contingent and as something which never has applied or can apply to every man, hence as not binding upon all men universally. Thus, "not they who say Lord! Lord! but they who do the will of God,"[1] they who seek to become well-pleasing to Him not by praising Him (or His envoy, as a being of divine origin) according to revealed concepts

---

[1] [Matthew VII, 21: "Not every one that saith unto me, Lord, Lord, shall enter into the kingdom of heaven; but he that doeth the will of my Father which is in heaven."]

which not every man can have, but by a good course of life, regarding which everyone knows His will—these are they who offer Him the true veneration which He desires.

But when we regard ourselves as obliged to behave not merely as men but also as *citizens* in a divine state on earth, and to work for the existence of such a union, under the name of a church, then the question: How does God wish to be honored in *a church* (as a congregation of God)? appears to be unanswerable by reason alone and to require statutory legislation of which we become cognizant only through revelation, *i.e.*, an historical faith which, in contradistinction to pure religious faith, we can call ecclesiastical faith.

For pure religious faith is concerned only with what constitutes the essence[1] of reverence for God, namely, obedience, ensuing from the moral disposition, to all duties as His commands; a church, on the other hand, as the union of many men with such dispositions into a moral commonwealth, requires a *public* covenant,[2] a certain ecclesiastical form dependent upon the conditions of experience. This form is in itself contingent and manifold, and therefore cannot be apprehended as duty without divine statutory laws. But the determination of this form must not be regarded forthwith as the concern of the divine Lawgiver; rather are we justified in assuming that it is the divine will that we should ourselves carry into effect the rational idea of such a commonwealth and that, although men may have tried many a type of church with unhappy result, yet on no account should they cease to strive after this goal, with new attempts if necessary, avoiding so far as possible the mistakes of the earlier ones—inasmuch as this task, which is for them a duty as well, is entirely committed to them alone. We therefore have no reason straightway to take the laws constituting the basis and form of any church as divine *statutory* laws; rather is it presumptuous to declare them to be such, in order to save ourselves the trouble of still further improving the church's form, and it is a usurpation of higher authority to seek, under pretense of a divine commission, to lay a yoke upon the multitude by means of ecclesiastical dogmas. Yet it would be as great self-conceit to deny peremptorily that the way in which a church is organized may perhaps be a special divine arrangement, if, so far as we can see, it is completely harmonious with the moral religion—and if, in addition, we cannot

---

[1] [*Materie*]
[2] [*Verpflichtung*]

conceive how it could have appeared all at once without the requisite initiatory progress of the public in religious conceptions.

In the indecision over the problem of whether God or men themselves should found a church, there is evidenced man's propensity to *a religion of divine worship* (*cultus*) and—since such a religion rests upon arbitrary precepts—to belief in divine statutory laws, on the assumption that some divine legislation, not to be discovered through reason but calling for revelation, must supplement the best life-conduct (conduct which man is always free to adopt under the guidance of the pure moral religion). Herein consideration is given to the veneration of the Highest Being directly (and not by way of that obedience to His laws which is already prescribed to us by reason). Thus it happens that men will regard neither union into a church, nor agreement with respect to the form which it is to take, nor yet *public* institutions, as in themselves necessary for the promotion of the moral element in religion, but only, as they say, for the service of their God, through ceremonies, confessions of faith in revealed laws, and observance of the ordinances requisite to the form of the church (which is itself, after all, only a means). All these observances are at bottom morally indifferent actions; yet, just because they are to be performed merely for His sake, they are held to be all the more pleasing to Him. In men's striving towards an ethical commonwealth, ecclesiastical faith thus naturally precedes† pure religious faith; *temples* (buildings consecrated to the public worship of God) were before *churches* (meeting-places for the instruction and quickening of moral dispositions), *priests* (consecrated stewards of pious rites) before *divines* (teachers of the purely moral religion); and for the most part they still are first in the rank and value ascribed to them by the great mass of people. Since, then, it remains true once for all that a statutory *ecclesiastical faith* is associated with pure religious faith as its vehicle and as the means of public union of men for its promotion, one must grant that the preservation of pure religious faith unchanged, its propagation in the same form everywhere, and even a respect for the revelation assumed therein, can hardly be provided for adequately through *tradition*, but only through *scripture;* which, again, as a revelation to contemporaries and posterity, must itself be an object of esteem, for the necessities of men require this in order that they may be sure of their duty in

† Morally, this order ought to be reversed.

divine service. A holy book arouses the greatest respect even among those (indeed, most of all among those) who do not read it, or at least those who can form no coherent religious concept therefrom; and the most sophistical reasoning avails nothing in the face of the decisive assertion, which beats down every objection: *Thus it is written*. It is for this reason that the passages in it which are to lay down an article of faith are called simply *texts*.¹ The appointed expositors of such a scripture are themselves, by virtue of their occupation, like unto consecrated persons; and history proves that it has never been possible to destroy a faith grounded in scripture, even with the most devastating revolutions in the state, whereas the faith established upon tradition and ancient public observances has promptly met its downfall when the state was overthrown. How fortunate,* when such a book, fallen into men's hands, contains, along with its statutes, or laws of faith, the purest moral doctrine of religion in its completeness—a doctrine which can be brought into perfect harmony with such statutes ([which serve] as vehicles for its introduction). In this event, both because of the end thereby to be attained and because of the difficulty of rendering intelligible according to natural laws the origin of such enlightenment of the human race as proceeds from it, such a book can command an esteem like that accorded to revelation.

* * * * * * * * * * *

And now a few words touching this concept of a belief in revelation.

There is only *one* (true) *religion;* but there can be *faiths* of several kinds. We can say further that even in the various churches, severed from one another by reason of the diversity of their modes of belief, one and the same true religion can yet be found.

It is therefore more fitting (as it is more customary in actual practice) to say: This man is of this or that *faith* (Jewish, Mohammedan, Christian, Catholic, Lutheran), than: He is of this or that religion. The second expression ought in justice never to be used in addressing the general public (in catechisms and sermons), for it

---

* An expression for everything wished for, or worthy of being wished for, which we can neither foresee nor bring about through our own endeavors according to the laws of experience; for which, therefore, if we wish to name its source, we can offer none other than a gracious Providence.

¹ [*Sprüche*]

is too learned and unintelligible for them; indeed, the more modern languages possess no word of equivalent meaning. The common man always takes it to mean his ecclesiastical faith, which appeals to his senses, whereas religion is hidden within and has to do with moral dispositions.

One does too great honor to most people by saying of them: They profess this or that religion. For they know none and desire none—statutory ecclesiastical faith is all that they understand by the word. The so-called religious wars which have so often shaken the world and bespattered it with blood, have never been anything but wrangles over ecclesiastical faith; and the oppressed have complained not that they were hindered from adhering to their religion (for no external power can do this) but that they were not permitted publicly to observe their ecclesiastical faith.

Now when, as usually happens, a church proclaims itself to be the one church universal (even though it is based upon faith in a special revelation, which, being historical, can never be required of everyone), he who refuses to acknowledge its (peculiar) ecclesiastical faith is called by it an *unbeliever* and is hated wholeheartedly; he who diverges therefrom only in part (in non-essentials) is called *heterodox* and is at least shunned as a source of infection. But he who avows [allegiance to] this church and yet diverges from it on essentials of its faith (namely, regarding the practices connected with it), is called, especially if he spreads abroad his false belief, a *heretic*,* and, as a rebel, such a man is held more culpable than a foreign foe, is expelled from the church with an anathema (like that which the Romans pronounced on him who crossed the

---

* According to the *Alphabetum Tibetanum* of Georgius,[1] Mongols call Tibet "Tangut-Chazar," or the land of the house-dwellers, to distinguish its inhabitants from themselves as nomads living in the desert under tents. From this has originated the name Chazars, and from this name that of a *Ketzer* [=heretic], since the Mongols adhered to the Tibetan faith (of the Lamas) which agrees with Manicheanism, perhaps even arose from it, and spread it in Europe during their invasions; whence, too, for a long time the names *Hæretici* and *Manichæi* were synonymous in usage.[2]

[1] [*Alphabetum Tibetanum missionum apostolicarum commodo editum* . . . studio et labore Fr. Augustini Antonii Georgii eremitae Augustinui, Romae, 1762.]

[2] ["This etymological explanation is certainly incorrect. In all probability, *Ketzer* is related to *Gazzari*, the Lombardish word for *Kathari* = καθαροί. The Kathari (the "pure ones") were the most important heretical sect with which the church in the Middle Ages (especially in the twelfth and thirteenth centuries) had to deal. The Manichaean element in the movement is unmistakable." (Note in Berlin Edition.)]

Rubicon against the Senate's will) and is given over to all the gods of hell. The exclusive correctness of belief in matters of ecclesiastical faith claimed by the church's teachers or heads is called *orthodoxy*. This could be sub-divided into *despotic* (*brutal*) or *liberal* orthodoxy.

If a church which claims that its ecclesiastical faith is universally binding is called a *catholic* church, and if that which protests against such claims on the part of others (even though oftentimes it would gladly advance similar claims itself, if it could) is called a *protestant* church, an alert observer will come upon many laudable examples of protestant Catholics and, on the other hand, still more examples, and offensive ones, of arch-catholic Protestants: the first, men of a cast of mind (even though it is not that of their church) *leading to self-expansion;* to which the second, with their *circumscribed* cast of mind, stand in sharp contrast—not at all to their own advantage.

VI. Ecclesiastical Faith Has Pure Religious Faith as its Highest Interpreter

We have noted that a church dispenses with the most important mark of truth, namely, a rightful claim to universality, when it bases itself upon a revealed faith. For such a faith, being historical (even though it be far more widely disseminated and more completely secured for remotest posterity through the agency of scripture) can never be universally communicated so as to produce conviction. Yet, because of the natural need and desire of all men for something *sensibly tenable*, and for a confirmation of some sort from experience of the highest concepts and grounds of reason (a need which really must be taken into account when the universal *dissemination* of a faith is contemplated), some historical ecclesiastical faith or other, usually to be found at hand, must be utilized.

If such an empirical faith, which chance, it would seem, has tossed into our hands, is to be united with the basis of a moral faith (be the first an end or merely a means), an exposition of the revelation which has come into our possession is required, that is, a thorough-going interpretation of it in a sense agreeing with the universal practical rules of a religion of pure reason. For the theoretical part of ecclesiastical faith cannot interest us morally if it does not conduce to the performance of all human duties as divine commands (that which constitutes the essence of all religion). Frequently this interpretation may, in the light of the text (of the revelation), appear forced—it may often really be forced; and yet if the text can possibly support it, it must be preferred to a literal interpretation which either contains nothing at all [helpful] to morality or else actually works counter to moral incentives.†

We shall find, too, that this has always been done with all types of faith, old and new, some of them recorded in holy books, and that wise and thoughtful teachers of the people kept on interpreting them until, gradually, they brought them, as regards their essential content, into line with the universal moral dogmas. The moral philosophers among the Greeks, and later among the Romans, did exactly this with the fabulous accounts of the gods. They were able in the end to interpret the grossest polytheism as mere symbolic representation of the attributes of the single divine Being, and to supply the various wicked actions [of the gods] and the wild yet lovely fancies of the poets with a mystical meaning which made a popular faith (which it would have been very inadvisable

† As an illustration of this, take Psalm LIX, 11–16, where we find a *prayer* for *revenge* which goes to terrifying extremes. Michaelis (*Moral*, Part II, p. 202) approves of this prayer, and adds: "The Psalms are *inspired;* if in them punishment is prayed for, it cannot be wrong, and *we must have no morality holier than the Bible.*" Restricting myself to this last expression, I raise the question as to whether morality should be expounded according to the Bible or whether the Bible should not rather be expounded according to morality. Without considering how the passage in the New Testament,[1] "It was said to them of old times, etc. . . . But I say unto you, Love your enemies, *bless them that curse you,* etc. . . . ,'" which is also inspired, can agree with the other, I should try, as a first alternative, to bring the New Testament passage into conformity with my own self-subsistent moral principles (that perhaps the reference is here not to enemies in the flesh but rather to invisible enemies which are symbolized by them and are far more dangerous to us, namely, evil inclinations which we must desire to bring wholly under foot). Or, if this cannot be managed, I shall rather have it that this passage is not to be understood in a moral sense at all but only as applying to the relation in which the Jews conceived themselves to stand to God as their political regent. This latter interpretation applies to still another passage in the Bible, where it is written: "Vengeance is mine. I will repay, saith the Lord."[2] This is commonly interpreted as a moral warning against private revenge, though probably it merely refers to the law, valid for every state, that satisfaction for injury shall be sought in the courts of justice of the overlord, where the judge's permission to the complainant to ask for a punishment as severe as he desires is not to be taken as approval of the complainant's craving for revenge.

[1] [Cf. Matthew V, 21 ff., 44 ff.]
[2] [Cf. Romans XII, 19: Deuteronomy XXXII, 35]

to destroy, since atheism, still more dangerous to the state, might perhaps have resulted) approach a moral doctrine intelligible to all men and wholly salutary. The later Judaism, and even Christianity itself, consist of such interpretations, often very forced, but in both instances for ends unquestionably good and needful for all men. The Mohammedans (as Reland[1] shows) know very well how to ascribe a spiritual meaning to the description of their paradise, which is dedicated to sensuality of every kind; the Indians do exactly the same thing in the interpretation of their Vedas, at least for the enlightened portion of their people.

That this can be done without ever and again offending greatly against the literal meaning of the popular faith is due to the fact that, earlier by far than this faith, the predisposition to the moral religion lay hidden in human reason; and though its first rude manifestations took the form merely of practices of divine worship, and for this very purpose gave rise to those alleged revelations, yet these manifestations have infused even into the myths, though unintentionally, something from the nature of their supersensible origin. Nor can we charge such interpretations with dishonesty, provided we are not disposed to assert that the meaning which we ascribe to the symbols of the popular faith, even to the holy books, is exactly as intended by them, but rather allow this question to be left undecided and merely admit the *possibility* that their authors may be so understood. For the final purpose even of reading these holy scriptures, or of investigating their content, is to make men better; the historical element, which contributes nothing to this end, is something which is in itself quite indifferent, and we can do with it what we like. (Historical faith "is dead, being alone";[2] that is, of itself, regarded as a creed, it contains nothing, and leads to nothing, which could have any moral value for us.)

Hence, even if a document is accepted as a divine revelation, the highest criterion of its being of divine origin will be: "All scripture given by inspiration of God is profitable for doctrine, for reproof, for improvement, etc.";[3] and since this last, to wit, the moral improvement of men, constitutes the real end of all religion of reason, it will comprise the highest principle of all Scriptural exegesis.

[1] [Adrian Reland (1676–1718), a Dutch Orientalist, wrote *De religione mohammedica ibri duo*, second edition, 1717; cf. II, xvii.]
[2] [Cf. James II, 17]
[3] [Cf. II Timothy III, 16]

This religion is "the Spirit of God, who guides us into all truth";[1] and this it is which in *instructing* us also *animates* us with basic principles for action, and wholly subjects whatever Scripture may contain for historical faith to the rules and incentives of pure moral faith, which alone constitutes the element of genuine religion in each ecclesiastical faith. All investigation and interpretation of Scripture must from the start be based on a search for this Spirit in it, and "eternal life can be found therein only so far as it [Scripture] testifies of this principle."[2]

Now placed beside this Scriptural interpreter, but subordinated to him, is another, namely, the *Scriptural scholar*. The authority of Scripture, as the most worthy instrument, and at present the only instrument in the most enlightened portion of the world, for the union of all men into one church, constitutes the ecclesiastical faith, which, as the popular faith, cannot be neglected, because no doctrine based on reason alone seems to the people qualified to serve as an unchangeable norm. They demand divine revelation, and hence also an historical certification of its authority through the tracing back of its origin. Now human skill and wisdom cannot ascend so far as heaven in order itself to inspect the credentials validating the mission of the first Teacher. It must be content with evidence that can be elicited, apart from the content, as to the way in which such a faith has been introduced—that is, with human reports which must be searched out little by little from very ancient times, and from languages now dead, for evaluation as to their historical credibility. Hence *Scriptural scholarship* will [ever] be required to maintain in authority a church founded upon Holy Scripture, ([though] not a religion, which, to be universal, must always be founded upon reason alone), even though this scholarship settles no more than that there is nothing in the origin of Scripture to render impossible its acceptance as direct divine revelation; for this would suffice to provide security for those who fancy that they find in this idea [of a revealed Scripture] special fortification of their moral faith, and who therefore gladly accept it. Yet not only the *authentication* of Holy Scripture, but its *interpretation* as well, stands in need of scholarship, and for the same reason. For how are the unlearned, who can read it only in transla-

[1] [Cf. John XVI, 13: "Howbeit when he, the Spirit of truth, is come, he will guide you into all truth, etc."]
[2] [Cf. John V, 39: "Search the scriptures; for in them ye think ye have eternal life: and they are they which testify of me."]

tion, to be certain of its meaning? Hence the expositor, in addition to being familiar with the original tongue, must also be a master of extended historical knowledge and criticism, in order that from the conditions, customs, and opinions (the popular faith) of the times in question he may be able to derive the means wherewith to enlighten the understanding of the ecclesiastical commonwealth.

Rational religion and Scriptural learning are thus the properly qualified interpreters and trustees of a sacred document. It is obvious that they must on no account be hindered by the secular arm in the public use of their judgments and discoveries in this field, or bound to certain dogmas; for otherwise the *laity* would compel the *clergy* to concur in their opinion, which, after all, they have acquired only from the clergy's instruction. So long as the state takes care that there is no dearth of scholars and of men in morally good repute who have authority in the entire church body and to whose consciences the state entrusts this commission, it has done all that its duty and capacity require. But to insist that the legislator should carry this matter into the schools and concern himself with their quarrels (which, if they are not proclaimed from the pulpit, leave the church-public quite undisturbed)—such a burden the public cannot thrust upon him without arrogance, for it is beneath his dignity.

A third claimant contests the office of interpreter, the man who needs neither reason nor scholarship, but merely an inner *feeling*, to recognize the true meaning of Scripture as well as its divine origin. Now we certainly cannot deny that "he who follows its teachings and *does* what it commands will surely find that it is of God,"[1] and that the very impulse to good actions and to uprightness in the conduct of life, which the man who reads Scripture or hears it expounded must feel, cannot but convince him of its divine nature; for this impulse is but the operation of the moral law which fills man with fervent respect and hence deserves to be regarded as a divine command. A knowledge of laws, and of their morality, can scarcely be derived from any sort of feeling; still less can there be inferred or discovered from a feeling certain evidence of a direct divine influence; for the same effect can have more than one cause. In this case, however, the bare morality of the law (and the doctrine), known through reason, is the source [of the law's validity];

---

[1] [Cf. John VII, 17: "If any man will do his will, he shall know of the doctrine, whether it be of God. . . ."]

and even if this origin were no more than barely possible, duty demands that it be thus construed unless we wish to open wide the gates to every kind of fanaticism, and even cause the unequivocal moral feeling to lose its dignity through affiliation with fantasy of every sort. Feeling is private to every individual and cannot be demanded of others [even] when the law, from which and according to which this feeling arises, is known in advance; therefore one cannot urge it as a touchstone for the genuineness of a revelation, for it teaches absolutely nothing, but is merely the way in which the subject is affected as regards pleasure or displeasure—and on this basis can be established no knowledge whatever.

There is therefore no norm of ecclesiastical faith other than Scripture, and no expositor thereof other than pure *religion of reason* and *Scriptural scholarship* (which deals with the historical aspect of that religion). Of these, the first alone is *authentic* and valid for the whole world; the second is merely *doctrinal*, having as its end the transformation of ecclesiastical faith for a given people at a given time into a definite and enduring system. Under this system, historical faith must finally become mere faith in Scriptural scholars and their insight. This does not, indeed, particularly redound to the honor of human nature; yet it is a situation which can be corrected through public freedom of thought—and such freedom is the more justified since only if scholars submit their interpretations to public examination, while they themselves ever hope for and remain open and receptive to better insight, can they count on the community's confidence in their decisions.

VII. The Gradual Transition of Ecclesiastical Faith to the Exclusive Sovereignty of Pure Religious Faith is the Coming of the Kingdom of God

The token of the true church is its *universality;* the sign of this, in turn, is its necessity and its determinability in only one possible way. Historical faith (which is based upon revelation, regarded as an experience) has only particular validity, to wit, for those who have had access to the historical record upon which this faith rests; and like all empirical knowledge it carries with it the consciousness not that the object believed in *must* be so and not otherwise, but merely that it *is* so; hence it involves as well the consciousness of its contingency. Thus historical faith can become an ecclesiastical faith (of which there can be several), whereas only pure religious faith, which bases itself wholly upon reason, can be accepted as necessary and therefore as the only one which signalizes the *true* church.

When, therefore, (in conformity with the unavoidable limitation of human reason) an historical faith attaches itself to pure religion, as its vehicle, but with the consciousness that it is only a vehicle, and when this faith, having become ecclesiastical, embraces the principle of a continual approach to pure religious faith, in order finally to be able to dispense with the historical vehicle, a church thus characterized can at any time be called the *true* church; but, since conflict over historical dogmas can never be avoided, it can be spoken of only as the church *militant*, though with the prospect of becoming finally the changeless and all-unifying church *triumphant!* We call the faith of every individual who possesses moral capacity (worthiness) for eternal happiness a *saving* faith. This also can be but a single faith; amid all diversity of ecclesiastical faiths [or creeds] it is discoverable in each of these in which, moving toward the goal of pure religious faith, it is practical. The faith of a religion of divine worship, in contrast, is a *drudging* and mercenary faith (*fides mercenaria, servilis*) and cannot be regarded as saving because it is not moral. For a moral faith must be free and based upon an ingenuous disposition of the heart (*fides ingenua*). Ecclesiastical faith fancies it possible to become well-pleasing to God through actions (of *worship*) which (though irksome) yet possess in themselves no moral worth and hence are merely acts induced by fear or hope—acts which an evil man also can perform. Moral faith, in contrast, presupposes that a morally good disposition is requisite.

Saving faith involves two elements, upon which hope of salvation is conditioned, the one having reference to what man himself cannot accomplish, namely, undoing lawfully (before a divine judge) actions which he has performed, the other to what he himself can and ought to do, that is, leading a new life conformable to his duty. The first is the faith in an atonement (reparation for his debt, redemption, reconciliation with God); the second, the faith that we can become well-pleasing to God through a good course of life in the future. Both conditions constitute but one faith and necessarily belong together. Yet we can comprehend the necessity of their union only by assuming that one can be derived from the other, that is, either that the faith in the absolution from the debt resting upon us will bring forth good life-conduct, or else that the genuine and active disposition ever to pursue a good course of life will engender the faith in such absolution according to the law of morally operating causes.

Here now appears a remarkable antinomy of human reason with itself, whose solution, or, were this not possible, at least whose adjustment can alone determine whether an historical (ecclesiastical) faith must always be present as an essential element of saving faith, over and above pure religious faith, or whether it is only a vehicle which finally—however distant this future event may be—can pass over into pure religious faith.

1. If it is assumed that atonement has been made for the sins of mankind, it is indeed conceivable that every sinner would gladly have it applied to himself and that were it merely a matter of *belief* (which means no more than an avowal that he wishes the atonement to be rendered for him also), he would not for an instant suffer misgivings on this score. However, it is quite impossible to see how a reasonable man, who knows himself to merit punishment, can in all seriousness believe that he needs only to credit the news of an atonement rendered for him, and to accept this atonement *utiliter* (as the lawyers say), in order to regard his guilt as annihilated,—indeed, so completely annihilated (to the very root) that good life-conduct, for which he has hitherto not taken the least pains, will in the future be the inevitable consequence of this faith and this acceptance of the proffered favor. No thoughtful person can bring himself to believe this, even though self-love often does transform the bare wish for a good, for which man does nothing and can do nothing, into a hope, as though one's object were to come of itself, elicited by mere longing. Such a persuasion can be regarded as possible only if the individual regards this belief as itself instilled in him by heaven and hence as something concerning which he need render no further account to his reason. If he cannot think this, or if he is still too sincere artificially to produce in himself such a confidence, as a mere means of ingratiation, he can only, with all respect for such a transcendent[1] atonement, and with every wish that it be available for him also, regard it as conditioned. That is, he must believe that he must first improve his way of life, so far as improvement lies in his power, if he is to have even the slightest ground for hope of such a higher gain. Where-

[1] *überschwenglich*]

fore, since historical knowledge of the atonement belongs to ecclesiastical faith, while the improved way of life, as a condition, belongs to pure moral faith, *the latter must take precedence over the former*.

2. But if men are corrupt by nature, how can a man believe that by himself, try as hard as he will, he can make himself a new man well-pleasing to God, when—conscious of the transgressions of which up to the present he has been guilty—he still stands in the power of the evil principle and finds in himself no capacity adequate for future improvement? If he cannot regard justice, which he has provoked against himself, as satisfied through atonement by another,[1] and cannot regard himself reborn, so to speak, through this faith and so for the first time able to enter upon a new course of life—and this would follow from his union with the good principle—upon what is he to base his hope of becoming a man pleasing to God? Thus faith in a merit not his own, whereby he is reconciled with God, must precede every effort to good works. But this goes counter to the previous proposition, [that good works must *precede* faith in divine atonement]. This contradiction cannot be resolved through insight into the causal determination of the freedom of a human being, *i.e.*, into the causes which bring it about that a man becomes good or bad; hence it cannot be resolved theoretically, for it is a question wholly transcending the speculative capacity of our reason. But practically, the question arises: What, in the use of our free will[w], comes first, (not physically[2] but morally)? Where shall we start, *i.e.*, with a faith in what God has done on our behalf, or with what we are to do to become worthy of God's assistance (whatever this may be)? In answering this question we cannot hesitate in deciding for the second alternative.

The acceptance of the first requisite for salvation, namely, faith in a vicarious atonement, is in any case necessary only for the theoretical concept; in no other way can we *make comprehensible* to ourselves such absolution. In contrast, the necessity for the second principle is practical and, indeed, purely moral. We can certainly hope to partake in the appropriation of another's atoning merit, and so of salvation, only by qualifying for it through our own efforts to fulfil every human duty—and this obedience must be the effect of our own action and not, once again, of a foreign

---

[1] [*fremde*]
[2] [*i.e.*, not in time.]

influence in the presence of which we are passive. For since the command to do our duty is unconditioned, it is also necessary that man shall make it, as maxim, the basis of his belief, that is to say that he shall begin with the improvement of his life as the supreme condition under which alone a saving faith can exist.

Ecclesiastical faith, being historical, rightly starts with the belief in atonement; but since it merely constitutes the vehicle for pure religious faith (in which lies the real end), the maxim of *action*, which in religious faith (being practical) is the condition, must take the lead, and the maxim of *knowledge*, or theoretical faith, must merely bring about the strengthening and consummation of the maxim of action.

In this connection it might also be remarked that, according to the ecclesiastical principle, the faith in a vicarious atonement would be imputed to man as a duty, whereas faith in good life-conduct, as being effected through a higher agency, would be reckoned to him as of grace. According to the other principle the order is reversed. For according to it the *good course of life*, as the highest condition of grace, is unconditioned *duty*, whereas atonement from on high[1] is purely a *matter of grace*. Against the first faith is charged (often not unjustly) the *superstitious belief* of divine worship, which knows how to combine a blameworthy course of life with religion; against the second, *naturalistic unbelief*, which unites with a course of life, perhaps otherwise exemplary, indifference or even antagonism to all revelation. This [latter attitude] would constitute cutting the knot (by means of a practical maxim) instead of disentangling it (theoretically)—a procedure which is after all permitted in religious questions. However, the theoretical demand can be satisfied in the following manner.

The living faith in the archetype of humanity well-pleasing to God (in the Son of God) is bound up, *in itself*, with a moral idea of reason so far as this serves us not only as a guide-line but also as an incentive; hence it matters not whether I start with it as a *rational* faith, or with the principle of a good course of life. In contrast, the faith in the self-same archetype *in its [phenomenal] appearance* (faith in the God-Man), as an *empirical* (historical) faith, is not interchangeable with the principle of the good course of life (which must be wholly rational), and it would be quite a

[1] [*höhere*]

different matter to wish to start with such a faith† and to deduce the good course of life from it. To this extent, then, there would be a contradiction between the two propositions above. And yet, in the appearance of the God-Man [on earth], it is not that in him which strikes the senses and can be known through experience, but rather the archetype, lying in our reason, that we attribute to him (since, so far as his example can be known, he is found to conform thereto), which is really the object of saving faith, and such a faith does not differ from the principle of a course of life well-pleasing to God.

Here, then, are not two principles which in themselves so differ that to begin with the one, or the other, would be to enter upon opposing paths, but only one and the same practical idea from which we take our start, this idea representing the archetype now as found in God and proceeding from Him, and now, as found in us, but in both instances as the gauge for our course of life. The antinomy is therefore only apparent, since, through a misunderstanding, it regards the self-same practical idea, taken merely in different references, as two different principles. If one wished, however, to make the historical faith in the reality of such an appearance, taking place in the world on a single occasion, the condition of the only saving faith, there would, indeed, be two quite different principles (the one empirical, the other rational) regarding which a real conflict of maxims would arise—whether one should begin with and start out from the one or the other. This conflict no reason would ever be able to resolve.

The proposition: We must believe that there was once a man (of whom reason tells us nothing) who through his holiness and merit rendered satisfaction both for himself (with reference to his duty) and for all others (with their shortcomings, in the light of their duty), if we are to hope that we ourselves, though in a good course of life, will be saved by virtue of that faith alone—this proposition says something very different from the following: With all our strength we must strive after the holy disposition of a course of life well-pleasing to God, to be able to believe that the love (already assured us through reason) of God toward man, so far as man does endeavor with all his strength to do the will of God, will make good, in consideration of an upright disposition, the deficiency of the deed, whatever this deficiency may be. The first

† Which must base the existence of such a person on historical evidence.

belief is not in the power of everyone (even of the unlearned). History testifies that in all forms of religion this conflict between two principles of faith has existed; for all religions have involved expiation, on whatever basis they put it, and the moral predisposition in each individual has not failed, on its side, to let its claims be heard. Yet at all times the priests have complained more than the moralists: the former (with summons to the authorities to check the mischief) protesting loudly against the neglect of divine worship, which was instituted to reconcile the people with heaven and to ward off misfortune from the state; the latter complaining, on the other hand, about the decline of morals, a decline which they zealously set to the account of those means of absolution whereby the priests made it easy for anyone to make his peace with the Deity over the grossest vices. In point of fact, if an inexhaustible fund is already at hand for the payment of debts incurred or still to be incurred, so that man has merely to reach out (and at every claim which conscience makes one would be sure, first of all, to reach out) in order to free himself of sin, while he can postpone resolving upon a good course of life until he is first clear of those debts—if this were possible it is not easy to conceive any other consequences of such a faith. Yet were this faith to be portrayed as having so peculiar a power and so mystical (or magical) an influence, that although merely historical, so far as we can see, it is yet competent to better the whole man from the ground up (to make a new man of him) if he yields himself to it and to the feelings bound up with it, such a faith would have to be regarded as imparted and inspired directly by heaven (together with, and in, the historical faith), and everything connected even with the moral constitution of man would resolve itself into an unconditioned decree of God: "He hath mercy on whom he will, and whom he will he *hardeneth*,"[1]* which, taken according to the letter, is the *salto mortale* of human reason.

* This can, indeed, be interpreted as follows. No one can say with certainty why this man becomes good, that man evil (both comparatively), because the predisposition to one of these characters or the other often seems to be discoverable at birth, and because contingencies of life as well, which no one can foresee, seem to tip the scale. No more can one say what a man may develop into. In all this therefore we must entrust judgment to the All-Seeing; but this is expressed in the text as though His decree, pronounced upon men

[1] [Cf. Romans IX, 18]

Hence a necessary consequence of the physical and, at the same time, the moral predisposition in us, the latter being the basis and the interpreter of all religion, is that in the end religion will gradually be freed from all empirical determining grounds and from all statutes which rest on history and which through the agency of ecclesiastical faith provisionally unite men for the requirements of the good; and thus at last the pure religion of reason will rule over all, "so that God may be all in all."[1] The integuments within which the embryo first developed into a human being must be laid aside when he is to come into the light of day. The leading-string of holy tradition with its appendages of statutes and observances, which in its time did good service, becomes bit by bit dispensable, yea, finally, when man enters upon his adolescence, it becomes a fetter. While he (the human race) "was a child he understood as a child"[2] and managed to combine a certain amount of erudition, and even a philosophy ministering to the church, with the propositions which were bestowed on him without his cooperation: "but when he becomes a man he puts away childish things."[2] The humiliating distinction between *laity* and *clergy* disappears, and equality arises from true freedom, yet without anarchy, because, though each obeys the (non-statutory) law which he prescribes to himself, he must at the same time regard this law as the will of a World-Ruler revealed to him through reason, a will which by invisible means unites all under one common government into one state—a state previously and inadequately represented and prepared for by the visible church. All this is not to be expected from an external revolution, because such an upheaval produces its effect tempestuously and violently, an effect, quite dependent on circumstances. Moreover whatever mistake has once been made in the establishment of a new constitution, is regretfully retained

---

before they were born, had prescribed to each the role which he was some day to play. *Prevision* regarding the order of appearances is at the same time *predestination* for a World-Creator, when, in this connection, He is conceived of in terms of human senses.[3] But in the supersensible order of things, according to the laws of freedom, where time drops out, it is only an *all-seeing knowledge;* and yet it is impossible to explain why one man conducts himself in one way, and another according to opposite principles and to harmonize [this knowledge of causes] with the freedom of the will.

[1] [Cf. I Corinthians XV, 28]
[2] [Cf. I Corinthians XIII, 11]
[3] [*anthropopathisch*]

throughout hundreds of years, since it can no longer be changed or at least only through a new (and at any time dangerous) revolution. The basis for the transition to that new order of affairs must lie in the principle that the pure religion of reason is a continually occurring divine (though not empirical) revelation for all men. Once this basis has been grasped with mature reflection, it is carried into effect, so far as this is destined to be a human task, through gradually advancing reform. As for revolutions which might hasten this progress, they rest in the hands of Providence and cannot be ushered in according to plan without damage to freedom.

We have good reason to say, however, that "the kingdom of God is come unto us"[1] once the principle of the gradual transition of ecclesiastical faith to the universal religion of reason, and so to a (divine) ethical state on earth, has become general and has also gained somewhere a *public* foothold, even though the actual establishment of this state is still infinitely removed from us. For since this principle contains the basis for a continual approach towards such a consummation, there lies in it (invisibly), as in a seed which is self-developing and in due time self-fertilizing, the whole, which one day is to illumine and to rule the world. But truth and goodness—and in the natural predisposition of every man there lies a basis of insight into these as well as a basis of heartfelt sympathy with them—do not fail to communicate themselves far and wide once they have become public, thanks to their natural affinity with the moral predisposition of rational beings generally. The obstacles, arising from political and civil causes, which may from time to time hinder their spread, serve rather to make all the closer the union of men's spirits with the good (which never leaves their thoughts after they have once cast their eyes upon it).*   *   *   *   *   *   *

* Without either renouncing the service of ecclesiastical faith or attacking it, one can recognize its useful influence as a vehicle and at the same time deny to it, taken as the illusory duty of divine worship, all influence upon the concept of genuine (that is, moral) religion. Thus, amid the diversity of statutory forms of belief, a mutual compatibility of the adherents to these forms can be established through the basic principles of the one and only religion of reason, toward which the teachers of all such dogmas and observances should direct their interpretations; until, in time, by virtue of the true enlightenment (conformity to law, proceeding from moral freedom) which has

[1] [Cf. Matthew XII, 28]

Such, therefore, is the activity of the good principle, unnoted by human eyes but ever continuing—erecting for itself in the human race, regarded as a commonwealth under laws of virtue, a power and kingdom which sustains the victory over evil and, under its own dominion, assures the world of an eternal peace.

---

now prevailed, the form of a debasing means of constraint can be exchanged, by unanimous consent, for an ecclesiastical form which squares with the dignity of a moral religion, to wit, the religion of a free faith. To combine a unity of ecclesiastical belief with freedom in matters of faith is a problem toward whose solution the idea of the objective unity of the religion of reason continually urges us, through the moral interest which we take in this religion; although, when we take human nature into account, there appears small hope of bringing this to pass in a visible church. It is an idea of reason which we cannot represent through any [sensuous] intuition adequate to it, but which, as a practical regulative principle, does have objective reality, enabling it to work toward this end, *i.e.*, the unity of the pure religion of reason. In this it is like the political idea of the rights of a state so far as these are meant to relate to an international law which is universal and *possessed of power*. Here experience bids us give over all hope. A propensity seems to have been implanted (perhaps designedly) in the human race causing every single state to strive if possible to subjugate every other state and to erect a universal monarchy, but, when it has reached a certain size, to break up, of its own accord, into smaller states. In like manner every single church cherishes the proud pretension of becoming a church universal; yet as soon as it has extended itself and commenced to rule, a principle of *dis*solution and schism into different sects at once shows itself.†

† The premature and therefore (since it comes before men have become morally better) the harmful fusion of states into one is chiefly hindered—if we are permitted here to assume a design of Providence—through two mightily effective causes, namely, difference of tongues, and difference of religions.

HISTORICAL ACCOUNT OF THE GRADUAL ESTABLISHMENT OF
THE SOVEREIGNTY OF THE GOOD PRINCIPLE ON EARTH

We can expect no *universal history* of religion (in the strictest
meaning of the word) among men on earth; for, since it is based
upon pure moral faith, it has no public status,[1] and each man
can become aware only in and for himself of the advances which he
has made in it. Hence it is only of ecclesiastical faith that we can
expect a universal historical account, in which its varied and
changing form is compared with the single, unchanging, pure religious faith. At the point where the first of these publicly recognizes its dependence upon the qualifying conditions of the second
and the necessity of conformity to them, the *church universal* commences to fashion itself into an ethical state of God and to march
toward the consummation of this state under a steadfast principle
which is one and the same for all men and for all times. We can
see in advance that this history will be nothing but the narrative
of the enduring conflict between the faith of divine worship and
the moral faith of religion, the first of which, as historical faith,
man is continually inclined to put foremost, while, on the other
hand, the second has never relinquished its claim to the priority
to which it is entitled as the only faith bettering the soul—a claim
which it will certainly, in the end, make good.

Now this historical account can have unity only if it is confined
wholly to that portion of the human race in which the predisposition to the unity of the universal church is already approaching
its [complete] development, that is, when the problem of the difference between the faiths of reason and of history has already been
publicly propounded and its solution made a matter of the greatest
moral importance; for an historical account merely of the dogmas
of diverse peoples, whose faiths stand in no connection with one
another, can reveal no [such example of] church unity. It cannot
be taken as an instance of this unity that in one and the same
people a certain new faith once arose and distinguished itself by
name from the faith previously dominant, even though the latter
afforded the *occasional* causes of the new product. For there must
exist a unity of principle if we are to construe the succession of
different types of belief following one another as modifications of

1 [*Zustand*]

one and the same church; and it is really with the history of this church that we are now concerned.

So we can deal, under this heading, only with the history of that church which contained within itself, from its first beginning, the seed and the principles of the objective unity of the true and *universal* religious faith, to which it is gradually brought nearer. And first of all it is evident that the Jewish faith stands in no essential connection whatever, *i.e.*, in no unity of concepts, with this ecclesiastical faith whose history we wish to consider, though the Jewish immediately preceded this (the Christian) church and provided the physical occasion for its establishment.

The *Jewish faith* was, in its original form, a collection of mere statutory laws upon which was established a political organization; for whatever moral additions were then or later *appended* to it in no way whatever belong to Judaism as such. Judaism is really not a religion at all but merely a union of a number of people who, since they belonged to a particular stock, formed themselves into a commonwealth under purely political laws, and not into a church; nay, it was *intended* to be merely an earthly state so that, were it possibly to be dismembered through adverse circumstances, there would still remain to it (as part of its very essence) the political faith in its eventual reestablishment (with the advent of the Messiah). That this political organization has a theocracy as its basis (visibly, an aristocracy of priests or leaders, who boast of instructions imparted directly by God), and that therefore the name of God, who after all is here merely an earthly regent making absolutely no claims upon, and no appeals to, conscience, is respected—this does not make it a religious organization. The proof that Judaism has not allowed its organization to become religious is clear. *First*, all its commands are of the kind which a political organization can insist upon and lay down as coercive laws, since they relate merely to external acts; and although the Ten Commandments are, to the eye of reason, valid as ethical commands even had they not been given publicly, yet in that legislation they are not so prescribed as to induce obedience by laying requirements upon the *moral disposition* (Christianity later placed its main emphasis here); they are directed to absolutely nothing but outer observance. From this it is also clear that, *second*, all the consequences of fulfilling or transgressing these laws, all rewards or punishments, are limited to those alone which can be allotted to all men in this world, and not even these [are distributed] according to ethical concepts, since both rewards and punishments were to reach a posterity which has taken no practical part in these deeds or misdeeds. In a political organization this may indeed be a prudent device for creating docility, but in an ethical organization it would be contrary to all right. Furthermore, since no religion can be conceived of which involves no belief in a future life, Judaism, which, when taken in its purity is seen to lack this belief, is not a religious faith at all. This can be further supported by the following remark. We can hardly question that the Jews, like other peoples, even the most savage, ought [normally] to have had a belief in a future life, and therefore in a heaven and a hell; for this belief automatically obtrudes itself upon everyone by virtue of the universal moral predisposition in human nature. Hence it certainly came about *intentionally* that the law-giver of this people, even though he is represented as God Himself, *wished* to pay not the slightest regard to the future life. This shows that he must have wanted to found merely a political, not an ethical commonwealth; and to talk, in a political state, of rewards and punishments which cannot become apparent here in this life would have been, on that premise, a wholly inconsequential and unsuitable procedure. And though, indeed, it cannot be doubted that the Jews may, subsequently, and each for himself, have framed some sort of religious faith which was mingled with the articles of their statutory belief, such religious faith has never been part and parcel of the legislation of Judaism. *Third,* Judaism fell so far short of constituting an era suited to the requirements of the *church universal,* or of setting up this universal church itself during its time, as actually to exclude from its communion the entire human race, on the ground that it was a special people chosen by God for Himself—[an exclusiveness] which showed enmity toward all other peoples and which, therefore, evoked the enmity of all. In this connection, we should not rate too highly the fact that this people set up, as universal Ruler of the world, a one and only God who could be represented through no visible image. For we find that the religious doctrines of most other peoples tended in the same direction and that these made themselves suspected of polytheism only by the *veneration* of certain mighty undergods subordinated to Him. For a God who desires merely obedience to commands for which absolutely no improved moral disposition is requisite is, after all, not really the moral Being the concept of whom we need for a religion. Religion would be more likely to arise from a belief in many mighty invisible beings of this order, provided a people conceived of these as all agreeing, amid their "departmental" differences, to bestow their good pleasure only upon the man who cherishes virtue with all his heart—more likely, I say, than when faith is bestowed upon but one Being, who, however, attaches prime importance to mechanical worship.

We cannot, therefore, do otherwise than begin general church history, if it is to constitute a system, with the origin of Christianity, which, completely forsaking the Judaism from which it sprang, and grounded upon a wholly new principle, effected a thoroughgoing revolution in doctrines of faith. The pains which teachers of Christianity take now, and may have taken in the beginning, to join Judaism and Christianity with a connecting strand by trying to have men regard the new faith as a mere continuation of the old (which, they allege, contained in prefiguration all the events of the new)—these efforts reveal most clearly that their problem is and was merely the discovery of the most suitable means of *introducing* a purely moral religion in place of the old worship, to which the people were all too well habituated, without directly offending the people's prejudices. The subsequent dispensing with the corporal sign which served wholly to separate this people from others warrants the judgment that the new faith, not bound to the statutes of the old, nor, indeed, to any statutes whatever, was to comprise a religion valid for the world and not for one single people.

Thus Christianity arose suddenly, though not unprepared for, from Judaism. The latter, however, was no longer patriarchal and unmixed, standing solely upon its political constitution (for even this was by that time sorely unsettled), but was already interfused, by reason of moral doctrines gradually made public within it, with a religious faith—for this otherwise ignorant people had been able to receive much foreign (Greek) wisdom. This wisdom presumably had the further effect of enlightening Judaism with concepts of virtue and, despite the pressing weight of its dogmatic faith, of preparing it for revolution, the opportunity being afforded by the diminished power of the priests, who had been subjugated to the rule of a people[1] which regarded all foreign popular beliefs

[1] [*i.e.*, the Romans]

with indifference. The Teacher of the Gospel announced himself to be an ambassador from heaven. As one worthy of such a mission, he declared that servile belief (taking the form of confessions and practices on days of divine worship) is essentially vain and that moral faith, which alone renders men holy "as their Father in Heaven is holy"[1] and which proves its genuineness by a good course of life, is the only saving faith. After he had given, in his own person, through precept and suffering even to unmerited yet meritorious death,* an example conforming to the archetype of a

* With which the public record of his life ends (a record which, as public, might serve universally as an example for imitation). The more secret records, added as a sequel, of his *resurrection* and *ascension*, which took place before the eyes only of his intimates, cannot be used in the interest of religion within the limits of reason alone without doing violence to their historical valuation. (If one takes these events merely as ideas of reason, they would signify the commencement of another life and entrance into the seat of salvation, *i.e.*, into the society of all the good.) This is so not merely because this added sequel is an historical narrative (for the story which precedes it is that also) but because, taken literally, it involves a concept, *i.e.*, of the materiality of all worldly beings, which is, indeed, very well suited to man's mode of sensuous representation but which is most burdensome to reason in its faith regarding the future. This concept involves both the *materialism of personality* in men (psychological materialism), which asserts that a personality can exist only as always conditioned by the same *body*, as well as the *materialism of necessary existence in a world*, a world which, according to this principle, must be *spatial* (cosmological materialism). In contrast, the hypothesis of the spirituality of rational world-beings asserts that the body can remain dead in the earth while the same person is still alive, and that man, as a spirit (in his non-sensuous quality), can reach the seat of the blessed without having to be transported to some portion or other of the endless space which surrounds the earth (and which is also called heaven). This hypothesis is more congenial to reason, not only because of the impossibility of making comprehensible a matter which thinks, but especially because of the contingency to which materialism exposes our existence after death by claiming that such existence depends solely upon the cohering of a certain lump of matter in a certain form, and denying the possibility of thinking that a simple substance can persist based upon its [own] nature. On the latter supposition (of spirituality) reason can neither take an interest in dragging along, through eternity, a body which, however purified, must yet (if the personality is to rest upon the body's identity) consist of the self-same stuff which constitutes the basis of its organization and for which, in life, it never achieved any great love; nor can it render conceivable that this calcareous earth, of which the body is composed, should be in heaven, *i.e.*, in another region of the universe, where presumably other

[Cf. Matthew V, 48; also I Peter I, 16]

humanity alone pleasing to God, he is represented as returning to heaven, whence he came. He left behind him, by word of mouth, his last will (as in a testament); and, trusting in the power of the memory of his merit, teaching, and example, he was able to say that "he (the ideal of humanity well-pleasing to God) would still be with his disciples, even to the end of the world."[1] Were it a question of *historical belief* concerning the derivation and the rank, possibly supermundane, of his person, this doctrine would indeed stand in need of verification through miracles; although, as merely belonging to moral soul-improving faith, it can dispense with all such proofs of its truth. Hence, in a holy book miracles and mysteries find a place; the manner of making these known, in turn, is also miraculous, and demands a faith in history; which, finally, can be authenticated, and assured as to meaning and import, only by scholarship.

Every faith which, as an historical faith, bases itself upon books, needs for its security a *learned public* for whom it can be controlled, as it were, by writers who lived in those times, who are not suspected of a special agreement with the first disseminators of the faith, and with whom our present-day scholarship is connected by a continuous tradition. The pure faith of reason, in contrast, stands in need of no such documentary authentication, but proves itself. Now at the time of the revolution in question there was present among the people (the Romans), who ruled the Jews and who had spread into their very domain, a learned public from whom the history of the political events of that period has indeed been handed down to us through an unbroken series of writers. And although the Romans concerned themselves but little with the religious beliefs of their non-Roman subjects, they were by no means incredulous of the miracles alleged to have taken place publicly in their midst. Yet they made no mention, as contemporaries, either of these miracles or of the revolution which the miracles produced (in respect to religion) in the people under their dominion, though the revolution had taken place quite as publicly. Only later, after more than a generation, did they institute inquiries into the nature of this change of faith which had re-

---

materials might constitute the condition of the existence and maintenance of living beings.

[1] [Cf. Matthew XXVIII, 20]

mained unknown to them hitherto (but which had occurred not without public commotion), but they did not inquire into the history of its first beginning, in order to learn this history from its own records. So from this period to the time when Christendom could furnish a learned public of its own, its history is obscure and we remain ignorant of what effect the teaching of Christianity had upon the morality of its adherents—whether the first Christians actually were morally improved men or just people of the common run. At any rate, the history of Christendom, from the time that it became a learned public itself, or at least part of the universal learned public, has served in no way to recommend it on the score of the beneficent effect which can justly be expected of a moral religion.

For history tells how the mystical fanaticism in the lives of hermits and monks, and the glorification of the holiness of celibacy, rendered great masses of people useless to the world; how alleged miracles accompanying all this weighed down the people with heavy chains under a blind superstitution; how, with a hierarchy forcing itself upon free men, the dreadful voice of *orthodoxy* was raised, out of the mouths of presumptuous, exclusively "called," Scriptural expositors, and divided the Christian world into embittered parties over credal opinions on matters of faith (upon which absolutely no general agreement can be reached without appeal to pure reason as the expositor); how in the East, where the state meddled in an absurd manner with the religious statutes of the priests and with priestdom, instead of holding them within the narrow confines of a teacher's status (out of which they are at all times inclined to pass over into that of ruler)—how, I say, this state had finally to become, quite inescapably, the prey of foreign enemies, who at last put an end to its prevailing faith; how, in the West, where faith had erected its own throne, independent of worldly power, the civil order together with the sciences (which maintain this order) were thrown into confusion and rendered impotent by a self-styled viceroy of God; how both Christian portions of the world became overrun by barbarians, just as plants and animals, near death from some disease, attract destructive insects to complete their dissolution; how, in the West, the spiritual head ruled over and disciplined kings like children by means of the magic wand of his threatened excommunication, and incited them to depopulating foreign wars in another portion of the

world (the Crusades), to the waging of war with one another, to
the rebellion of subjects against those in authority over them, and
to bloodthirsty hatred against their otherwise-minded colleagues
in one and the same universal Christendom so-called; how the root
of this discord, which even now is kept from violent outbreaks
only through political interest, lies hidden in the basic principle of
a despotically commanding ecclesiastical faith and still gives cause
for dread of events like unto these—this history of Christendom
(which indeed could not eventuate otherwise if erected upon an
historical faith), when surveyed in a single glance, like a painting,
might well justify the exclamation: *tantum religio potuit suadere
malorum*,[1] did not the fact still shine forth clearly from its
founding that Christianity's first intention was really no other
than to introduce a pure religious faith, over which no conflict
of opinions can prevail; whereas that turmoil, through which the
human race was disrupted and is still set at odds, arises solely from
this, that what, by reason of an evil propensity of human nature,
was in the beginning to serve merely for the introduction of pure
religious faith, *i.e.*, to win over for the new faith the nation habituated to the old historical belief through its own prejudices, was in
the sequel made the foundation of a universal world-religion.

If now one asks, What period in the entire known history of the
church up to now is the best? I have no scruple in answering, *the
present*. And this, because, if the seed of the true religious faith,
as it is now being publicly sown in Christendom, though only by
a few, is allowed more and more to grow unhindered, we may look
for a continuous approximation to that church, eternally uniting
all men, which constitutes the visible representation (the schema)
of an invisible kingdom of God on earth. For reason has freed itself, in matters which by their nature ought to be moral and soul-
improving, from the weight of a faith forever dependent upon the
arbitrary will[w] of the expositors, and has among true reverers of
religion in all the lands of this portion of the world universally
(though indeed not in all places publicly) laid down the following
principles. The *first* is the principle of reasonable *modesty* in pronouncements regarding all that goes by the name of revelation.
For no one can deny the *possibility* that a scripture which, in
practical content, contains much that is godly, may (with respect
to what is historical in it) be regarded as a genuinely divine revela-

---

[1] [Lucretius, *De rerum natura*, I, 101: "Such evil deeds could religion prompt!"]

tion. It is also possible that the union of men into one religion cannot feasibly be brought about or made abiding without a holy book and an ecclesiastical faith based upon it. Moreover, the contemporary state of human insight being what it is, one can hardly expect a new revelation, ushered in with new miracles. Hence the most intelligent and most reasonable thing to do is from now on to use the book already at hand as the basis for ecclesiastical instruction and not to lessen its value through useless or mischievous attacks, yet meanwhile not forcing belief in it, as requisite to salvation, upon any man. The *second* principle is this: that, since the sacred narrative, which is employed solely on behalf of ecclesiastical faith, can have and, taken by itself, ought to have absolutely no influence upon the adoption of moral maxims, and since it is given to ecclesiastical faith only for the vivid presentation of its true object (virtue striving toward holiness), it follows that this narrative must at all times be taught and expounded in the interest of morality; and yet (because the common man especially has an enduring propensity within him to sink into passive* belief) it must be inculcated painstakingly and repeatedly that true religion is to consist not in the knowing or considering of what God does or has done for our salvation but in what we must do to become worthy of it. This last can never be anything but what possesses in itself undoubted and *unconditional* worth, what therefore can alone make us well-pleasing to God, and of whose necessity every man can become wholly certain without any Scriptural learning whatever. Now it is the duty of rulers not to hinder these basic principles from becoming public. On the contrary, very much is risked and a great responsibility assumed by one who intrudes upon the process of divine Providence and, for the sake of certain historical ecclesiastical doctrines which at best have in their favor only a probability discoverable by scholars, exposes to tempta-

---

* One of the causes of this propensity lies in the principle of security; that the defects of a religion in which I am born and brought up, instruction therein not having been chosen by me nor in any way altered through my own ratiocination, are charged not to my account but to that of my instructors or teachers publicly appointed for the task. This is also a ground for our not easily giving our approval to a man's public change of religion: although here, no doubt, there is another (and deeper) ground, namely, that amid the uncertainty which every man feels within himself as to which among the historical faiths is the right one, while the moral faith is everywhere the same, it seems highly unnecessary to create a stir about the matter.

tion* the consciences of the subjects through the offer, or denial, of
certain civil advantages otherwise open to all: all this, apart from
the damage done thereby to a freedom which in this case is holy,
can scarcely produce good citizens for the state. Who among those
proffering themselves to hinder such a free development of godly
predispositions to the world's highest good, or even proposing
such a hindrance, would wish, after thinking it over in communion
with his conscience, to answer for all the evil which might arise
from such forcible encroachments, whereby the advance in goodness intended by the Governor of the world, though it can never
be wholly destroyed through human might or human contrivance,
may perhaps be checked for a long time, yea, even turned into a
retrogression!

As regards its guidance by Providence, the kingdom of heaven
is represented in this historical account not only as being brought
ever nearer, in an approach delayed at certain times yet never

---

* When a government wishes to be regarded as not coercing man's conscience because it merely prohibits the *public utterance* of his religious opinions
and hinders no one from *thinking* to himself in secrecy whatever he sees fit,
we usually jest about it and say that in this the government grants no freedom
at all, for it cannot in any case hinder thinking. Yet what the greatest secular
power cannot do, spiritual power can—that is, forbid thought itself and really
hinder it; it can even lay such a compulsion—the prohibition even to think
other than it prescribes—upon those in temporal authority over it. For because of men's propensity to the servile faith of divine worship, which they
are automatically inclined not only to endow with an importance greater
than that of moral faith (wherein man serves God truly through the performance of his duties) but also to regard as unique and compensating for every
other deficiency, it is always easy for the custodians of orthodoxy, the shepherds of souls, to instil into their flock a pious terror of the slightest swerving
from certain dogmas resting on history, and even of all investigation—a terror
so great that they do not trust themselves to allow a doubt concerning the
doctrines forced upon them to arise, even in their thoughts, for this would be
tantamount to lending an ear to the evil spirit. True, to become free from
this compulsion one needs but *to will* (which is not the case when the sovereign
compels public confessions); but it is precisely this willing against which a
rule has been interposed internally. Such forcing of conscience is indeed bad
enough (for it leads to inner hypocrisy); yet it is not as bad as the restriction
of external freedom of belief. For the inner compulsion must of itself gradually
disappear through the progress of moral insight and the consciousness of one's
own freedom, from which alone true respect for duty can arise, whereas this
external pressure hinders all spontaneous advances in the ethical community
of believers—which constitutes the being of the true church—and subjects
its form to purely political ordinances.

wholly interrupted, but also as arriving. When to this narrative is added (in the Apocalypse) a prophecy (like those in the Sibylline books) of the consummation of this great world-change, in the image of a visible kingdom of God on earth (under the government of His representative and viceroy, again descended to earth), and of the happiness which is to be enjoyed under him in this world after the separation and expulsion of the rebels who once again seek to withstand him, and also of the complete extirpation of these rebels and their leader, and when, thus, the account closes with *the end of the world*, all this may be interpreted as a symbolical representation intended merely to enliven hope and courage and to increase our endeavors to that end. The Teacher of the Gospel revealed to his disciples the kingdom of God on earth only in its glorious, soul-elevating moral aspect, namely, in terms of the value of citizenship in a divine state, and to this end he informed them of what they had to do, not only to achieve it themselves but to unite with all others of the same mind and, so far as possible, with the entire human race. Concerning happiness, however, which constitutes the other part of what man inevitably wishes, he told them in advance not to count on it in their life on earth. Instead he bade them be prepared for the greatest tribulations and sacrifices; yet he added (since man cannot be expected, while he is alive, wholly to renounce what is physical in happiness): "Rejoice and be exceeding glad: for great is your reward in heaven."[1] The supplement, added to the history of the church, dealing with man's future and final destiny, pictures men as ultimately *triumphant, i.e.*, as crowned with happiness while still here on earth, after all obstacles have been overcome. The separation of the good from the evil, which, during the progress of the church toward its consummation, would not have conduced to this end (since their mixture with one another was needed, partly to spur the good on to virtue, partly to withdraw the bad from evil through the others' example), is represented as following upon the completed establishment of the divine state and as its last consequence; whereto is added, as the final proof of the state's stability and might, its victory over all external foes who are also regarded as forming a state (the state of hell). With this all earthly life comes to an end, in that "the last enemy (of good men), death, is

---

[1] [Cf. Matthew V, 12. Luther's translation reads *belohnet* instead of Kant's *vergolten*.]

destroyed";[1] and immortality commences for both parties, to the salvation of one, the damnation of the other. The very form of a church is dissolved, the viceroy becomes at one with man who is raised up to his level as a citizen of heaven, and so God is all in all.*

This sketch of a history of after-ages, which themselves are not yet history, presents a beautiful ideal of the moral world-epoch, brought about by the introduction of true universal religion and in faith *foreseen* even to its culmination—which we cannot *conceive* as a culmination in experience, but can merely *anticipate*, *i.e.*, prepare for, in continual progress and approximation toward the highest good possible on earth (and in all of this there is nothing mystical, but everything moves quite naturally in a moral fashion). The appearance of the Antichrist, the milennium, and the news of the proximity of the end of the world—all these can take on, before reason, their right symbolic meaning; and to represent the last of these as an event not to be seen in advance (like the end of life, be it far or near) admirably expresses the necessity of standing ready at all times for the end and indeed (if one attaches the intellectual meaning to this symbol) really to consider ourselves always as chosen citizens of a divine (ethical) state. "When, therefore, cometh the kingdom of God?"[2] "The kingdom of God cometh not in visible form. Neither shall they say, Lo here; or lo there! *For, behold, the kingdom of God is within you,*" (Luke XVII, 21–2).**

---

* This expression (if one sets aside what is mysterious, what reaches out beyond the limits of all possible experience, and what belongs merely to sacred *history* and so in no way applies to us practically) can be taken to mean that historical faith, which, as ecclesiastical, stands in need of a sacred book as a leading-string for men, but, for that very reason, hinders the unity and universality of the church, will itself cease and pass over into a pure religious faith equally obvious to the whole world. To this end we ought even now to labor industriously, by way of continuously setting free the pure religon from its present shell, which as yet cannot be spared.†

† Not that it is to cease (for as a vehicle it may perhaps always be useful and necessary) but that it be able to cease; whereby is indicated merely the inner stability of the pure moral faith.

[1] [Cf. I Corinthians, XV, 26]
[2] [Cf. Luke XVII, 20–21: "And when he was demanded of the Pharisees when the kingdom of God should come, he answered them and said, the kingdom of God cometh not with observation. Neither shall, etc."]

** Here a kingdom of God is represented not according to a particular covenant (*i.e.*, not Messianic) but *moral* (knowable through unassisted reason). The former (*regnum divinum pactitium*) had to draw its proofs from history; and there it is divided into the *Messianic* kingdom according to the *old* and according to the *new* covenant. Now it is worthy of notice that the followers of the former (the Jews) have continued to maintain themselves as such, though scattered throughout the world; whereas the faith of other religious fellowships has usually been fused with the faith of the people among whom they have been scattered. This phenomenon strikes many as so remarkable that they judge it to be impossible according to the nature of things, but to be an extraordinary dispensation for a special divine purpose. Yet a people which has a written religion (sacred books) never fuses together in one faith with a people (like the Roman Empire, then the entire civilized world) possessing no such books but only rites; instead, sooner or later it makes proselytes. This is the reason why, after the Babylonian captivity (following which, it seems, their sacred books were for the first time read publicly), the Jews were no longer chargeable with their propensity to run after strange gods; though the Alexandrian culture, which must also have had an influence upon them, could have been favorable to their giving this propensity a systematic form. Thus also the Parsees, followers of the religion of Zoroaster, have kept their faith up to the present despite their dispersion; for their *dustoors*[1] possessed the Zendavesta. These Hindus, on the other hand, who under the name of gipsies are scattered far and wide, have not escaped a mixture with foreign faiths, for they came from the dregs of the people (the Pariahs) who are forbidden even to read in the sacred books of the Hindus. What the Jews would not have achieved of themselves, the Christian and later the Mohammedan religions brought about—especially the former; for these religions presupposed the Jewish faith and the sacred books belonging to it (even though Mohammedanism declares that these books have been falsified). For the Jews could ever and again seek out their old documents among the Christians (who had issued forth from them) whenever, in their wanderings, the skill in reading these books, and so the desire to possess them, was lost, as may often have happened, and when they merely retained the memory of having formerly possessed them. Hence we find no Jews outside the countries referred to, if we except the few on the coast of Malabar and possibly a community in China (and of these the first could have been in continual commercial relation with their co-religionists in Arabia). Although it cannot be doubted that they spread throughout those rich lands,[2] yet, because of the lack of all kinship between their faith and the types of belief found there, they came wholly to forget their own. To base edifying remarks upon this preservation of the Jewish people, together with their religion, under circumstances so disadvantageous to them, is very hazardous, for both sides believe that they find in it [confirmation of] their own opinions.

[1] [High priests]
[2] [*i.e.*, lands not Christian or Mohammedan.]

One man sees in the continuation of the people to which he belongs, and in his ancient faith which remained unmixed despite the dispersion among such diverse nations, the proof of a special beneficent Providence saving this people for a future kingdom on earth; the other sees nothing but the warning ruins of a disrupted state which set itself against the coming of the kingdom of heaven —ruins, however, which a special Providence still sustains, partly to preserve in memory the ancient prophecy of a Messiah arising from this people, partly to offer, in this people, an example of punitive justice [visited upon it] because it stiff-neckedly sought to create a political and not a moral concept of the Messiah.

GENERAL OBSERVATION

Investigation into the inner nature of all kinds of faith which concern religion invariably encounters a *mystery*, *i.e.*, something *holy* which may indeed be *known* by each single individual but cannot be *made known* publicly, that is, shared universally. Being something *holy*, it must be moral, and so an object of reason, and it must be capable of being known from within adequately for practical use, and yet, as something *mysterious*, not for theoretical use, since in this case it would have to be capable of being shared with everyone and made known publicly.

Belief in what we are yet to regard as a holy mystery can be looked upon as *divinely prompted* or as *a pure rational faith*. Unless we are impelled by the greatest need to adopt the first of these views, we shall make it our maxim to abide by the second. Feelings are not knowledge and so do not indicate [the presence of] a mystery; and since the latter is related to reason, yet cannot be shared universally, each individual will have to search for it (if ever there is such a thing) solely in his own reason.

It is impossible to settle, *a priori* and objectively, whether there are such mysteries or not. We must therefore search directly in the inner, the subjective, part of our moral predisposition to see whether any such thing is to be found in us. Yet we shall not be entitled to number among the holy mysteries the *grounds* of morality, which are inscrutable to us; for we can thus classify only that which we can know but which is incapable of being communicated publicly, whereas, though morality can indeed be communicated publicly, its cause remains unknown to us. Thus freedom, an attribute of which man becomes aware through the determinability of his will[w] by the unconditioned moral law, is no mystery, because the knowledge of it can be *shared* with everyone; but the ground, inscrutable to us, of this attribute is a mystery because this ground is *not given* us as an object of knowledge. Yet it is this very freedom which, when applied to the final object of practical reason (the realization of the idea of the moral end), alone leads us inevitably to holy mysteries.*

* Similarly, the *cause* of the universal gravity of all matter in the world is unknown to us, so much so, indeed, that we can even see that we shall never know it: for the very concept of gravity presupposes a primary motive force

The idea of the highest good, inseparably bound up with the purely moral disposition, cannot be realized by man himself (not only in the matter of the happiness pertaining thereto, but also in the matter of the union of men necessary for the end in its entirety); yet he discovers within himself the duty to work for this end. Hence he finds himself impelled to believe in the cooperation or management of a moral Ruler of the world, by means of which alone this goal can be reached. And now there opens up before him the abyss of a mystery regarding what God may do [toward the realization of this end], whether indeed *anything* in general, and if so, *what* in particular should be ascribed to God. Meanwhile man knows concerning each duty nothing but what he must himself do in order to be worthy of that supplement, unknown, or at least incomprehensible, to him.

This idea of a moral Governor of the world is a task presented to our practical reason. It concerns us not so much to know what God is in Himself (His nature) as what He is for us as moral beings; although in order to know the latter we must conceive and comprehend all the attributes of the divine nature (for instance, the unchangeableness, omniscience, omnipotence, etc. of such a Being) which, in their totality, are requisite to the carrying out of

---

unconditionally inhering in it. Yet gravity is no mystery but can be made public to all, for its *law* is adequately known. When Newton represents it as similar to divine omnipresence in the [world of] appearance (*omnipræsentia phænomenon*), this is not an attempt to explain it (for the existence of God in space involves a contradiction), but a sublime analogy which has regard solely to the union of corporeal beings with a world-whole, an incorporeal cause being here attributed to this union. The same result would follow upon an attempt to comprehend the self-sufficing principle of the union of rational beings in the world into an ethical state, and to explain this in terms of that principle. All we know is the duty which draws us toward such a union; the possibility of the achievement held in view when we obey that duty lies wholly beyond the limits of our insight.

There are mysteries which are hidden things in nature (*arcana*), and there can be mysteries (secrecies, *secreta*) in politics which *ought* not to be known publicly; but both *can*, after all, become known to us, inasmuch as they rest on empirical causes. There can be no mystery with respect to what all men are in duty bound to know (*i.e.*, what is moral); only with respect to that which God alone can do and the performance of which exceeds our capacity, and therefore our duty, can there be a genuine, that is, a holy mystery (*mysterium*) of religion; and it may well be expedient for us merely to know and understand that there is such a mystery, not to comprehend it.

the divine will in this regard. Apart from this context we can know nothing about Him.

Now the universal true religious belief conformable to this requirement of practical reason is belief in God (1) as the omnipotent Creator of heaven and earth, *i.e.*, morally as *holy* Legislator, (2) as Preserver of the human race, its *benevolent* Ruler and moral Guardian, (3) as Administrator of His own holy laws, *i.e.*, as *righteous* Judge.

This belief really contains no mystery, because it merely expresses the moral relation of God to the human race; it also presents itself spontaneously to human reason everywhere and is therefore to be met with in the religion of most civilized peoples.* It is present likewise in the concept of a people regarded as a commonwealth, in which such a threefold higher power (*pouvoir*) will always be descried, except that this commonwealth is here represented as ethical: hence this threefold quality of the moral Governor of the human race, which in a juridico-civil state must of necessity be divided among three different departments [legislative, executive, and judicial], can be thought of as combined in one and the same Being.†

* In the sacred prophetic story of "the last things," the *judge of the world* (really he who will separate out and take under his dominion, as his own, those who belong to the kingdom of the good principle) is not represented and spoken of as God but as the Son of Man. This seems to indicate that *humanity itself*, knowning its limitation and its frailty, will pronounce the sentence in this selection [of the good from the bad]— a benevolence which yet does not offend against justice. In contrast, the Judge of men, represented in His divinity (the Holy Ghost), *i.e.*, as He speaks to our conscience according to the holy law which we know, and in terms of our own reckoning, can be thought of only as passing judgment according to the rigor of the law. For we ourselves are wholly ignorant of how much can be credited, in our behalf, to the account of our frailty, and have moreover before our eyes nothing but our transgression, together with the consciousness of our freedom, and the violation of duty for which we are wholly to blame; hence we have no ground for assuming benevolence in the judgment passed upon us.

† We cannot discover the cause for the agreement of so many ancient peoples in this idea, unless it is that the idea is present universally in human reason whenever man wants to conceive of civil government or (by analogy therewith) of world government. The religion of Zoroaster had these three divine persons, Ormazd, Mithra, and Ahriman; that of the Hindus had Brahma, Vishnu, and Siva—but with this difference, that Zoroastrians represent the third person as creator, not only of *evil* so far as it is punishment, but even of *moral evil* for which man is punished, whereas the Hindus represent

And since this faith which, on behalf of religion in general, has cleansed the moral relation of men to the Supreme Being from harmful anthropomorphism, and has harmonized it with the genuine morality of a people of God, was first set forth in a particular (the Christian) body of doctrine and only therein made public to the world, we can call the promulgation of these doctrines a revelation of the faith which had hitherto remained hidden from men through their own fault.

These doctrines assert, *first*, that we are to look upon the Supreme Lawgiver as one who commands not *mercifully* or with *forbearance* (indulgently) for men's weakness, or *despotically* and merely according to His unlimited right; and we are to look upon His laws not as arbitrary and as wholly unrelated to our concepts of morality, but as laws addressed to man's holiness. *Second*, we must place His beneficence not in an unconditioned *good-will* toward His creatures but in this, that He first looks upon their moral character, through which they can be *well-pleasing* to Him, and only then makes good their inability to fulfil this requirement of themselves. *Third*, His justice cannot be represented as *beneficent* and *exorable* (for this involves a contradiction); even less can it be represented as dispensed by Him in his character of *holy* Lawgiver (before Whom no man is righteous); rather, it must be thought of as beneficence which is limited by being conditioned upon men's agreement with the holy law so far as they, as *sons of men*, may be able to measure up to its requirement. In a word, God wills to be served under three specifically different moral aspects. The naming of the different (not physically, but morally different) persons of one and the same Being expresses this not ineptly. This symbol of faith gives expression also to the whole of

---

him as merely judging and punishing. The religion of Egypt had its Ptah, Kneph, and Neith, of whom, so far as the obscurity of the earliest records of this people allows of conjecture, the first was intended to represent spirit, distinguished from matter, as *World-Creator*, the second, a principle of sustaining and *ruling* benevolence, the third, wisdom setting limits to this benevolence, *i.e.*, *justice*. The Goths honored their Odin (father of all), their Freya (also Freyer, beneficence), and Thor, the judging (punishing) god. Even the Jews seem to have followed these ideas during the last period of their hierarchical constitution. For in the complaint of the Pharisees that Christ had called himself a *Son of God*, they seem to have attached no special weight of blame to the doctrine that God had a son, but merely to Christ's having wished to be this son of God.

pure moral religion which, without this differentiation, runs the risk of degenerating into an anthropomorphic servile faith, by reason of men's propensity to think of the Godhead as a human overlord (because in man's government rulers usually do not separate these three qualities from one another but often mix and interchange them).

But if this very faith (in a divine tri-unity) were to be regarded not merely as a representation of a practical idea but as a faith which is to describe what God is in Himself, it would be a mystery transcending all human concepts, and hence a mystery of revelation, unsuited to man's powers of comprehension; in this account, therefore, we can declare it to be such. Faith in it, regarded as an extension of the theoretical knowledge of the divine nature, would be merely the acknowledgment of a symbol of ecclesiastical faith which is quite incomprehensible to men or which, if they think they can understand it, would be anthropomorphic, and therefore nothing whatever would be accomplished for moral betterment. Only that which, in a practical context, can be thoroughly understood and comprehended, but which, taken theologically (for the determining of the nature of the object in itself), transcends all our concepts, is a mystery (in one respect) and can yet (in another) be revealed. To this type belongs what has just been mentioned; and this can be divided into three mysteries revealed to us through our reason.

1. The mystery of the divine *call* (of men, as citizens, to an ethical state). We can conceive of the universal *unconditioned* subjection of men to the divine legislation only so far as we likewise regard ourselves as God's *creatures;* just as God can be regarded as the ultimate source of all natural laws only because He is the creator of natural objects. But it is absolutely incomprehensible to our reason how beings can be *created* to a free use of their powers; for according to the principle of causality we can assign to a being, regarded as having been brought forth, no inner ground for his actions other than that which the producing cause has placed there, by which, then, (and so by an external cause) his every act would be determined, and such a being would therefore not be free. So the legislation which is divine and holy, and therefore concerns free beings only, cannot through the insight of our reason be reconciled with the concept of the creation of such beings; rather must one regard them even now as existing free beings who

are determined not through their dependence upon nature by virtue of their creation but through a purely moral necessitation possible according to laws of freedom, *i.e.*, a call to citizenship in a divine state. Thus the call to this end is morally quite clear, while for speculation the possibility of such a calling is an impenetrable mystery.

2. The mystery of *atonement*. Man, as we know him, is corrupt and of himself not in the least suited to that holy law. And yet, if the goodness of God has called him, as it were, into being, *i.e.*, to exist in a particular manner (as a member of the kingdom of Heaven), He must also have a means of supplementing, out of the fullness of His own holiness, man's lack of requisite qualifications therefor. But this contradicts spontaneity (which is assumed in all the moral good or evil which a man can have within himself), according to which such a good cannot come from another but must arise from man himself, if it is to be imputable to him. Therefore, so far as reason can see, no one can, by virtue of the superabundance of his own good conduct and through his own merit, take another's place; or, if such vicarious atonement is accepted, we would have *to assume it* only from the moral point of view, since for ratiocination it is an unfathomable mystery.

3. The mystery of *election*. Even if that vicarious atonement be admitted as possible, still a morally-believing acceptance of it is a determination of the will toward good that already presupposes in man a disposition which is pleasing to God; yet man, by reason of his natural depravity, cannot produce this within himself through his own efforts. But that a heavenly *grace* should work in man and should accord this assistance to one and not to another, and this not according to the merit of works but by an unconditioned *decree;* and that one portion of our race should be destined for salvation, the other for eternal reprobation—this again yields no concept of a divine justice but must be referred to a wisdom whose rule is for us an absolute mystery.

As to these mysteries, so far as they touch the moral life-history of every man—how it happens that there is a moral good or evil at all in the world, and (if the evil is present in all men and at all times) how out of evil good could spring up and be established in any man whatever, or why, when *this* occurs in some, others remain deprived thereof—of this God has revealed to us nothing and can reveal nothing since we would not *understand* it.† It is as though we wished to *explain* and to *render comprehensible* to ourselves in terms of a man's freedom what happens to him; on this question God has indeed revealed His will through the moral law in us, but the *causes* due to which a free action on earth occurs or does not occur He has left in that obscurity in which human investigation must leave whatever (as an historical occurrence, though yet springing from freedom) ought to be conceived of according to the laws of cause and effect.†† But all that we need concerning the objective rule of our behavior is adequately revealed to us (through reason and Scripture), and this revelation is at the same time comprehensible to every man.

That, through the moral law, man is called to a good course of life; that, through unquenchable respect for this law lying in him, he finds in himself justification for confidence in this good spirit and for hope that, however it may come about, he will be able to satisfy this spirit; finally, that, comparing the last-named expectation with the stern command of the law, he must continually test himself as though summoned to account before a judge—reason, heart, and conscience all teach this and urge its fulfilment. To demand that more than this be revealed to us is presumptuous, and

† We commonly have no misgivings in requiring of novices in religion a belief in mysteries; for the fact that we do not *comprehend* them, *i.e.*, that we cannot see into the possibility of their objective existence,[1] could no more justify our refusal to accept them than it could justify our not accepting, say, the procreative capacity of organisms, which likewise no man comprehends yet which we cannot on that account refuse to admit, even though it is and will remain a mystery to us. But we *understand* very well what this expression means to convey and we have an empirical concept of this capacity, together with the consciousness that it harbors no contradiction. Now we can with justice require of every mystery offered for belief that we *understand* what it is supposed to mean; and this does not happen when we merely understand the words by which it is designated *one by one*, *i.e.*, attaching a meaning to each word—rather, these words, taken together in one concept, must admit of another meaning and not, thus taken in conjunction, frustrate all thought. It is unthinkable that God could allow this knowledge to come to us through *inspiration* whenever we on our part wish earnestly for it; for such knowledge cannot inhere in us at all because our understanding is by nature unsuited to it.

†† Hence we understand perfectly well what freedom is, practically (when it is a question of duty), whereas we cannot without contradiction even think of wishing to understand theoretically the causality of freedom (or its nature).

[1] [*Gegenstand*]

were such a revelation to occur, it could not rightly be reckoned among man's universal needs.

Although that great mystery, comprising in one formula all that we have mentioned, can be made comprehensible to each man through his reason as a practical and necessary religious idea, we can say that, in order to become the moral basis of religion, and particularly of a public religion, it was, at that time, first revealed when it was *publicly* taught and made the symbol of a wholly new religious epoch. *Ceremonial formulas* are usually couched in a language of their own, intended only for those who belong to a particular union (a guild or society), a language at times mystical and not understood by everyone, which properly (out of respect) ought to be made use of only for a ceremonial act (as, for instance, when some one is to be initiated as a member of a society which is exclusive). But the highest goal of moral perfection of finite creatures—a goal to which man can never completely attain—is love of the law.

The equivalent in religion of this idea would be an article of faith, "God is love": in Him we can *revere* the loving One (whose love is that of moral *approbation* of men so far as they measure up to His holy law)—the *Father;* in Him also, so far as He reveals Himself in His all-inclusive idea, the archetype of humanity reared and beloved by Him, we can revere His *Son;* and finally, so far as He makes this approbation dependent upon men's agreement with the condition of that approving love, and so reveals love as based upon wisdom, we can revere the *Holy Ghost.** Not that we

---

* This Spirit, in and through which the love of God, as the Author of salvation (really our own responding love proportioned to His), is combined with the fear of God as Lawgiver, *i.e.*, the conditioned with the condition, and which can therefore be represented as "issuing forth from both,"[1] not only "leads to all truth"[2] (obedience to duty), but is also the real Judge of men (at the bar of conscience). For judgment can be interpreted in two ways, as concerning either merit and lack of merit, or guilt and absence of guilt. God, regarded as *love* (in His Son), judges men so far as merit is attributable to them over and above their indebtedness, and here the verdict is: *worthy,* or *unworthy.* He separates out as His own those to whom such merit can still be accredited. Those who are left depart empty-handed. On the other hand the sentence of the Judge in terms of *justice*[3] (of the Judge properly so called,

[1] ["As it is expressed in the Western (Augustinian) form of the doctrine of the Trinity; whereas the Eastern form asserts the emanance of the Holy Ghost from the Father alone. Cf. John XV, 26." (Note in the Berlin Edition.)]

[2] [Cf. John XVI, 13]

[3] [*Berechtigkeit;* where the context is theological, we have usually translated this word as *righteousness;* otherwise, as *justice.*]

should actually *invoke* Him in terms of this multiform personality
(for to do so would suggest a diversity of entities, whereas He is
ever but single); but we can call upon Him in the name of that
object loved of Him, which He Himself esteems above all else,
with which to enter into moral union is [our] desire and also [our]
duty. Over and above this, the theoretical avowal of faith in the

---

under the name of the Holy Ghost) upon those for whom no merit is forthcoming, is *guilty* or *not guilty*, i.e., condemnation or acquittal. This *judging*
signifies first of all the *separation* of the deserving from the undeserving, both
parties competing for a prize (salvation). By *desert* is here meant moral excellence, not in relation to the law (for in the eyes of the law no balance of
obedience to duty over and above our indebtedness can accrue to us), but
only in comparison with other men on the score of their moral disposition. And
worthiness always has a merely negative meaning (not unworthiness), that
is, the moral receptivity for such goodness.

Hence he who judges in the first capacity (as *brabeuta*[1]) pronounces a judgment of choice between *two* persons (or parties) striving for the prize (of salvation); while he who judges in the second capacity (the real judge) passes sentence upon *one and the same* person before a court (conscience) which declares
the final verdict between the prosecution and the defense. If now it is admitted that, though indeed all men are guilty of sin, some among them may
be able to achieve merit, then the verdict of *Him who judges from love* becomes effective. In the absence of this judgment, only a *verdict of rejection*
could follow, whose inescapable consequence would be the *judgment of condemnation* (since the man now falls into the hands of Him who judges in
righteousness). It is thus, in my opinion, that the apparently contradictory
passages, "The Son will come again to judge the quick and the dead,"[2] and,
"God sent not his Son into the world to condemn the world; but that the
world through him might be saved" (John III, 17), can be reconciled, and
they can agree with the other passage which reads, "He that believeth not in
him is condemned *already*" (John III, 18), namely, by the Spirit, of whom it
is said: "He will judge the world because of sin and righteousness."[3] Anxious
solicitude over such distinctions in the domain of bare reason, for whose sake
they have really been instituted here, might well be regarded as a useless and
burdensome subtlety; and it would indeed be such if it were directed to an
inquiry into the divine nature. But since men are ever prone, in matters of
religion, to appeal, respecting their transgressions, to divine benignity, though
they cannot circumvent His righteousness, and since a *benign judge*, as one
and the same person, is a contradiction in terms, it is very evident that, even
from a practical point of view, men's concepts on this subject must be very
wavering and lacking in internal coherence, and that the correction and precise determination of these concepts is of great practical importance.

[1] [One who presided at public games and assigned the prizes.]
[2] [Cf. II Timothy IV, 1]
[3] [Cf. John XVI, 8: ". . . he will reprove the world of sin and of righteousness and
of judgment."]

divine nature under this threefold character is part of what is merely the classic formula of an ecclesiastical faith, to be used for the distinguishing of this faith from other modes of belief deriving from historical sources. Few men are in the position of being able to combine with this faith a concept [of the Trinity] which is clear and definite (open to no misinterpretation); and its exposition concerns, rather, teachers in their relation to one another (as philosophical and scholarly expositors of a Holy Book), that they may agree as to its interpretation, since not everything in it is suited to the common capacity of comprehension, nor to the needs of the present, and since a bare literal faith in it hurts rather than improves the truly religious disposition.

BOOK FOUR

CONCERNING SERVICE AND PSEUDO-SERVICE
UNDER THE SOVEREIGNTY OF THE GOOD
PRINCIPLE, OR, CONCERNING RELIGION
AND CLERICALISM

The dominion of the good principle begins, and a sign that "the kingdom of God is at hand"[1] appears, as soon as the basic principles of its constitution first become *public;* for (in the realm of the understanding) that is already here whose causes, which alone can bring it to pass, have generally taken root, even though the complete development of its appearance in the sensuous world is still immeasurably distant. We have seen that it is a duty of a peculiar kind (*officium sui generis*) to unite oneself with an ethical commonwealth, and that, if everyone alike heeded his own private duty, we could indeed infer therefrom an *accidental agreement* of all in a common good, even without the necessity of a special organization; yet, [we must admit] that such a general agreement cannot be hoped for unless a special business be made of their union with one another for the self-same end, and of the establishment of a COMMONWEALTH under moral laws, as a federated and therefore stronger power to withstand the assaults of the evil principle (for otherwise men are tempted, even by one another, to serve this principle as its tools). We have also seen that such a commonwealth, being a KINGDOM OF GOD, can be undertaken by men only through *religion,* and, finally, in order that this religion be public (and this is requisite to a commonwealth), that it must be represented in the visible form of a *church;* hence the establishment of a church devolves upon men as a task which is committed to them and can be required of them.

To found a church as a commonwealth under religious laws seems, however, to call for more wisdom (both of insight and of good disposition) than can well be expected of men, especially since it seems necessary to *presuppose* the presence in them, for this purpose, of the moral goodness which the establishment of such a church has in view. Actually it is nonsensical to say that *men* ought to *found* a kingdom of God (one might as well say

[1] [Cf. Matthew VI, 20; Luke XI, 2]

of them that they could set up the kingdom of a human monarch); God himself must be the founder of His kingdom. Yet, since we do not know what God may do directly to translate into actuality the idea of His kingdom—and we find within ourselves the moral destiny to become citizens and subjects in this kingdom—and since we do know how we must act to fit ourselves to become members thereof, this idea, whether it was discovered and made *public* to the human race by reason or by Scripture, will yet obligate us to the establishment of a church of whose *constitution*, in the last analysis, God Himself, as Founder of the kingdom, is the Author, while men, as members and free citizens of this kingdom, are in all cases the creators of the *organization*. Then those among them who, in accordance with this organization, manage its public business, compose its *administration*, as servants of the church, while the rest constitute a co-partnership, the *congregation*, subject to their laws.

Now since a pure religion of reason, as public religious faith, permits only the bare idea of a church (that is, an invisible church), and since only the visible church, which is grounded upon dogmas, needs and is susceptible of organization by men, it follows that service under the sovereignty of the good principle cannot, in the invisible church, be regarded as ecclesiastical service, and that this religion has no legal servants, acting as *officials* of an ethical commonwealth; every member of this commonwealth receives his orders directly from the supreme legislator. But since, with respect to all our duties (which, collectively, we must at the same time look upon as divine commands) we also stand at all times in the service of God, the *pure religion of reason* will have, as its *servants* (yet without their being *officials*) all right-thinking men; except that, so far, they cannot be called servants of a church (that is, of a visible church, which alone is here under discussion). Meanwhile, because every church erected upon statutory laws can be the true church only so far as it contains within itself a principle of steadily approximating to pure rational faith (which, when it is practical, really constitutes the religion in every faith) and of becoming able, in time, to dispense with the churchly faith (that in it which is historical), we shall be able to regard these laws, and the officials of the church established upon them, as constituting a [true] *service* of the church (*cultus*) so far as these officials steadily direct their teachings and regulations toward that final end (a public religious faith). On the other hand, the servants of a church who do not at all have this in view, who rather interpret the maxim of continual approximation thereto as damnable, and allegiance to the historical and statutory element of ecclesiastical faith as alone bringing salvation, can rightly be blamed for the *pseudo-service* of the church or of what is represented through this church, namely, the ethical commonwealth under the dominion of the good principle. By a *pseudo-service* (*cultus spurius*) is meant the persuasion that some one can be served by deeds which in fact frustrate the very ends of him who is being served. This occurs in a commonwealth when that which is of value only *indirectly*, as a means of complying with the will of a superior, is proclaimed to be, and is substituted for, what would make us *directly* well-pleasing to him. Hereby his ends are frustrated.

PART ONE

CONCERNING THE SERVICE OF GOD IN RELIGION IN GENERAL

Religion is (subjectively regarded) the recognition of all duties as divine commands.* That religion in which I must know in advance that something is a divine command in order to recognize

* By means of this definition many an erroneous interpretation of the concept of a religion in general is obviated. *First*, in religion, as regards the theoretical apprehension and avowal of belief, no assertorial knowledge is required (even of God's existence), since, with our lack of insight into supersensible objects, such avowal might well be dissembled; rather is it merely a *problematical* assumption (hypothesis) regarding the highest cause of things that is presupposed speculatively, yet with an eye to the object toward which our morally legislative reason bids us strive—an *assertorial* faith, practical and therefore free, and giving promise of the realization of this its ultimate aim. This faith needs merely *the idea of God*, to which all morally earnest (and therefore confident) endeavor for the good must inevitably lead; it need not presume that it can certify the objective reality of this idea through theoretical apprehension. Indeed, the *minimum* of knowledge (it is possible that there may be a God) must suffice, subjectively, for whatever can be made the duty of every man. *Second*, this definition of a religion in general obviates the erroneous representation of religion as an aggregate of *special* duties having reference directly to God; thus it prevents our taking on (as men are otherwise very much inclined to do) *courtly obligations* over and above the ethico-civil duties of humanity (of man to man) and our seeking, perchance, even to make good the deficiency of the latter by means of the former. There are no special duties to God in a universal religion, for God can receive nothing from us; we cannot act for Him, nor yet upon Him. To wish to transform a guilty awe of Him into a duty of the sort described is to forget that awe is not a special act of religion but rather the religious temper in all our actions done in conformity with duty. And when it is said: "We ought to obey God rather than men,"[1] this means only that when statutory commands, regarding which men can be legislators and judges, come into conflict with duties which reason prescribes unconditionally, concerning whose observance or transgression God alone can be the judge, the former must yield precedence to the latter. But were we willing to regard the statutory commands, which are given out by a church as coming from God, as constituting that wherein God must be obeyed more than man, such a principle might easily become the war-cry, often heard, of hypocritical and ambitious clerics in revolt against their civil superiors. For that which is permissible, *i.e.*, which the civil authorities command, is *certainly* duty; but whether something which is indeed permissible in itself, but cognizable by us only through divine revelation, is really commanded by God—that is (at least for the most part) highly uncertain.

[1] [Cf. Acts V, 29]

142

it as my duty, is the *revealed* religion (or the one standing in need of a revelation); in contrast, that religion in which I must first know that something is my duty before I can accept it as a divine injunction is the *natural* religion. He who interprets the natural religion alone as morally necessary, *i.e.*, as duty, can be called the *rationalist* (in matters of belief); if he denies the reality of all supernatural divine revelation he is called a *naturalist;* if he recognizes revelation, but asserts that to know and accept it as real is not a necessary requisite to religion, he could be named a *pure rationalist;* but if he holds that belief in it is necessary to universal religion, he could be named the pure *supernaturalist* in matters of faith.

The rationalist, by virtue of his very title, must of his own accord restrict himself within the limits of human insight. Hence he will never, as a naturalist, dogmatize, and will never contest either the inner possibility of revelation in general or the necessity of a revelation as a divine means for the introduction of true religion; for these matters no man can determine through reason. Hence the question at issue can concern only the reciprocal claims of the pure rationalist and the supernaturalist in matters of faith, namely, what the one or the other holds as necessary and sufficient, or as merely incidental, to the unique true religion.

When religion is classified not with reference to its first origin and its inner possibility (here it is divided into natural and revealed religion) but with respect to its characteristics which make it *capable of being shared widely with others*, it can be of two kinds: either the *natural* religion, of which (once it has arisen) everyone can be convinced through his own reason, or a *learned* religion, of which one can convince others only through the agency of learning (in and through which they must be guided). This distinction is very important: for no inference regarding a religion's qualification or disqualification to be the universal religion of mankind can be drawn merely from its origin, whereas such an inference is possible from its capacity or incapacity for general dissemination, and it is this capacity which constitutes the essential character of that religion which ought to be binding upon every man.

Such a religion, accordingly, can be *natural*, and at the same time *revealed*, when it is so constituted that men *could and ought to have discovered it* of themselves merely through the use of their reason, although they *would* not have come upon it so early, or over so wide an area, as is required. Hence a revelation thereof at a given time and in a given place might well be wise and very advantageous to the human race, in that, when once the religion thus introduced is here, and has been made known publicly, everyone can henceforth by himself and with his own reason convince himself of its truth. In this event the religion is *objectively* a natural religion, though *subjectively* one that has been revealed; hence it is really entitled to the former name. For, indeed, the occurrence of such a supernatural revelation might subsequently be entirely forgotten without the slightest loss to that religion either of comprehensibility, or of certainty, or of power over human hearts. It is different with that religion which, on account of its inner nature, can be regarded only as revealed. Were it not preserved in a completely secure tradition or in holy books, as records, it would disappear from the world, and there must needs transpire a supernatural revelation, either publicly repeated from time to time or else enduring continuously within each individual, for without it the spread and propagation of such a faith would be impossible.

Yet in part at least every religion, even if revealed, must contain certain principles of the natural religion. For only through reason can thought add revelation to the concept of a *religion*, since this very concept, as though deduced from an obligation to the will of a *moral* legislator, is a pure concept of reason. Therefore we shall be able to look upon even a revealed religion on the one hand as a *natural*, on the other as a *learned* religion, and thus to test it and decide what and how much has come to it from one or the other source.

If we intend to talk about a revealed religion (at least one so regarded) we cannot do so without selecting some specimen or other from history, for we must devise instances as examples in order to be intelligible, and unless we take these from history their possibility might be disputed. We cannot do better than to adopt, as the medium for the elucidation of our idea of revealed religion in general, some book or other which contains such examples, especially one which is closely interwoven with doctrines that are ethical and consequently related to reason. We can then examine it, as one of a variety of books which deal with religion and virtue on the credit of a revelation, thus exemplifying the procedure, useful in itself, of searching out whatever in it may be for us a pure and therefore a universal religion of reason. Yet we do not wish thereby to encroach upon the business of those to whom is entrusted the exegesis of this book, regarded as the summary of positive doctrines of revelation, or to contest their interpretation based upon scholarship. Rather is it advantageous to scholarship, since scholars and philosophers aim at one and the same goal, to wit, the morally good, to bring scholarship, through its own rational principles, to the very point which it already expects to reach by another road. Here the New Testament, considered as the source of the Christian doctrine, can be the book chosen. In accordance with our intention we shall now offer our demonstration in two sections, first, the Christian religion as a natural religion, and, second, as a learned religion, with reference to its content and to the principles which are found in it.

SECTION ONE

THE CHRISTIAN RELIGION AS A NATURAL RELIGION

Natural religion, as morality (in its relation to the freedom of the agent) united with the concept of that which can make actual its final end (with the concept of *God* as moral Creator of the world), and referred to a continuance of man which is suited to this end in its completeness (to immortality), is a pure practical idea of reason which, despite its inexhaustible fruitfulness, presupposes so very little capacity for theoretical reason that one can convince every man of it sufficiently for practical purposes and can at least require of all men as a duty that which is its effect. This religion possesses the prime essential of the true church, namely, the qualification for universality, so far as one understands by that a validity for everyone (*universitas vel omnitudo distributiva*), *i.e.*, universal unanimity. To spread it, in this sense, as a world religion, and to maintain it, there is needed, no doubt, a body of servants (*ministerium*) of the invisible church, but not officials (*officiales*), in other words, teachers but not dignitaries, because in the rational religion of every individual there does not yet exist a church as a universal *union* (*omnitudo collectiva*), nor is this really contemplated in the above idea.

Yet such unanimity could not be maintained of itself and hence could not, unless it became a visible church, be propagated in its universality; rather is this possible only when a collective unanimity, in other words a union of believers in a (visible) church under the principles of a pure religion of reason, is added; though this church does not automatically arise out of that unanimity nor, indeed, were it already established, would it be brought by its free adherents (as was shown above) to a permanent status as a *community* of the faithful (because in such a religion none of those who has seen the light believes himself to require, for his religious sentiments, fellowship with others). Therefore it follows that unless there are added to the natural laws, apprehensible through unassisted reason, certain statutory ordinances attended by legislative prestige (authority), that will still be lacking which constitutes a special duty of men, and a means to their highest end, namely, their enduring union into a universal visible church; and the authority mentioned above, in order to be a founder of such a church, presupposes a realm of fact[1] and not merely the pure concepts of reason.

Let us suppose there was a teacher of whom an historical record (or, at least, a widespread belief which is not basically disputable) reports that he was the first to expound publicly a pure and searching religion, comprehensible to the whole world (and thus natural). His teachings, as preserved to us, we can in this case test for ourselves. Suppose that all he did was done even in the face of a dominant ecclesiastical faith which was onerous and not conducive to moral ends (a faith whose perfunctory worship can serve as a type of all the other faiths, at bottom merely statutory, which were current in the world at the time). Suppose, further, we find that he had made this universal religion of reason the highest and indispensable condition of every religious faith whatsoever, and then had added to it certain statutes which provided forms and observances designed to serve as means of bringing into existence a church founded upon those principles. Now, in spite of the adventitiousness of his ordinances directed to this end, and the elements of arbitrariness[2] in them, and though we can deny the name of true universal church to these, we cannot deny to him himself the prestige due the one who called men to union in this church; and this without further adding to this faith burdensome new ordinances or wishing to transform acts which he had initiated into peculiar holy practices, required in themselves as being constituent elements of religion.

After this description one will not fail to recognize the person

---

[1] [*ein Factum*]
[2] [*Willkürlichen*]

who can be reverenced, not indeed as the *founder* of the *religion* which, free from every dogma, is engraved in all men's hearts (for it does not have its origin in an arbitrary will),[1] but as the founder of the first true *church*. For attestation of his dignity as of divine mission we shall adduce several of his teachings as indubitable evidence of religion in general, let historical records be what they may (since in the idea itself is present adequate ground for its acceptance); these teachings, to be sure, can be no other than those of pure reason, for such alone carry their own proof, and hence upon them must chiefly depend the attestation of the others.

First, he claims that not the observance of outer civil or statutory churchly duties but the pure moral disposition of the heart alone can make man well-pleasing to God (Matthew V, 20–48); that sins in thought are regarded, in the eyes of God, as tantamount to action (V, 28) and that, in general, holiness is the goal toward which man should strive (V, 48); that, for example, to hate in one's heart is equivalent to killing (V, 22); that injury done one's neighbor can be repaired only through satisfaction rendered to the neighbor himself, not through acts of divine worship (V, 24), and that, on the point of truthfulness, the civil device for extorting it, by oath,* does violence to respect for truth itself (V, 34–37); that the natural but evil propensity of the human heart

---

* It is hard to understand why this clear prohibition against this method of forcing confession before a civil tribunal of religious teachers—a method based upon mere superstition, not upon conscientiousness—is held as so unimportant. For that it is superstition whose efficacy is here most relied on is evident from the fact that the man whom one does not trust to tell the truth in a solemn statement, on the truthfulness of which depends a decision concerning the rights of a human being (the holiest of beings in this world) is yet expected to be persuaded to speak truly, by the use of a formula through which, over and above that statement, he simply calls down upon himself divine punishments (which in any event, with such a lie, he cannot escape), just as though it rested with him whether or not to render account to this supreme tribunal. In the passage of Scripture cited above, the mode of confirmation by oath is represented as an *absurd* presumption, the attempt to make actual, as though with magical words, what is really not in our power. But it is clearly evident that the wise Teacher who here says that whatever goes beyond Yea, Yea, and Nay, Nay, in the asseveration of truth comes of evil, had in view the bad effect which oaths bring in their train—namely, that the greater importance attached to them almost sanctions the common lie.

[1] [Our phrase "arbitrary will" translates *"willkürlichen Ursprunge"*]

is to be completely reversed, that the sweet sense of revenge must be transformed into tolerance (V, 39, 40) and the hatred of one's enemies into charity (V, 44). Thus, he says, does he intend to do full justice to the Jewish law (V, 17); whence it is obvious that not scriptural scholarship but the pure religion of reason must be the law's interpreter, for taken according to the letter, it allowed the very opposite of all this. Furthermore, he does not leave unnoticed, in his designations of the strait gate and the narrow way, the misconstruction of the law which men allow themselves in order to evade their true moral duty and, holding themselves immune through having fulfilled their churchly duty (VII, 13).* He further requires of these pure dispositions that they manifest themselves also in *works* (VII, 16) and, on the other hand, denies the insidious hope of those who imagine that, through invocation and praise of the Supreme Lawgiver in the person of His envoy, they will make up for their lack of good works and ingratiate themselves into favor (VII, 21). Regarding these works he declares that they ought to be performed publicly, as an example for imitation (V, 16), and in a cheerful mood, not as actions extorted from slaves (VI, 16); and that thus, from a small beginning in the sharing and spreading of such dispositions, religion, like a grain of seed in good soil, or a ferment of goodness, would gradually, through its inner power, grow into a kingdom of God (XIII, 31–33). Finally, he combines all duties (1) in one *universal* rule (which includes within itself both the inner and the outer moral relations of men), namely: Perform your duty for no motive[1] other than unconditioned esteem for duty itself, *i.e.*, love God (the Legislator of all duties) above all else; and (2) in a *particular* rule, that, namely, which concerns man's external relation to other men as universal duty: Love every one as yourself, *i.e.*, further his welfare from good-will that is immediate and not derived from motives of self-advantage. These commands are not mere laws of virtue but precepts of *holiness* which we ought to pursue, and the very pursuit of them is called *virtue*.

* The *strait gate* and the narrow way, which leads to life, is that of good life-conduct; the *wide gate* and the broad way, found by many, is the *church*. Not that the church and its doctrines are responsible for men being lost, but that the *entrance* into it and the knowledge of its statutes or celebration of its rites are regarded as the manner in which God really wishes to be served.

[1] [*Triebfeder*]

Accordingly he destroys the hope of all who intend to wait upon this moral goodness quite passively, with their hands in their laps, as though it were a heavenly gift which descends from on high. He who leaves unused the natural predisposition to goodness which lies in human nature (like a talent entrusted to him) in lazy confidence that a higher moral influence will no doubt supply the moral character and completeness which he lacks, is confronted with the threat that even the good which, by virtue of his natural predisposition, he may have done, will not be allowed to stand him in stead because of this neglect (XXV, 29).

As regards men's very natural expectation of an allotment of happiness proportional to a man's moral conduct, especially in view of the many sacrifices of the former which must be undergone for the sake of the latter, he promises (V,11, 12) a reward for these sacrifices in a future world, but one in accordance with the differences of disposition in this conduct between those who did their duty *for the sake of the reward* (or for release from deserved punishment) and the better men who performed it merely for its own sake; the latter will be dealt with in a different manner. When the man governed by self-interest, the god of this world, does not renounce it but merely refines it by the use of reason and extends it beyond the constricting boundary of the present, he is represented (Luke XVI, 3–9) as one who, in his very person [as servant], defrauds his master [self-interest] and wins from him sacrifices in behalf of "duty." For when he comes to realize that sometime, perhaps soon, the world must be forsaken, and that he can take along into the other world nothing of what he here possessed, he may well resolve to strike off from the account what he or his master, self-interest, has a legal right to exact from the indigent, and, as it were, thereby to acquire for himself bills of exchange, payable in another world. Herein he acts, no doubt, *cleverly* rather than *morally*, as regards the motives of such charitable actions, and yet in conformity with the moral law, at least according to the letter of that law; and he can hope that for this too he may not stand unrequited in the future.* Compare with

* We know nothing of the future, and we ought not to seek to know more than what is rationally bound up with the incentives of morality and their end. Here belongs the belief that there are no good actions which will not, in the next world, have their good consequences for him who performs them; that, therefore, however reprehensible a man may find himself at the end of

this what is said of charity toward the needy from sheer motives of duty (Matthew XXV, 35–40), where those, who gave succor to the needy without the idea even entering their minds that such action was worthy of a reward or that they thereby obligated heaven, as it were, to recompense them, are, for this very reason, because they acted thus without attention to reward, declared by the Judge of the world to be those really chosen for His kingdom, and it becomes evident that when the Teacher of the Gospel spoke of rewards in the world to come he wished to make them thereby not an incentive to action but merely (as a soul-elevating representation of the consummation of the divine benevolence and wisdom in the guidance of the human race) an object of the purest respect and of the greatest moral approval when reason reviews human destiny in its entirety.

Here then is a complete religion, which can be presented to all men comprehensibly and convincingly through their own reason; while the possibility and even the necessity of its being an archetype for us to imitate (so far as men are capable of that imitation) have, be it noted, been made evident by means of an example without either the truth of those teachings nor the authority and the worth of the Teacher requiring any external certification (for which scholarship or miracles, which are not matters for everyone, would be required). When appeals are here made to older (Mosaic) legislation and prefiguration, as though these were to serve the Teacher as means of confirmation, they are presented not in support of the truth of his teachings but merely for the introduction of these among people who clung wholly, and blindly, to the old. This introduction, among men whose heads, filled with statutory dogmas, have been almost entirely unfitted for the religion of reason, must always be more difficult than when this religion is to be brought to the reason of people uninstructed but also unspoiled. For this reason no one should be astonished to find an exposition, that adapted itself to the prejudices of those times, now puzzling and in need of pains-taking exegesis; though indeed

---

his life, he must not on that account refrain from doing at least *one* more good deed which is in his power, and that, in so doing, he has reason to hope that, in proportion as he possesses in this action a purely good intent, the act will be of greater worth than those actionless absolutions which are supposed to compensate for the deficiency of good deeds without providing anything for the lessening of the guilt.

it everywhere permits a religious doctrine to shine forth and, in addition, frequently points explicitly to that which must be comprehensible and, without any expenditure of learning, convincing to all men.

To the extent to which a religion propounds, as necessary, dogmas which cannot be known to be so through reason, but which are none the less to be imparted uncorrupted (as regards essential content) to all men in all future ages, it must be viewed (if we do not wish to assume a continuous miracle of revelation) as a sacred charge entrusted to the guardianship of *the learned*. For even though *at first*, accompanied by miracles and deeds, this religion, even in that which finds no confirmation in reason, could obtain entry everywhere, yet the very report of these miracles, together with the doctrines which stand in need of confirmation through this report, requires *with the passage of time* the written, authoritative, and unchanging instruction of posterity.

The acceptance of the fundamental principles of a religion is faith *par excellence* (*fides sacra*). We shall therefore have to examine the Christian faith on the one hand as a pure *rational faith*, on the other, as a *revealed faith* (*fides statutaria*). The first may be regarded as a faith freely assented to by everyone (*fides elicita*), the second, as a faith which is commanded (*fides imperata*). Everyone can convince himself, through his own reason, of the evil which lies in human hearts and from which no one is free; of the impossibility of ever holding himself to be justified before God through his own life-conduct, and, at the same time, of the necessity for such a justification valid in His eyes; of the futility of substituting churchly observances and pious compulsory services for the righteousness which is lacking, and, over and against this, of the inescapable obligation to become a new man: and to become convinced of all this is part of religion.

But from the point where the Christian teaching is built not upon bare concepts of reason but upon facts, it is no longer called merely the Christian *religion*, but the Christian *faith*, which has been made the basis of a church. The service of a church consecrated to such a faith is therefore twofold: what, on the one hand, must be rendered the church according to the historical faith, and, on the other, what is due it in accordance with the practical and moral faith of reason. In the Christian church neither of these can be separated from the other as adequate in itself; the second is indispensable to the first because the Christian faith is a religious faith, and the first is indispensable to the second because it is a learned faith.

The Christian faith, as a *learned* faith, relies upon history and, so far as erudition (objectively) constitutes its foundation, it is not in itself a *free faith* (*fides elicita*) or one which is deduced from insight into adequate theoretical proofs. Were it a pure rational faith it would have to be thought of as a free faith even though the moral laws upon which it, as a belief in a divine Legislator, is based, command unconditionally—and it was thus presented in Section One. Indeed, if only this believing were not made a duty, it could be a free theoretical faith even when taken as an historical faith, provided all men were learned. But if it is to be valid for all men, including the unlearned, it is not only a faith which is commanded but also one which obeys the command blindly (*fides servilis*), *i.e.*, without investigation as to whether it really is a divine command.

In the revealed doctrines of Christianity, however, one cannot by any means start with *unconditional belief* in revealed propositions (in themselves hidden from reason) and then let the knowledge of erudition follow after, merely as a defense, as it were, against an enemy attacking it from the rear; for if this were done the Christian faith would be not merely a *fides imperata*, but actually *servilis*. It must therefore always be taught as at least a *fides historice elicita;* that is, *learning* should certainly constitute in it, regarded as a revealed credal doctrine, not the rearguard but the vanguard, and then the small body of textual scholars (the clerics), who, incidentally, could not at all dispense with secular learning, would drag along behind itself the long train of the unlearned (the laity) who, of themselves, are ignorant of the Scripture (and to whose number belong even the rulers of world-states). But if this, in turn, is to be prevented from happening, recognition and respect must be accorded, in Christian dogmatic, to universal human reason as the supremely commanding principle in a natural religion, and the revealed doctrine, upon which a church is founded and which stands in need of the learned as interpreters and conservers, must be cherished and cultivated as merely a means, but a most precious means, of making this doctrine comprehensible, even to the ignorant, as well as widely diffused and permanent.

This is the *true service* of the church under the dominion of the good principle; whereas that in which revealed faith is to precede religion is *pseudo-service*. In it the moral order is wholly reversed and what is merely means is commanded unconditionally (as an end). Belief in propositions of which the unlearned can assure themselves neither through reason nor through Scripture (inasmuch as the latter would first have to be authenticated) would here be made an absolute duty (*fides imperata*) and, along with other related observances, it would be elevated, as a compulsory service, to the rank of a saving faith even though this faith lacked moral determining grounds of action. A church founded upon this latter principle does not really have *servants* (*ministri*), like those of the other organization, but commanding high *officials* (*officiales*). Even when (as in a Protestant church) these officials do not appear in hierarchical splendor as spiritual officers clothed with external power—even when, indeed, they protest verbally against all this— they yet actually wish to feel themselves regarded as the only chosen interpreters of a Holy Scripture, having robbed pure rational religion of its merited office (that of being at all times Scripture's highest interpreter) and having commanded that Scriptural learning be used solely in the interest of the churchly faith. They transform, in this way, the *service* of the church (*ministerium*) into a *domination* of its members (*imperium*) although, in order to conceal this usurpation, they make use of the modest title of the former. But this domination, which would have been easy for reason, costs the church dearly, namely, in the expenditure of great learning. For, "blind with respect to nature, it brings down upon its head the whole of antiquity and buries itself beneath it."[1]

The course of affairs, once brought to this pass, is as follows. First, that procedure, wisely adopted by the first propagators of the teaching of Christ in order to achieve its introduction among the people, is taken as a part of religion itself, valid for all times and peoples, with the result that one is obliged to believe *that every Christian must be a Jew whose Messiah has come.* Yet this does not harmonize with the fact that a Christian is really bound by no law of Judaism (as statutory), though the entire Holy Book of this people is none the less supposed to be accepted faithfully

[1] [The source of this quotation has not been found.]

as a divine revelation given to all men.† Yet the authenticity of this Book involves great difficulty (an authenticity which is certainly not proved merely by the fact that passages in it, and indeed the entire sacred history appearing in the books of the Christians, are used for the sake of this proof). Prior to the beginning of Christianity, and even prior to its considerable progress, Judaism had not gained a foothold among the *learned public*, that is, was not yet known to its learned contemporaries among other peoples; its historical recording was therefore not yet subjected to control and so its sacred Book had not, on account of its antiquity, been brought into historical credibility. Meanwhile, apart from this, it is not enough to know it in translations and to pass it on to posterity in this form; rather, the certainty of churchly faith based thereon requires that in all future times and among all peoples

---

† Mendelssohn[1] very ingeniously makes use of this weak spot in the customary presentation of Christianity wholly to reject every demand upon a son of Israel that he change his religion. For, he says, since the Jewish faith itself is, according to the avowal of Christians, the substructure upon which the superstructure of Christianity rests, the demand that it be abandoned is equivalent to expecting someone to demolish the ground floor of a house in order to take up his abode in the second story. His real intention is fairly clear. He means to say: First wholly remove Judaism itself out of your *religion* (it can always remain, as an antiquity, in the historical account of the faith); we can then take your proposal under advisement. (Actually nothing would then be left but pure moral religion unencumbered by statutes.) Our burden will not be lightened in the least by throwing off the yoke of outer observances if, in its place, another yoke, namely confession of faith in sacred history—a yoke which rests far more heavily upon the conscientious—is substituted in its place.

In any case, the sacred books of this people will doubtless always be preserved and will continue to possess value for scholarship even if not for the benefit of religion: since the history of no other people dates back, with some color of credibility, so far as does this, into epochs of antiquity (even to the beginning of the world) in which all secular history known to us can be arranged; and thus the great hiatus, which must be left by the latter, is filled by the former.

---

[1] [Moses Mendelssohn, 1729–1786, (father of Felix Mendelssohn, the composer) was a prominent Jewish philosopher and theologian. Kant and Mendelssohn were familiar, over a long period of years, with each other's writings, and in 1763 both submitted essays for a prize offered by the Royal Academy in Berlin; Mendelssohn won the prize, Kant having been given second place, and their two essays were published together in 1764.

Kant here refers to Mendelssohn's *Jerusalem, oder über religiöse Macht und Judenthum*, ("Jerusalem, or concerning Religious Power and Judaism"). Cf. Kant's *Streit der Facultäten*, Berlin Edition, 1907, p. 52 n.]

there be scholars who are familiar with the Hebrew language (so far as knowledge is possible of a language in which we have only a single book). And it must be regarded as not merely a concern of historical scholarship in general but one upon which hangs the salvation of mankind, that there should be men sufficiently familiar with Hebrew to assure the true religion for the world.

The Christian religion has had a similar fate, in that, even though its sacred events occurred openly under the very eyes of a learned people, its historical recording was delayed for more than a generation before this religion gained a foothold among this people's learned public; hence the authentication of the record must dispense with the corroboration of contemporaries. Yet Christianity possesses the great advantage over Judaism of being represented as coming *from the mouth of the first Teacher* not as a statutory but as a moral religion, and as thus entering into the closest relation with reason so that, through reason, it was able of itself, without historical learning, to be spread at all times and among all peoples with the greatest trustworthiness. But the first founders of the *Christian communities*[1] did find it necessary to entwine the history of Judaism with it; this was managed wisely in view of the situation at the time, and perhaps with reference to that situation alone; thus this history too has come down to us in the sacred legacy of Christianity. But the founders of the *church* incorporated these episodical means of recommendation among the essential articles of faith and multiplied them either with tradition, or with interpretations, which acquired legal force from the Councils or were authenticated by means of scholarship. As for this scholarship, or its extreme opposite, the inner light to which every layman can pretend, it is impossible to know how many changes the faith will still have to undergo through these agencies; but this cannot be avoided so long as we seek religion without and not within us.

[1] [*Gemeinde*, congregations]

PART TWO

CONCERNING THE PSEUDO-SERVICE OF GOD IN A
STATUTORY RELIGION

The one true religion comprises nothing but laws, that is, those practical principles of whose unconditioned necessity we can become aware, and which we therefore recognize as revealed through pure reason (not empirically). Only for the sake of a church, of which there can be different forms, all equally good, can there be statutes, *i.e.*, ordinances held to be divine, which are arbitrary and contingent as viewed by our pure moral judgment. To deem this statutory faith (which in any case is restricted to one people and cannot comprise the universal world-religion) as essential to the service of God generally, and to make it the highest condition of the divine approval of man, is *religious illusion** whose consequence is a *pseudo-service*, that is, pretended honoring of God through which we work directly counter to the service demanded by God Himself.

1. Concerning the Universal Subjective Ground of the Religious Illusion

Anthropomorphism, scarcely to be avoided by men in the theoretical representation of God and His being, but yet harmless enough (so long as it does not influence concepts of duty), is highly dangerous in connection with our practical relation to His will, and

---

* Illusion [*Wahn*] is the deception of regarding the mere representation of a thing as equivalent to the thing itself. Thus a rich miser is subject to the *covetous* illusion of holding the idea of being able sometime or other to make use of his riches, when he may wish to do so, as an adequate substitute for never using them. The illusion of *honor* ascribes to praise by others, which is at bottom merely the outward expression of their regard (perhaps inwardly not entertained by them at all) the worth which ought to be attached solely to the regard itself. Here too belongs the passion for titles and orders, since these are but outward representations of a superiority over others. Even *madness* is so named [*Wahnsinn*] because it commonly takes a mere representation (of the imagination) for the presence of the thing itself and values it accordingly. Now the consciousness of possessing a means to some end or other (before one has availed oneself of this means) is the possession of the end in representation only; hence to content oneself with the former, just as though it could take the place of the latter, is a *practical illusion*, which is all we are speaking of here.

even for our morality; for here *we create a God for ourselves,*† and we create Him in the form in which we believe we shall be able most easily to win Him over to our advantage and ourselves escape from the wearisome uninterrupted effort of working upon the innermost part of our moral disposition. The basic principle which man usually formulates for himself in this connection is that everything which we do solely in order to be well-pleasing to the Godhead (provided it does not actually run counter to morality, though it may not contribute to it in the very least) manifests to God our willingness to serve Him as obedient servants, well-pleasing to Him through this very obedience; and that thus we also serve God (*in potentia*). Not only through sacrifices, man believes, can he render this service to God; festivals and even public games, as among the Greeks and Romans, have often had to perform this function, and still suffice, according to men's illusion, to make the Godhead propitious to a people or even to a single individual. Yet the former (penances, castigations, pilgrimages, and the like) were always held to be more powerful, more efficacious upon the the favor of heaven, and more apt to purify of sin, because they serve to testify more forcefully to unbounded (though not moral) subjection to His will. The more useless such self-castigations are and the less they are designed for the general moral improvement of the man, the holier they seem to be; just because they are of no use whatsoever in the world and yet cost painful effort they seem to be directly solely to the attestation of devotion to God. Even though God has not in any respect been served by by the act, men say, He yet sees herein the good will, the heart, which is indeed too weak to obey His moral commands but which, through its attested willingness on this score, makes good that deficiency. Now here is apparent the propensity to a procedure

† Though it does indeed sound dangerous, it is in no way reprehensible to say that every man *creates a God* for himself, nay, must make himself such a God according to moral concepts (and must add those infinitely great attributes which characterize a Being capable of exhibiting, in the world, an object commensurate with Himself), in order to honor in Him *the One who created him.* For in whatever manner a being has been made known to him by another and described as God, yea, even if such a being had appeared to him (if this is possible), he must first of all compare this representation with his ideal in order to judge whether he is entitled to regard it and to honor it as a divinity. Hence there can be no religion springing from revelation alone, *i.e.*, without *first* positing that concept, in its purity, as a touchstone. Without this all reverence for God would be *idolatry.*

which has no moral value in itself, except perhaps as a means of elevating the powers of sense-imagery to comport with intellectual ideas of the end, or of suppressing them* when they might work counter to these ideas. For in our thinking we attribute to this procedure the worth of the end itself, or what amounts to the same thing, we ascribe to the frame of mind (called *devotion*) attuned to acquiring dispositions dedicated to God the worth belonging to those dispositions themselves. Such a procedure, therefore, is merely a religious illusion which can assume various forms, in some of which it appears more moral than in others; but in all forms it is not merely an inadvertent deception but is rather a maxim of attributing to a means an intrinsic value instead of the value deriving from the end. Hence the illusion, because of this maxim, is equally absurd in all these forms and, as a hidden bias toward deception, it is reprehensible.

2. *The Moral Principle of Religion Opposed to the Religious Illusion*

To begin with, I take the following proposition to be a principle requiring no proof: *Whatever, over and above good life-conduct, man fancies that he can do to become well-pleasing to God is mere religious illusion and pseudo-service of God.* I say, what man believes that *he* can do; for here it is not denied that beyond all that *we* can do there may be something in the mysteries of the highest wisdom that God alone can do to transform us into men well-pleasing to

---

* For those who believe that the critique of pure reason contradicts itself whenever my distinctions between the sensuous and the intellectual are not wholly congenial to them, I here remark that, when mention is made of sensuous means furthering what is intellectual (of the pure moral disposition), or of the former opposing the latter, the influence of two such heterogeneous principles must not be thought of as *direct*. That is, as sensuous beings we can work against the law, or for its behoof, only in the *appearances of the intellectual principle, i.e.,* in the determination of our physical powers through *free choice*[w] which expresses itself in actions; so that cause and effect may be represented as actually homogeneous. But in what concerns the supersensible (the subjective principle of morality in us, that which lies hidden in the incomprehensible attribute of freedom), for example, the pure religious disposition, we have insight only into its law (though this, indeed, suffices) touching the relation of cause and effect in man; that is, we cannot *explain* to ourselves the possibility of actions, as events in the sensuous world, in terms of the moral constitution of man, as imputable to him, just because these are free acts and because the grounds of explanation of all events must be derived from the sensuous world.

Him. Yet even should the church proclaim such a mystery as revealed, the notion that *belief* in such a revelation, as the sacred history recounts it to us, and *acknowledgment* of it (whether inwardly or outwardly) are in themselves means whereby we render ourselves well-pleasing to God, would be a dangerous religious illusion. For this belief, as an inner confession of his steadfast conviction, is so genuinely an *action* which is compelled by fear that an upright man might agree to any other condition sooner than to this; for in the case of all other compulsory services he would at most be doing something merely superfluous, whereas here, in a declaration, of whose truth he is not convinced, he would be doing violence to his conscience. The confession, then, regarding which man persuades himself that in and of itself (as acceptance of a good proffered him) it can make him well-pleasing to God, is something which he fancies he can render over and above good life-conduct in obedience to moral laws which are to be put into practice on earth, on the ground that in this service [of confession] he turns directly to God.

In the *first* place, reason does not leave us wholly without consolation with respect to our lack of righteousness valid before God. It says that whoever, with a disposition genuinely devoted to duty, does as much as lies in his power to satisfy his obligation (at least in a continual approximation to complete harmony with the law), may hope that what is not in his power will be supplied by the supreme Wisdom *in some way or other* (which can make permanent the disposition to this unceasing approximation). Reason says this, however, without presuming to determine the manner in which this aid will be given or to know wherein it will consist; it may be so mysterious that God can reveal it to us at best in a symbolic representation in which only what is practical is comprehensible to us, and that we, meanwhile, can not at all grasp theoretically what this relation of God to man might be, or apply concepts to it, even did He desire to reveal such a mystery to us. Suppose, now, that a particular church were to assert that it knows with certainty the manner in which God supplies that moral lack in the human race, and were also to consign to eternal damnation all men who are not acquainted with that means of justification which is unknown to reason in a natural way, and who, on this account, do not accept and confess it as a religious principle: who, indeed, is now the unbeliever? Is it he who trusts, without knowing how that for which he hopes will come to pass; or he who absolutely insists on knowing the way in which man is released from evil and, if he cannot know this, gives up all hope of this release? Fundamentally the latter is not really so much concerned to know this mystery (for his own reason already teaches him that it is of no use to him to know that regarding which he can do nothing); he merely wishes to know it so that he can make for himself (even if it be but inwardly) a divine service out of the *belief*, acceptance, confession, and cherishing of all that has been revealed—a service which could earn him the favor of heaven prior to all expenditure of his own powers toward a good life-conduct, in a word, quite gratuitously; a service which could produce such conduct, mayhap, in supernatural fashion, or, where he may have acted in opposition, could at least make amends for his transgression.

Second: if man departs in the very least from the above maxim, the pseudo-service of God (superstition) has *no other limits*, for once beyond this maxim everything (except what directly contradicts morality) is arbitrary. He proffers everything to God, from lip-offerings, which cost him the least, to the donation of earthly goods, which might better be used for the advantage of mankind, yea, even to the immolation of his own person, becoming lost to the world (as a hermit, fakir, or monk)—everything except his moral disposition; and when he says that he also gives his heart to God he means by this not the disposition to a course of life well-pleasing to Him but the heart-felt wish that those sacrifices may be accepted in lieu of that disposition. (*Natio gratis adhelans, multa agendo nihil agens.* Phaedrus.[1])

Finally, when once a man has gone over to the maxim of a service presumed to be in itself well-pleasing to God, and even, if need be, propitiating Him, yet not purely moral, there is no essential difference among the ways of serving Him, as it were, mechanically, which would give one way a priority over another. They are all alike in worth (or rather worthlessness), and it is mere affectation to regard oneself as more excellent, because of a *subtler*

---

[1] [*Fables* II, 5. Kant draws upon this passage (lines 1–3):

> Est ardelionum quaedam Romae natio,
> Trepide concursans, occupata in otio
> Gratis anhelans, multa agendo nil agens.

"There is a certain set of busybodies at Rome, hurriedly running to and fro, busily engaged in idleness, out of breath for no reason, doing much but achieving naught."]

deviation from the one and only intellectual principle of genuine respect for God, than those who allow themselves to become guilty of an assumedly *coarser* degradation to sensuality. Whether the devotee betakes himself to *church* according to rule or whether he undertakes a pilgrimage to the sanctuaries in Loretto or in Palestine; whether he brings his formulas of prayer to the court of heaven with his *lips*, or by means of a *prayer-wheel*, like the Tibetan (who believes that his wishes will reach their goal just as well if they are set down in writing, provided only they be *moved* by something or other, by the wind, for example, if they are written on flags, or by the hand, if they are enclosed in a sort of revolving cylinder)—whatever be substituted for the moral service of God, it is all one and all equal in value. What matters here is not a difference in the external form; everything depends upon the adoption or rejection of the unique principle of becoming well-pleasing to God—upon whether we rely on the moral disposition alone, so far as this disposition exhibits its vitality in actions which are its appearances, or on pious playthings and on inaction.* But is there not also perhaps a dizzying *illusion of virtue*, soaring above the bounds of human capacity, which might be reckoned, along with the cringing religious illusion, in the general class of self-deceptions? No! The disposition of virtue occupies itself with something *real* which of itself is well-pleasing to God and which harmonizes with the world's highest good.[1] True, an illusion of self-sufficiency may attach itself thereto, an illusion of regarding oneself as measuring up to the idea of one's holy duty; but this is merely contingent. To ascribe the highest worth to that disposition is not an illusion, like faith in the devotional exercises of the church, but is a direct contribution which promotes the highest good of the world.

Furthermore, it is customary (at least in the church) to give

* It is a psychological phenomenon that the adherents of a denomination wherein somewhat less of the statutory is offered for belief, feel themselves, by virtue of this fact, somewhat ennobled and more enlightened, even though they have still retained so much of this statutory belief that they are not entitled to look down with contempt (as they actually do), from their fancied heights of purity, upon their brothers in churchly illusion. The reason for this is that, because of this difference of belief, however slight it be, they find themselves a little nearer to pure moral religion, even though they remain attached to the illusion of wishing to supplement it by means of pious observances in which reason is only less passive.

[1] [*Weltbesten*]

the name of *nature* to that which men can do by dint of the principle of virtue, and the name of *grace* to that which alone serves to supplement the deficiency of all our moral powers and yet, because sufficiency of these powers is also our duty, can only be wished for, or hoped for, and solicited; to regard both together as active causes of a disposition adequate for a course of life well-pleasing to God; and not only to distinguish them from one another but even to set them over against one another.

The persuasion that we can distinguish the effects of grace from those of nature (virtue) or can actually produce the former within ourselves, is *fanaticism;* for we cannot, by any token, recognize a supersensible object in experience, still less can we exert an influence upon it to draw it down to us; though, to be sure, at times there do arise stirrings of the heart making for morality, movements which we cannot explain and regarding which we must confess our ignorance: "The wind bloweth where it listeth . . . but thou canst not tell whence it cometh, etc."[1] To wish to *observe* such heavenly influences in ourselves is a kind of madness, in which, no doubt, there can be method (since those supposed inner revelations must always be attached to moral, and hence to rational, ideas), but which none the less remains a self-deception prejudicial to religion. To believe that there may be works of grace and that perhaps these may even be necessary to supplement the incompleteness of our struggle toward virtue—that is all we can say on this subject; beyond this we are incapable of determining anything concerning their distinctive marks and still less are we able to do anything to produce them.

The illusion of being able to accomplish anything in the way of justifying ourselves before God through religious acts of worship is religious *superstition*, just as the illusion of wishing to accomplish this by striving for what is supposed to be communion with God is religious *fanaticism*. It is a superstitious illusion to wish to become well-pleasing to God through actions which anyone can perform without even needing to be a good man (for example, through profession of statutory articles of faith, through conformity to churchly observance and discipline, etc.). And it is called superstitious because it selects merely natural (not moral) means which in themselves can have absolutely no effect upon what is not nature (*i.e.*, on the morally good). But an illusion is called

---

[1] [Cf. John III, 8]

fanatical when the very means it contemplates, as supersensible, are not within man's power, leaving out of account the inaccessibility of the supersensible end aimed at by these means; for this feeling of the immediate presence of the Supreme Being and the distinguishing of this from every other, even from the moral feeling, would constitute a receptivity for an intuition for which there is no sensory provision in man's nature. Because the superstitious illusion contains the means, available to many an individual, enabling him at least to work against the obstacles in the way of a disposition well-pleasing to God, it is indeed thus far allied to reason, and is only contingently objectionable in transforming what is no more than a means into an object immediately well-pleasing to God. The fanatical religious illusion, in contrast, is the moral death of reason; for without reason, after all, no religion is possible, since, like all morality in general, it must be established upon basic principles.

So the basic principle of an ecclesiastical faith, a principle that remedies or prevents all religious illusion, is this, that such a faith must contain within itself, along with the statutory articles with which it cannot as yet wholly dispense, still another principle, of setting up the religion of good life-conduct as the real end, in order, at some future time, to be able entirely to dispense with the statutory articles.

3. Concerning Clericalism† as a Government in the Pseudo-Service of the Good Principle

The veneration of mighty invisible beings, which was extorted from helpless man through natural fear rooted in the sense of his

† This name (*Pfaffentum*), signifying merely the authority of a spiritual father[1] (πάππα), possesses a censorious meaning as well, only because of the attendant concept of a spiritual despotism, to be found in all forms of ecclesiasticism, however unpretentious and popular they may declare themselves. I do not by any means want to be understood as desiring, in my comparison of the sects, to treat with contempt one of them, with its practices and ordinances, as contrasted with another. All deserve the same respect so far as their forms are the attempts of poor mortals to render perceptible to the senses the kingdom of God on earth, but also the same blame when they take the form of the representation of this idea (in a visible church) to be the thing itself.

[1] [*Papacy* would, in this context, best translate *Pfaffentum;* but we have used *clericalism* here and elsewhere since Kant is referring to the Protestant as well as to the Roman Catholic clergy.]

impotence, did not begin with a religion but rather with a slavish worship of a god (or of idols). When this worship had achieved a certain publicly legalized form it was a *temple service*,[1] and it became a *church worship*[1] only after the moral culture of men was gradually united with its laws. An historical faith constituted the basis of both of these, until man finally came to regard such a faith as merely provisional, and to see in it the symbolic presentation, and the means of promotion, of a pure religious faith.

We can indeed recognize a tremendous difference in *manner*, but not in *principle*, between a *shaman* of the Tunguses and a European *prelate* ruling over church and state alike, or (if we wish to consider not the heads and leaders but merely the adherents of the faith, according to their own mode of representation) between the wholly sensuous *Wogulite* who in the morning places the paw of a bearskin upon his head with the short prayer, "Strike me not dead!" and the sublimated *Puritan* and Independent in Connecticut: for, as regards principle, they both belong to one and the same class, namely, the class of those who let their worship of God consist in what in itself can never make man better (in faith in certain statutory dogmas or celebration of certain arbitrary observances). Only those who mean to find the service of God solely in the disposition to good life-conduct distinguish themselves from those others, by virtue of having passed over to a wholly different principle and one which is far nobler than the other, the principle, namely, whereby they confess themselves members of an (invisible) church which includes within itself all right-thinking people and, by its essential nature, can alone be the true church universal.

The intention of all of them is to manage to their own advantage the invisible Power which presides over the destiny of men; they differ merely in their conceptions of how to undertake this feat. If they hold that Power to be an intelligent Being and thus ascribe to Him a will from which they await their lot, their efforts can consist only in choosing the manner in which, as creatures subjected to His will, they can become pleasing to Him through what they do or refrain from doing. If they think of Him as a moral Being they easily convince themselves through their own reason that the condition of earning His favor must be their morally good life-conduct, and especially the pure disposition as the sub-

[1] [*Tempeldienst, Kirchendienst*]

jective principle of such conduct. But perhaps the Supreme Being may wish, in addition, to be served in a manner which cannot become known to us through unassisted reason, namely, by actions wherein, in themselves, we can indeed discover nothing moral, but which we freely[1] undertake, either because He commanded them or else in order to convince Him of our submissiveness to Him. Under either mode of procedure, if it provides for us a unified whole of systematically ordered activities, our acts constitute in general a *service* of God. Now if the two are to be united, then each of them must be regarded as a way in which one may be well-pleasing to God directly, or else one of them must be regarded as but a means to the other, the real service of God. It is self-evident that the moral service of God (*officium liberum*) is directly well-pleasing to Him. But this service cannot be recognized as the highest condition of divine approval of man (this approval is already contained in the concept of morality) if it be possible for hired service (*officium mercenarium*) to be regarded as, *alone and of itself*, well-pleasing to God; for then no one could know which service was worthier in a given situation, in order to decide thereby regarding his duty, or how they supplemented each other. Hence actions which have no moral value in themselves will have to be accepted as well-pleasing to Him only so far as they serve as means to the furtherance of what, in the way of conduct, is immediately good (*i.e.*, so far as they promote morality), or in other words, so far as they are performed *for the sake of the moral service of God*.

Now the man who does make use of actions, as means, which in themselves contain nothing pleasing to God (*i.e.*, nothing moral), in order to earn thereby immediate divine approval of himself and therewith the attainment of his desires, labors under the illusion that he possesses an art of bringing about a supernatural effect through wholly natural means. Such attempts we are wont to entitle *sorcery*. But (since this term carries with it the attendant concept of commerce with the evil principle, whereas the above-mentioned attempt can be conceived to be undertaken, through misunderstanding, with good moral intent) we desire to use in place of it the word *fetishism*, familiar in other connections. A supernatural effect induced by a man would be one whose possibility would rest, as he conceives the matter, upon a supposition that he works on God and uses Him as a means to bring about a

[1] [*willkürlich*]

result in the world for which his own powers, yea, even his insight into whether this result may be well-pleasing to God, would, of themselves, not avail. But this involves an absurdity even in his own conception of it.

But if a man, not only by means which render him immediately an object of divine favor (by the active disposition to good life-conduct) but also through certain formalities, seeks to make himself *worthy* of the supplementation of his impotence through supernatural assistance, and if he thinks that he is merely making himself *capable of receiving* the object of his good moral desires by conforming, with this intent, to observances which indeed have no immediate value but yet serve as means to the furthering of the moral disposition—then, to be sure, he is counting on something *supernatural* to supplement his natural impotence, yet not on what is *effected by man* (through influence upon the divine will) but on what is received, on what he can hope for but can not bring to pass. But if it is his idea that actions, which in themselves, so far as we can see, contain nothing moral or well-pleasing to God, are to serve as a means, nay as a condition, whereby he can expect the satisfaction of his wishes directly from God, then he is a victim of illusion; *viz.*, the illusion that, though he possesses neither physical control over, nor yet moral receptivity for, this supernatural assistance, he can yet produce it through *natural* acts, which in themselves are in no way related to morality (and the performance of which calls for no disposition well-pleasing to God, and which can be put into practice by the most wicked man quite as well as by the best)—through formulas of invocation, through profession of a mercenary faith, through churchly observances, and so on—and that he can thus, as it were, *conjure up* divine assistance by magic. For between solely physical means and a morally efficacious cause there is no connection whatsoever according to any law of which reason can conceive, in terms of which the moral cause could be represented as determinable to specific activities through the physical.

Hence whoever assigns priority to obedience to statutory laws, requiring a revelation, as being necessary to religion, and regards this obedience not merely as a means to the moral disposition but as the objective condition of becoming immediately well-pleasing to God, and whoever thus places endeavor toward a good course of life below this historical faith (instead of requiring the latter, which can be well-pleasing to God only *conditionally*, to adapt it-self to the former, which alone is *intrinsically* well-pleasing to Him)—whoever does this transforms the service of God into a mere *fetishism* and practises a pseudo-service which is subversive to all endeavors toward true religion. So much depends, when we wish to unite two good things, upon the order in which they are united! True *enlightenment* lies in this very distinction; therein the service of God becomes first and foremost a free and hence a moral service. If man departs from it there is laid upon him, in place of the freedom of the children of God,[1] the yoke of a law (the statutory law), and this yoke, as an unconditional require-ment of belief in what can only be known historically and there-fore cannot be an object of conviction for everyone, is for a con-scientious man a far heavier yoke* than all the lumber of piously ordained observances could ever be. For the solemnization of these suffices to secure a man's conformity with an established churchly commonwealth, and he need not either inwardly or out-wardly profess the belief that he regards them as institutions *founded by God;* and it is by confession of the latter sort that con-science is really burdened.

Clericalism, therefore, is the constitution of a church to the ex-tent to which a *fetish-worship* dominates it; and this condition is always found wherever, instead of principles of morality, statu-

---

* "That yoke is easy, and the burden is light"[2] where the duty, which binds every man, can be regarded as imposed on him by himself and through his own reason; and that yoke he therefore so far takes upon himself freely as his own. Only the moral laws, however, taken as divine commands, are of this sort; of these alone the Founder of the true church could say, "My com-mandments are not grievous."[3] This expression merely means that these com-mands are not *burdensome* because everyone of himself perceives the neces-sity of their obedience and so nothing is here forced upon him; whereas des-potically imperative ordinances, in which we can see no use, though they are imposed upon us for our best interests (yet not through our own reason), are a kind of vexation (drudgery) to which we subject ourselves only under com-pulsion. In themselves, however, the actions, regarded in the purity of their source, which are commanded by those moral laws, are precisely those which man finds the hardest, and in place of which he would gladly undertake the most burdensome pious drudgery were it possible to offer this in payment for the other.

[1] [Cf. Romans VIII, 21]
[2] [Cf. Matthew XI, 30]
[3] [Cf. I John V, 3]

tory commands, rules of faith, and observances constitute the basis and the essence of the church. Now there are, indeed, various types of church in which the fetishism is so manifold and so mechanical that it appears to crowd out nearly all of morality, and therefore religion as well, and to seek to occupy their place; such fetishism borders very closely on paganism. But it is not a question of more or less here, where worth or worthlessness rests on the nature of the principle which is supremely binding. When this principle imposes not free homage, as that which *first and foremost* must be paid to the moral law, but submission to precepts as a compulsory service; then, however few the imposed observances, so long as these are laid down as unconditionally necessary the faith remains a fetish-faith through which the masses are ruled and robbed of their moral freedom by subservience to a church (not to religion). The structure of this hierarchy can be monarchical or aristocratic or democratic; this is merely a matter of organization; its constitution is and ever remains despotic in all these forms. Wherever credal statutes find a place among the laws of the constitution, a *clergy* rules which believes that it can actually dispense with reason and even, finally, with Scriptural learning, because it has authority, as the uniquely authorized guardian and interpreter of the will of the invisible Legislator, exclusively to administer the prescriptions of belief and so, furnished with this power, needs not convince but *merely command*. But since aside from the clergy all that remains is the *laity* (the head of the political commonwealth not excepted), the church in the end rules the state not exactly with force but through its influence upon men's hearts, and in addition through a dazzling promise of the advantage which the state is supposed to be able to draw from an unconditioned obedience to which a spiritual discipline has inured the very *thought* of the people. Thus, however, the habit of hypocrisy undermines, unnoticed, the integrity and loyalty of the subjects, renders them cunning in the simulation of service even in civil duties and, like all erroneously accepted principles, brings about the very opposite of what was intended.

* * * * * * * * * *

Now all this is the inevitable consequence of what at first sight appears to be a harmless transposition of the principles of the uniquely saving religious faith, since it was a question of which one should be assigned first place as the highest condition (to which the other is subordinated). It is fair, it is reasonable, to assume that not only "wise men after the flesh,"[1] the learned or sophisticated, will be called to this enlightenment touching their true welfare—for the entire human race is to be susceptible of this faith; "the foolish things of the world"[2] as well, even those who are most ignorant and most circumscribed conceptually, must be able to lay claim to such instruction and inner conviction. It does indeed seem as though an historical faith, especially if the concepts which it requires for the understanding of its documents are wholly anthropological and markedly suited to sense-perception, satisfies this description perfectly. For what is easier than to take in so sensuously depicted and simple a narrative and to share it with others, or to repeat the words of mysteries when there is no necessity whatsoever to attach a meaning to them! How easily does such a faith gain universal entrance, especially in connection with great promised advantage, and how deeply rooted does belief in the truth of such a narrative become, when it bases itself, moreover, upon a report accepted as authentic for a long time past! Such a faith, therefore, is indeed suited even to the commonest human capacities. Now even though the announcement of such an historical event, as well as the faith in rules of conduct based upon it, cannot be said to have been vouchsafed solely or primarily to the learned or the wise of the world, these latter are yet not excluded from it; consequently there arise so many doubts, in part touching its truth, and in part touching the sense in which its exposition is to be taken, that to adopt such a belief as this, subjected as it is to so many controversies (however sincerely intentioned), as the supreme condition of a universal faith alone leading to salvation, is the most absurd course of action that can be conceived of.

There exists meanwhile a practical knowledge which, while resting solely upon reason and requiring no historical doctrine, lies as close to every man, even the most simple, as though it were engraved upon his heart—a law, which we need but name to find ourselves at once in agreement with everyone else regarding its authority, and which carries with it in everyone's consciousness *unconditioned* binding force, to wit, the law of morality. What is

[1] [Cf. I Corinthians I, 26]
[2] [Cf. I Corinthians I, 27]

more, this knowledge either leads, alone and of itself, to belief in God, or at least determines the concept of Him as that of a moral Legislator; hence it guides us to a pure religious faith which not only can be comprehended by every man but also is in the highest degree worthy of respect. Yea, it leads thither so naturally that, if we care to try the experiment we shall find that it can be elicited in its completeness from anyone without his ever having been instructed in it. Hence to start off with this knowledge, and to let the historical faith which harmonizes with it follow, is not only an act of prudence; it is also our duty to make such knowledge the supreme condition under which alone we can hope to become participants in whatever salvation a religious faith may promise. So true is this that only as warranted by the interpretation which pure religious faith gives to the historical can we hold the latter to be universally binding or are we entitled to allow its validity (for it does contain universally valid teaching); meanwhile the moral believer is ever open to historical faith so far as he finds it furthering the vitality of his pure religious disposition. Only thus does historical faith possess a pure moral worth, because here it is free and not coerced through any threat (for then it can never be honest).

Now even when the service of God in a church is directed preeminently to the pure moral veneration of God in accordance with the laws prescribed to humanity in general, we can still ask whether, in such a service, the *doctrine of godliness* alone or that of *virtue* as well, or peculiarly the one or the other, should constitute the content of religious teaching. The first of these appellations, that is, the *doctrine of godliness*, perhaps best expresses the meaning of the word *religio* (as it is understood today) in an objective sense.

Godliness comprises two determinations of the moral disposition in relation to God: *fear* of God is this disposition in obedience to His commands from *bounden* duty (the duty of a subject), *i.e.*, from respect for the law; *love* of God, on the other hand, is the disposition to obedience from one's own *free choice* and from approval of the law (the duty of a son). Both involve, therefore, over and above morality, the concept of a supersensible Being provided with the attributes which are requisite to the carrying out of that highest good which is aimed at by morality but which transcends our powers. Now if we go beyond the moral relation of the idea of this Being to us, to a concept of His *nature*, there is always a danger that we shall think of it anthropomorphically and hence in a manner directly hurtful to our basic moral principles. Thus the idea of such a Being cannot subsist of itself in speculative reason; even its origin, and still more its power, are wholly grounded in its relation to our self-subsistent determination to duty. Which, now, is the more natural in the first instruction of youth and even in discourses from the pulpit: to expound the doctrine of virtue before the doctrine of godliness, or that of godliness before that of virtue (without perhaps even mentioning the doctrine of virtue at all)? Both obviously stand in necessary connection with one another. But, since they are not *of a kind*, this is possible only if one of them is conceived of and explained as end, the other merely as means. The doctrine of virtue, however, subsists of itself (even without the concept of God), whereas the doctrine of godliness involves the concept of an object which we represent to ourselves, in relation to our morality, as the cause supplementing our incapacity with respect to the final moral end. Hence the doctrine of godliness cannot of itself constitute the final goal of moral endeavor but can merely serve as a means of strengthening that which in itself goes to make a better man, to wit, the virtuous disposition, since it reassures and guarantees this endeavor (as a striving for goodness, and even for holiness) in its expectation of the final goal with respect to which it is impotent. The doctrine of virtue, in contrast, derives from the soul of man. He is already in full possession of it, undeveloped, no doubt, but not needing, like the religious concept, to be rationalized into being by means of logistics. In the purity of this concept of virtue, in the awakening of consciousness to a capacity which otherwise we would never surmise (a capacity of becoming able to master the greatest obstacles within ourselves), in the dignity of humanity which man must respect in his own person and human destiny, toward which he strives, if he is to attain it—in all this there is something which so exalts the soul, and so leads it to the very Deity, who is worthy of adoration only because of His holiness and as Legislator for virtue, that man, even when he is still far from allowing to this concept the power of influencing his maxims, is yet not unwillingly sustained by it because he feels himself to a certain extent ennobled by this idea already, even while the concept of a World-Ruler who transforms this duty into a command to us, still lies far from him. But to commence with this latter concept would incur the danger of dashing man's courage (which goes to constitute the essence of virtue) and transforming godliness into a fawning slavish subjection to a despotically commanding might. The courage to stand on one's own feet is itself strengthened by the doctrine of atonement, when it follows the ethical doctrine, in that this doctrine portrays as wiped out what cannot be altered, and opens up to man the path to a new mode of life; whereas, when this doctrine is made to come first, the futile endeavor to render undone what has been done (expiation), the fear regarding appropriation of this atonement, the idea of his complete incapacity for goodness, and the anxiety lest he slip back into evil must rob* a man of his courage and reduce him to a state of sighing moral passivity in which nothing great or good is undertaken

* The various kinds of belief among peoples seem to give them, after a time, a character, revealing itself outwardly in civil relations, which is later attributed to them as though it were universally a temperamental trait. Thus Judaism in its original economy, under which a people was to separate itself from all other peoples by means of every conceivable, and some arduous, observances and was to refrain from all intermingling with them, drew down upon itself the charge of *misanthropy*. Mohammedanism is characterized by *arrogant pride* because it finds confirmation of its faith not in miracles but in victories and the subjugation of many peoples, and because its devotional practices are all of the spirited sort.† The Hindu faith gives its adherents the character of *pusillanimity* for reasons which are directly op-

† This remarkable phenomenon (of the pride of an ignorant though intelligent people in its faith) may also originate from the fancy of its founder that he alone had once again renewed on earth the concept of God's unity and of His supersensible nature. He would indeed have ennobled his people by release from image-worship and the anarchy of polytheism could he with justice have credited himself with this achievement. As regards the characteristic of the third type of religious fellowship [the Christian], which is based upon a misconceived humility, the depreciation of self-conceit in the evaluation of one's own moral worth, through consideration of the holiness of the law, should bring about not contempt for oneself but rather the resolution, conformable to this noble predisposition in us, to approach ever nearer to agreement with this law. Instead of this, however, virtue, which really consists in the courage for this improvement, has, as a name already suspected of self-conceit, been exiled into paganism, and sycophantic courting of favor is extolled in its place.

Devotional hypocrisy (bigotry, *devotia spuria*) consists in the habit of identifying the practice of piety not with well-pleasing actions (in the performance of all human duties) but with direct commerce with God through manifestations of awe. This practice must then be classed as *compulsory service* (*opus operatum*), except that it adds to this superstition the fanatical illusion of imagined supersensible (heavenly) feelings.

and everything is expected from the mere wishing for it. In that which concerns the moral disposition everything depends upon the highest concept under which one subsumes one's duties. When reverence for God is put first, with virtue therefore subordinated to it, this object [of reverence] becomes an *idol*, that is, He is thought of as a Being whom we may hope to please not through morally upright conduct on earth but through adoration and ingratiation; and religion is then idolatry. But godliness is not a surrogate for virtue, whereby we may dispense with the latter; rather is it virtue's consummation, enabling us to be crowned with the hope of the ultimate achievement of all our good ends.

4. Concerning the Guide of Conscience in Matters of Faith

The question here is not, how conscience ought to be guided (for conscience needs no guide; to have a conscience suffices), but how it itself can serve as a guide in the most perplexing moral decisions.

Conscience is a state of consciousness which in itself is duty. But how is it possible to conceive of such a state of consciousness, since the consciousness of all our representations seems to be necessary only for logical purposes and therefore only in a conditioned manner (when we want to clarify our representations), and so cannot be unconditioned duty?

It is a basic moral principle, which requires no proof, that *one ought to hazard nothing that may be wrong (quod dubitas, ne feceris!* Pliny[1]). Hence the *consciousness* that an action *which I intend to*

---

posed to those productive of the temper just mentioned [the Mohammedan].

Now surely it is not because of the inner nature of the Christian faith but because of the manner in which it is presented to the heart and mind, that a similar charge can be brought against it with respect to those who have the most heartfelt intentions toward it but who, starting with human corruption, and despairing of all virtue, place their religious principle solely in *piety* (whereby is meant the principle of a passive attitude toward a godliness which is to be awaited from a power above). Such men never place any reliance in themselves, but look about them, in perpetual anxiety, for a supernatural assistance, and in this very self-abnegation (which is not humility) fancy themselves to possess a means of obtaining favor. The outward expression of this (in pietism or in spurious devotion) signalizes a *slavish* cast of mind.

[1] [*Epistles*, I,18: Si tutius putas illud cautissimi cuiusque præceptum: quod dubites, ne feceris. ". . . if you consider more safe that rule of a certain extremely cautious man: 'What you have doubts about, do not do.' "]

perform is right, is unconditioned duty. The understanding, not conscience, judges whether an action is really right or wrong. Nor is it absolutely necessary to know, concerning all possible actions, whether they are right or wrong. But concerning the act which *I* propose to perform I must not only judge and form an opinion, but I must be *sure* that it is not wrong; and this requirement is a postulate of conscience, to which is opposed *probabilism*,[1] *i.e.*, the principle that the mere opinion that an action may well be right warrants its being performed. Hence conscience might also be defined as follows: it is *the moral faculty of judgment, passing judgment upon itself;* only this definition would stand in great need of a prior elucidation of the concepts contained in it. Conscience does not pass judgment upon actions as cases which fall under the law; for this is what reason does so far as it is subjectively practical (hence the *casus conscientiae* and casuistry, as a kind of dialectic of conscience). Rather, reason here judges itself, as to whether it has really undertaken that appraisal of actions (as to whether they are right or wrong) with all diligence, and it calls the man himself to witness *for* or *against* himself whether this diligent appraisal did or did not take place.

Take, for instance, an inquisitor, who clings fast to the uniqueness of his statutory faith even to the point of [imposing] martyrdom, and who has to pass judgment upon a so-called heretic (otherwise a good citizen) charged with unbelief. Now I ask whether, if he condemns him to death, one might say that he has judged according to his conscience (erroneous though it be), or whether one might not rather accuse him of absolute *lack of conscience*, be it that he merely erred, or consciously did wrong; for we can tell him to his face that in such a case he could never be quite certain that by so acting he was not possibly doing wrong. Presumably he was firm in the belief that a supernaturally revealed Divine Will (perhaps in accord with the saying, *compellite intrare*[2]) permitted him, if it did not actually impose it as a duty, to extirpate pre-

---

[1] ["As it was methodically developed by the Jesuits and the Redemptorists (Alphons Liguori). The classical formula of probabilism—laid down as early as 1577 by the Dominican Bartholomew Medina—runs as follows: si est opinio probabilis, licitum est eam sequi, licet opposita est probabilior." (Note in Berlin Edition.) The Latin may be translated: "If an opinion is probable, to follow it is allowable, even granted that the opposite opinion is more probable."]

[2] ["Compel them to come in." Cf. Luke XIV, 23: "Go out into the highways and hedges and compel them to come in." "This phrase (*coge intrare*) Augustine early used (*Epistles* 93 and 185) as evidencing the duty of states to support the church in coercive measures against idolaters, heretics, and schismatics." (Note in Berlin Edition.)]

sumptive disbelief together with the disbelievers. But was he really strongly enough assured of such a revealed doctrine, and of this interpretation of it, to venture, on this basis, to destroy a human being? That it is wrong to deprive a man of his life because of his religious faith is certain, unless (to allow for the most remote possibility) a Divine Will, made known in extraordinary fashion, has ordered it otherwise. But that God has ever uttered this terrible injunction can be asserted only on the basis of historical documents and is never apodictically certain. After all, the revelation has reached the inquisitor only through men and has been interpreted by men, and even did it appear to have come to him from God Himself (like the command delivered to Abraham to slaughter his own son like a sheep) it is at least possible that in this instance a mistake has prevailed. But if this is so, the inquisitor would risk the danger of doing what would be wrong in the highest degree; and in this very act he is behaving unconscientiously. This is the case with respect to all historical and visionary faith; that is, the *possibility* ever remains that an error may be discovered in it. Hence it is unconscientious to follow such a faith with the possibility that perhaps what it commands or permits may be wrong, *i.e.*, with the danger of disobedience to a human duty which is certain in and of itself.

And further: even were an act commanded by (what is held to be) such a positive revealed law allowable in itself, the question arises whether spiritual rulers or teachers, after presumably becoming convinced of it themselves, should impose it upon the people as an *article of faith* for their acceptance (on penalty of forfeiting their status). Since assurance on this score rests on no grounds of proof other than the historical, and since there ever will remain in the judgment of the people (if it subjects itself to the slightest test) the absolute possibility of an error which has crept in through their interpretation or through previous classical exegesis, the clergyman would be requiring the people at least inwardly to confess something to be as true as is their belief in God, *i.e.*, to confess, as though in the presence of God, something which they do not know with certainty. Such, for instance, would be the acknowledgment, as a part of religion directly commanded by God, of the setting aside of a certain day for the periodic public cultivation of godliness; or, again, the confession of firm belief in a mystery which the layman does not even understand. Here the layman's spiritual superior would himself go counter to conscience in forcing others to believe that of which he himself can never be wholly convinced; he should therefore in justice consider well what he does, for he must answer for all abuse arising out of such a compulsory faith. Thus there may, perhaps, be truth in what is believed but at the same time untruthfulness[1] in the belief (or even in the mere inner confession thereof), and this is in itself damnable.

Although, as was noted above,[2] men who have made but the merest beginning in the freedom of thought,* because previously they were under a slavish yoke of belief (*e.g.*, the Protestants), forthwith hold themselves to be, as it were, the more ennobled the less they need to believe (of what is positive and what belongs to clerical precepts); the exact contrary holds concerning those who have so far not been able, or have not wished, to make an attempt of this kind, for their principle is: It is expedient to believe too much rather than too little, on the ground that what we do over and above what we owe will at least do no harm and might even help. Upon this illusion, which makes dishonesty in religious confessions a basic principle (to which one subscribes the more easily since religion makes good every mistake, and hence that of dishonesty along with the rest), is based the so-called maxim of certainty in matters of faith (*argumentum a tuto*): If that which I profess regarding God is true, I have hit the mark; if it is untrue,

* I grant that I cannot really reconcile myself to the following expressions made use of even by clever men: "A certain people (engaged in a struggle for civil freedom) is not yet ripe for freedom"; "The bondmen of a landed proprietor are not yet ready for freedom"; and hence, likewise; "Mankind in general is not yet ripe for freedom of belief." For according to such a presupposition, freedom will never arrive, since we cannot *ripen* to this freedom if we are not first of all placed therein (we must be free in order to be able to make purposive use of our powers in freedom). The first attempts will indeed be crude and usually will be attended by a more painful and more dangerous state than that in which we are still under the orders and also the care of others; yet we never ripen with respect to reason except through *our own* efforts (which we can make only when we are free). I raise no protest when those who hold power in their hands, being constrained by the circumstances of the times, postpone far, very far, into the future the sundering of these three[3] bonds. But to proceed on the principle that those who are once sub-

¹ [*Unwahrhaftigkeit, i.e.*, insincerity.]
² [See p. 161 n.]
³ [Civil, economic or domestic, and religious, corresponding to the quoted expressions at the opening of the note.]

and in addition not something in itself forbidden, I have merely believed it superfluously and have burdened myself with what was indeed not necessary but was after all only an inconvenience, not a transgression. *The hypocrite regards as a mere nothing* the danger arising from the dishonesty of his profession, *the violation of conscience*, involved in proclaiming even before God that something is certain, when he is aware that, its nature being what it is, it cannot be asserted with unconditional assurance. The genuine maxim of certainty, which alone is compatible with religion, is just the reverse of the former: Whatever, as the means or the condition of salvation, I can know not through my own reason but only through revelation, and can incorporate into my confession only through the agency of an historical faith, and which, in addition, does not contradict pure moral principles—this I cannot, indeed, believe and profess as certain, but I can as little reject it as being surely false; nevertheless, without determining anything on this score, I may expect that whatever therein is salutary will stand me in good stead so far as I do not render myself unworthy of it through defect of the moral disposition in good life-conduct. In this maxim there is genuine moral certainty, namely, certainty in the eye of conscience (and more than this cannot be required of a man); on the other hand, the greatest danger and uncertainty attend the supposedly prudential device of craftily evading the harmful consequences which might accrue to me from non-profession, in that, through seeking the favor of both parties, I am liable to incur the disfavor of both.

Let the author of a creed, or the teacher of a church, yea, let every man, so far as he is inwardly to acknowledge a conviction regarding dogmas as divine revelations, ask himself: Do you really trust yourself to assert the truth of these dogmas in the sight of Him who knows the heart and at the risk of losing all that is valuable and holy to you? I must needs have a very disparaging conception of human nature (which is, after all, not wholly unsusceptible of goodness) not to anticipate that even the boldest teacher

---

jected to these bonds are essentially unfit for freedom and that one is justified in continually removing them farther from it is to usurp the prerogatives of Divinity itself, which created men for freedom. It is certainly more convenient to rule in state, household, and church if one is able to carry out such a principle. But is it also more just?

of faith would have to tremble at such a question.† But if this is so, how is it consistent with conscientiousness to insist, none the less, upon such a declaration of faith as admits of no reservation, and even to proclaim that the very audacity of such an asseveration is in itself a duty and a service to God, when thereby human freedom, which is absolutely required in all moral matters (such as the adoption of a religion) is wholly crushed under foot and no place is even left for the good will, which says: "Lord, I believe; help thou my unbelief!"[1] ††

† The very man who has the temerity to say: He who does not believe in this or that historical doctrine as a sacred truth, that man *is damned*, ought to be able to say also: If what I am now telling you is not true, *let me be damned!* Were there anyone who could make such a dreadful declaration, I should advise the conduct toward him suggested by the Persian proverb concerning a *hadji:* If a man has been in Mecca once (as a pilgrim), move out of the house in which he is living; if he has been there twice, leave the street on which he is to be found; but if he has been there three times, forsake the city, or even the land, which he inhabits!

†† *O sincerity!* Thou Astraea, that hast fled from earth to heaven, how mayst thou (the basis of conscience, and hence of all inner religion) be drawn down thence to us again? I can admit, though it is much to be deplored, that candor (in speaking the *whole* truth which one knows) is not to be found in human nature. But we must be able to demand *sincerity* (that *all that one says* be said with truthfulness), and indeed if there were in our nature no predisposition to sincerity, whose cultivation merely is neglected, the human race must needs be, in its own eyes, an object of the deepest contempt. Yet this sought-for quality of mind is such that it is exposed to many temptations and entails many a sacrifice, and hence calls for moral strength, or virtue (which must be won); moreover it must be guarded and cultivated earlier than any other, because the opposed propensity is the hardest to extirpate if it has been allowed firmly to root itself. And if now we compare with the kind of instruction here recommended our usual mode of upbringing, especially in the matter of religion, or better, in doctrines of faith, where fidelity of memory in answering questions relating to these doctrines, without regard to the fidelity of the confession itself (which is never put to the test) is accepted as sufficient to make a believer of him who does not even understand what he declares to be holy, no longer shall we wonder at the lack of sincerity which produces nothing but inward hypocrites.

[1][Cf. Mark IX, 24]

GENERAL OBSERVATION

Whatever good man is able to do through his own efforts, under laws of freedom, in contrast to what he can do only with supernatural assistance, can be called *nature*, as distinguished from *grace*. Not that we understand by the former expression a physical property distinguished from freedom; we use it merely because we are at least acquainted with the *laws* of this capacity (laws of *virtue*), and because reason thus possesses a visible and comprehensible clue to it, considered as *analogous to [physical] nature;* on the other hand, we remain wholly in the dark as to when, what, or how much, *grace* will accomplish in us, and reason is left, on this score, as with the supernatural in general (to which morality, if regarded as *holiness*, belongs), without any knowledge of the laws according to which it might occur.

The concept of a supernatural accession to our moral, though deficient, capacity and even to our not wholly purified and certainly weak disposition to perform our entire duty, is a transcendent concept, and is a bare idea, of whose reality no experience can assure us. Even when accepted as an idea in nothing but a practical context it is very hazardous, and hard to reconcile with reason, since that which is to be accredited to us as morally good conduct must take place not through foreign influence but solely through the best possible use of our own powers. And yet the impossibility thereof (*i.e.*, of both these things occurring side by side) cannot really be proved, because freedom itself, though containing nothing supernatural in its conception, remains, as regards its possibility, just as incomprehensible to us as is the supernatural factor which we would like to regard as a supplement to the spontaneous but deficient determination of freedom.

Now we at least know the *laws* of freedom (the moral laws), according to which it is to be determined. But we cannot know anything at all about supernatural aid—whether a certain moral power, perceptible to us, really comes from above or, indeed, on what occasions and under what conditions it may be expected. Hence, apart from the general assumption that grace will effect in us what nature cannot, provided only we have made the maximum use of our own powers, we will not be able to make any further use of this idea, either as to how (beyond a constant striving after a good life) we might draw down to us its cooperation, or how we might determine on what occasions to expect it. This idea is wholly transcendent; and it is even salutary to hold it, as a sacred thing, at a respectful distance, lest, under the illusion of performing miracles ourselves or observing miracles within us, we render ourselves unfit for all use of reason or allow ourselves to fall into the indolence of awaiting from above, in passive leisure, what we should seek within.

Now *means* are all the intermediate causes, which man *has in his power*, whereby a certain purpose may be achieved. There is no other means (and there can be no other) of becoming worthy of heavenly assistance than earnest endeavor to better in every possible way our moral nature and thus render ourselves susceptible of having the fitness of this nature perfected for divine approval, so far as this perfecting is not in our power; for that divine aid, which we await, itself really aims at nothing but our morality. It was already to be expected *a priori* that the impure man would not seek this aid here but rather in certain sensuous contrivances (which he does, indeed, have in his power but which, in themselves, cannot make a man better, and yet herein are supposed to achieve this very result in supernatural fashion); and this is what actually happens. The concept of a so-called *means of grace*, although it is internally self-contradictory (in accordance with what has just been said), serves here none the less as a means of self-deception which is as common as it is detrimental to true religion.

The true (moral) service of God, which the faithful must render as subjects belonging to His kingdom but no less as citizens thereof (under laws of freedom), is itself, indeed, like the kingdom, invisible, *i.e.*, a *service of the heart* (in spirit and in truth). It can consist solely in the disposition of obedience to all true duties as divine commands, not in actions directed exclusively to God. Yet for man the invisible needs to be represented through the visible (the sensuous); yea, what is more, it needs to be accompanied by the visible in the interest of practicability and, though it is intellectual, must be made, as it were (according to a certain analogy), perceptual. This is a means of simply picturing to ourselves our duty in the service of God, a means which, although really indispensable, is extremely liable to the danger of misconstruction; for, through an *illusion* that steals over us, it is easily held to be the *service of God* itself, and is, indeed, commonly thus spoken of.

This alleged service of God, when brought back to its spirit and its true meaning, namely, to a disposition dedicating itself to the kingdom of God within us and without us, can be divided, even by reason, into four observances of duty; and certain corresponding rites, which do not stand in a necessary relation to these observances, have yet been associated with them, because the rites are deemed to serve as schemata[1] for the duties and thus, for ages past, have been regarded as useful means for sensuously awakening and sustaining our attention to the true service of God. They base themselves, one and all, upon the intention to further the morally good and are: (1) (private prayer)—firmly to establish this goodness *in ourselves*, and repeatedly to awaken the disposition of goodness in the heart; (2) (church-going)—the *spreading abroad* of goodness through public assembly on days legally dedicated thereto, in order that religious doctrines and wishes (together with corresponding dispositions) may be expressed there and thus be generally shared; (3) (in the Christian religion, baptism)—the *propagation* of goodness in posterity through the reception of newly entering members into the fellowship of faith, as a duty; also their instruction in such goodness; (4) (communion)—the *maintenance of this fellowship* through a repeated public formality which makes enduring the union of these members into an ethical body and this, indeed, according to the principle of the mutual equality of their rights and joint participation in all the fruits of moral goodness.

Every initiatory step in the realm of religion, which we do not take in a purely moral manner but rather have recourse to as *in itself* a means of making us well-pleasing to God and thus, through Him, of satisfying all our wishes, is a *fetish-faith*. This is the persuasion that what can produce no effect at all according either to natural laws or to moral laws of reason, will yet, of itself, bring about what is wished for, if only we firmly believe that it will do so, and if we accompany this belief with certain formalities. Even where the conviction has taken hold that everything in religion depends upon moral goodness, which can arise only from action, the sensuous man still searches for a secret path by which to evade that arduous condition, with the notion, namely, that if

---

[1] [A schema is a spatio-temporal or sensuous form of what, in its essence, does not possess this character. The "certain analogy," parenthetically referred to above, is presumably the doctrine of the schema in the *Critique of Pure Reason* (Transcendental Analytic, Book II, Chap. I).]

only he honors the *custom* (the formality), God will surely accept it in lieu of the act itself. This would certainly have to be called an instance of transcendent grace on God's part, were it not rather a grace dreamed of in slothful trust, or even in a trust which is itself feigned. Thus in every type of public belief man has devised for himself certain practices, as *means of grace*, though, to be sure, in all these types the practices are not, as they are in the Christian, related to practical concepts of reason and to dispositions conformable to them. (There are, for instance, the five great commands in the Mohammedan type of belief: washing, praying, fasting, almsgiving, and pilgrimage to Mecca. Of these, almsgiving alone would deserve to be excepted were it to take place from a truly virtuous and at the same time religious disposition, as a human duty, and would thus really merit regard as a genuine means of grace; but the fact is, on the contrary, that it does not deserve to be thus distinguished from the rest because, under this faith, almsgiving can well go hand in hand with the extortion from others of what, as a sacrifice, is offered to God in the person of the poor.)

There can, indeed, be three kinds of *illusory faith* that involve the possibility of our overstepping the bounds of our reason in the direction of the supernatural (which is not, according to the laws of reason, an object either of theoretical or practical use). *First,* the belief in knowing through experience something whose occurrence, as under objective laws of experience, we ourselves can recognize to be impossible (the faith in *miracles*). *Second,* the illusion of having to include among our rational concepts, as necessary to our best moral interests, that of which we ourselves can form, through reason, no concept (the faith in *mysteries*). *Third,* the illusion of being able to bring about, through the use of merely natural means, an effect which is, for us, a mystery, namely, the influence of God upon our morality (the faith in *means of grace*). We have dealt with the first two of these artificial modes of belief in the General Observations following the two immediately preceding Books of this work. It still remains, therefore, for us to treat of the means of grace (which are further distinguished from *works of grace,*†*i.e.*, supernatural moral influences in relation to which we are merely passive; but the imagined experience of these is a fanatical illusion pertaining entirely to the emotions).

1. *Praying,* thought of as an *inner formal* service of God and

† See the General Observation at the end of Book One.

hence as a means of grace, is a superstitious illusion (a fetish-making); for it is no more than a *stated wish* directed to a Being who needs no such information regarding the inner disposition of the wisher; therefore nothing is accomplished by it, and it discharges none of the duties to which, as commands of God, we are obligated; hence God is not really served. A heart-felt wish to be well-pleasing to God in our every act and abstention, or in other words, the disposition, accompanying all our actions, to perform these as though they were being executed in the service of God, is the *spirit of prayer* which can, and should, be present in us "without ceasing."[1] But to clothe* this wish (even though it be but inwardly) in words

* In the heart-felt wish which is the spirit of prayer, man seeks but to work upon himself (for the quickening of his disposition by means of the *idea of God*); whereas, in the other, where he declares himself in words, and so outwardly, he tries to work *upon* God. In the first sense, a prayer can be offered with perfect sincerity even though the man praying does not presume to be able to affirm that the existence of God is wholly certain; in its second form, as an *address*, he supposes this Supreme Being to be present in person, or at least he adopts an attitude (even inwardly) as though he were convinced of His presence, with the idea that, even if this be not so, his acting thus can at least do him no harm and is more likely to get him favor. Hence such complete sincerity cannot be found in the latter (verbal) prayer as it can in the former (the pure spirit of prayer).

Anyone will find the truth of this last remark confirmed if he conceives of a pious and well-meaning man, but one who is circumscribed in respect of these purified religious concepts, whom some one else takes unawares, I will not say in praying aloud, but merely in behavior indicative of prayer. Everyone will of himself, of course, without my saying so, expect a man thus surprised to fall into confusion or embarrassment, as though in a situation whereof he should of ashamed. But why? It is because a man caught talking aloud to himself is suspected for the moment of having a slight attack of madness; and thus do we also judge a man (and not altogether unjustly) when we find him, all alone, in an occupation or attitude which can properly belong only to one who sees some one else before him—and in the example we have given this is not the case.

Now the Teacher of the Gospel has expressed the spirit of prayer most admirably in a formula which has at once rendered dispensable not only all this, but also the prayer itself (as a verbal utterance). One finds in it nothing but the resolution to good life-conduct which, taken with the consciousness of our frailty, carries with it the persistent desire to be a worthy member in the kingdom of God. Hence it contains no actual request for something which God in His wisdom might well refuse us, but simply a wish which, if it is genuine (active), of itself achieves its object (to become a man well-pleasing to God). Even the wish for the means of sustaining our existence (for bread) for one

[1] [Cf. I Thessalonians V, 17]

and formulas can, at best, possess only the value of a means where-

---

day, since this wish is expressly not directed to its continuance but is the effect of a felt need which is merely animal, is more a confession of what *nature* in us *demands* than a special deliberate request for what the *man* [in us] *wills*. The latter's request would be for bread for another day; but this is here clearly enough ruled out.

A prayer of the kind described above arises in the moral disposition (animated solely by the idea of God), and, as the moral spirit of prayer, brings about its object (being well-pleasing to God) of itself. Only such a prayer can be prayed with *faith*, and by this faith we mean the assurance that the prayer will *be heard*. But only morality in us gives rise to this assurance, for even were the petition to be for this day's bread alone, no one can be assured that it will be heard, *i.e.*, that its granting stands in necessary conjunction with God's wisdom; it may perhaps comport better with this wisdom to let the suppliant die today for lack of bread. It is, further, not only a preposterous but also a presumptuous illusion to try to divine whether, through the persistent importunity of one's request, God cannot be diverted (to our present advantage) from the plan of His wisdom. Hence we cannot hold that any prayer which is for a non-moral object is sure to be heard, that is, we cannot pray for such an object *in faith*. Nay, more: even were the object indeed moral, but yet possible only through supernatural influence (or at least awaited by us from this source alone because we do not wish to trouble ourselves to bring it about—as, for example, the change of heart, the putting on of the new man, called rebirth) it is at least so very uncertain that God will find it conformable to His wisdom to supplement in supernatural fashion our (self-incurred) deficiency that we have reason, rather, to expect the opposite. Man cannot therefore pray even for this in faith.

In the light of the foregoing we can explain what might be the status of a miracle-working faith (which would at the same time always be united with an inner prayer). Since God can lend man no power to bring about effects supernaturally (for that is a contradiction), and since man, on his part, cannot determine, according to the concepts which he forms for himself of good ends possible on earth, what the divine Wisdom judges in these matters, and so cannot, by means of the wish he himself nurtures within him, make use of the divine Power for his purposes, it follows that a gift of miracles, I mean, a gift wherein it rests with man himself whether he has it or not ("If ye had faith as a grain of mustard-seed, etc."[1]), is, taken literally, not to be thought of. Such a faith, therefore, if it is to mean anything at all, is simply an idea of the overwhelming importance of man's moral nature, were he to possess it in its entire God-pleasing completeness (which, indeed, he never does), greater than all other moving causes which God in His supreme wisdom may have [at His disposal]; it is therefore a basis upon which we can be confident that, were we now, or eventually, to become *wholly* what we ought to be and (in continued approximation) could be, nature would have to heed our wishes, which, under these circumstances, however, would by the same token never be unwise.

[1] [Cf. Matthew XVII, 20; Luke XVII, 6]

by that disposition within us may be repeatedly quickened, and can have no direct bearing upon the divine approval; and for this very reason it cannot be a duty for everyone. For a means can be prescribed only to him who *needs* it for certain ends; but certainly not all men stand in need of this means (of conversing within and really *with onself*, but ostensibly of speaking the more intelligibly *with God*). Rather must one labor to this end through continued clarification and elevation of the moral disposition, in order that this spirit of prayer alone be sufficiently quickened within us and that the letter of it (at least as directed to our own advantage) finally fall away. For the letter, like everything which is aimed at a given end indirectly, rather weakens the effect of the moral idea (which, taken subjectively, is called *devotion*). Thus the contemplation of the profound wisdom of the divine creation in the smallest things, and of its majesty in the great—which may indeed have already been recognized by men in the past, but in more recent times has grown into the highest wonder—this contemplation is a power which cannot only transport the mind into that sinking mood, called *adoration*, annihilating men, as it were, in their own eyes; it is also, in respect of its own moral determination, so soul-elevating a power that words, in comparison, even were they those of the royal suppliant David (who knew little of all those marvels),

---

As regards the *edification* sought in attendance at church, here too public prayer is indeed no means of grace; yet it is a moral ceremony, whether it consists in united singing of the hymn of faith, or in the *address* formally directed to God, through the mouth of the clergyman and in the name of the whole congregation, and embracing all the moral concerns of men. Such an address, since it presents these last as a public concern, wherein the wish of each individual ought to be represented as united with the wishes of all toward the same ends (the ushering in of the kingdom of God), cannot only raise the feelings to the point of moral exaltation (whereas private prayers, because they are uttered without this sublime idea, lose little by little, through habituation, their influence upon the heart); it also possesses in itself a more rational basis than does private prayer for clothing the moral wish, which constitutes the spirit of prayer, in a formal mode of address—and it does this without picturing the Supreme Being as present, or thinking of the special power of this rhetorical device as a means of grace. For here there is a special purpose, namely, to set in more active motion the moral motivating forces of each individual through a public ceremony, representing *the union of all men* in a common desire for the kingdom of God; and this cannot be accomplished more appropriately than by speaking to the Head of this kingdom just as though He were specially present in that very place.

must needs pass away as empty sound because the emotion arising from such a vision of the hand of God is inexpressible. Men, are prone, moreover, when their hearts are disposed to religion, to transform what really has reference solely to their own moral improvement into a courtly service, wherein the humiliations and glorifications usually are the less felt in a moral way the more volubly they are expressed. It is therefore the more necessary carefully to inculcate set forms of prayer in children (who still stand in need of the letter), even in their earliest years, so that the language (even language spoken inwardly, yea, even the attempts to attune the mind to the comprehension of the idea of God, which is to be brought nearer to intuition) may possess here no value in itself but may be used merely to quicken the disposition to a course of life well-pleasing to God, those words being but an aid to the imagination. Otherwise all these devout attestations of awe involve the danger of producing nothing but hypocritical veneration of God instead of a practical service of Him—a service which never consists in mere feelings.

2. *Church-going*, thought of as the ceremonial *public service of God* in a church, *in general*, is, considered as a sensuous representation of the community of believers, not only a means to be valued by each *individual* for his own *edification** but also a duty

* If we seek for a meaning proper to this term, probably none can be ascribed to it other than that it is to be understood as the *moral result produced upon the subject by devotion*. Now this result does not consist in feelings (this is already comprised in the very concept of devotion), even though most men, presumed to be devout (and therefore called *devotees*), identify it entirely with such feelings; hence the word *edification* [*Erbauung*] must signify the *result* of devotion in the actual improvement of the man. But this improvement becomes actual only if man systematically sets to work, lays deep in his heart firm basic principles squaring with well-understood concepts, erects thereupon dispositions measurable to the differing weight of the duties connected with these principles, strengthens and secures them against the onslaughts of the desires, and thus, as it were, *builds up* a new man as a *temple of God*.[1] One can easily see that this building can progress but slowly; yet it must at least be possible to see that something has been *accomplished*. But men believe themselves to be mightily *edified* [*erbaut*] (through listening or reading and singing) while absolutely nothing has been *built up* [*gebauet*], yea, where no hand has been put to the work. They believe this, presumably, because they hope that this moral edifice will rise up of itself, like the walls of Thebes, to the music of sighs and yearning wishes.

¹ [Cf. Ephesians II, 21–22]

directly obligating them as a *group*, as citizens of a divine state which is to appear here on earth; provided, that this church contains no formalities which might lead to idolatry and so burden the conscience, *e.g.*, certain prayers to God, with His infinite mercy personified under the name of a man—for such sensuous representation of God is contrary to the command of reason: "Thou shalt not make unto thee any graven image, etc."[1] But to wish to use it as, in itself, a *means of grace*, as though thereby God were directly served and as though He had attached special *favors* to the celebration of this solemnity (which is merely a sensuous representation of the *universality* of religion), is an illusion which does, indeed, well comport with the cast of mind of a good *citizen in a political commonwealth*, and with external propriety, yet which not only contributes nothing to the character of such a man, as a *citizen in the kingdom of God*, but rather debases it, and serves, by means of a deceptive veneer, to conceal the bad moral content of his disposition from the eyes of others, and even from his own eyes.

3. The ceremonial *initiation*, taking place but once, into the church-community, that is, one's first acceptance *as a member of a church* (in the Christian church through *baptism*) is a highly significant ceremony which lays a grave obligation either upon the initiate, if he is in a position himself to confess his faith, or upon the witnesses who pledge themselves to take care of his education in this faith. This aims at something holy (the development of a man into a citizen in a divine state) but this act performed by others is not in itself holy or productive of holiness and receptivity for the divine grace in this individual; hence it is no *means of grace*, however exaggerated the esteem in which it was held in the early Greek church, where it was believed capable, in an instant, of washing away all sins—and here this illusion publicly revealed its affinity to an almost more than heathenish superstition.

4. The oft-repeated ceremony (*communion*) of a *renewal, continuation, and propagation of this churchly community* under laws of *equality*, a ceremony which indeed can be performed, after the example of the Founder of such a church (and, at the same time, in memory of him), through the formality of a common partaking at the same table, contains within itself something great, expanding the narrow, selfish, and unsociable cast of mind among men,

[1] [Cf. Exodus XX, 4]

especially in matters of religion, toward the idea of a cosmopolitan *moral community;* and it is a good means of enlivening a community to the moral disposition of brotherly love which it represents. But to assert that God has attached special favors to the celebration of this solemnity, and to incorporate among the articles of faith the proposition that this ceremony, which is after all but a churchly act, is, in addition, a *means of grace*—this is a religious illusion which can do naught but work counter to the spirit of religion. *Clericalism* in general would therefore be the dominion of the clergy over men's hearts, usurped by dint of arrogating to themselves the prestige attached to exclusive possession of means of grace.

* * * * * * * * * *

All such artificial self-deceptions in religious matters have a common basis. Among the three divine moral attributes, holiness, mercy, and justice, man habitually turns directly to the second in order thus to avoid the forbidding condition of conforming to the requirements of the first. It is tedious to be a good *servant* (here one is forever hearing only about one's duties); man would therefore rather be a *favorite,* where much is overlooked or else, when duty has been too grossly violated, everything is atoned for through the agency of some one or other favored in the highest degree—man, meanwhile, remaining the servile knave he ever was. But in order to satisfy himself, with some color of truth, concerning the feasibility of this intention of his, he has the habit of transferring his concept of a man (including his faults) to the Godhead; and just as, even in the best *ruler of our race,* legislative rigor, beneficent grace, and scrupulous justice do not (as they should) operate separately, each by itself, to produce a moral effect upon the actions of the subject, but *mingle* with one another in the thinking of the human ruler when he is making his decisions, so that one need only seek to circumvent one of these attributes, the fallible wisdom of the human will, in order to determine the other two to compliance; even so does man hope to accomplish the same thing with God by applying himself solely to His *grace.* (For this reason it was important for religion that the attributes, or rather the relations of God to man, which were conceived of, should be separated through the idea of a triune personality, wherein God is to be thought of analogously to this idea in order that each attribute or relation be made specifically cognizable.) To this end man busies himself with every conceivable formality, designed to indicate how greatly he *respects* the divine commands, in order that it may not be necessary for him to *obey* them; and, that his idle wishes may serve also to make good the disobedience of these commands, he cries: "Lord, Lord," so as not to have to "do the will of his heavenly Father."[1] Thus he comes to conceive of the ceremonies, wherein certain means are used to quicken truly practical dispositions, as in themselves means of grace; he even proclaims the belief, that they are such, to be itself an essential part of religion (the common man actually regards it as the whole of religion); and he leaves it to all-gracious Providence to make a better man of him, while he busies himself with *piety* (a passive respect for the law of God) rather than with *virtue* (the application of one's own powers in discharging the duty which one respects)—and, after all, it is only the latter, *combined with the former*, that can give us the idea which one intends by the word *godliness* (true *religious disposition*).

When the illusion of this supposed favorite of heaven mounts to the point where he fanatically imagines that he feels special works of grace within himself (or even where he actually presumes to be confident of a fancied occult *intercourse* with God), virtue comes at last actually to arouse his loathing, and becomes for him an object of contempt. Hence it is no wonder that the complaint is made publicly, that religion still contributes so little to men's improvement, and that the inner light ("under a bushel"[2]) of these favored ones does not shine forth outwardly in good works also, yea, (as, in view of their pretensions, one could rightly demand) *preeminently*, above other men of native honesty who, in brief, take religion unto themselves not as a substitute for, but as a furtherance of, the virtuous disposition which shows itself through actions, in a good course of life. Yet the Teacher of the Gospel has himself put into our hands these external evidences of outer experience as a touchstone, [by telling us that] we can know men by their fruits and that every man can know himself. But thus far we do not see that those who, in their own opinion, are extraordinarily favored (the chosen ones) surpass in the very least the naturally

---

[1] [Cf. Matthew VII, 21. "Not every one that saith unto me, Lord, Lord, shall enter into the kingdom of heaven; but he that doeth the will of my Father which is in heaven."]

[2] [Cf. Matthew V, 15]

honest man, who can be relied upon in social intercourse, in business, or in trouble; on the contrary, taken as a whole, the chosen ones can scarcely abide comparison with him, which proves that the right course is not to go from grace to virtue but rather to progress from virtue to pardoning grace.

INDEX

Abbott, T. K., cxxiv, cxxxv–cxxxvi
Abraham, 175
Accountability, lxxxvii ff., cxvii ff., 17, 21 n., 28, 30, 31, 32, 33, 34, 36, 52, 65 ff., 123, 131 n., 134
Adam, 37 ff., 68 n., 74
Adickes, E., lxv–lxvi, cxl–cxlii
"All's well that ends well," 64 n., 72
Analogy, 59 n.
Angels, 81
Animality, in man, 21–2, 30; not ground of evil, cxi ff.
Anselm, xlii, 66 n., 67 n.
Anthropomorphism, lxi, 58 n., 133, 157 ff., 171
Antinomy, xl, xlv–xlvi, xcvii, cxxxii, 107 ff.
Archetype, 54 ff., 69 n., 109 ff., 119, 136, 150. See Son of God
Arndt, Johann, xii
Atheism, 102
Atonement, cxxxi–cxxxiv, 66 ff., 106 ff., 111, 134, 172. See Justification
Aufklärung, defined, xi; its pietism, xii–xiv; its rationalism, xiv–xx; its un-historical attitude corrected by Lessing, xx–xxii; in Königsberg, xxii–xxvii
Augustine, St., cxxiii, 38 n., 51 n., 136 n., 174 n.
Author of Evil, see Evil Principle
Autonomy, see Freedom

Badness, see Evil
Bahrdt, K. F., 76 n.
Baptism, 181, 187
Baumgarten, A. B., xv n.
Baumgarten, S. J., xv and n.
Beck, L. W., lxxxiii
Belief, honesty of, 173–8. See Faith
Bergson, xlv n.
Berkeley, xxxviii
Bernard, J. H., lxviii n.
Bible, pietists' attitude to, xii–xiii; Wolff's attitude to, xv, xvii–xviii; Reimarus' attitude to, xx; Semler's historical approach to, xix; Lessing's conception of, xx–xxi. See Scripture, Holy
Blame (and Praise), see Accountability
Borowski, L. E., xix n., xxviii
Broad, C. D., cxviii n.
British Parliament, 34

Caird, E., xxxvii n., lxviii, lxx n.
Call, divine, 133

Carlyle, T., xxvii
Casuistry, 174
Catechism, 13, 88
Categorical Imperative, liii, lxvi; its possibility, lxxxi ff., xciii ff., xcvii ff., civ, cxxiv–cxxv, cxxx–cxxxi; Christian formulation of, 148. See Moral Law, Duty and Freedom.
Catholic, 100, 163 n.
Causality, 135 and n., 158 n. See Freedom and Determinism
Censorship, xxxii–xxxvi, 7–10, 104, 123–4 and n.
Certainty, maxim of, 177
Charlevoix, 73 n.
Christ, 57 ff., 66 ff., 103; Reimarus' attitude to, xix; Lessing's attitude to, xxii; Knutzen's attitude to, xxvi–xxvii; birth, life and death, 74–8; teachings of, 147 ff.; as Teacher of the Gospel, 119, 125, 146 ff., 183 n., 189; as an example, 77, 79, 110, 119 and n., 120, 146 ff., 150, 187; as Ideal of Humanity, 120; resurrection and ascension of, 119 n.; faith in, 109 ff. See Archtype and Son of God
Christianity, 47, 78, 102, 116; pietists' attitude to, xii–xiv; Knutzen's conception of, xxv–xxvii; origin and development of, 118 ff., 127 n.; as natural religion, 145–51; as a revealed and learned religion, 151–5; relation to Judaism, 153–5 and n.; practices of, 181 ff.
Church, 91 ff., 94 ff., 103 ff., 105 ff., 139 ff., 146 ff., 148 n., 151, 164; pietists' criticism of the Lutheran, xii–xiv; visible, 112 ff. and n., 115 ff., 122, 140, 145 ff.; invisible, 122, 140, 145; universal, 115 ff., 126 n.; unity of, 115–6; founding of, 139–41; attendance, 181 ff. See Commonwealth, ethical
Civilization, 28–9
Clergy and Laity, 104, 112, 140 ff., 152, 168, 175–6
Clergyman, 63 n., 72 n., 82
Clericalism, 67 n., 124 n., 142 n., 153, 163–8, 188
Collegium Friedericianum, xxiii, xxiv, xxviii–xxx, lxxv
Collins, xv
Commonwealth, types of, 86; political (juridico-civil), 87–8, 131; ethical, 87 ff., 90 ff., 139 ff., see Church and Kingdom of God

cxlvii

INDEX TO BIBLICAL REFERENCES